THE LAST REFUGE

THE LAST REFUGE

YEMEN, AL-QAEDA, AND AMERICA'S WAR IN ARABIA

Gregory D. Johnsen

W. W. NORTON & COMPANY
New York • London

Printed in the United States of America
First Edition

For information about special discounts for bulk purchases, please contact W. W. Norton Special Sales at specialsales@wwnorton.com or 800-233-4830

Manufacturing by Courier Westford
Book design by Chris Welch
Production manager: Julia Druskin

Library of Congress Cataloging-in-Publication Data

Johnsen, Gregory D.
The last refuge : Yemen, al-Qaeda, and
America's war in Arabia / Gregory D. Johnsen.
p. cm.
Includes bibliographical references and index.
ISBN 978-0-393-08242-5 (hbk.)
1. Terrorism—Yemen (Republic) 2. Qaida (Organization)
3. Terrorism—Persian Gulf Region—Prevention.
4. War on Terrorism, 2001-2009. 5. United States—Military policy.
I. Title.
HV6433.Y4J64 2013
363.32509533—dc23

2012027875

W. W. Norton & Company, Inc.
500 Fifth Avenue, New York, N.Y. 10110
www.wwnorton.com

W. W. Norton & Company Ltd.
Castle House, 75/76 Wells Street, London W1T 3QT

1 2 3 4 5 6 7 8 9 0

For my mother,

who read to me as a child

CONTENTS

Map of Yemen ix
Prologue xi

I

RISE AND FALL

1 A Far-Off Land 3
2 The Next Afghanistan 19
3 The Dogs of War 35
4 Faith and Wisdom 48
5 The Southern Job 65
6 Allies 81
7 A New War 93
8 Attrition 107
9 Victory 119

II

FORGETTING

10 Rehab 135

11 A Revolt in the North 148

12 Prison Cells 160

13 Policy Shift 176

III

THE NEXT GENERATION

14 The Great Escape 191

15 Resurrecting al-Qaeda 206

16 Echoes of Battles 220

17 The Merger 235

18 Targets 251

19 Out of the Shadows 269

Principal Characters 289

Acknowledgments 295

Note on Sources and Transliteration 301

Notes 303

Index 333

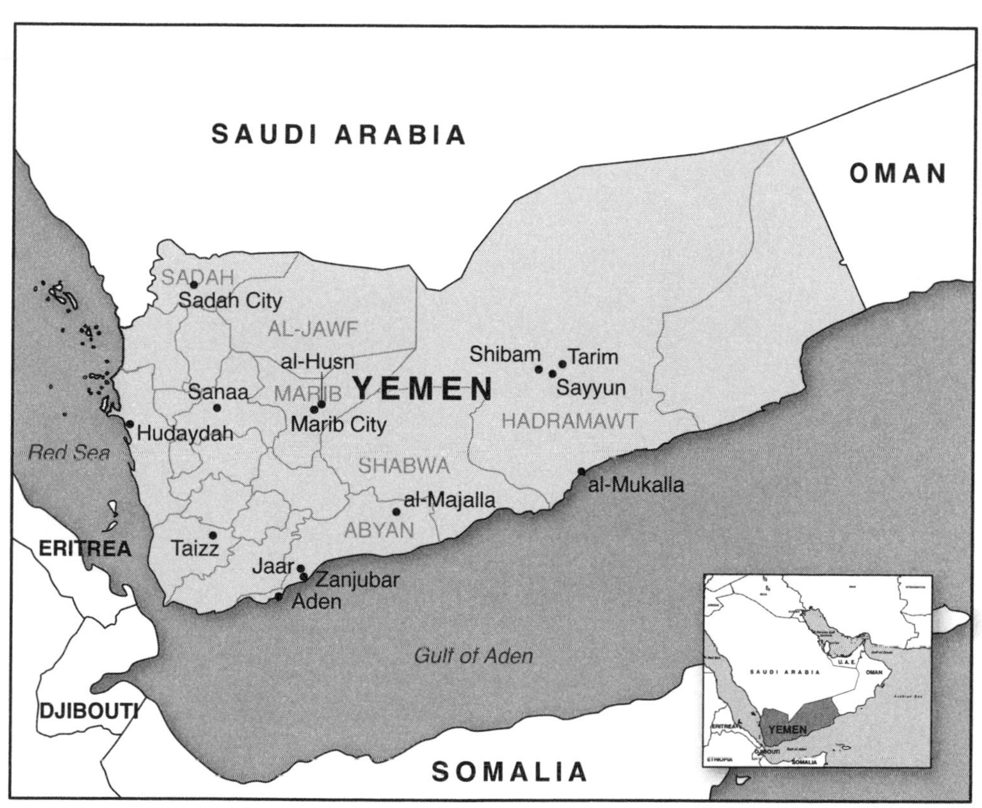
SAUDI ARABIA
OMAN
SADAH
Sadah City
AL-JAWF
al-Husn
MARIB
Marib City
YEMEN
Sanaa
Hudaydah
Red Sea
Shibam
Tarim
Sayyun
HADRAMAWT
SHABWA
al-Mukalla
al-Majalla
ABYAN
Taizz
ERITREA
Jaar
Zanjubar
Aden
Gulf of Aden
DJIBOUTI
SOMALIA
SAUDI ARABIA
U.A.E.
OMAN
ERITREA
YEMEN
ETHIOPIA
DJIBOUTI
SOMALIA

PROLOGUE

Centuries ago, somewhere in the middle of the Arabian desert, an illiterate former shepherd gathered together his band of rebels and outcasts for some final words. Most of the men had broken with their families and tribes—the social glue of seventh-century Arabia—to follow the former shepherd and his stories of an angelic revelation. Muhammad's claims had scandalized much of Mecca, on Arabia's western coast. Chased out of his hometown by an assassination plot, Muhammad had fled north looking for help. He had already dispatched some of his followers across the Red Sea into what is now Ethiopia, keeping only a handful of supporters by his side. Exhausted and on the run, it looked like the end for the small band of men who remained. Looking at the few who had followed him into the desert that day, Muhammad said, "When disaster threatens, seek refuge in Yemen." If this failed, if Muhammad didn't survive, those were their orders. Yemen was the last refuge.

History, of course, turned around. Muhammad's desperate flight north didn't fail. It was a success, the modest beginnings of an empire that would soon stretch across continents. That flickering moment of despair and doubt passed, but his words would remain, instructions for what to do in case of emergency. Muhammad was speaking to more than just the present; he was speaking to the future. Someday disaster would come and his followers would need a last refuge. Those were the men he addressed that day in the desert: the future generation who would flee to Yemen. His words were for them, whoever they might be.

FOR MOST MUSLIMS, Muhammad's desperate order to flee to Yemen is apocryphal. But for others, the handfuls of men and women down the years who considered themselves the only true believers left, his instruction spoke to them and their situation. And for that, if for no other reason, it was believed. Faith trumped evidence.

Scattered around the world in isolated pockets and secluded villages, the small bands of believers never quite needed the refuge that Yemen promised. There was always another mountain hideout, another untouchable sanctuary where they could find safety. Kings and rulers, mortal men bound by time and space, had their limits. But by the end of the twentieth century, those ancient bonds were slipping. A global power had arisen that could strike anywhere in the world. Robotic drones fired missiles at their meetings, while warships and planes harassed them out of their homes and villages. More than 1,400 years after Muhammad's battlefield speech, the moment had finally come. Surely, this was the disaster their prophet had foreseen. The men and women of the early twenty-first century were his chosen generation, and they needed a last refuge.

IN EARLY JANUARY 2009, several of these men gathered for a meeting in a tiny two-story safe house in the Yemeni highlands, just north of the capital, Sanaa. They came from all over the Arab world—Saudi Arabia, Egypt, and the Gulf—from Africa and south Asia. Within months, a handful of Americans and at least a few

Europeans would join them. For such young men, they had surprisingly long histories. Nearly all of them had fought and failed elsewhere. Some had been imprisoned, locked away in some of the world's darkest corners. In Iran and Saudi Arabia, Guantánamo Bay and Yemen, they had paid for their failures. In dank prison cells, the men had been tortured and interrogated, deprived of sleep and burned. But they had survived, and now they had fallen back on Muhammad's last refuge.

The men in the safe house that day had come to Yemen in boats, smuggled across the Gulf of Aden by human traffickers, lost in the daily waves of refugees from Africa. Some of the Saudis had driven south, speeding across the invisible line in the sand that acted as an international border. Others had landed at Sanaa International Airport claiming to be Arabic students or tourists. At least one of them had, like Muhammad's earliest supporters, ridden his camel to this latest jihad, crossing hundreds of miles of desert to reach the safe house. No matter how they arrived, they were all ready for what was coming.

Halfway around the world, President-elect Barack Obama was not prepared for what was about to happen. Sitting in a temporary office at the luxurious Hay–Adams Hotel next door to the White House, the new president was preparing to implement the changes he had promised during his campaign. At the top of his list was closing the prison at Guantánamo Bay. The detention facility had bothered him for years, harming America's image abroad and splitting voters at home. Domestic courts picked away at its legal underpinnings while stories of torture spilled out of Guantánamo's metal cages.

Although Obama didn't know it at the time, the handful of men meeting in the Yemeni safe house were about to force his hand. In the coming days, they would compel him to renege on his campaign pledge and, in the process, pose one of the most difficult questions of his administration: how could the US fight an agile and stateless enemy without yet another costly invasion that would only make the problem worse?

Obama came into office prepared to deal with wars in Afghanistan and Iraq, but he'd spent little time on Yemen. In the early days of January 2009, Yemen was still a secondary issue, but it wouldn't stay that way. By the end of his first week in office, Obama would need an answer to the question Yemen and its militants posed, and he hadn't even started thinking about the problem yet.

A few days before Obama's inauguration ceremony, the handful of men in the dusty building staged their own coming-out party. It had none of the pomp of a major international event, just four men sitting cross-legged on the ground in front of a white sheet and a black flag. The rest of the world wouldn't hear about it until days later, well after President Obama had signed an executive order announcing his intent to close Guantánamo Bay. But the men in Yemen knew what they were doing. From their cramped desert hideout, using only a camera and a few laptop computers, they embarrassed the President of the United States and his Arab allies—the Saudis and Yemenis—with a single video. Even the way they released the information was calculated to maximize its impact. First a teaser: a press statement posted on jihadi Web forums in the days leading up to the inauguration; and then, only after Obama was sworn in, the finished product.

THE NINETEEN-MINUTE video confirmed the worst fears of the US: someone who had once been in custody was now free and threatening to kill Americans. Said al-Shihri, a former Guantánamo Bay detainee from Saudi Arabia whom the US had released more than a year earlier, had rejoined al-Qaeda. Sitting on the ground in a black robe with a bandolier of bullets draped over one shoulder and a rocket launcher resting on the floor in front of him, he shook his finger at the camera. He was here, he said, to announce the merger of the Yemeni and Saudi branches of al-

Qaeda into a single organization: al-Qaeda in the Arabian Peninsula. As he spoke, al-Qaeda technicians flashed his name, title, and internment serial number at Guantánamo, 372, across the bottom of the screen.

Shihri wasn't alone. Another former Guantánamo Bay detainee from Saudi Arabia, Muhammad al-Awfi, also appeared in the video. Sitting next to Shihri, wearing a suicide vest and a red-checked headdress, was a Yemeni named Qasim al-Raymi, the group's new military commander. In the center of the semicircle, dwarfed by the two large Saudis on either side of him, sat AQAP's new commander, Nasir al-Wihayshi. The tiny Yemeni with a jutting beard and soft-spoken manner had spent four years as Osama bin Laden's understudy in Afghanistan. He had been the al-Qaeda commander's personal secretary and aide-de-camp, and now he was branching off on his own.

Yemen was back in play. Five years earlier, it had been a US success story, an early victory in the war against al-Qaeda. Now those gains were lost and al-Qaeda was back. President Obama and his staff would need to figure out how to fight a different kind of war, and they were going have to do it in one of the most inhospitable countries in the world, a place that was collapsing into civil war and violence as food prices soared and wells ran dry.

This is that story. It is the story of the rise, the fall, and the ultimate resurrection of al-Qaeda in Yemen. It is a story of success and failure, the challenges of a new century and a new way of understanding the world. It is a story of America at war.

I

RISE AND FALL

1

A Far-Off Land

1980s

The call came late in the morning, the sharp ringing of the telephone echoing off the heavy stones in a Sanaa house. On the other end of the line, an unfamiliar voice crackled through miles of static. "Hisham has been martyred," the man announced. "Congratulations."

That was all the family would get, a handful of words from a stranger 2,000 miles away. There was no body to bury and no final message to pass along. By the time the call came through from Pakistan, Hisham had been dead twelve days.

A member of one of Yemen's great religious families, Hisham al-Daylami had left for Afghanistan months earlier to fight in the jihad against the Soviets. Abd al-Wahhab, the patriarch of the family, had twelve sons and a handful of daughters, but Hisham was his favorite. Physically, the two looked nothing alike. Abd al-Wahhab was tall and thin with a lopsided face that sloped down toward his right shoulder. A wiry beard forked down off his chin in a pair of red tangles that he liked to tug at when he was deep in thought. Hisham often made the same motion, stroking his hairless chin in imitation of his father, though the pudgy teenager lacked his father's beard and his tall, striking looks. Still, the two shared a special bond that had been obvious since Hisham was a boy. When his friends were outside playing soccer, Hisham was studying the Quran. When they discovered girls in high school, shadowing them through Sanaa's twisting streets, he was devouring the works of the Egyptian radical Sayyid Qutb. Nothing touched the heart of the forty-nine-year-old religious shaykh quite like the sight of his chubby son hunched over his books.

An exacting father, Abd al-Wahhab made no secret of his preference. He loved his other sons, but Hisham was special. And now those other sons, who had received the phone call while their father was out, had to give him the news. It was September 12, 1987, and Abd al-Wahhab's favorite son was dead.

SEPTEMBER IS ONE of the most beautiful times of the year in Sanaa. The mid-afternoon rains from the monsoon clouds that get caught in Yemen's high northern mountains as they blow off the Indian Ocean in late summer have passed, but the morning frost of winter has yet to set in and turn dawn prayers uncomfortably cold. Temperatures in the early fall are mild enough for shirtsleeves and sandals as the city's inhabitants shuffle across the hourglass-shaped mountain basin upon which the city is built. On a clear day, one can easily make out the peak of Nabi Shuayb in the distance, which, at just over 12,000 feet, is the highest point in the Arabian peninsula.

On that September morning in 1987, Abd al-Wahhab struggled to speak as he listened to his sons tell him about the phone call from Pakistan. As they talked, Abd al-Wahhab's mind drifted back to the ancient story of Jacob, and how the Hebrew patriarch had handled the loss of his own favorite son. But there was little comfort in that either. "My heart was sad and my eyes welled up," he recalled. "I wanted my son."

Eventually the full story emerged. Days earlier, Hisham had been part of an operation against Soviet forces in Afghanistan.

The nineteen-year-old had attempted to fire a rocket without a launcher—an incredibly risky procedure that required balancing the rocket on a rock while using a string as a trigger—and miscalculated, killing himself and wounding two others, who like him had no previous military experience. The teenagers had been posted to a windy outpost in eastern Afghanistan known only as Maasada, or the Lion's Den, under the command of a young Saudi named Osama bin Laden.

In the years leading up to his son's death, Abd al-Wahhab had been part of a loose network of clerics and shaykhs who recruited for the jihad, encouraging young men like Hisham to travel to Afghanistan. The clerics preached wherever they could, in unfinished mosques of rebar and bare concrete and in the tiny back rooms of sympathetic shopkeepers. Across the Middle East, mainstream preachers in gleaming mosques ignored the wild-eyed clerics and their ranting sermons, but for the frustrated youths and unemployed young men their simple message struck a chord. Like Muhammad, who had built an army out of society's discards, clerics like Abd al-Wahhab transformed a movement of ex-cons and outcasts into a jihad. Drawing them in with his rhythmic and strangely looping speeches, Abd al-Wahhab had been one of the best, convincing dozens to travel thousands of miles to a land they had never heard of.

By 1986, the years of listening to his father's sermons had convinced Hisham. On a trip to Saudi Arabia to perform the hajj, the pilgrimage Islam requires of all believers, the precocious teenager told his father he was dropping out of high school to travel to Afghanistan. Standing in the shadow of the Kaabah, the large cubic structure at the center of Mecca's massive mosque and the holiest site in Islam, Abd al-Wahhab listened to his son's carefully rehearsed speech. He was surprised but not really shocked, and eventually promised Hisham his blessing on the condition that he graduated from high school first.

Even though he followed his father's instructions and waited an extra year, Hisham was still a child when he arrived in Peshawar, Pakistan—the dusty gateway to the war next door in Afghanistan. A border town full of shifting loyalties and backbiting politicians, Peshawar was nothing like the Islamic utopia he had dreamed of back in Sanaa. There was no sense of purpose and little unity. Instead of towering warriors and Islamic heroes, Hisham found a city of refugees.

In a picture taken days after he stepped off the plane in Pakistan, Hisham looks lost, a little boy drowning in his father's clothes. Within weeks of the snapshot he was dead, a martyr to the jihad. His father was supposed to be congratulated, not consoled. In time, Abd al-Wahhab would find the comfort his religion promised, even taking pride in his son's sacrifice, but on that day in September 1987 the pain was still too new. He wanted his son.

AFGHANISTAN NEVER SHOULD have been Hisham's war. A Cold War struggle in central Asia, it had little to do with Islam and nothing to do with Yemen. On the checkerboard of great power politics, religion was an accident of geography. But driven by something deeper, something more elusive than politics or power, the Arabs were drawn to the war in Afghanistan, stumbling into a country they never quite understood.

The Afghanistan these Arab volunteers found was one of long, colorless winters and bleached deserts that cracked and crumbled underfoot. The bunched mountains in the east, twisted and broken with jagged, river-laced valleys, were nothing like the sweeping deserts and cramped cities most of the jihadis called home. The gritty backwash of a country at war was played out through fractious tribes and drugged-out warlords, petty criminals, spies, and prostitutes. That was the Afghanistan of history and experience. But there was another Afghanistan that existed beyond the chaos and mess. Nurtured to life in the pristine minds of teenage boys like Hisham who would come to form terrorism's popular armies of the next century, their Afghanistan had always been more of an idea than a destination.

The Soviet Union's 1979 Christmas Day deployment to shore up the Communist government in Kabul sparked the initial fighting. But the Arabs soon transformed war into jihad. They hadn't traveled thousands of miles to stem the tide of Communism or fight for national liberation. Instead, the Arabs saw themselves as part of a long tradition dating back to the prophet. Just as Muhammad had fought unbelievers and infidels, they were battling atheists and Communists. It was a myth, of course, but in time the myth created its own reality.

Unlike other Arab governments, who publicly supported the jihad while privately discouraging their young men from traveling to Afghanistan, North Yemen, then a separate state, sent scores of its best and brightest. For an entire generation of young Yemenis, a trip to the front lines in Afghanistan became a rite of passage. There were three channels that fed Yemen's pipeline to Afghanistan. The first was the government headed by President Ali Abdullah Salih, a short, leathery military commander who in the mid-1980s favored an Afro and aviator shades. He had come to power nearly a decade earlier, in 1978, as North Yemen's fifth president. Salih invited recruits to the presidential palace, seating the awkward teenagers in huge, overstuffed chairs. Lost in the flowery opulence and gilded edges of the presidential décor, the boys listened as Salih compared them to Muhammad's earliest companions.

The second channel drew from Yemen's tribes, which often acted as a state in their own right, controlling territory and imposing their own laws in the country's rugged mountains. North of Sanaa two large tribal confederations, Hashid and Bakil, held sway. Referred to as the two wings of the state, the tribes were Yemen's most enduring social institution. Shaykh Abdullah al-Ahmar, the stately-looking head of the massive Hashid tribal confederation and its thousands of armed fighters, often hosted video parties at his walled compound in downtown Sanaa, screening grainy videos from the front lines and organizing lectures by returning fighters from Afghanistan.

The third channel was Yemen's network of mosques. Every Friday, in sermons across the country, clerics echoed government ministers and tribal shaykhs, telling their congregations that they had a duty to fight. Along with Abd al-Wahhab al-Daylami, Abd al-Majid al-Zindani, a tall, well-built preacher with a carrot-colored beard, spearheaded the effort. A former student actor who had found religion in the late 1950s, Zindani knew how to work a room. He mesmerized audiences with tales from his trips to Afghanistan. Zindani told the eager-eyed young men of the miracles of jihad: of angels falling to earth to fight beside men and of corpses refusing to decompose. With signs like these, he explained in a booming voice, God was calling them forward.

OUTSIDE SANAA, part-time preachers in small villages across Yemen took their cues from clerics like Abd al-Wahhab and Zindani, repeating from their own pulpits the stories they had heard in the capital. Around the same time Hisham was petitioning his father for permission to go to Afghanistan, another young Yemeni was coming to a similar decision. Mustafa Badi, a curly-haired Yemeni in his twenties, was just back from a stint working in Saudi Arabia when he headed to the local mosque one Friday with his cousin. "The sermon that day," he remembered years later, "changed the course of my life forever."

The village shaykh spoke about Afghanistan, a place few in the audience had ever heard of. "I didn't even know where Afghanistan was," Badi confessed. Glancing at his cousin kneeling beside him, he asked in a whisper if he knew. His cousin shrugged a response with his eyes.

Afghanistan, the shaykh's voice rang out from the front of the mosque, is a land where Muslims are under attack. Soviet pilots strike from the air, murdering entire families in their homes as they sleep, he said. Communists rape women and disguise mines as toys, maiming children too young to pray. As he spoke, a few of the men kneeling in front of him started to cry. Slowly the sobs worked their way back through the congregation, washing over the worshippers. Touching his cheek with his hand, Badi felt his own tears.

Armed with nothing but their faith in God, the shaykh continued, the Afghans were fighting back. But they needed help. Pausing slightly in his delivery, the shaykh waited for the sniffling and muffled sobs to fade. He wanted every man's face turned toward his. His eyes swept across the room, taking in the worshippers and the wordless promises that were already forming. When he spoke again, his voice was a challenge. Badi didn't need to hear any more. The next morning he bought a ticket to Pakistan.

Days later, on the flight to Karachi, Badi considered what he was doing. He didn't know anyone in Pakistan or Afghanistan and had no idea what to do or where to go when the plane landed. A week earlier he hadn't even heard of Afghanistan, and now he was on his way there.

In line to use the plane's lavatory, he struck up a conversation with a pair of young Yemeni men. The two listened as Badi repeated the shaykh's sermon, telling them of the crimes the Soviets were committing in Afghanistan. The men had told Badi they were students on their way to the Islamic University in Pakistan, but as the plane crossed over the Arabian Sea, they let slip that they too were headed to Afghanistan. The Yemenis took Badi under their care, guiding him through the wild port city of Karachi to a quiet hotel and getting him a ticket on their flight across the country to Peshawar.

In the arrivals lounge a Palestinian, who introduced himself simply as Abu Turab, was waiting for them. Along with a grubby Afghan fighter who didn't seem to speak, the jihadi packed the

Yemenis into a tiny bus, dropping them across town in front of a house in the University Town section of Peshawar. This, Abu Turab explained, was the Services Bureau, a hostel and bureaucratic clearinghouse for Arab volunteers run by Abdullah Azzam, the godfather of the Arab jihad in Afghanistan. Inside, the three surrendered their passports, identity cards, and money and selected new identities. The jihadi names, they were told, would protect them during their time in Peshawar's underground. Badi chose the name Ibrahim after his favorite prophet, the Old Testament and Quranic figure Abraham. For the rest of his time in Afghanistan he would be known only as Abu Ibrahim.

ABDULLAH AZZAM BECAME a father figure to the young men who showed up at his door in Peshawar. In Azzam's deep voice and expressive eyes, the teenagers and young men like Hisham and Badi found a man who could articulate the secret desires of their hearts. Azzam even looked like a leader. In Afghanistan, he had adopted the *pakul*, a soft woolen cap favored by the mujahidin, and let his beard grow until it reached past his collar; two white streaks that turned back to black beneath his chin.

A Palestinian by birth, Azzam was seven years old when the state of Israel was created in 1948, and the shock of its founding shaped the arc of his life. Two decades later, the 1967 Arab–Israeli war pushed him out of Palestine and into exile. A graduate student at the time, Azzam moved to Cairo, where he completed his doctorate at the prestigious al-Azhar University in 1973 before accepting a university position in Saudi Arabia. Throughout the 1960s, Egypt and Saudi Arabia had struggled for supremacy of the Arab world, fighting their own version of a cold war on proxy battlefields across the Middle East. Egyptian dissidents found refuge in Saudi Arabia, while the kingdom's critics fled to Cairo. In Saudi Arabia, Azzam fell in with Egyptian exiles like Muhammad Qutb, the younger brother of Sayyid Qutb, the radical thinker and Islamist who had been sent to his death by Egyptian president Gamal Abd al-Nasser in 1966. Saudi Arabia put Egyptians like Qutb on salary, giving them positions in state mosques and schools where they would go on to mold a generation of students with their understanding of the Quran and jihad.

By the time the Soviets invaded Afghanistan in 1979, Azzam was ready to put his theories into practice. He took a job at the Islamic University in Islamabad in 1980. But life in the quiet, tree-lined Pakistani capital was still too far from the war he sought. Within months of his arrival in Pakistan, Azzam had uprooted his family a second time and moved them 120 miles west to Peshawar. Here, in the shadow of the Khyber Pass and the jihad that lay just beyond its snowcapped mountains, he found his life's work.

On trips across the border, Azzam watched the Afghan mujahidin push back repeated Soviet offensives with little more than antique rifles and their faith in God. Their courage under fire impressed the Palestinian exile, who believed his own homeland had been stolen by invaders. Soon Azzam was back in Peshawar, developing a vision for a pan-Arab army that would travel the world liberating Muslim lands from foreign occupation. In 1984, he distilled his thinking down to a religious ruling known as a fatwa. In it, Azzam argued that jihad in Afghanistan was a duty incumbent on all Muslims. That same year he established the guesthouse and office in Peshawar that he called the Services Bureau. The nerve center of Arab efforts in Afghanistan, the Services Bureau was designed to catch the expected flow of volunteers. But for the first few years after Azzam's fatwa there was only a trickle, teenagers and young men like Hisham and Badi.

When the men wouldn't come to Afghanistan, Azzam brought Afghanistan to them. On recruiting trips across the Middle East, he roused crowds with his booming voice and onstage theatrics. "Jihad and the rifle alone," he shouted, shaking a rifle in the air. He repeated the performance wherever there were Muslims, traveling to Europe and the US to recruit fighters for his war. The US, eager to see the Soviets bogged down in their own Vietnam, allowed Azzam to establish satellite centers across the country, in cities like Brooklyn, Kansas City, and Tucson. The broad-shouldered Palestinian in his Afghan cap was a tireless recruiter, screening videos and delivering speeches night after night. "Your brothers and sisters in Afghanistan need you," he beseeched the uncertain crowds.

Listening to Azzam, one jihadi recalled years later, "made me want to find a blanket and withdraw from the world." The men that emerged were Azzam's soldiers, pledging their loyalty and obedience to him. Everything Azzam did—the lectures, the videos, and especially his battlefield stories, when he would grab his listener by the hand, clenching his callused fist around their fingers while he whispered what he'd seen on the front lines—was designed to attract the pious and the adventurous.

By the late 1980s, just as the Soviets were preparing to withdraw, the trickle of Arab volunteers had turned into a flood. Many of these men gravitated to Azzam and his Saudi protégé, Osama bin Laden on February 15, 1989. The final Soviet soldier in Afghanistan, General Boris Gromov, walked across the concrete and steel Friendship Bridge and into Soviet Uzbekistan. That doesn't matter, bin Laden told the legions of new fighters who had gathered around him in Peshawar. The Soviets had left behind a puppet government in Kabul, and bin Laden wanted to finish the job. The thirty-one-year-old Saudi was full of confidence after the Soviet retreat, and he was planning one final trip over the border into Afghanistan. No one expected much of a fight. In Langley, Virginia, CIA analysts agreed with the mujahidin's analysis, and together with Pakistani intelligence they put together a plan to support the rebel fighters as they pushed west out of Pakistan toward Kabul. Already the subject of fawning articles back home in Saudi Arabia, bin Laden wanted to reach a wider audience. His march to Kabul would be a victory lap that would secure his reputation as a hero of the jihad.

On the other side of the Khyber Pass, the Arabs reassembled in the freezing mountains outside the city of Jalalabad in eastern Afghanistan. Tucked inside the city, protected by a winding river fed by the winter snows and lines of Russian mines, sat several thousand soldiers loyal to Afghanistan's Communist government. Along with bin Laden's Arabs, several groups of Afghan mujahidin had taken up positions in the mountains around the city in March and April, all hoping to deliver the knockout blow before advancing on Kabul, just over 100 miles to the west. This was the loose alliance of shaggy-haired rebels and warlords that had impressed Azzam years earlier and eventually chased the Soviets out of Afghanistan. Despite a decade of war, few of the mujahidin commanders had experience in taking a city. They had been guerrilla fighters, slipping out of the mountains to disable Soviet tanks or popping up from behind pine trees to bring down low-flying helicopters with Stinger missiles. Many of the commanders had been rivals for the foreign funding and arms that fueled the war, and the years of competition had fostered a culture of mistrust.

Early efforts to take the city failed, as Communist fighters easily turned back the mujahidin's wild frontal assaults. Suspicious commanders, who worried their rivals were playing a double game and holding out for more cash now that the war was winding down, blamed one another for the setbacks. Instead of the quick romp to victory predicted by the CIA, the mujahidin coalition fractured and fell apart. Bin Laden tried to steer clear of the rivalries and suspicions in the Afghan ranks, but he couldn't defeat the Communists on his own. Most days, the Saudi commander dispatched fresh raiding parties from his mountain base in a vain attempt to break the stalemate. Through the spring, dozens of Arab fighters lost their lives in bin Laden's poorly planned forays. One Yemeni fighter was killed when he attempted to rush a tank position. Others were killed in the steady bombardment of missiles and cluster bombs from the Afghan Communists' aging fleet of fighter planes.

Fifteen weeks after that first hopeful rush, in the heat of late summer in Afghanistan, Jalalabad finally fell to the mujahidin. The victory was a hollow one. The fissures that the siege of Jalalabad had exposed continued to grow as the fighting in Afghanistan collapsed into civil war between the various mujahidin commanders. Instead of enjoying his victory, bin Laden withdrew back to Pakistan in disgust, having lost more than eighty men in the weeks of fighting.

BOTH AZZAM AND bin Laden were troubled by the debacle at Jalalabad and the bickering fallout among their Afghan allies. Azzam wondered if his dream of a pan-Arab army had been a mistake, while bin Laden tried to figure out where his battle plan had gone wrong. Each went looking for answers. Azzam traveled eight days on foot through the Hindu Kush to the northern Panjshir Valley on the border with Soviet Tajikistan to visit Ahmad Shah Massoud, a brilliant guerrilla commander who had stayed out of the fighting at Jalalabad. Bin Laden sought solitude and space. In late 1989, shortly after Azzam returned to Peshawar, the two spoke one final time. Then bin Laden flew home.

Azzam remained in Peshawar and tried to rebuild his dream. In November, Abd al-Majid al-Zindani, the Yemeni cleric with the carrot-colored beard, arrived in Peshawar to consult with his old friend and mentor. Zindani wanted to talk about the future and what to do after Afghanistan. Let's speak after Friday prayers, Azzam told him. The Palestinian commander was exhausted from the political backbiting in the border town, which by now had attracted thousands of unaffiliated fighters looking for a war. In the face of so many men entering Peshawar, Azzam had lost control of the movement. Like the Afghan mujahidin, the Arab alliance was breaking down. The Services Bureau couldn't keep up with the paperwork of registering everyone in Azzam's antiquated database, and newer fighters began gravitating toward uncompromising figures like the Egyptian radical Ayman al-Zawahiri, who whispered that Azzam was the problem. Rumors and lies swirled through the city's markets and mosques. Instead of uniting Azzam's fighters, victory had divided them.

On November 24, 1989, the day Azzam was scheduled to meet with Zindani after Friday prayers, the veteran jihadi said goodbye to his wife and left for the mosque with two of his sons. Azzam's afternoon was packed with meetings, and he wanted some quiet time before prayers. As their car neared the mosque, a bomb that had been hidden in a drainage culvert exploded, splitting the car into two jagged pieces and killing all three men instantly. The forty-four pounds of TNT were powerful enough to propel the body of Azzam's twenty-three-year-old son, Muhammad, into a nearby tree, while the legs of his younger son, fourteen-year-old Ibrahim, got tangled in electrical wires overhead. The boy's hands landed across the street in a gory spray of metal and body parts that coated nearby buildings. Azzam's body, however, was barely touched. "There was just a little blood coming from his mouth," his nephew recalled.

A final miracle or not, the godfather of the Afghan jihad was dead. Weeks earlier, a cleaning crew at the mosque had discovered a massive bomb hidden under the pulpit he used for Friday sermons. Yes, there are threats, admitted Azzam at the time, telling one journalist, "My destiny is already written. Nothing I can do will prevent what is meant to happen."

At Azzam's funeral, days later, a brokenhearted Zindani tried to hold the movement together. Standing before hundreds of mourners on a hill outside Peshawar, he made an impassioned plea, his voice rising and falling in the microphone, as he praised Azzam's ability to reconcile different factions and called for unity now that Azzam was gone. But Zindani couldn't replace Azzam. No one could.

Azzam's death ended whatever command-and-control structure existed among the squabbling Arabs. Absent the Soviets and Azzam's guiding hand, the fighting in Afghanistan went on, directionless and purposeless, a nationwide crime spree masquerading as war. Frustrated and outmaneuvered, Zindani gave up on Afghanistan, following bin Laden back to Saudi Arabia, where the ruling family set him up in his own institution. Within months, the shine was off the new position. Lecturing and research was dull compared to a decade of jihad. Like Azzam, Zindani couldn't find it in his heart to be an academic. He hadn't even finished the two degrees he had started. His first, in pharmacy studies, he'd abandoned when he found religion in Cairo. His next attempt, in Islamic studies at al-Azhar University, had been similarly short-lived. Looking to recapture some of the lost magic of the Afghanistan campaign, Zindani turned his back on Saudi Arabia's oil money and headed home to Yemen. He would soon find a new jihad.

WITH TIME TO think away from the battlefields in Afghanistan, bin Laden reflected on Azzam's assassination and his own failure at Jalalabad. Like Azzam, he had dreamed of a movement that would unite the Muslim world, restoring it to the greatness of the early caliphate, when Islam had reigned over an empire that stretched from Spain to Asia. The problem in Afghanistan, bin Laden believed, was a lack of unity. But he could fix that. Along with Tariq al-Fadhli, a twenty-two-year-old Yemeni veteran of Afghanistan, bin Laden was already working on plans for the next jihad. This time, he would be in control.

Fadhli was a thin, hawk-faced fighter with a goatee who favored the same oversized black turban that the Taliban would later make famous. He had been with bin Laden in the mountains around Jalalabad, and had even been wounded in the fighting. Both men had grown up in Saudi Arabia, but each saw Yemen as his homeland. Bin Laden's father, Muhammad, had been a Yemeni day laborer who traveled north to the new kingdom of Saudi Arabia and turned himself into a construction magnate. Nasir al-Fadhli, on the other hand, had been born into leadership as the heir to the sultanate of Abyan, a region in southern Yemen famous for its coastal fishing and rugged mountains. Backed by the British Empire, which had established Aden as a Crown colony, the Fadhli family thrived for much of the early twentieth century. But in 1967, months after Tariq was born, the British abandoned Aden, leaving their former friends exposed. Marxist militias soon forced the Fadhli family off their farms and into exile in Saudi Arabia. Growing up in the kingdom, Fadhli was indoctrinated in the same theological school that would produce bin Laden and eventually al-Qaeda. By the time young Saudis started to head to Afghanistan in the mid-1980s, Fadhli had been uniquely prepared by both his father's stories and Saudi Arabia's strong anti-Communist ideology to combat the Soviets and their allies. The twin pillars of his life, family and faith, were allied against the same enemy.

Many of the Saudi volunteers who went to Afghanistan were rich dilettantes playing at jihad. But for Fadhli, fighting Communism was less an adventure vacation than a proving ground. Afghanistan prepared him for his real jihad in Yemen. The boy who went off to central Asia on jihad came home a leader of men. Fadhli had seen war and survived. The vague, youthful expression was gone, replaced by creases of tension around his eyes that deepened and widened as he aged.

Recovering in Saudi Arabia from the wound he sustained at Jalalabad, Fadhli was as shocked by the news of Azzam's assassination as bin Laden had been. Both men had trouble recognizing the movement they had helped mold. In Peshawar, Azzam's would-be heirs were bickering over the future of jihad, but in the steamy Saudi port city of Jeddah, bin Laden and Fadhli charted their own course. Bin Laden talked less than the others, but he planned more. And he had something no one else had: money.

In the months after Azzam's assassination, bin Laden and Fadhli sat up late in the evening, enjoying the cool sea breeze, as they sketched out the future of jihad in bin Laden's apartment. They were both drawn to Yemen, the land of their fathers, a place they knew only through family stories and snapshots. Said to be the Arab world's Afghanistan, Yemen was full of tribes and mountains and, at least in the south, was ruled by Socialists. But mostly it was a blank map onto which the two young jihadis could project their ambitions.

After months of conversations and lengthy strategy sessions, the pair produced a plan that looked remarkably like the one Azzam had used in Afghanistan. Bin Laden would supply the funding while Fadhli led a group of Arab fighters into the southern mountains, where they would initiate a guerrilla war. In bin Laden's mind, the Yemen campaign would be the first in a series of steps to renew and reinvigorate the Muslim world. But first he had to rid the Arab world of the Communists. The jihadis, bin Laden believed, had defeated them in Afghanistan; surely they could beat them in Yemen. At once grandiose in objective and simple in design, bin Laden's plan, like Azzam's original, would benefit from decisions made elsewhere. As in Afghanistan, a state and a band of jihadis were about to find they had a common enemy.

2

The Next Afghanistan

1990–1993

In late 1989, Yemeni president Ali Abdullah Salih was preparing for unification. Over the past several months, while Osama bin Laden and Tariq al-Fadhli had been plotting their new jihad, Salih had been laying the groundwork for expansion. Quietly shuttling between his capital, Sanaa, and the whitewashed port city of Aden in South Yemen, Salih pitched the idea to Ali Salim al-Bid (pronounced "Beed"), his Socialist counterpart. It wasn't a difficult case to make. The Cold War was ending, and both North and South Yemen were in trouble.

After the British fled Aden in 1967, with clients like the Fadhlis close behind, leftist militias seized control of South Yemen. Within three years, a radical Marxist faction had taken over, establishing the People's Democratic Republic of Yemen in 1970 and outlawing every political party except their own. The Marxists had then embarked on a curious social experiment that attempted to mix Islam and socialism into a workable unity. The result was a strange amalgamation of competing symbols in which mosques sat uneasily next to beer gardens and bikini beaches. By the late 1980s, the grand experiment was unraveling, as the Socialist government found itself an international pariah thanks to its support of leftist terrorist groups, and nearly broke as Soviet aid began to run dry. In the north, Salih's republic was almost as badly off. Less a president than a shaykh with a state, Salih ruled North Yemen like a giant tribe, and his patronage-based government barely functioned. Salih thrived on making deals, playing rivals against one another in a process he flippantly referred to as dancing on the heads of snakes.

Oil and greed pushed both sides toward a deal. For years Salih and Bid had watched their neighbors on the Arabian peninsula get rich while they scraped by on pennies. Test wells in the border region between the two countries suggested that a united Yemen might have oil reserves of its own, but first the two presidents had to set aside their political differences. Excited at the prospect of oil wealth, Salih and Bid initiated a secret dialogue.

In late 1989, Salih paid a final visit to Aden. Later that day, Yemen's two Alis announced the impending unification of their two countries. Despite the platitudes, both men must have known that only one of them could win. A united Yemen needed one president, not two. Salih had already shown he could survive in the ruthless world of North Yemeni politics. His two immediate predecessors had been assassinated within months of one another. The first was gunned down in a murky gang-style hit along with his brother and a pair of women described by newspapers as prostitutes. All four bodies were then doused with alcohol and dumped. North Yemen's next president, Ahmad al-Ghashmi, fared even worse. Nine months after being sworn in he was assassinated in a drug deal gone wrong. Ghashmi had sent qat—a leafy stimulant grown primarily in the north—south to the socialist president in Aden. When the socialist envoy returned with payment, the briefcase that was supposed to contain cash exploded in Ghashimi's face. Despite rumors that Salih may have had a hand in one or both assassinations, he succeeded Ghashmi as North Yemen's fifth president. At the time, hardly anyone in Yemen thought Salih, a no-name officer from a tiny tribe, could survive. CIA officials even took bets on how long the curly-haired military officer would last. One analyst told the *Washington Post* in early 1979 that Salih wouldn't make it six months. But he did, surviving an attempted coup three months into his rule before restructuring the military and intelligence command structures until they resembled his tribal family tree.

Bid's rise to the top had been even bloodier. Four years before unification, during a midmorning politburo meeting in January 1986, a presidential bodyguard walked into the room and started shooting. Apparently under instructions from Ali Nasir Muhammad, the sitting president, the bodyguard killed the vice president, the minister of defense, and a politburo member. Bid, another politburo member who was in the room at the time, escaped out the window down a makeshift rope of curtains. The fighting that followed lasted for ten days. Thousands died in a bloodbath that confused the Socialists' allies in Moscow before Muhammad, the president who had ordered the preemptive counter-coup, fled the country. As one of the few high-ranking officials left in the country, Bid outmaneuvered his domestic opponents to be elected general secretary.

With so much blood behind them, both presidents moved toward unification cautiously. They devised a five-man "collective presidency" with Salih as chair and Bid as deputy chairman. Bid also agreed, in a nod to the north's greater population, to Sanaa as the capital instead of Aden. But almost as soon as they'd announced the newly unified Yemen, each started looking for ways to undercut the other. Bid thought he could sow enough chaos north of the old border to divide Salih's base into a series of petty power blocs. Salih had essentially the same plan for Bid and the south.

The Socialists had spent close to three decades trying to suppress the tribes and the reactionary thinking they believed the tribal system nurtured. Salih wanted to undo their work, retribalizing the south in an effort to outflank the Socialists in their own backyard. Salih reached out to Tariq al-Fadhli, who was still planning the

Yemen jihad with bin Laden in Saudi Arabia, and dozens of other tribal exiles. Nearly all of them had lost land when the Socialists came to power, and they were ready to return home.

Along with the tribesmen came scores of Arab fighters from Afghanistan. After their victory over the Soviets, most of them had found that they were no longer welcome in their home countries. But Yemen was different. Aware that the veteran fighters might prove useful in his brewing struggle against the Socialists, Salih turned a blind eye to the jihadis flooding into Yemen in the months after unification in early 1990. The foreign fighters, many of whom were connected to bin Laden, scattered across the country, setting up camps near the Saudi border and in the desert province of Marib. In the south, Fadhli provided the bridge between Salih's retribalization strategy and bin Laden's jihad. Fadhli was loyal to bin Laden and the plan they had made together, but he was also bound to his father's tribe and their lands in the south. There were other ties to consider as well. One of Salih's relatives and top generals, Ali Muhsin al-Ahmar, had married into the Fadhli clan, wedding Fadhli's sister. But for the moment at least, Fadhli didn't have to choose. In the early 1990s, Salih and the jihadis were on the same side.

EAST OF ADEN, halfway along the coastal road toward the port city of al-Mukalla, sits a rugged range of mountains known as al-Maraqishah. Barely 10 miles from the dazzling blue Gulf of Aden, the mountains jut up like a jagged row of teeth. Amid these cracked and broken peaks the few roads that exist are mostly rough dirt tracks grafted over old shepherd trails. It was here, among bunched outcroppings of rock and twisted desert trees, that Fadhli and his men set up camp in the summer of 1990. After more than two decades of exile, he had finally come home. These were the mountains that had formed the backdrop to his childhood bedtime stories. This was where his grandfather had learned to hunt and where his father had become a ruler. This was Abyan, the land of his birth.

Below the peaks, stretching toward the coast, was the massive cotton farm where he had been born twenty-three years earlier. Like everything else the family once owned, the Socialists had seized it in 1967. The state divided the land into tiny parcels, redistributing the sections to tribesmen it called the proletariat. What the Socialists didn't give away they kept for themselves, nationalizing the most profitable pieces. One house they converted into a police station, another they made over into a headquarters for state security. They renamed the main farm after Lenin, displaying busts of the bald visionary in the very rooms where Fadhli's mother had once rocked him to sleep.

Fadhli's motivations ran deeper than the loss of money and property, however. Handfuls of his uncles and cousins had stayed behind to fight the Marxist guerrillas when the rest of the family fled to safety in 1967. The bodies of those men were now scattered across the region, buried where they fell in unmarked graves. Fadhli would later tell reporters that he hadn't returned to Yemen for revenge, but at the time, as a veteran of the jihad in Afghanistan and as his father's heir, he must have felt the heavy weight of family and tribal expectations. With his elderly father still in exile, it fell to the twenty-three-year-old to reclaim the family's honor.

Fadhli slowly added to his army of Afghan Arabs, as the men who had fought in Afghanistan called themselves. In tribal councils across southern Yemen, he appealed to his father's former tribesmen, calling on them to follow him as they had once followed his father. Falling back on lessons of leadership he'd learned under fire in Afghanistan, the young jihadi rallied the tribal remnant that remained in Abyan. Within months of returning to Yemen in 1990, Fadhli was ready to put bin Laden's plan into action. For the fighters who had been with him in Afghanistan, the campaign had a similar feel. Once again they were on jihad, fighting Socialists in the mountains.

East of Fadhli's Abyan camp, dozens of other Yemeni fighters, along with a smattering of foreign Arabs, used bin Laden's seemingly endless supply of money to set up their own camps in 1990. The Saudi financier paid the men a small salary and promised them cars and guns in return for their service. Much like Fadhli, bin Laden felt the self-imposed weight of liberating his father's homeland. From his apartment in Jeddah, bin Laden tracked the raids and assassinations his men carried out across the south. Yemen was his passion that summer, and he spent freely out of the fortune his father had left. Much like the Services Bureau in Peshawar, bin Laden's apartment in Jeddah now doubled as a recruiting center.

Friends in Saudi Arabia cautioned bin Laden against meddling in Yemen, warning him that it wouldn't end well. But bin Laden was unyielding, often quoting a *hadith*, or saying of the Prophet Muhammad: "Expel the infidels from the Arabian peninsula." That, bin Laden's expression seemed to suggest, should end the discussion. The Socialists were infidels; they had to be expelled. A year earlier, in 1989, just as the jihad in Afghanistan was drawing to a close, bin Laden had created a small organization he called al-Qaeda. Yemen was supposed to be the new group's first test.

BEFORE BIN LADEN could fully mobilize his private army, he had to put his plans on hold. On August 2, 1990, Saddam Hussein invaded Kuwait. Bin Laden, who had never liked the secular Iraqi leader, saw an opportunity to get royal backing for his army of jihadis. With Fadhli and the others handling the jihad in Yemen, bin Laden approached several members of the Saudi royal family to lobby for the chance to defend the kingdom. The princes, who were suddenly confronting Saddam's rumored million-man army only miles from their eastern oil fields, were not impressed with bin Laden's battle plans. "There are no caves in the desert," one prince scoffed. "What will you do when he lobs missiles at you with chemical and biological weapons?"

Instead of the jihadis, the Saudis turned to the US for help. Bin Laden was stunned. He had spent the last year fighting to expel infidels from the Arabian peninsula in Yemen and at home his own government was inviting them to build military bases on holy ground. For bin Laden and the rest of the jihadis, the difference between Socialists and capitalists was one of degrees; they divided the world between Muslim and infidel. Fed up with his complaints and criticism, the princes told bin Laden to keep quiet and know his place. For all his money and connections, he was still a commoner. The jihadi hero had no place in the kingdom's foreign policy.

In Sanaa, President Salih was similarly distracted. After Yemen's unification, the Arab League had, in a rare moment of unity, granted the new country the "Arab seat" on the UN Security Council. In the wake of Saddam's invasion, this harmless diplomatic favor had turned into a crisis for Salih's new government. Saddam Hussein was a close friend and someone Salih modeled himself after, but the Yemeni president couldn't ignore the pressure from the other side. The US, Saudi Arabia, and Kuwait's exiled, though still wealthy, royal family were all major donors to Yemen and its faltering economy. Uncertain which way to turn, Salih decided to split the difference and directed his diplomats at the UN to pursue what he called a middle course. In New York, Yemen's ambassador to the UN abstained from the initial resolution condemning the invasion.

US president George H. W. Bush warned Salih that Yemen was making the wrong choice. Bush wanted to make the Gulf crisis—the first post–Cold War conflict—a showcase for the new world order. To do that, the US needed a broad, multinational coalition. Yemen's grandstanding and calls for an "Arab" solution to the crisis were ruining the show. Making matters worse, Yemen was scheduled to take over the presidency of the UN Security Council on

December 1, 1990. As dictated by its charter, the Security Council presidency rotates monthly along alphabetical lines and allows that country's ambassador to set the agenda and oversee any crisis as well as serve as the body's spokesperson. The US wanted any vote on the use of force in Iraq to take place before Yemen assumed the presidency. Days before that happened, Bush tried again. While he was in Saudi Arabia visiting the troops for Thanksgiving, he directed Secretary of State James Baker, whom he had brought along, to fly to Yemen for a personal conversation with Salih. Bush knew it was a long shot. Salih viewed Iraq's invasion and the Gulf crisis as a minor diplomatic flap. "This is like a summer storm," he said. "It will blow over." The Saudis, who knew the temperamental Yemeni leader well, also warned Baker that he was wasting his time.

Salih was evasive during the meeting, shrugging noncommittally over the mutton his chefs had prepared when Baker suggested that Yemen stood to lose $70 million in annual aid from the US alone. A seasoned diplomat, Baker tried to feel the president out. Salih wouldn't give him a straight answer. When the meeting ended, the two men stepped out to face the press. Salih suddenly grew more animated in the presence of cameras, telling reporters that Yemen would not support the resolution. Frustrated and embarrassed by Salih's performance, Baker flew back to Saudi Arabia; it would be another twenty years before a US secretary of state again visited Yemen.

Nearly one month later, on the night before the final vote in the Security Council, an exhausted Baker put it as bluntly as he knew how in a conversation with Yemen's ambassador to the UN, Abdullah al-Ashtal. "This will be the most expensive 'no' vote you ever cast," Baker told the diplomat. Ashtal shrugged. He had his orders. The next day, the Yemeni ambassador spoke first in the debate. Reading from a prepared text, he strongly condemned the US and the resolution. As the slight diplomat sat down, Baker slipped a scribbled note to an aide. "Yemen's permanent representative just enjoyed about $200 to $250 million worth of applause for that speech."

Baker's prediction came true almost immediately. Within days of the vote, Saudi Arabia retaliated. In mid-September, after Yemen's first Security Council abstention, the kingdom had expelled nearly one million Yemeni migrant workers, who had previously enjoyed easy access to employment. This time Saudi Arabia cut off millions in aid. What good was helping out your neighbor, King Fahd wondered, if your neighbor wouldn't help you?

Remittances from Saudi Arabia had been Yemen's safety net for decades, and the sudden reversal was a shock. Overnight Yemen lost a steady stream of cash and gained a million newly unemployed workers. The US and Kuwait also followed through on Baker's threat and canceled most of their own aid packages. The cuts sent a sharp message, but also dealt Yemen a blow from which it has yet to recover. Instead of reaping the benefits of a newly unified democracy in the post–Cold War world, Yemen was diplomatically isolated and in the middle of a cash crisis. Already struggling to integrate two vastly different systems of government and their competing bureaucracies, Yemen was ill prepared for the loss in aid. Its currency went into freefall, losing more than half its value in months. There were riots across the country as the government was forced to cut back on food subsidies. Stung by his foray into international politics, Salih turned inward, refocusing on the struggle in the south.

AS US AND coalition troops romped to victory in Iraq during January and February 1991, coming within 150 miles of Baghdad before opting to leave a weakened Saddam Hussein in power, Yemen descended into chaos. Fadhli and the rest of the Arab Afghans, acting on bin Laden's broad instructions, roamed across the south, ambushing Socialist leaders and assassinating politicians.

North of the former border, other politicians were dying as well, in a series of seemingly random attacks that were never solved. To most Yemenis it wasn't clear if the killings were personal vendettas being played out against the backdrop of a country coming apart, or something different. In the midst of the disorder and confusion, Fadhli and the jihadis thrived. They were doing exactly what he and bin Laden had planned two years earlier in Jeddah.

North of the war he had unleashed in Yemen, bin Laden was growing increasingly frustrated with his role in Saudi Arabia's politics. He'd returned from Afghanistan in 1989 to a stream of praise in the press and at mosques around the kingdom. But during the 1990–91 Gulf War, he learned how little the royal family valued his efforts. In the months after the war, bin Laden watched in anger as US soldiers expanded their bases in Saudi Arabia instead of leaving as they had promised. Ostensibly a hedge against a weakened Saddam Hussein in Iraq, the continued presence of US troops and the decision to leave the Iraqi dictator in power appeared to bin Laden to be part of an American plot to take control of his beloved Arabian peninsula. In conversations with friends, bin Laden fumed about the shame and embarrassment he felt. As if American soldiers weren't bad enough, the US contingent also included females. "Women," he sputtered, "defending Saudi men." Slowly bin Laden realized that if he was ever going to be free to pursue his dream of restoring the Islamic world to the glory of history, he would have to abandon his homeland. Bin Laden didn't reach this decision lightly. But once it was made, he took some comfort from a precedent he found in the life of the Prophet. In 622, Muhammad fled Mecca with a handful of followers ahead of a plot to assassinate him. That journey would become known as the *hijrah*, or migration, and the starting point of the Islamic calendar. Bin Laden saw his decision to leave Saudi Arabia in similarly stark terms. Perhaps in an effort to strengthen the parallel, bin Laden told friends he was worried that Saudi intelligence might try to kill him for his outspoken opposition to the king.

In March 1992, bin Laden set off on his own *hijrah*, traveling to Afghanistan where he offered his services as a mediator in the brewing civil war among the mujahidin. When none of his old friends would listen to his advice, he reversed course and flew back across the Middle East to Sudan. Hasan al-Turabi, Sudan's Islamist leader, had been begging him to come to Africa for years, and with few other options bin Laden finally accepted.

Soon after he arrived in Sudan, another piece of bin Laden's imagined conspiracy fell into place. On December 3, 1992, the UN Security Council voted to allow "all necessary means to establish as soon as possible a secure environment for humanitarian relief operations in Somalia." As part of the US action plan for Operation Restore Hope, which President Bush announced the day after the vote, the Pentagon proposed using the Yemeni port of Aden as a jumping-off point for the peacekeeping mission in war-torn Somalia. On the map it looked perfect: separated from the fighting by the Gulf of Aden, but close enough that soldiers could be on the ground in Somalia in less than an hour. Eager to work his way back into favor after his Security Council misstep two years earlier, Salih agreed to the US request. For bin Laden, the move was further evidence of US designs on the peninsula.

From the farm he had purchased outside the Sudanese capital of Khartoum, bin Laden contemplated his options. He wanted to send a message, but he wasn't sure he was ready to strike the US directly. Despite his exile, bin Laden still nurtured thoughts of one day returning to Saudi Arabia, and he was certain that any attack linked to him or his al-Qaeda network would destroy those chances. Across the Red Sea in Yemen, al-Qaeda members kept him up-to-date with calls and personal briefings. Reports flooded into the Khartoum farm of soldiers stationed in hotels and planes at the airport in Aden. But still bin Laden wavered, haunted by a single thought. He had done nothing when US soldiers came to Saudi Arabia and now, more than a year after the war ended, they were still there. He couldn't shake the feeling that if he failed to act a second time, the Americans would never leave Arabia. Finally, after days of indecision, bin Laden gave the order to strike. From this point on, there would be no way out. Bin Laden had made his choice.

ON DECEMBER 23, shortly after bin Laden made up his mind in Sudan, a handful of Fadhli's men ambushed a Socialist politician in Abyan. At the same time, several miles west along the coast, Jamal al-Nahdi, another bin Laden ally from Afghanistan, was holding a meeting in an Aden apartment. Like bin Laden's father, Nahdi had been born in Hadramawt, the angled governorate of dust and rocks in Yemen's eastern desert. In 1989, Nahdi had also been one of the first men to swear the *bay'a*, or oath of allegiance that signified membership in al-Qaeda, to bin Laden at an early meeting in Afghanistan. With Fadhli busy carrying out raids from his hideout in Abyan, bin Laden turned to Nahdi for the strike on the US Marines in Aden. Already bin Laden understood the dangers of micromanaging his men, preferring what he would later call a philosophy of "centralization of decision and decentralization of execution." Bin Laden ordered the attack, but the details were up to his operatives on the ground.

Nahdi laid out a simple plan that Wednesday in Aden. He divided his men, many of whom had spent time at a training camp near the Saudi border under the tutelage of a Libyan instructor paid for by bin Laden, into two teams. The first group would hit Aden's airport, near the heart of downtown along the harbor's eastern shore. Their goal would be the destruction of a US Navy transport plane, a C-5 Galaxy, which the jihadis had glimpsed parked on the tarmac. Nahdi himself would supervise the second, trickier part of the plot: simultaneous bombings of the two hotels where the US Marines were staying. Intuitively, the Yemeni veteran of Afghanistan grasped the power of the synchronized strikes that would come to characterize al-Qaeda attacks in the years to come.

Five days after Nahdi's planning session, on the eve of the attack, his men contacted him with an urgent request. Socialist security forces in Aden, always on the lookout for jihadi sympathizers, had arrested the two men Nahdi had tasked with hitting the airport. Worried their cover was blown, the rest of the cell wanted to call off the attack. Nahdi heard them out, but he had already made his decision. The explosives were in place, buried near one of the fences surrounding the airport, and bin Laden wanted that plane. Turning to a muscular, African-looking Yemeni at his side, Nahdi asked if he was prepared to take over the airport job. "Absolutely," the man replied.

Nahdi had recruited the man, Salih al-Khanabashi, a year earlier. Like many young Yemenis, Khanabashi had been indoctrinated by glory-inducing sermons about the jihad in Afghanistan that told of how a band of outnumbered Arabs armed only with guns and God's blessing had defeated the mighty Soviet army. By the time he met Nahdi in 1991, two years after the Soviet withdrawal, Khanabashi thought he had missed his chance at jihad. Nahdi explained it differently, telling the young Somali-born Yemeni that the jihad hadn't ended; rather, it had moved from Afghanistan back to Yemen. "Brother," the veteran fighter continued, "we are in need of men to declare war on God's enemies"—a reference to Yemen's Socialists.

One year after that recruiting pitch, Khanabashi was about to get the chance he thought he had missed. Nahdi briefed him on the plan, telling him where the smuggled explosives were buried and instructing a second man to help with the attack.

When the two men reached the airport the following evening, December 29, they found only some churned-up ground where the explosives had been. Across town, in the parking lot of the Movenpick Hotel, Nahdi was having his own problems. He had already planted one bomb at the Gold Mohur, a luxury hotel just off the beach, but as he tinkered with the second bomb a faulty detonator exploded, nearly severing his hand. While his men struggled to stop the gushing blood, they heard the first bomb go off. The blast ripped through one of the upper floors in the Gold Mohur, shattering windows and fracturing support beams, killing two people. Nahdi didn't know it at the time, but he hadn't even got that one right. Instead of the Marines he'd targeted, the bomb killed an Austrian tourist and a hotel employee. The Marines were staying across town in a different hotel. Dazed from the loss of blood and with the remains of his hand hanging limply at his side, Nahdi and his men were picked up within minutes by police units as they worked to salvage the second bomb at the Movenpick. Al-Qaeda's first terrorist attack had failed.

SHORTLY AFTER THE failed bombings, Vice President Ali Salim al-Bid ordered Socialist military units into Abyan to track down the jihadis. The terms of Yemen's unity agreement had failed to integrate the two armies, and Bid still had several units under his direct command. The bombings in Aden finally gave him the excuse he had been looking for to go after the jihadis. The Socialist Third Armored Division surrounded Fadhli's camp in Abyan and several other training camps further east in the mountains of Shabwa. From Sanaa, Salih watched the developing situation closely. In an attempt to outflank Bid's military units, Salih dispatched a mediation team south to meet with Fadhli and his besieged men. The president's men laid out the choices: Fadhli could surrender himself to Salih and travel back to Sanaa, or he could fight Bid and lose. Reluctantly, Fadhli agreed to return to Sanaa under the president's umbrella of protection. Bid was livid, but Salih promised him and the international community that there would be a full investigation.

Not everyone enjoyed Fadhli's level of protection, however. In Shabwa, the next governorate to the east, Khanabashi had sought refuge in one of the mountain camps Bid's soldiers were now shelling. Late in the evening of January 9, 1993, a local tribesman slipped down the gravelly slopes and into camp. "Can you hold them off for another month?" he asked. The fighters stared at him disbelief. "I need that much time to get more men and weapons," he explained.

Khanabashi shook his head; he doubted they could last another day. Leaving a few men to cover their escape, the rest of the jihadis abandoned the camp. Most of them went north, traveling back to the camp in Sadah, near the Saudi border, where they had trained for the Aden attacks. But their Libyan instructor was gone and there wasn't much for them to do. The attitude of the country had changed as well. After the Aden bombings, people started to question what exactly the Afghan Arabs were doing in Yemen. Over the next few weeks, worried fathers and irate tribal shaykhs arrived at the camp to drag their sons home. Without a tribal affiliation, Khanabashi watched the numbers dwindle until only a few men were left.

One day, as Khanabashi struggled to figure out his next move, a well-built man with a full, dark beard and deep-set eyes arrived at the camp. Khanabashi knew him only as Abu Ali, one of bin Laden's top lieutenants in Yemen and the founder of the camp they were in. The thirty-seven-year-old tribesman looked around at his nearly abandoned creation and the depressed young fighters, and immediately took charge. Like nearly all of al-Qaeda's earliest members, Abu Ali al-Harithi had fought in Afghanistan. But he also had professional military training, having served in the UAE's army as a young man, and he had used that experience to organize the camp in Sadah as well as those in Marib and Shabwa. Harithi listened as the frustrated fighters poured out the details of the last few weeks, telling him about their failures and the arrests. It's all right, Harithi consoled them. These things happen.

The few men Harithi found in the camps had nowhere to go. Most of them had been born outside Yemen, and none of them knew if they could go home now that they were on the run. Harithi brushed their concerns aside. You are under my protection, he said. "I am your father."

Despite the failure in Aden, al-Qaeda found something to cheer about. On January 2, 1993, citing security concerns, the Pentagon had announced that it would no longer use Yemen as a support base. Bin Laden's men had botched the attacks, but his larger plan succeeded. The US pulled out of Aden. Bin Laden would recall this lesson often in the years to come. In bin Laden's simplified version, he did nothing in Saudi Arabia and the Americans stayed. But when he hit them in Yemen, they ran.

3

The Dogs of War

1993–1994

Bin Laden agonized over the fate of Jamal al-Nahdi and the men he had ordered into action in Yemen. After their arrest, the Socialists put the men in al-Mansurah prison, just across Aden's harbor from the two hotels they had attacked. Like the Yemenis in al-Qaeda, bin Laden knew al-Mansurah's history. Built by the British in the late 1950s, the prison's four white-washed square towers had witnessed the bloody end of empire in Aden. Under the Socialists, al-Mansurah became notorious as a torture center, and bin Laden hated the thought of his men there.

In the middle of the summer, as the temperature at his farm outside Khartoum neared 100 degrees Fahrenheit, bin Laden received some good news. Days earlier, on July 17, 1993, six of the men, including Nahdi, had managed to break out of the prison with the help of sympathetic guards. Bin Laden immediately sent word to Harithi to get the men out of Yemen. They were all to join him in Sudan.

Harithi smuggled the six fugitives and Khanabashi, whom he had taken under his protection, out of the country. In Sudan, the men soon settled into the easy pace of life bin Laden had found at his properties along the Nile. They relaxed around the farm and in town, recuperating after the months in prison. Harithi set up a modified printing press for forging passports, while Khanabashi stayed in the country to manage one of bin Laden's farms. After the failure in Aden, the muscular African-born Yemeni seemed to enjoy looking after the cows. When bin Laden saw he could trust the young fighter, he made Khanabashi a manager, giving him control over the paddocks and pastures. Khanabashi liked the fact that most of the proceeds from the farm went back into the organization. Four years after bin Laden had established al-Qaeda in a valley in eastern Afghanistan, it was becoming more of a self-sufficient business empire than the private army he had envisioned.

Other members of al-Qaeda hung around bin Laden, chatting with their commander most evenings in the open salon he held in Khartoum. Life kept to this gentle rhythm for months. Men came and went as they pleased, rotating among bin Laden's different holdings. Even bin Laden seemed to relax in the dry air of central Sudan. Business was good, and he was more popular than ever. Men from all over the Islamic world flocked to Khartoum just to talk to him. After years of war and an embarrassing exile from Saudi Arabia, the attention must have been flattering.

Despite the setback in Aden, bin Laden had not given up on liberating south Yemen. He continued to follow the news, especially reports of political problems between Salih and the Socialists. But the man jihadis called simply "the shaykh" seemed quiet and content, contemplative even. Bin Laden ate with his men and talked with them like an older brother or a father figure. In Sudan, he appeared to his followers as a man with "money and honor." It was a rare moment of peace and calm in al-Qaeda's history. It wouldn't last.

In February 1994, a group of wild young renegades shattered bin Laden's Sudanese idyll. Frustrated with the al-Qaeda commander and his seeming lack of activity, the young jihadis under the command of a Libyan named Muhammad al-Khulayfi had declared him an infidel. If bin Laden was truly Islamic, they reasoned, he would be doing more with his wealth and power. The group nominated themselves to carry out the execution their judgment required. Like Abdullah Azzam, bin Laden was now a target of the very forces he had unleashed.

Late in the evening on February 4, Khulayfi and his followers shot up the mosque bin Laden usually attended. They missed the al-Qaeda commander, who wasn't there at the time, but managed to kill sixteen worshippers and wound several others. Bin Laden, who must have known about the attack, apparently didn't realize he was the target until Khulayfi and his men returned the next day to complete the job.

Bin Laden had a house across the street from his office in Khartoum, where he often stayed when he was in town. As one of the wealthiest and most popular figures in the Sudanese capital, bin Laden's schedule was public knowledge. Each afternoon, following a short rest at home, he returned to the office for one of his open salons with whoever might be in town. These sessions were popular among the growing numbers of Islamists in Khartoum, who liked to listen to bin Laden expound on the problems of the day.

That afternoon, Khulayfi and his men drove up the street toward bin Laden's office. They could see the guests arriving, and the shaykh's loose contingent of bodyguards was already in place outside his office. The renegades opened up with a shotgun and several machine guns, but again they missed bin Laden. The al-Qaeda commander had been delayed at home by an argument with his eldest son, Abdullah. The boy hated life in Sudan and wanted to return to the easy luxury of Saudi Arabia. Perhaps embarrassed by this latest dispute with his son, bin Laden had sent his men across the street ahead of him to welcome the guests. The move, which fooled the attackers into thinking he was in the office, probably saved his life.

As soon as bin Laden heard the gunfire across the street, he grabbed a gun and handed another one to Abdullah. Their argument forgotten, the two peeked out the window. Across the street they could see men running back and forth, firing into the office. One of bin Laden's Yemeni guards lay on the ground bleeding from a wound in the stomach, and Harithi had a bullet in his thigh. Bin Laden and Abdullah moved out of the house, flanking the kidnappers, who were now caught in a vicious crossfire between bin Laden, his son, and the al-Qaeda guards across the street. Firing off several rounds, the men brought down Khulayfi and killed several other attackers.

Rattled but unhurt, bin Laden checked on the rest of his men. A number of men, including Jamal al-Nahdi, were down with bullet wounds and needed medical attention. Bin Laden's options were limited. Sudan didn't have the facilities he needed, and he couldn't send the men to Saudi Arabia, Egypt, or Yemen, all of which were on the lookout for members of al-Qaeda. Pakistan was similarly tricky. The last time he had been there, two years earlier, Pakistani intelligence had acted strangely and bin Laden worried they might sell him out to the Saudis. Instead, he instructed Khanabashi to take Nahdi and four others to India for treatment. As always, bin Laden paid for their trip and medical expenses.

THE INDIA TRIP turned out well for Khanabashi. While he hung around the hospital waiting for the men to recover, he met and eventually married a young Indian girl. Back home in Yemen, however, things continued to fall apart. The country's first parliamentary elections in April 1993 had destroyed the illusion of a unity government. Salih's party crushed the Socialists at the polls, but the real damage came when Islah, an Islamist party backed by Salih, outgained the Socialists and took a ten-seat advantage in Yemen's new parliament.

After the elections, Bid had left Sanaa in a huff, flying to the US for an unscheduled meeting with Vice President Al Gore. Bid had bypassed normal diplomatic channels, using Yemen's ambassador to Cairo, a fellow Socialist, to set up the meeting instead of the Salih loyalist in Washington. The country's diplomatic corps was breaking down along regional lines, as southerners and northerners working in the same building ignored each other and cleared their actions through their preferred president. When Bid returned to Yemen, things continued to deteriorate. He refused to take the oath of office twice, standing Salih up both times. Despite some frantic diplomacy by concerned neighbors, Yemen's unity was broken. On April 27, 1994, the one-year anniversary of the parliamentary elections, the war many had predicted started at a military base north of Sanaa.

At the presidential palace in Sanaa, the same polished stone building where he had recruited for the jihad in Afghanistan, Salih reacted to the news of the battle by calling Abd al-Majid al-Zindani, the radical preacher with the carrot-colored beard who had also played a major role in sending Yemenis abroad to fight. A member of Islah, Zindani held the party's seat on the five-man presidential council, and his alliance with Salih gave the president a three-to-two advantage over the Socialists on every vote. Salih also reached out to Abd al-Wahhab al-Daylami, the lanky cleric with the lopsided face. Hisham al-Daylami, the chubby child jihadi, had been dead for almost a decade, but his father hadn't changed. If anything, Abd al-Wahhab had become even more extreme since his son's death. Just as in the 1980s, Salih needed the clerics to help him mobilize support for a jihad, only this time it would be fought in Yemen. It was bin Laden and Fadhli's Jeddah strategy, yoked to the ambitions of a strongman.

Zindani and Daylami immediately released fatwas in support of Salih and the north. The Socialists, both men ruled, were infidels and could be killed with impunity. With his conservative flank secure, Salih made his next move. The outbreak of civil war put an end to the charade of Fadhli's house arrest in Sanaa. Salih commissioned the young jihadi as a colonel in the Yemeni army and sent him south to Abyan to reorganize his fighters and march on Aden.

In India, Khanabashi and the recovering al-Qaeda operatives followed early reports of the fighting. Eager to finally crush the Socialists they had been fighting for years, the men booked a flight back to Sanaa. From Sudan, other Yemeni members of al-Qaeda rushed home, with bin Laden's blessing. After the assassination attempt in February, bin Laden had run into another problem. On March 5, an envoy from the Saudi king had arrived in Sudan and demanded the exiled al-Qaeda commander surrender his passport. Without a passport, bin Laden would be at the mercy of Sudan and Hassan al-Turabi, its erratic president. Frustrated and out of options, bin Laden lost his temper and threw the slim green booklet at the king's messenger. "Take it, if having it dictates anything on my behalf," he cried. Still, the al-Qaeda commander wasn't about to let these problems distract him from his goal of defeating the Socialists in Yemen. When the war started, bin Laden sent his Yemenis home to fight. Once again, Salih and the jihadis were on the same side.

IN SANAA, SALIH and his generals formed a battle plan. Ali Muhsin, the paunchy, bucktoothed general who had married Fadhli's sister, would take his First Armored Division south in a straight line, descending out of the mountains like an arrow aimed at Aden. Meanwhile, his brother-in-law Fadhli would march on Aden from the east with his band of jihadis and tribesmen. This pincer movement, Salih believed, would cut the south in half, separating Aden from its hinterlands to the east, where the bulk of the Socialist army was concentrated.

As always in Yemen, the tribes were the wild card. Salih didn't think he needed them to win, but he had to make sure they didn't try to leverage the chaos at the center by supporting the south. If he couldn't get their backing, he at least needed their neutrality. Salih reached out to Shaykh Abdullah al-Ahmar, the old man of Yemeni politics who had parlayed his tribal clout into being named speaker of parliament as the head of the Islah party. A distinguished-looking tribesman with a carefully trimmed gray goatee and piercing eyes, Shaykh Abdullah had what Salih, an army officer from a minor tribe, did not: the elusive quality Yemenis refer to as *jah*. A combination of reputation, honor, and dignity, *jah* gets things done in Yemen's tribal territories.

From his heavily fortified compound in downtown Sanaa, where he ran a private prison for unruly tribesmen, Shaykh Abdullah worked the phones. He convinced shaykhs along the army's route south that now was not the time to press for position against the state. As Salih's army rushed south to Aden, the tribes remained on the sidelines. This would be a war between armies.

TAKING OFF UNDER the cover of darkness on May 4, one week after the opening shots in the north, Socialist warplanes left Aden, flying low over the black-and-white sea and sand before turning north toward the mountains. Several minutes later, the Soviet-era jets made a quick ring around Sanaa, darting past the imposing mountain east of the capital before dropping their bombs on the sleeping city. Below them, a corner of the presidential palace was on fire, and across town they hit the airport as tardy anti-aircraft fire echoed in their wake. On the Red Sea coast, near the border with Saudi Arabia, another squadron struck the north's only deep-water port at Hudaydah.

Inside the presidential palace, Salih escaped the bombing and quickly ordered a retaliatory strike. Minutes later, word came back that Salih's jets couldn't manage a nighttime takeoff from the burning airport across town. The man aides called "the boss" was furious. Salih fumed through the night, barking orders at his commanders as he waited for morning. Shortly after daybreak on May 5, Salih's fighters finally got airborne. Concentrating all their firepower on Aden International Airport, which doubled as an air force base, the northern jets pounded the parallel runways, effectively grounding the Socialist fleet.

While his planes were on their way south, Salih announced a state of emergency over state radio, officially dismissing Bid as his vice president and warning Yemenis to stay off the major roads. The time for negotiation had passed. This was all-out war. The sharp rhetoric, coupled with what to nervous diplomats and aid workers on the ground felt like indiscriminate bombing runs, sparked an exodus of foreigners. Handfuls of students and oil workers living in Sanaa were evacuated on US military transport planes. In Aden, a French warship took on 300 foreigners fleeing the fighting. Without the use of its air force, the Socialists fell back on their preunification arsenal, launching a handful of Scud missiles at Sanaa. The Soviet-made missiles performed no better than when Saddam had lobbed them at Israel during the first Gulf War.

Meanwhile, Ali Muhsin stuck to Salih's war plan, moving south toward Aden. By May 8, the army was within striking distance of the port city, and residents could hear artillery shells exploding in the distance. In the east, Fadhli's militants had linked up with other northern units and were fighting their way toward Aden. Behind them, in the eastern mountains of Shabwa, other jihadis tied down Socialist troops in a series of firefights. A third group of jihadis, under the command of Abu Ali al-Harithi, was also converging on Aden. Their progress had been slowed when Harithi was shot in the foot, his second gun wound in four months, but the burly fighter whittled a rough pair of crutches out of tree branches and kept going.

On May 21, with the fighting in full swing, an obviously fatigued Ali Salim al-Bid emerged from hiding to appear on Aden television, where he announced that the south was seceding. Bid's declaration of independence, on the eve of what would have been

Yemen's fourth anniversary, was his last card. Aden was about to fall and once it did, the rest of the south would follow. Bid was convinced that in order to get outside help, particularly from Saudi Arabia and Kuwait, whose leaders still harbored a grudge against Salih for backing Saddam during the Gulf War, he needed to formally secede. Secession, Bid hoped, would be the trigger that allowed for international recognition and would permit the south to buy weapons on the open market. Saudi Arabia and Kuwait had already been supplying the Socialists with under-the-table arms deals and cash, but the south needed more.

Bid's announcement, which he hadn't cleared with top Socialist leaders, split the party. Most were opposed to Salih's heavy-handed dominance, but not all were certain secession was the answer. None of them knew if an independent south was even viable in a post-Soviet world. The south had few resources and hardly any money. Did the Socialists really want Bid speaking for them, leading them into a war they could never win? Doubters including Abd Rabu Mansur Hadi, a top military official from Abyan and Yemen's future president, defected to Salih. Others, who couldn't bear to join forces with Salih, feigned medical problems and fled the country. In the face of so many desertions, Bid abandoned Aden for the port city of al-Mukalla, 400 miles east along the Indian Ocean. Far from the main thrust of Salih's troops, the tightly bunched, whitewashed city at the foot of a series of low-slung mountains was the main entry point for weapons and artillery into the south.

In Aden, Abd al-Rahman al-Jifri, a fifty-one-year-old statesman with a Saudi passport, took over the day-to-day operations of the new government. Widely believed to be Riyadh's man in the south, Jifri maintained close contact with Saudi Arabia. At the United Nations, both the Saudis and Kuwait pushed for a UN Security Council resolution demanding a ceasefire, which might have offered their clients in the south a chance to regroup and come to some sort of negotiated settlement. But while the Arab world focused on the fighting in Yemen, the rest of the international community was waking up to the horror of genocide in Rwanda. The gruesome images of bodies hacked to death with machetes focused international attention in a way Yemen's confusing conflict never could.

On July 3, six weeks after his announcement of secession, Bid went into exile, captaining a lonely convoy of tanks and missile launchers east across the desert to Oman. Al-Mukalla fell the next day. Two days later, on July 6, what remained of the Socialist leadership in Aden fled as well, motoring across the Gulf of Aden that night in high-powered speedboats for Djibouti with what was later rumored to be millions in state funds. As the politicians escaped, northern troops were already slipping into the burning city.

ALONG WITH THE soldiers came the jihadis. Tired and thinned by weeks of war, the ragged, bearded fighters entered Aden in a caravan of battered Land Cruisers and bullet-scarred pickups. Salih wanted to drive home the point that there was a price to pay for crossing him. And just as the jihadis had formed part of Salih's two-pronged assault on Aden, so too would they share in his postwar lesson.

Ali Muhsin al-Ahmar, the conquering general, rode into the defeated city early on the morning of July 7. Several of his men, who had infiltrated the city by decorating their tanks with pictures of Ali Salim al-Bid, greeted him. Everyone else watched from behind closed doors as Salih's most-trusted general took stock of the badly damaged city. He commandeered the Aden Hotel for his headquarters, and then watched from his window as the sack of the city got underway. Tanks rumbled into position at traffic circles as huge trucks spread out across the volcanic slopes that formed Aden's near-perfect port. Next came the jihadis, shooting their guns into the air and screaming "Allahu Akbar." Aden would be the victory party they never got in Afghanistan.

As the day wore on, Aden's once pristine beach turned grimy with human waste and burning trash. Jihadis and soldiers set up camp wherever they could, sleeping on the beach or in abandoned stores. This wasn't going to be a brief moment of post-victory looting. Salih wanted the south to remember this moment for years. In Aden's wide, British-built thoroughfares, broken glass lay everywhere as soldiers smashed windows and display cases, carting off the booty as partial payment for their services. Some men simply backed their trucks up to buildings and disassembled them piece by piece, stripping the walls down to bare concrete before shipping them north. Years later, when his political loyalties had shifted, Tariq al-Fadhli would compare the looting by northern groups to a swarm of locusts. Everything—telephones, computers, carpets, chairs, and even the electrical wires—was hauled off.

ON THE OTHER side of the looting and violence stood men like Abdullah, a tall, sophisticated Adeni with a sloping forehead and a refined air who cherished the city's cosmopolitan history. A secretary for a British company, Abdullah was well aware of Salih's reputation and scared to death of the jihadi militias. When a group with "long beards and wild looks" showed up at his office, he kept his eyes down and did what they ordered. Quick and efficient, the men moved from room to room, taking everything they could carry. When they came to the bathroom, they turned to Abdullah.

"Give us the key," one of them said. After his foreign bosses abandoned the city weeks earlier at the start of the war, Abdullah had piled all of his company's computers and records in a tiny bathroom near the back wall, and he wanted to protect them. Abdullah felt himself start to sweat, but he kept his voice level, swearing that his British manager had taken the key with him when he fled the country. "Look," he continued, "you can break the door down if you want, but it is only the bathroom."

After a hurried discussion, one of the men shrugged and they walked out the door. "Idiots," Abdullah remembered years later, "they can't even use a computer and now they rule the country."

Not every Adeni was so lucky. Nor was the sack of the city just about what could be carried off. Both Salih and bin Laden wanted to erase all traces of the past. The bikini beaches were closed and the beer gardens wiped away by sweaty men with guns and beards. It was time for a new start.

In the city's cemeteries, Harithi led small teams armed with stone hammers and machine guns as they methodically destroyed the white tombstones and grave markers they believed distracted from God. For al-Qaeda's purists, any sort of memorial was a slippery slope. First, people visited graves to pay their respects to deceased relatives, but soon enough they would be praying to the dead to intercede with God on their behalf. That the fighters couldn't allow; people should pray to God, not to the dead. Better to avoid the problem altogether, al-Qaeda reasoned with uncompromising certainty. Over the course of a few days in early July, the jihadis crushed centuries of memories into rubble.

Outside the city, Khanabashi directed a group of al-Qaeda fighters toward the brewery. Three years earlier, during his recruiting meeting with Jamal al-Nahdi, Khanabashi had told the veteran fighter he wanted to destroy Aden's only brewery, calling it the "corrupter of Islamic morals." That dream was about to come true. Lining up in front of the square structure, the men took turns launching shoulder-fired missiles and rocket-propelled grenades at the building. The target practice soon became a free-for-all as the walls crumbled. Few in Yemen seemed aware that a new, uncompromising strand of activism had entered the local political scene. Smashing gravestones and destroying buildings was not simply vandalism. It was part of a larger political project that was just beginning to take root.

The orgy of violence and destruction served Salih's immediate purpose of intimidating an entire population into submission. After the sack of Aden, Salih left the city untouched, pointedly refusing to repair scarred buildings and damaged infrastructure, a warning every bit as gruesome as the premodern Yemeni practice of affixing the heads of prisoners to spikes on the city wall. In the same city where Salih and Bid had stood hand in hand as they announced the unification of Yemen, their experiment came to its bloody end. Salih had won the four-year battle for the state. But he wasn't alone in victory. The jihadis had won as well, and they had a different vision for the future.

4

Faith and Wisdom

1994–1999

In late 1994, months after the civil war ended, a squat-looking Egyptian with oversized glasses and a large purple bruise on his forehead stepped off the plane in Sanaa. The mark above his eyes, which resembled an egg-shaped birthmark, came from years of vigorously pressing his head to the ground in prayer. Ayman al-Zawahiri had been a cell leader for Egyptian radical groups since 1966, when as a fifteen-year-old high school student he had seen Nasser's government execute his hero Sayyid Qutb. Rarely in the nearly three decades that followed had Zawahiri been as desperate at he was at this moment. His latest attack, an attempted assassination of Egypt's prime minister Atif Sidqi in November 1993, had gone horribly wrong. Instead of the prime minister, the car bomb killed a young schoolgirl who was standing nearby. Egyptian society was outraged. The police cracked down, arresting hundreds of operatives in Zawahiri's al-Jihad organization. By the time he landed in Yemen, the operatives that weren't in jail had scattered across the Middle East.

Known in jihadi circles as the "land of faith and wisdom," after a famous saying of the Prophet, Yemen offered an inviting base. Mountainous and tribal, Yemen reminded Zawahiri of

Afghanistan, and he thought it represented his best chance to start over. More than just its geography, Yemen's politics presented an opening. During the civil war, Salih had relied on a number of Egyptian jihadis to help him defeat the Socialists. One of these men, Dr. Fadl, a square-faced radical, had spent most of the war as a volunteer physician, treating northern soldiers at al-Thawrah hospital in Sanaa. Zawahiri and Dr. Fadl, whose real name was Sayyid Imam al-Sharif, were old friends. Both had come of age in Egypt's Islamic underground of the 1960s and 1970s. They worked together at a Kuwaiti-backed Red Crescent hospital in Peshawar during the 1980s, where Dr. Fadl's views on *takfir*, the practice of excommunicating fellow Muslims, influenced the younger Zawahiri. Other Egyptian members of Zawahiri's al-Jihad organization, like Ahmad al-Najjar, a veteran of the jihadi circuit, had played a more active role in the civil war. In Zawahiri's mind, Salih owed him for al-Jihad's participation in the civil war, and the Egyptian was coming to collect. At the very least, Zawahiri hoped to leverage the memory of this support into a tacit acceptance of al-Jihad's presence in Yemen.

Waiting in a safe house across town were several of Zawahiri's oldest and dearest friends: men like Dr. Fadl and Zawahiri's younger brother, Muhammad. It wasn't home, but for an Egyptian on the run in 1994, Sanaa was as close as he was likely to get. Dozens of other Egyptians were spread throughout the country, putting down roots, taking up jobs, and marrying local women. Zawahiri had come to Yemen to reorganize this remnant of al-Jihad. In the north, several operatives, including the group's master forger, Ibrahim al-Banna, had rented a large farm in the mountains of Amran. That could be one training camp. Other possibilities were scattered down south, where some Egyptians were still affiliated with Fadhli in Abyan. This was Zawahiri's immediate future, reorganizing and planning. Over the next year, Zawahiri toured safe houses and fledgling training camps his men had established as he worked to rebuild al-Jihad into an organization that could once again challenge Egyptian president Hosni Mubarak for control of the state.

It was the same thing on the other side of the Red Sea in Sudan, where some operatives had fled after the crackdown in Egypt. Bin Laden still lived in Khartoum and the two terrorist leaders knew each other well. At the tail end of the jihad in Afghanistan, Zawahiri had often acted as bin Laden's doctor, taking care of the tall Saudi during his frequent bouts of illness. And although they would often coordinate activities and training for al-Qaeda and al-Jihad, each man maintained his independence. Both were proud, often haughty leaders, and in early 1995 they had different goals. Bin Laden sought to change the world with al-Qaeda, while Zawahiri and al-Jihad were obsessively focused on Mubarak and Egypt. It was this singular goal that drew Zawahiri back to Africa in the summer of 1995. Mubarak was scheduled to fly to Ethiopia on June 26 for a meeting of the Organization of African Unity, an oddly anachronistic organization that many joked was little more than a dictators' club. Zawahiri had known about the trip for more than a year, and along with Sudanese intelligence officers, who wanted to export their own Islamic revolution, he laid a trap. Bin Laden had also kicked in money and men to the plot. Weeks before the conference, Zawahiri flew to Sudan for a motivational talk with the attackers before traveling to Ethiopia, where he walked the road Mubarak's motorcade would travel. There would be an initial ambush, with a backup team farther down the road in case the first group failed to take out Mubarak's car.

The Egyptian president arrived ahead of schedule, as Zawahiri's team scrambled to get in position, their rocket-propelled grenade launcher misfired. The assault deteriorated quickly as the assailants fired wildly into the motorcade, killing two policemen as Mubarak's armored limousine absorbed the hail of gunfire. Instead of attempting to power through the ambush toward the second team, as Zawahiri had anticipated, Mubarak's dented car reversed course and returned to the airport, where the Egyptian president held a press conference. "Suddenly I found a blue van blocking the road and somebody jumped to the ground," the sixty-seven-year-old Mubarak calmly told the shocked reporters. "I saw those who shot at me." It was the twelfth time Zawahiri had tried and failed to kill him.

In the wake of the failed assassination, Zawahiri's Sudanese branch collapsed. The UN imposed sanctions on Sudan for its role in the attack, and once again al-Jihad was forced to scatter. Zawahiri kept prodding, however, looking for a weakness in Egypt's defenses, and that fall he believed he found one. Leaving Ahmad al-Najjar in charge of al-Jihad's network in Yemen, Zawahiri left Sanaa for Pakistan to coordinate an attack on the Egyptian embassy in Islamabad, which took place on November 19, 1995, killing seventeen people. But minus their leader and his determination, the group in Yemen atrophied.

SOON AFTER ZAWAHIRI left Yemen, it became clear that Salih was going to disappoint the Egyptians of al-Jihad. Nothing had worked out as they had expected. The tribes were always at each other's throats, fighting over some confusing issue that only they seemed to understand. Accustomed to the straightforward dictatorship of Mubarak's Egypt, the exiles struggled to make sense of Yemen's multiple power centers. Politicians and tribal shaykhs would pledge their support only to withdraw it at the worst possible moment. In this they seemed to take their cue from their president. Salih went from hot to cold with the Egyptian jihadis, who could never quite grasp his true feelings. The promises Salih had made during the 1994 civil war were forgotten as soon as the fighting ended. The defeat of the Socialists hadn't been the first step toward the implementation of Shariah law; instead, it was merely a centralization of power at the top. Salih had used the jihadis when he needed them, and now that the war was over he ignored them. Meanwhile, Tariq al-Fadhli got to keep his colonel's salary and was given a seat in Yemen's upper, and presidentially appointed, house of parliament, while Jamal al-Nahdi, with his mangled hand from the failed Movenpick bombing years earlier, was made a permanent member of the high committee for Salih's ruling party. But Fadhli and Nahdi were local powerbrokers Salih could use to rule. The Egyptians had nothing the Yemeni strongman needed.

On the international front, things were just as troubled for al-Jihad. Zawahiri went off the grid for months in the winter of 1996. Accustomed to constant communication from their micromanaging leader, his followers were disoriented by the sudden silence. It later emerged that Zawahiri had been in a Russian jail, arrested as he attempted to cross the border from Azerbaijan without a visa. But at the time, all his men in Yemen knew was that he wasn't responding to their requests. When Zawahiri was released in June 1997, after the Russians failed to determine his true identity, he started work on his next plot. The result was the bloodbath at Luxor five months later, in which fifty-eight tourists and four Egyptians were gunned down at the temple of Queen Hatshepsut in Upper Egypt. The carnage cost Zawahiri's men what little support they still had in Egypt. From Yemen, his increasingly disheartened network wondered what their leader was up to.

In February 1998, Zawahiri reconnected with bin Laden in Afghanistan, where the al-Qaeda leader had been forced to flee after being expelled from Sudan two years earlier as part of Hasan al-Turabi's attempt to rehabilitate his country in the face of international sanctions. Along with several other terrorist leaders, Zawahiri and bin Laden issued a fatwa entitled "Jihad against the Jews and Crusaders." The declaration of war urged "every Muslim" to kill Americans and Jews wherever they found them. Zawahiri's followers in Yemen were stunned. They hadn't been consulted. What was their boss doing? Criticism poured in from around the Middle

East, Africa, and Europe as members of al-Jihad struggled to come to terms with Zawahiri's about-face. They were supposed to be fighting Mubarak's regime, and now Zawahiri wanted them to kill Americans.

An al-Jihad official in Yemen wrote to Zawahiri that his signature on the fatwa was a dereliction of duty. He was abandoning the struggle for the soul of Egypt in favor of a war they could never win. Zawahiri snapped back that his decision to align al-Jihad with bin Laden's al-Qaeda network was a necessary step toward overthrowing Mubarak. Convinced their leader had lost touch, al-Jihad operatives around the world started announcing their resignation. In an attempt to stem the loss of personnel, Zawahiri returned to Yemen for a series of face-to-face meetings.

As he flew west from Afghanistan, crossing the Persian Gulf and most of the Arabian peninsula, the stocky Egyptian physician still had little understanding of how al-Jihad's Yemen network had deteriorated in his absence. Breezing through Sanaa's airport security on yet another forged passport, he met a waiting car at the curb. Instead of the safe house in Sanaa, which was deemed too dangerous, Zawahiri's men drove him to the central highland city of Taizz, 140 miles south of the capital. Zawahiri wanted a quick trip. He was desperate to get back to Afghanistan and continue working on his next big attack. But first he had to ease the group's fears and reenlist some of his disgruntled supporters.

Things started off poorly. His brother Muhammad, who had often served as his top deputy, refused to reconsider his resignation. The years apart had changed the two men. Married with six children, Muhammad was working for an electrical engineering company and providing for his family. He didn't understand what his older brother was doing declaring war on the US. Neither did anyone else in Yemen. One of Zawahiri's most trusted operatives, a former Egyptian house painter named Ahmad Nasrallah, became so frustrated with Zawahiri that he lost faith in the entire enterprise of jihad. A self-taught student of dense religious texts, Nasrallah had a long history of militancy dating back to the 1970s. He had been active on the fringes of the Egyptian extremist group Takfir wa Hijra, which was responsible for murdering an Egyptian minister in 1977, and he had spent time in Afghanistan before coming to Yemen with the wave of Egyptian exiles in the early 1990s. But the years on the move and Zawahiri's apparent betrayal of their mission had taken a toll. Nasrallah wanted out and he thought he had found a way to make his life after jihad more comfortable.

Shortly after Zawahiri arrived in Yemen, Nasrallah walked into the headquarters of the Interior Ministry in Sanaa, which ran several competing intelligence arms, and offered up his former commander along with the rest of group's network in Yemen. The Interior Minister, Husayn Arab, a frumpy former military officer with a protruding gut and a thick mustache, was intrigued enough by Nasrallah's story to meet with him three different times over the course of a few days. But Arab, an ex-Socialist from the south, was unsure of his footing in postwar Yemen and took his time with Nasarallah's information. Worried that Zawahiri might return to Afghanistan and upset his chance at a reward before Arab made his move, Nasrallah abandoned his efforts with the minister and approached Yemen's top intelligence agency, the Political Security Organization (PSO).

A secretary gave Nasarallah an appointment with the deputy director, Muhammad al-Surmi, an overweight official in his fifties who agreed to meet the Egyptian at a Sanaa hotel. After listening to Nasrallah's rambling take on the state of Zawahiri's network in Yemen, the deputy director instructed him to wait in the hotel room while he made a call. Four hours later Abd al-Salam al-Hilah, a thirty-year-old colonel in the PSO, arrived to take control of the case and supervise al-Jihad's traitor.

The PSO had a long history with the jihadis dating back to the 1980s, when it had been part of Yemen's efforts to send fighters to

Afghanistan. After unification in 1990, the spy agency had helped settle returning foreign fighters in the country, and it had been instrumental in using some of those same men to defeat the Socialists in the 1994 civil war. A rising star in the agency, Hilah was a tribesman from just outside Sanaa who typically dressed in a Western suit and tie. He had a well-groomed black beard that partially masked a protruding jaw, and as the PSO's point man on jihadis he controlled the agency's Islamist file. Surmi introduced him to Nasrallah as his case officer.

Hilah immediately transported Nasrallah across town to a PSO safe house for debriefing. Sitting in the tiny apartment in downtown Sanaa, Nasrallah went over his story a third time. He gave Hilah the address of Zawahiri's hideout in Taizz as well as several other secure locations al-Jihad was using across the country. Nasrallah even offered himself as a mole, telling Hilah that he could travel south to spy on the remains of Fadhli's group, which had fragmented after the civil war as their leader abandoned jihad in the wake of the Socialists' defeat and the return of his family's land in Abyan. Many of those men, Nasrallah explained, had coalesced around a man named Zayn al-Abidin al-Mihdhar. Or, if the PSO wasn't interested in that, he could travel to Afghanistan and collect information on bin Laden. Whatever the PSO asked of him, he would do. He just wanted out. Hilah listened patiently, occasionally prodding the Egyptian for more details. The PSO safe house was equipped with a hidden video camera and Hilah wanted to get everything on tape.

As he walked out of the apartment, Hilah made his decision. Within minutes the Yemeni spy dialed a number he knew well and informed the man who answered that he had a traitor in his ranks.

The news shocked the jihadi community in Yemen. One of their own had betrayed them. Zawahiri finally understood how bad things had gotten. The remnants of his disheartened organization hustled him out of the country as other operatives seized Nasrallah. The men held him bound and gagged for days in one of the safe houses in Sanaa that Nasrallah had offered up to the authorities. Eventually, after several rounds of torture, they extracted his confession. This time the camera was in plain sight and the broken Egyptian stared directly into it.

No one knew what to do with Nasrallah. Messages flew back and forth among the jihadi leadership in Yemen and Afghanistan. Some wanted to execute him right away; others called for caution and a full tribunal. The cash-strapped group in Yemen swore they didn't have enough money for a ticket to Afghanistan. If the contractor wanted him, they said, using bin Laden's code name, he was going to have to send the money himself. The cash came, but Nasrallah evaded his captors at the airport and managed to board a flight to Egypt. Mubarak's agents, who were on the lookout for members of al-Jihad, arrested Nasrallah as he landed in Cairo. But the damage had been done. In addition to Zawahiri, dozens of other operatives abandoned Yemen. After Nasarallah's betrayal, their network had been compromised. Some scattered to Europe and Africa but most made their way to Afghanistan, where they joined bin Laden and Zawahiri in Kandahar. Along with them came a new generation of fighters.

THE BOLD DECLARATION of war in the joint fatwa with bin Laden may have split Zawahiri's old guard of Egyptians, but for a generation of younger Arabs it produced the opposite effect. The teenagers who heeded bin Laden's new call had grown up with stories of the jihad in Afghanistan, watching grainy videos from the 1980s as they listened to preachers extol the glories of fighting abroad. In Yemen, many of these new recruits came from the nearly 1,000 private religious institutes that had sprouted in the 1970s and 1980s. By the time bin Laden and Zawahiri called for an all-out war on Americans and Jews, the schools had produced more than 600,000 graduates. Taught by Egyptian and Saudi exiles, the institutes didn't necessarily turn students into terrorists, but they did create a student more prepared for al-Qaeda's message. They were gateway schools, innocuous on the surface but deadly in retrospect.

One of these recent graduates was Nasir al-Wihayshi, a tiny, frail-looking twenty-two-year-old with a sharp nose and sunken cheeks. Wihayshi had grown up in the mountains of the al-Mukayras region of northern Abyan, an economically stunted backwater with few roads or opportunities, nearly 100 miles inland from the Gulf of Aden. After graduation in 1998, Wihayshi could recite the Quran and debate the finer points of Islamic law, but those skills were useless in helping him find a job. Instead, the young scholar left his home in southern Yemen for Afghanistan. It would be five long years before he returned.

Shortly after Wihayshi arrived at a training camp near the Afghan city of Khost, one of bin Laden's scouts spotted him. The al-Qaeda commander was always on the lookout for special talent, and after days of observation he thought he recognized something of himself in the short Yemeni. Both were soft-spoken thinkers, silently ambitious men who saw further than those around them. One day, bin Laden pulled Wihayshi aside for a private conversation. Bin Laden told the young volunteer that he saw great things in his future. As Wihayshi listened to the al-Qaeda commander lay out his vision for the future, he found himself falling under bin Laden's spell. Soon he had sworn the oath of allegiance and joined al-Qaeda. Bin Laden had always preferred to surround himself with Yemeni bodyguards, but he had a different plan for his newest recruit. Too short to be intimidating and too smart to be wasted, bin Laden made him his personal secretary and apprentice, an aide-de-camp who handled both his correspondence and his schedule. For the next four years, Wihayshi was bin Laden's shadow. The two were "always together," one fighter remembered. Other young Yemenis soon followed Wihayshi into al-Qaeda's Afghanistan training camps. A decade later these same young men would go on to form al-Qaeda in the Arabian Peninsula (AQAP).

WHILE THE NEW generation was bound for Afghanistan, in thrall to bin Laden's vision of a global war against Americans and Jews, fragments of the old one struggled to make an impact in Yemen. In the south, Zayn al-Abidin al-Mihdhar, the same man al-Jihad's traitor Nasrallah had warned the Yemeni government about, was putting together an army. His motley collection of Yemenis, Egyptians, and a smattering of other Arabs were mostly Fadhli's leftovers. After the civil war in 1994, Salih returned most of Fadhli's land and allowed him to keep his colonel's salary in return for services rendered during the war. "I walked into the Republican Palace without an appointment," Fadhli later told people about that time in his life. "I was in the highest authority." Not all of Fadhli's men felt the same way, and among those who hadn't fought for land or money there were dark mutterings of discontent and frustration. Along with the foreign jihadis, who thought Fadhli had sold out, they gravitated toward Mihdhar and his uncompromising brand of jihad.

The thirty-two-year-old Mihdhar was an obvious choice. Tall and almost savagely handsome, he was a local Yemeni with jihadi credentials from Afghanistan who had refused to fight in the civil war against the Socialists. He had declared it a war of darkness and ignorance. At one point during the fighting, he had even driven into Fadhli's camp to lecture him on the dangers of participating in such a war. "You are fighting under Ali Abdullah Salih's banner, not under the Prophet's," he railed amidst the campfires. "This is not jihad."

Fadhli had listened politely while Mihdhar was in camp. But as soon as he left, Fadhli had started badmouthing his record. "This is someone who refused to fight on the front lines in Afghanistan," he said. We aren't fighting for Salih; we are fighting against the Socialists, Fadhli continued. That distinction, however, failed to survive the postwar fallout and Fadhli's eventual defection to Salih's camp. When the defeat of the Socialists didn't result in an Islamic state, the men remembered Mihdhar's warning.

Mihdhar called his group of malcontents the Aden–Abyan Islamic Army, taking the name from a prophetic saying that in the last days an army of 12,000 men will rise up in the regions around Aden and Abyan to defend Islam. By most accounts, the group never numbered more than a few handfuls of followers—hardly an army—but they were ambitious.

In the fall of 1998, the Aden–Abyan Islamic Army began releasing a series of statements through Abu Hamza al-Masri, an Egyptian cleric who had lost both hands and one eye in a land mine explosion in Afghanistan. Masri later replaced one of his hands with a hook and often used a patch to cover his damaged eye. As the head of the Finsbury Park Mosque in north London, Masri had easy access to the city's journalists. Mihdhar and Masri had met in Peshawar's mixing pot of jihadis in the early 1990s. At the time, the younger Mihdhar saw the Egyptian cleric as a spiritual mentor; a decade later, when the Yemeni formed the Aden–Abyan Islamic Army, he reached out to Masri for guidance. Like bin Laden, the men were worried about the growing US presence on the Arabian peninsula. With Saudi Arabia having played host to US military bases since the Gulf War in 1990, and the rest of the countries in the Gulf following suit, Mihdhar and Masri were convinced that Yemen was the only "independent" state left on the Arabian peninsula. But even this was changing.

Eight years after Yemen's disastrous performance on the UN Security Council, the US was finally getting around to forgiving Salih. In a sign of the growing goodwill, the US Navy negotiated a deal to use Aden as a refueling base, and the US Ambassador to Yemen, a trim, no-nonsense career diplomat from Missouri named

Barbara Bodine, was increasingly visible around the country. The US's first female ambassador to Yemen, her unveiled, angular good looks came as a shock to many in the conservative country. More worrying still for the jihadis under Mihdhar's command was the steady stream of US military officials visiting Sanaa.

On December 12, 1998, General Anthony Zinni, a square-shouldered Marine officer with a jutting chin, touched down in Sanaa for a meeting with President Salih. The previous August, Zinni had been named head of US Central Command, the regional military command center responsible for operations in the Middle East, central Asia, and the Horn of Africa. He was in Yemen to discuss ongoing efforts to demine the south after the civil war and to talk about future joint military exercises between the US and Yemen. For Mihdhar and Masri it was too much. They had been keeping count, and Zinni was the seventh US military official to visit Yemen that year. For a president who had needed jihadi help to hold his country together four years earlier, Salih was getting too close to the Americans.

TWO WEEKS LATER, on December 23, 1998, everything was in place for the response Mihdhar and Masri had warned of in their statements. The plan called for several British Muslims, including Masri's eldest son and a stepson, to carry out a series of coordinated attacks in Aden on Christmas day. They would then flee the country to London, which Masri liked to describe as "a paradise where you could do anything you wanted." Among the targets in Aden were the Anglican church, a restaurant popular with foreigners, the British consulate, the UN office, and the Movenpick Hotel, the site of Jamal al-Nahdi's failed attack in 1992. Overwhelming force, Mihdhar assured his followers in Yemen, was the only language the Americans understood. The creeping occupation of Yemen, he said, would end only when it proved too costly for them to remain.

Late in the evening on December 23, six men—five Britons and an Algerian who had flown in with them from Heathrow—left Mihdhar's camp in Abyan in a white sedan. Gingerly the men eased the car down the rocky dirt track for what must have seemed like hours before they reached the paved road to Aden. In the trunk were several mines, rocket launchers, and assorted bomb-making material, and none of them wanted it to explode prematurely.

By the time they reached the outskirts of Aden it was nearly midnight. As the car approached of the city's traffic circles, the driver, Malik Harhara, a young British citizen of Yemeni descent, fell back on old habits. Instead of driving around the circle in the counterclockwise direction favored in Yemen, Harhara went the way he drove at home in Britain. The curious visual of a car going around the circle the wrong way caught the attention of a traffic policeman, who flagged the men down. When the officer bent down to look into the vehicle and ask Harhara for his identification, the twenty-six-year-old panicked and sped away. Unsure of where he was in the dark, Harhara kept turning, hoping to lose the police, who were now pursuing the men through Aden's early morning traffic. Jolted by the adrenaline of the car chase, Harhara abandoned the caution of the previous few hours. Fishtailing around a corner, he slammed into an oncoming vehicle.

The six men in the car were shaken but miraculously unhurt. After a dazed moment, they opened the doors and spilled out into the cool night air, abandoning the car and its weapons to the police. But none of the men had any idea where they were, and within hours the police had arrested them all.

IN ABYAN, MIHDHAR scrambled to find a way to salvage the Christmas plot. A local contact told him that a group of Western tourists was scheduled for a safari-like tour of Abyan in the next few days, and Mihdhar hurriedly put together a plan to get his men back. Around 11 a.m. on December 28, Mihdhar's jihadis spotted the tourist convoy of five SUVs slowly picking its way down the narrow, sandswept road back toward Aden. As the first SUV passed their hiding spot, the jihadis raced a truck onto the pavement, blocking the road and cutting off the other four vehicles. The rest of the men, who had been hiding behind rocks and trees, suddenly stood up screaming "Allahu Akbar" and firing their guns into the air. For the tourists in the SUVs, the scene was surreal, a Hollywood western come to life. Scrambling down the rocky slope, Mihdhar's men rushed the convoy. One man flashed a grenade at a driver and ordered him out of the vehicle. As soon as the driver opened the door, the masked man pulled him to the ground and slammed his head with the butt of his gun. In the dusty chaos, one tourist and the driver of the first vehicle managed to escape. But the rest of the group—sixteen tourists from Britain, Australia, and the US, as well as four Yemeni drivers—was in Mihdhar's hands.

The jihadis piled into the SUVs and maneuvered them off the road onto a faint trail. For several minutes they drove north, easing their way past stunted trees and the low, rocky foothills of southern Yemen. After pulling into their base camp, the jihadis separated the tourists from the local drivers, keeping both groups under armed guard. On his satellite phone, Mihdhar placed several calls to the UK. "We've got the goods that were ordered—1,600 cartons marked British and American," he said in a transparent code.

From London, Masri agreed that the hostages should be exchanged for the members of their group, including his son and stepson, who had been arrested in Aden after the car chase in the early morning hours of Christmas Eve. Mihdhar sent a messenger to a local police outpost to inform the government of his demands. Then he sat back and waited. Kidnappings of foreigners happened frequently in Yemen and the government, eager to avoid negative international press, always caved. Mihdhar rejoined his men late in the evening for a meal of fresh meat cooked over open fires.

The men woke early to say their dawn prayers. Shortly after they finished, an elderly shaykh from a local tribe wandered into camp with tea and biscuits. He was looking to act as an intermediary between Mihdhar and the government, a common role for local dignitaries. The kidnappers were in his territory and, according to tribal law, he had a responsibility. But Mihdhar rebuffed his advances, telling him they had "higher contacts." The old man walked back out of camp confused that the kidnappers didn't want to negotiate.

The government also had no intention of bargaining. Yemeni soldiers had Mihdhar's camp surrounded, and Salih was certain he could get the tourists back without releasing the prisoners. Just as he had with the Socialists in Aden, Salih wanted to send a message to the jihadis. In Abyan, Salih's commanders ordered their men into action at eight o'clock that morning. The soldiers crept up to the camp slowly through a series of dry water channels. Spotting the commandos' advance through the boulders and shrunken trees, one of the outlying guards fired his gun in warning. Mihdhar's men scrambled the hostages to their feet to use as human shields, screaming that they would execute them if the soldiers didn't back off. In the confusion of RPG and bazooka fire four hostages were killed.

YEMEN PUT MIHDHAR and his men in the camp on trial and requested Masri's extradition from Britain, which Prime Minister Tony Blair refused. In Yemen, Mihdhar refused to recognize the state court. "I am a mujahid," he shrieked at the judge. "I am fighting for the establishment of Shariah law in Yemen." Days later, his story remained unchanged. "If you want to try us, you should convene an Islamic court," he said, suggesting Abd al-Majid al-Zindani and Abd al-Wahhab al-Daylami, the two clerics who had been most active in recruiting for Afghanistan, as suitable authorities. "We fought in Afghanistan and Chechnya and we will continue our struggle until the establishment of an Islamic state in Yemen."

Mihdhar's trial dragged on for months. One of the defendants testified that Mihdhar had met with a man he identified as Abu Ali al-Harithi in Sanaa. But his was one name among many and was soon lost in a blizzard of hearsay. In February 1999, the prosecution presented evidence taken from Mihdhar's house in Shabwa. Among the material were a number of pictures of Osama bin Laden. "Yes, three times yes," Mihdhar responded. "If we had ten men like him in the Muslim world they would liberate the people. We call on the mujahidin to gather round him."

On October 17, five months after he was sentenced, the Yemeni government ordered Mihdhar's execution. Four guards escorted the handcuffed prisoner into a public square in Sanaa. Ritually pure in a white robe, Mihdhar was given a chance to say his final prayers before the soldiers laid him facedown on a red carpet spread over a patch of dirt. Surrounded by a shoving, jeering crowd, the public executioner hovered over Mihdhar, straddling the prostrate man. He took a quick look around, as the onlookers hushed in anticipation. With an almost casual roll of his shoulders he fired a single shot. The bullet raced the three feet down into the back of Mihdhar's head. The crack of the gunsot held in the air for a brief moment, before the cheering overtook it. The jihadi was dead.

The grievances and anger that found form in Mihdhar did not end with his execution. Scattered throughout the country in tiny pockets of anger and rage, a number of jihadis wondered why they were being ignored instead of being asked to share in governing the country, as Salih had promised. The president would soon learn the price of ignoring unsavory proxies.

5

The Southern Job

2000–2001

At the al-Faruq training camp just outside Kandahar in southern Afghanistan, Osama bin Laden plotted his next move. It was late January 2000 and his plans for the millennium had failed. Two years earlier, after his fatwa declaring war on Americans and Jews, bin Laden's men in east Africa had carried out simultaneous bombings of US embassies in Kenya and Tanzania. The US responded three weeks later with missile strikes in Sudan and Afghanistan, which destroyed several of bin Laden's training camps, and since then al-Qaeda had struggled to hit back.

In December 1999, a cell of sixteen operatives had been arrested in Jordan as they prepared to strike at Western hotels. Days later, in the northwest corner of the US, an alert border guard had stopped a nervous Algerian as he attempted to cross the border into Washington from Canada. His intention, he later told investigators, was to bomb Los Angeles International Airport. A third strike had been scheduled to take place in Yemen on January 3, 2000. Under the supervision of Abd al-Rahim al-Nashiri, al-Qaeda's chief of operations for the Arabian peninsula, a small group of al-Qaeda operatives planned to bomb one of the US warships that used Aden as a refueling stop. But on a practice run shortly before the scheduled strike, they had overloaded the small boat with too many explosives and then watched as the attack vessel sank just offshore. When the men retrieved the boat, the waterlogged bricks of explosives were too damaged to use and Nashiri was forced to postpone the operation. Bin Laden didn't have a direct hand in any of the plots, continuing to favor his idea of centralization of decision and decentralization of execution; still, he expected better.

The frustration over the failed attacks mixed with bin Laden's personal restlessness that winter in Afghanistan. For much of his adulthood he'd had four wives, the maximum allowed under Islamic law. But for the past few years he'd been limited to three. During his exile in Sudan, bin Laden's fourth wife, Umm Ali, had asked for a divorce so she could return to the comfort of Saudi Arabia. Bin Laden had granted her request, but it pained him to do so. Nearly four years after that draining episode, he was ready to try again. A Yemeni friend made the initial arrangements, putting bin Laden in touch with the al-Sadah, a local family in Yemen. Natives of the mountain trading city of Ibb, nearly 100 miles south of Sanaa, the family was local aristocracy, famous for producing generations of religious scholars. Bin Laden's intermediaries described Amal al-Sadah, the fifteen-year-old bride-to-be, as beautiful and pious. As part of the traditional marriage contract, bin Laden had agreed to a bride price of $5,000.

Wary of wire transfers and unable to travel himself after the US attacks two years earlier, bin Laden needed a courier. He selected Nasir al-Bahri, a Yemeni bodyguard who had once saved his life by foiling an assassination attempt. Months earlier, bin Laden had arranged for Bahri and a Yemeni driver, Salim Hamdan, to marry a pair of Yemeni sisters. Now the roles were reversed, and bin Laden had to trust Bahri with the details of his own marriage.

WELL BUILT, with careful eyes, Bahri looks like a bodyguard. Known in the camps by his nickname, Abu Jandal, which roughly means "the powerful one," Bahri possesses a disarming sense of humor that often amused his boss. Like bin Laden, he was born to a Yemeni father in Saudi Arabia. Along with thousands of Arabs who came of age in the late 1980s, Bahri was inspired by jihadi stories from Afghanistan but also worried that, with the end of the Soviet occupation, he had missed his own chance at greatness. In 1993, a female schoolteacher in Saudi Arabia sponsored him for the new jihad in Bosnia, a common way for women and the elderly, who were unable to fight, to participate in jihad. Bahri used the woman's $2,000 to purchase equipment and pay for a ticket to Bosnia. After a short tour in Bosnia, the twenty-one-year-old fighter moved on to Somalia and then Tajikistan, which was in the midst of its own civil war. By early 1996, Bahri and the three dozen Arab fighters under his command had drifted into Afghanistan. Like most of the fighters on the jihadi circuit of the 1990s, the men were searching for a pure jihad. But everywhere they went, there were problems. In Bosnia, the European Muslims didn't seem to want their help or even trust them; in Somalia, they were fighting other Muslims; and in Tajikistan, they were drawn into a confusing clan-based conflict they didn't understand.

Within weeks, Bahri was ready to give up on Afghanistan as well. The people were too "treacherous," he confided to friends, and there was too much infighting among the different Islamic groups. The trusting Yemeni never knew whom to believe. "I had decided to return to Yemen to either settle there or to go to Chechnya to wage jihad," he remembered, explaining that in Chechnya, the groups were organized and the fighting made sense.

Bin Laden sought to change his mind. At the time, shortly after his arrival from Sudan, the al-Qaeda commander was hurting for recruits, and the news of Bahri and his three dozen Arab fighters traveled fast in Afghanistan. Bin Laden asked for a meeting. Bahri, however, had no interest in talking to the Saudi fugitive. "I am not the kind of man who likes to meet with bin Laden," he told intermediaries.

But the requests kept coming. When Bahri rebuffed one messenger, bin Laden sent another. Finally, one of them quoted a well-known saying of the Prophet that suggested Bahri owed bin Laden a response. Reluctantly, Bahri agreed to follow the envoy back to the camp at Jalalabad.

For three days, the traditional period of hospitality, bin Laden hosted the fighters. Perceptive as ever, he charmed the homesick Arabs. He had his cooks serve up Arab delicacies the men hadn't tasted in years, all the while telling them of his vision for jihad and the necessity of striking at the US. When bin Laden discovered Bahri's favorite food, a deliciously sweet mixture of flour, bananas, and sugar, he told the stocky fighter he was having that exact dish for breakfast the next day.

Almost in spite of himself, Bahri found himself attracted to bin Laden and his grandiose vision of the future. The rest of the young men, who had fought with Bahri in Tajikistan, looked to their twenty-four-year-old leader for guidance. "Every one of you is a man," Bahri told them. "You should all decide for yourself."

Eventually, nearly all of them followed Bahri's example and joined al-Qaeda. Like a teacher meeting with a student, bin Laden called the men into his room for a private audience. Those who agreed to join al-Qaeda recited the oath he required of every member: "I pledge before God my obedience to carry out both pleasant and unpleasant orders at good times and bad, and to work selflessly and not to disobey my commanders."

Exactly who swore the oath and who did not was kept secret. Recruits were instructed not to reveal whether they had given bin Laden the oath of allegiance. It was part of his plan to maintain secrecy and security. When Bahri's turn came, he walked into the shadow-filled room and sat down in front of his host.

"Are you ready?" bin Laden asked.

"Yes," al-Bahri replied, "although I have one condition."

"What is it?"

"If I should come out from under your umbrella and leave the area over which you are in command, then you will have no authority over me."

Bin Laden nodded his acceptance and asked if he was prepared for the oath. Bahri read it out, pausing only before the last clause about not disobeying commanders. He was willing to swear loyalty to bin Laden, but not to men he hadn't met. Bin Laden explained the line and walked him through the necessity of the chain of command. His fears eased, Bahri completed the oath. He was now a member of al-Qaeda.

For the next four years, Bahri served bin Laden, training in his camps and overseeing a guesthouse. After uncovering the plot to assassinate bin Laden, which al-Qaeda later blamed on Saudi intelligence, Bahri became bin Laden's chief bodyguard. He was entrusted with two bullets should "the shaykh" ever be surrounded with no chance of escape. When it came time to send someone to Yemen with a suitcase full of cash, Bahri was the only choice.

IN ADDITION TO bin Laden's marriage celebration, there was also whispered talk within the terrorist organization of another "wedding." The big one, as some of the men called it, had been in the works for years. Only a select group among al-Qaeda's leadership knew about the plot, but after Muhammad Atta and his men left the camps at the beginning of 2000, the circle had slowly begun to expand.

In August 2000, Abd al-Salam al-Hilah, the young Yemeni intelligence officer who had double-crossed al-Qaeda's traitor two years earlier, flew to Italy. A man he called Abu Salih met him at the airport in Bologna, along with a local preacher. The three greeted one another like old friends. Abu Salih hugged and kissed the younger man on the cheek, before leading him by the arm to his boxy Citroën. They didn't have much time before the meeting.

Abu Salih, whose real name was Abd al-Qadir al-Sayyid, was one of the Egyptians who had fled Yemen in the wake of Nasrallah's betrayal. Throughout the tumult of the past two years he had remained loyal to Zawahiri, never questioning his decision to align with bin Laden or target the US. Like others in al-Jihad, he was a talented forger, able to rework a passport or manufacture documents that could fool most immigration officers. Since arriving in Italy, he had been busy building up a network of supporters and stockpiling arms. Officially he was an imam at a local mosque, but preaching was only part of his job.

Abu Salih wanted to hear about the camps in Yemen, but Hilah couldn't wait. The camps are fine, he said. "They are in good hands. They are protected." He had bigger news to share with his old friend. As the car drove through Bologna's narrow streets, making its way toward the sports center where the three were scheduled to meet with a group of Islamists from around Europe, Hilah started telling Abu Salih about a madman.

"He's a madman," Hilah repeated, "but he's also a genius."

Using coded references and a strangely elliptical speech pattern, Hilah hinted at an upcoming attack. The strike would be a massive blow to the enemies of Islam, involving "airplanes" and "the sky." It "will be written about in all the newspapers of the world," Hilah continued. This is one that "will never be forgotten."

The cryptic comments about planes and the US made little sense to the Italian investigators who had bugged Abu Salih's car. The Italians had been tailing the Egyptian for nearly a year, but were struggling to put together a case. Hilah's excited speech was too vague to raise an alarm. The Italians dutifully passed the transcripts along to their US counterparts in the CIA, but the handful of intelligence operatives who reviewed Hilah's remarks couldn't make any sense of them either. The conversation was just one more data point in a world of sound.

As the tiny Citroën neared the sports center, Hilah addressed Abu Salih once more. "The fire is already lit, and is just waiting for the wind."

WHEN HILAH FLEW back to Yemen on his diplomatic passport days later, he wasn't the only jihadi returning to the country. Nasir al-Bahri was also coming home. And in the Persian Gulf, Abd al-Rahim al-Nashiri, al-Qaeda's skinny military commander, was preparing for another trip to Yemen. This was part of the genius of bin Laden's network. Compartmentalized cells, the centralization of decisions, and decentralization of execution meant that multiple plots could proceed simultaneously. Only bin Laden and a few other top leaders possessed the whole picture.

Nashiri had kept his small team together through the embarrassment of sinking their own boat ten months earlier on the eve of the millennium attack. They had withstood bin Laden's doubts and calls for a last minute shakeup. The men have learned from their mistake, Nashiri argued. Bin Laden acquiesced to his commander's decision, and by early October everything was ready for another attempt. A number of top al-Qaeda operatives, including Nashiri, flew to Yemen to oversee the operation. The US Navy had begun using Aden as a refueling stop in January 1999, and in the twenty-two months since warships had made thirty stops in the port city. Once Nashiri's team was in place, all they had to do was wait for the next ship.

Around 9:30 on the morning of October 12, it arrived. Gunmetal gray and nearly two football fields in length, the USS *Cole* was the latest in US naval technology. The destroyer had rolled off the assembly line at Norfolk, Virginia, in early 1995, at a cost of nearly a billion dollars. Almost halfway into a five-month deployment, the 281-person crew was looking forward to their upcoming port visit in nearby Bahrain. Several hundred yards offshore, Commander Kirk Lippold brought the ship in line with a floating mooring device known as a dolphin, and started the lengthy refueling process.

On shore, two al-Qaeda operatives maneuvered a tiny white boat into the water and shoved off. Hassan al-Khamiri, a Yemeni friend of Bahri's, must have known how lucky he was. The year before, Yemeni authorities had nabbed him in connection with a kidnapping plot. But he hadn't talked, and within a few weeks he was free again. His companion, Ibrahim al-Thawar, had also requested this suicide mission. They started their Yamaha outboard motor and weaved slowly through the maze of wooden fishing vessels that clogged the harbor. The two made sure to keep their speed down. Nashiri had been clear about that. Don't call attention to yourselves, he was always reminding them. Act normal.

At 11:17 a.m. they pulled alongside the destroyer. Smiling and waving at the US sailors above them, the bombers breathed in one final time.

The explosion punched a jagged 40-foot-square hole at the ship's waterline. Fire raced up the side of the ship, scorching the metal on its way to the top. Thick black smoke choked the air, while in the belly of the ship sailors were thrown off their feet by the strength of the blast. Nashiri's charges had done their job.

Inside the *Cole*, the crew wobbled to their feet, struggling to decipher the destruction around them. Slowly, as sound rushed back into their ears, their training took over. Command Master Chief James Parlier, who had years of experience as a corpsman, the navy's version of a medic, rushed topside. On his way up, he found a small knot of sailors staring at something on the floor. One of their shipmates lay horribly wounded on the metal at their feet.

Parlier took charge. Along with a couple of other men, he ripped a loosened door off its hinges and hauled the wounded man up to the deck on the temporary stretcher. As he leaned over the dying man, Parlier already knew it was too late. Still he kept pumping on his chest, giving him CPR. Finally, a chief put his hand on his shoulder.

"He's gone. You have to let him go."

Parlier sat up in a daze. He'd never had a man die on him before. The chief knelt down again; there were still others he could help.

"I said last rites," Parlier remembered. "I said a prayer and then we put him on the side somewhere so he wouldn't be in a position where he was dying in front of the crew and demoralizing the crew."

On Aden's sandy beach 650 yards away, members of al-Qaeda's support team peered through the black smoke, trying to judge the success of the mission. Fahd al-Qusa, a slender twenty-five-year-old from the al-Awaliq tribe in southern Yemen, was late joining them. Weeks earlier, Jamal al-Badawi, the logistics head, had arranged for the young tribesman to videotape the attack, giving him a pager and a secret code. When this goes off with the code, Badawi told him, that is your signal to set up the camera and start filming. Qusa, who came from the same tribe as Zayn al-Abidin al-Mihdhar, adored bin Laden and desperately wanted to do a good job. Always a bit of a screw-up, he had never quite been able to finish anything in his life. This would be his big chance.

On the morning of the attack he missed the signal, noticing too late he'd left the pager on vibrate. As he raced toward the safe house near the beach, he heard the blast. He could see the smoke billowing into the sky, a tall black column that fanned out as it rose.

The bombers hadn't sunk the ship, but they had crippled it. Within days, the al-Qaeda cell would have the final toll: seventeen dead and thirty-nine wounded. But even they knew this attack could not be measured by body bags alone. Two men in a tiny boat had struck the very face of American power.

AS THE SMOKE cleared in the harbor, the crew of the *Cole* began to take stock. Interior rooms had buckled and cracked like houses after an earthquake, the galley was a disaster, and other parts of the ship were nearly impassable due to debris and jagged metal. Marines from Bahrain were the first US military support staff to arrive on the scene, flying in hours after the attack. From the air they tried to assess the situation. Ali Soufan, an FBI agent, later said that the billion-dollar warship reminded him of a wounded lion, damaged and exposed as it swayed helplessly in the sea.

Barbara Bodine, the US ambassador, arrived in Aden within hours of the attack. She had lived through war before. In 1990, when Iraq invaded Kuwait, she was second-in-command at the US embassy in Kuwait, the deputy chief of mission. Her cool-headed demeanor throughout the four-month siege had won her the secretary of state's award for valor. She also had a long history with Yemen, serving first as a country officer in the late 1970s and then as the political–military officer for the Arabian peninsula. The ambassadorship was meant to cap an illustrious career. By the time she arrived in Aden, Bodine was certain of one thing. "The attack on the *Cole* was a hostile act, but this was not a hostile government or a hostile people."

Her counterpart in the FBI came to a similarly quick if opposing viewpoint. John O'Neill, the FBI's lead investigator, landed in Aden days later. He came, he liked to tell people, for one reason and one reason only: to catch the bad guys and bring them to justice. Loud and brash, and every bit as self-confident as Bodine, O'Neill was convinced that Yemen was part of the problem. "This is a country of 18 million people and 50 million guns," he wrote in reports home.

Bodine and O'Neill clashed almost as soon as the FBI team touched down in Yemen. First it was over accommodations and the weapons agents could carry, and then, as the investigation dragged on, over personnel and the size of the US footprint in the country. Bodine always wanted less and O'Neill always wanted more. Each the product of a particular bureaucracy, they both had their own way of doing things. "It is my job to make sure our actions don't subvert our goals," Bodine explained, referring to broader US policy in Yemen.

O'Neill couldn't understand why the ambassador didn't see the situation the way he did. The US had been attacked and it needed to find the guys responsible before they struck again. He regularly checked in with his home office in New York, updating them on his progress in conference calls. In the small talk before one of them he told a friend, "I have tried everything in my power to win this woman over with my O'Neill charm, but it just isn't working."

Bodine believed she understood O'Neill's argument. She simply disagreed with it. He was an intensely focused investigator who didn't understand the country he was working in. He had one narrow goal; she had many large ones. The relationship of the US with Yemen went far beyond the investigation of the USS *Cole* bombing. The US needed to apprehend those responsible, but it had to tread carefully. Otherwise, Bodine worried, it would just make a bad situation worse.

"The realities of a US investigative style inevitably collided headlong with the limited capabilities of Yemen," she later wrote in defense of her actions. "The Yemenis knew Aden and its people but lacked technical and professional competence; the FBI had the forensic and technical capability but could not operate 'on the street' in Aden."

But while O'Neill was trying the patience of diplomats on both sides, his sharp elbows were opening other doors. Painstakingly, in meeting after meeting, he built a relationship with Ghalib al-Qamish, the aging head of the PSO. Thin, with a leathery face that was partially hidden beneath a bristling mustache, the fifty-five-year-old Qamish was one of the few top security officials in Yemen not related to the president by blood. He was a cautious survivor in a cutthroat world. The US government worried about Qamish's organization and its loyalties—this was the same service that employed Abd al-Salam al-Hilah—but in the man himself O'Neill thought he had an ally. Initially Yemeni officials had treated the attack as a refueling accident. When US investigators presented them with undeniable evidence of a bomb, Yemen's intelligence services finally began to investigate, but they had already lost precious time which allowed Nashiri and others to flee the country.

Yemeni authorities approached the USS *Cole* investigation the way they did every major case. They arrested everyone they could find and then began the slow process of sorting them out. Suspects were guilty until proven innocent. This approach made no sense to the FBI officials, who were trying to put together a case that would stand up in a US court. But that was the environment, and O'Neill and his team tried to adapt.

Exhausted by the long hours and constant stress of working in what he considered enemy territory, O'Neill returned to the US shortly before Thanksgiving for a break. He was visibly changed. He'd lost weight and those who knew him thought he looked beaten. In his absence, the investigation bogged down. In Yemen, personal relationships are essential. The man matters more than the institution, and without O'Neill's constant pressing Yemen's cooperation slowed to a crawl. Qamish refused to take meetings with FBI deputies, shuffling them off to his own aides. Worried about what his team might miss if he wasn't there to lead, O'Neill felt personally responsible. He knew Qamish and the rest of the Yemeni intelligence infrastructure, and after years of study he knew al-Qaeda. Following the Christmas holiday he requested permission to return to Yemen. Bodine, who as ambassador had the final say on all US citizens in Yemen, refused.

The rejection stung. O'Neill tried to play it off to friends in the FBI, saying he was amused that the ambassador wouldn't let him back in the country. Barry Mawn, his boss in the New York office, watched O'Neill's frustration with FBI headquarters grow. The FBI, the organization that O'Neill had given twenty-four years of his life, failed to support him. "They decided that they weren't going to take that on," Mawn said. They didn't want a "turf battle with the State Department." But if O'Neill couldn't be on the ground, he couldn't lead his team or the investigation. He wasn't suited to be a desk agent. Seven months later, in August 2001, he retired from the FBI and took a job as head of security at the World Trade Center.

IN YEMEN, ONE of O'Neill's staff, a young Arabic-speaking officer named Ali Soufan, began to take more of a lead in the investigation. He had problems getting things done without his boss, but slowly, and in his own way, he started to make progress.

As the arrests mounted, Yemen managed to snag several local members of the attack team in its dragnet. In arresting so many people, the Yemenis had no idea who they held. Some were guilty, but most were not. The PSO detained Jamal al-Badawi, the logistics head of al-Qaeda, and in December it picked up Nasir al-Bahri, who hadn't even been aware of plans for an attack in Yemen. Security agents were also on the lookout for Fahd al-Qusa. Instead of wasting time and manpower on a manhunt, Yemeni security agents opted to flush him out of hiding. PSO officers visited Qusa's family home in Aden and arrested his father. As they led the old man away in handcuffs, they told the women of the family that Qusa knew what to do if he wanted his father released.

The PSO would hold Qusa's father, requiring the family to pay for his room and board in a local prison, until his son surrendered.

Within days, Qusa abandoned his hideout in Sanaa and turned himself in to the PSO. For the next two months Qamish, acting on orders from President Salih, refused to give US investigators access to the undersized prisoner. Finally, in early 2001, he relented and allowed Soufan and other agents into the room. The man the FBI found was a cheeky little tribesman with narrow eyes and a carefully trimmed goatee. Sitting in the interrogation room, he stared up at the American agents.

It was a form of torture, Qusa later told people: "The Americans had these Christian crosses around their necks, hanging down their chests." FBI agents dispute Qusa's allegations as well as his claim that he refused to cooperate. Qusa says he argued that the FBI agents were making a mockery of the Quran, citing a saying of the Prophet that suggested non-Muslims shouldn't be allowed to set foot on the Arabian peninsula.

Qusa wasn't the only one the FBI made uncomfortable. Not knowing how much time they had with the prisoner, the Americans' interrogation was blunt and to the point. They wanted to know what ties, if any, existed between officials in the Yemeni military and the bombers. The agents zeroed in on Ali Muhsin al-Ahmar, a fellow tribesman of President Salih and the head of the First Armored Division, who had overseen the sack of Aden. They knew about his work with Tariq al-Fadhli and the rest of the Afghan Arabs and they wondered if he was still involved. The FBI was also curious about Shaykh Abd al-Majid al-Zindani. Was he linked to the cell? They even asked Qusa about President Salih's eldest son, Ahmad, who was the head of Yemen's Special Forces and the country's powerful Republican Guard as well as being a member of parliament. The closer the questions got to the president's family, the more nervous the PSO became. After three weeks, Qamish put a halt to the interrogation. The FBI had managed to extract some good information, but the agents still had more questions than answers.

ON FEBRUARY 12, 2001, Italian officials recorded an outgoing call from Abu Salih, the Egyptian forger, to his old friend in Yemen. The phone rang in Abd al-Salam al-Hilah's house in Sanaa, but instead of the PSO colonel, Abu Salih got his younger brother. It didn't matter; both men knew what was going on.

"I heard you were going to America," Abu Salih said.

"I'm sorry to say we were not able to get in," the younger man answered. "It is our most important wish and our big target."

Much like the conversation recorded in Abu Salih's Citroën six months earlier, this one was too vague to be actionable. Again, the Italians shared the information with the CIA, but the CIA neglected to tell the FBI, who had a team in Yemen cooperating with the PSO. The pieces were starting to accumulate, and still no one was willing to share. Four months later, in July 2001, the surveillance ended when Abu Salih abruptly fled Italy for Afghanistan.

THE SUMMER OF 2001 was a big one for al-Qaeda. The normally calm bin Laden appeared more nervous than usual to his men, moving around constantly and holding secret meetings with al-Qaeda's military council. For years, recruits had been pouring into al-Qaeda training camps, and now bin Laden began to send them home. Throughout July and August, small groups of al-Qaeda operatives trickled back into Saudi Arabia and Yemen. They were bin Laden's vanguard, the men he hoped would spark a revolution in the heart of the Arab world. None of them had any idea what they were doing, but they trusted their leader. They had all sworn an oath and they went where he ordered.

In early August, bin Laden told Fawaz al-Rabi'i, an intense twenty-two-year-old Yemeni, that he too was being sent home. Rabi'i was young, but bin Laden liked what he had seen. Daring and charismatic, Rabi'i had been born in Saudi Arabia, the son of a Yemeni migrant worker. As a child he seemed almost destined for jihad. His heroes were the *mutatawwa*, Saudi Arabia's morality police. He idolized them, often walking with them as they made their daily rounds, making sure that women were properly veiled and that everyone said their prayers. The bearded volunteers encouraged their young pupil, pushing him to memorize the Quran and occasionally allowing him to use their correcting rods.

After the Gulf War and Saudi Arabia's expulsion of nearly a million Yemeni migrant workers in 1990 in retaliation for Salih's support for Saddam Hussein, Rabi'i had struggled to adjust to life in Sanaa. He was Yemeni by birth, but Saudi by training and experience. After he finished high school, he took a job as a clerk in the presidential office, and then in early 2000, along with a couple of friends including a former PSO agent, Rabi'i left for Afghanistan.

Rabi'i loved life in the camps. The young Yemeni was finally back among friends who thought and believed like he did. He had met Abu Musab al-Zarqawi, a one-time criminal turned jihadi who would go on to lead al-Qaeda in Iraq, and spent time talking with some of the eventual September 11 hijackers. In phone calls back to Yemen, Rabi'i encouraged his younger brother Salman to join him. This is the place to be, he said.

His new goal, he told his father at one point, was to "die a martyr." He told bin Laden the same thing. The al-Qaeda leader had other plans. "I'm making you a commander," bin Laden said when he sent him home, explaining that he was dispatching Rabi'i back to Yemen as the head of a twelve-man cell. Salman, who had arrived in Afghanistan only two months earlier, would remain behind for more training.

Bin Laden encouraged his young deputy, assuring him that he would know what to do when the time was right. Rabi'i packed his bags and said goodbye to his friends in the camp, but inside he must have wondered what the shaykh was planning.

6

Allies

Fall 2001

Fawaz al-Rabi'i and the rest of the jihadi cell flying back to Yemen in early August 2001 likely paid little attention to the desolate landscape of rocks and dust as they crossed over the Gulf of Oman to the Arabian peninsula. But for the FBI agents who would soon converge on Yemen, the miles of barren peaks and wide expanses of desert looked like some distant planet. Even from the air, the poverty was apparent. There were no rivers, no cities, and no green, just a single, unending collage of dusty grays and browns unfolding below like a rumpled quilt. At night it was worse. With most of the country off the electrical grid, there were none of the clustered constellations of lights that punctuate most flights. The only thing agents could see outside the frosted Plexiglas was a vast wilderness of darkness and shadows. Since the *Cole* bombing the year before, Ali Soufan and the rest of John O'Neill's team had made this trip several times and reentry always took a toll.

On August 22, the FBI was preparing for yet another flight to Yemen. Barbara Bodine was scheduled to transfer out of the country, and in New York O'Neill was on his way out as well. This was his last day as an FBI agent before starting his job as chief of security at the World Trade Center. Ordering his team back to Yemen had been his last official act. Pointedly, the FBI team waited until September, after Bodine had departed, to land in Yemen.

There wasn't much for the agents to do. The US never responded to the suicide attack on the *Cole* and the trail had gone cold. After the disastrous response to the African embassy bombings in 1998, which cost $40 million in munitions alone but did little real damage to al-Qaeda, President Clinton had balked at a second round of missile strikes. What could the US even hit in Afghanistan, some within his administration asked at the time. More tents and mud huts, which al-Qaeda could rebuild within days for a fraction of what it had cost to destroy them. Throughout late 2000 these discussions gradually hardened into a consensus: bin Laden was a job for the CIA, not the army. Term-limited and with the US in the middle of a tight presidential campaign between Vice President Al Gore and Texas governor George W. Bush, Clinton never struck back.

The moment soon passed, as the economy continued to grow and consumers spent extravagantly on second homes and extra cars. The public had little interest in a small terrorist attack in a country no one knew anything about. As the US watched a controversial election, transfixed by Florida's hanging chads, the *Cole* bombing faded from public memory. On January 19, 2001, the day before George W. Bush's inauguration, Clinton's outgoing secretary of defense, William Cohen, released his report on the *Cole* attack. Amidst the celebrations and inauguration balls in Washington, few paid any attention. George W. Bush had his own priorities, which included a strong focus on the economy and domestic politics. By the time Soufan and the rest of the agents flew to Yemen in late August 2001, hardly anyone in the government even noticed they were gone.

WITH THE *COLE* in a shipyard back in Mississippi and Bodine out of the country, Soufan and the rest of the team ran the investigation out of the US embassy, a low-slung fortified compound halfway up a hill on Sanaa's eastern edge. With the tight security measures stemming from the *Cole* attack still in place, the team was booked into the Sheraton, the only hotel deemed safe enough to host US officials. A depressingly bland 1970s-style hotel with leaky faucets and tasteless food, the Sheraton was at least familiar to the American agents. The rest of the city was unlike anything they'd ever seen.

One of the oldest continuously inhabited cities in the world, Sanaa was a museum piece desperately trying to be modern; tiny tea shops with battered shutters and dented tables jostled against mosques that predated the Crusades by centuries. For years, the religious rulers of Sanaa, which was built on a mountain plain surrounded by dozens of warring tribes, had ordered the fortified city's seven gates to be locked every evening after prayers. The civil war in the 1960s put an end to the imams and their protective custody. The city soon burst its walls, swelling from a population of 50,000 to nearly two million in thirty years.

By the time the FBI team arrived in early September 2001, Sanaa was in trouble. Three decades of uncontrolled growth had outpaced the city's antiquated infrastructure. Viewing the hazy sprawl of dirt and poverty from the Sheraton's eighth-floor bar, it was hard to imagine the Prophet Muhammad ever describing Sanaa as "the paradise of earthly paradises." The modern version of Sanaa looked more like a garbage dump. The agents could still see the scores of giant gingerbread houses the city was famous for, rising up like ancient sentries from the squalor and noise below. Clustered in the old city, the stunning towers were slowly dissolving into the sea of disorder that lapped at their feet. Everywhere else, traditional architecture gave way to modern shortcuts as people poured into the city looking for work.

Wherever the FBI team turned, there were crowded markets full of barking vendors shouting out their offers in rough, throaty

Arabic. Their clientele was just as strange. Men with long bushy beards and ankle-length robes brushed with mud and dirt regarded the foreigners with suspicion. The women, jokingly referred to as ninjas by some at the embassy, were ghostly figures in black cloaks known as abayas, slipping through the throngs completely covered and silent. The crowds kicked up dust that mixed with the smoke, sweat, and diesel fumes to form a sour-smelling haze. Choking on the nasty mix, the agents had little reason to venture into many of the city's newer neighborhoods. There was nothing to see, only streets of cheap, grubby buildings that spilled ever outward.

The weary apathy of life in Sanaa was easy to succumb to. Jumbled traffic jams of battered pickups and rusty taxis, unending noise, and the general lack of order all wore on the agents' nerves. More subtly but just as effectively, Yemen's bureaucracy did the same.

On September 5, days after the FBI team arrived in Sanaa, President Salih sat down with a journalist from al-Jazeera to talk about the USS *Cole* investigation. He had done everything in his power, he explained, to limit the FBI in Yemen. "We denied them access to Yemen with forces, planes, and ships," he offered in characteristic overstatement. "We put them under direct monitoring by our security forces." For the FBI agents, Salih's boasts were more of the same. Eleven months after the *Cole* attack, the agents were still hammering away at the same walls.

ON SEPTEMBER 11, Ali Soufan called his fiancée from an office at the US embassy in Sanaa. It was almost 5 p.m. in Yemen, but the eight-hour time difference between Sanaa and New York meant this was one of the few windows the two had. Minutes into their conversation, another FBI agent burst into the room.

"Ali," he gasped, "a plane hit the World Trade Center."

Hanging up the phone, Soufan dialed John O'Neill's number in New York. There was no answer. As Soufan tried a second time, the agent rushed back into the room. "Another plane just hit the World Trade Center!" he screamed. "It's a passenger plane. Oh my God, a big plane."

Hurriedly leaving a message on O'Neill's phone, Soufan rushed into Bodine's old office where the rest of the team was watching on the embassy's television. There was no doubt in the agents' minds; this was an attack. Soufan kept dialing the number to the FBI's office in New York, but no one was answering. Trained to be where the action was, the agents were stuck continents away, forced to watch the worst terrorist attack in US history unfold on the television's tiny screen.

Later that evening in Yemen, their orders finally came through. The FBI wanted the team to evacuate. "Yemen," they were told, "is deemed unsafe." As the agents prepared to board a plane early the next morning for the flight back to the US, a second call came through. The FBI wanted Soufan and a couple of other agents to remain in Yemen. The US didn't have many leads on the attacks, but already it looked like al-Qaeda, and the agents in Yemen were some of the country's only assets in the field.

Back at the embassy compound on a secure line, their full orders came in. The bureau authorized to them to use "any means necessary" to identify the hijackers. To Soufan, the message was clear: get something and get it fast. Racing across town to see Ghalib al-Qamish, the leathery head of the PSO who had developed a rapport with O'Neill, Soufan asked to see Fahd al-Qusa. Headquarters had said that Qusa, the would-be cameraman from the *Cole* attack, was important. Qamish was skeptical. The FBI had already had three weeks with Qusa. What more could they get?

"I'm not talking about the *Cole*," Soufan sputtered. Fighting back tears, he said that O'Neill was missing and feared dead. Qamish hesitated for a moment, then, as the agents watched, he picked up the phone and called the PSO prison in Aden where Qusa was being held. With the final flight to Sanaa about to take off that evening, his men told Qamish it was too late. They would transfer the prisoner tomorrow. Get him on that plane, Qamish barked. Worried that his men might not be quick enough, Qamish dialed the Aden airport and ordered the pilots not to take off until his prisoner was on board.

By midnight, Qusa was sitting in an interrogation room at PSO headquarters. The twenty-six-year-old was just as cocky as Soufan remembered. Evasive and full of himself, he wanted nothing to do with Soufan or the FBI. "You shouldn't even be in Yemen," he spat at the investigators. "Your presence is an insult to Islam."

Soufan was tired of his attitude. Some of his friends were dead and his country had been attacked. He was going to find out what Qusa really knew. Shortly before he went into the interrogation, CIA officials in Sanaa had handed him three photos of an al-Qaeda meeting Qusa had attended a year earlier. The photos gave Soufan an edge with Qusa, and he pressed it home. Night after night, Soufan interrogated the scrawny tribesman. Qusa didn't have much, but he did have a name. On the fifth day he gave it up: Abu Jandal. That was the nickname used in the camps by bin Laden's bodyguard, Nasir al-Bahri.

Bin Laden's former bodyguard had been picked up in the months after the attack on the USS *Cole*, but the PSO had refused to give the FBI access to Bahri, claiming he had nothing to do with the *Cole* attack. "Why is he in jail?" one of the agents asked the Yemenis.

"Suspicion," the guard replied.

Like hundreds of other suspects, Bahri was stuck. Even though the Yemenis didn't have anything on him, they were convinced he was too dangerous to let go. Instead, they just forgot about him. Bahri had left Afghanistan more than a year earlier and had nothing to do with the planning of 9/11, but at the moment he was all the US had. In the decade since the Soviet withdrawal from Afghanistan in 1989, the US had drastically scaled back its operations on the ground there, and the years of neglect were coming back to haunt the US at the worst possible moment.

But Qusa had just given the FBI a reason to interrogate the bodyguard. "We need to talk to Abu Jandal," Soufan told the Yemeni guard. "Quickly."

Angry at being imprisoned without charge and prevented from seeing his wife and two young children, Bahri was a tougher case than Qusa. The FBI worked on him for days, softening him up with small favors and challenging his assumptions about America and Islamic law. Soufan knew Bahri was tired of jihad, but the bodyguard still felt bound to the men in Afghanistan. They were men he had fought and bled with, men he had recruited. Plus there were his ties to bin Laden to consider. In addition to arranging Bahri's wedding, bin Laden had been present at the birth of Bahri's oldest son, where he honored the family by rubbing a piece of softened date on the newborn's palate in imitation of an early Islamic practice. And Bahri's brother-in-law, Salim Hamdan, was still in Afghanistan, working as a driver for bin Laden. Years earlier, before the men married a pair of Yemeni sisters, Bahri had convinced the chubby Yemeni to go to Afghanistan, and he still felt responsible for him.

One night during the interrogation, Soufan collapsed from exhaustion and had to be taken to the emergency room, but the next night he was back at the table questioning Bahri and arguing theology with him. A few nights later, Soufan slipped a book of mug shots in front of the weary prisoner. Bahri skimmed through the book quickly and then flipped it down on the table. Soufan picked the book up and gently slid it back across the table. "Look again," he said. Bahri glanced up at his Arabic-speaking interrogator and opened the book. On the third time through, Soufan pointed at a picture of Marwan al-Shihhi, one of the hijackers. "Are you claming you don't know al-Sharqi?" Soufan asked, using Shihhi's alias. Bahri looked away instead of responding and Soufan knew he had him. Thanks to the Qusa interrogation, Soufan already knew of Bahri's relationship with the balding hijacker. Caught in a lie, Bahri admitted he knew Shihhi and confirmed that they had spent time together in Afghanistan. The rest came quicker. As Bahri looked through the remaining photos, he identified six more men. They had all trained in bin Laden's camps, he admitted.

The US had its link. From an interrogation room in Sanaa, bin Laden's bodyguard tied the hijackers to al-Qaeda.

ON SEPTEMBER 11, the US was without an ambassador in Yemen. Bodine had left two weeks prior to the attacks and Congress had never acted on Clinton's nominee to replace her. Without someone to interpret his actions to the new administration in Washington, Salih worried that the US might do something drastic. Already the diplomatic rumor mill was churning with reports of sharp exchanges between US officials and key allies. Bush's bullish deputy secretary of state, Richard Armitage, told Pakistan's intelligence chief that the US would "bomb it back to the Stone Age" if it didn't cooperate. Other analysts on CNN and MSNBC suggested that Yemen was the next logical target after Afghanistan. Suddenly, Salih's comments on al-Jazeera a week before the attack about blocking the FBI looked much more sinister. The last time Salih had crossed the US was during the 1990 Gulf War, and the combination of US, Saudi, and Kuwaiti aid cuts had crippled the country. But this time, the US wasn't talking about economic retribution.

Salih's soft-spoken son-in-law, Abd al-Wahhab al-Hijri, Yemen's understated ambassador to the US, offered little help. George W. Bush was unpredictable. He had only been in office nine months and the US had never been attacked like this. In the confused days immediately after the attack, Hijri advised Salih to convince Bush that Yemen was an ally in America's new war.

"I'm sending you Abd al-Karim," Salih told his son-in-law, referring to Abd al-Karim al-Iryani.

A short, elfin-looking Yemeni, Iryani was Salih's preferred intermediary with the Americans and Europeans. As the nephew of North Yemen's second president, Iryani had spent a large part of his youth abroad, attending college and graduate school in Georgia before gaining a PhD in biochemical genetics from Yale in 1968. He spoke fluent, idiomatic English and, more importantly, he knew how to talk to Westerners. Diplomats and aid workers appreciated his direct approach and calm, studied manner. Dr. Abd al-Karim, as he was known to most, said what he meant. Only months earlier Salih had fired him as prime minister—Iryani's second time in charge of the cabinet—and now he was back in favor.

Iryani would be carrying a letter for President Bush, Salih told his ambassador.

In Washington, President Bush's top deputies met with Edmund Hull, Bush's nominee to replace Bodine in Yemen. On September 17, Secretary of State Colin Powell administered the oath of office to Hull, a trim, Arabic-speaking diplomat with a background in intelligence. Starting in the early 1970s when he was a Peace Corps volunteer in Tunisia, Hull had spent most of his career in the Arab world. His latest post had been as the State Department's deputy coordinator for counterterrorism, where he had worked on the *Cole* bombing. Bush liked that. The only issue that mattered in Yemen was counterterrorism, and Hull was an expert.

On September 27, Iryani arrived in Washington for a series of meetings at the State Department. That afternoon, late in the evening in Sanaa, he called Salih to tell him that everything looked good. There was a sense in Washington, Iryani told the president, that Yemen's calculus changed in the aftermath of the September 11 attacks. After the successful interrogations of Qusa and Bahri, the FBI reported that Yemen was cooperating, and other agencies seemed satisfied as well. Yemen is not a target, Iryani congratulated his boss.

Salih heard much the same thing from Hull, who had just arrived in the country. Presenting his credentials to the president, Hull assured him that the US had no plans to attack Yemen. Later, the new US ambassador told reporters that he believed President Salih had "chosen sides in this war on terrorism."

NOT EVERYONE IN the US was so sure. Intelligence analysts in the CIA worried about al-Qaeda operatives already in Yemen, and when Salih landed in the US on November 25 for a meeting with Bush, they were ready with a list of names. This was Salih's third official visit to the US; the previous two had both ended in disaster. In 1990, President George Bush had invited Salih to the White House ahead of Yemen's referendum on unification. The new country's coming-out party was spoiled months later when Salih refused to side with the US against Saddam Hussein. Ten years later, in 2000, Bill Clinton had given him a second chance. That visit was soon overshadowed by the attack on the USS *Cole*.

Salih knew the US wanted to work with him. He just wasn't sure what working with the US entailed. His intelligence agencies were already cooperating with the CIA and the FBI and, in the weeks after the attacks, Yemen had arrested dozens of suspected al-Qaeda operatives. Police had closed down bank accounts and shuttered businesses the US worried were funneling money to al-Qaeda.

With all his top security officials, including Ghalib al-Qamish, in tow, Salih was prepared to deal. He met with George Tenet at Yemen's official residence in northwest Washington on November 26. The stocky CIA director wasted little time. He had brought the list of names his agents had prepared. Earlier in November, the CIA had given their counterparts in Yemeni intelligence a similar list of suspects, only to watch most of them slip out of the country.

Frustrated analysts were convinced crooked agents in the PSO had tipped the suspects off.

This has to stop, Tenet warned, looking down the table at Qamish. Pausing briefly, he took out the list and handed it directly to Salih. No one in the room missed the move. The list was Salih's responsibility. If something went wrong, it would be on him.

At the top of Tenet's list was Abu Ali al-Harithi, the man who had set up al-Qaeda's first training camps in Yemen. American intelligence agents called him simply "the Godfather." He was bin Laden's top lieutenant in the country and the head of al-Qaeda in Yemen. We need this guy, Tenet said.

Right below him was Muhammad Hamdi al-Ahdal. Another Yemeni who had grown up in Saudi Arabia, Ahdal had a prosthetic leg from the fighting in Chechnya. According to US intelligence, Harithi and Ahdal were the two top al-Qaeda figures in Yemen. They were, in the words of one administration official, "the nuts and bolts of terrorism." This is how Yemen can demonstrate that it is on the side of the US, Tenet told Salih.

The next day, President Bush repeated the same message. Shortly after 9/11, on September 20, he had laid out his worldview in an extraordinary speech to a joint session of Congress. Standing in the well of the US House of Representatives in front of an enormous American flag, Bush gave his allies a stark choice. "Every nation, in every region, now has a decision to make. Either you are with us, or you are with the terrorists."

On November 27 in the Oval Office, Bush reiterated that choice to Salih. A good first step, Bush said, would be the arrest of Harithi and Ahdal. The list of names was a way for Yemen to demonstrate it supported the US, not al-Qaeda. Yemen had to take the fight to al-Qaeda. If it couldn't arrest or kill the men on the CIA's list of names, Bush continued, he would be more than happy to send in US Special Forces.

Salih blanched at the implied threat. Asking for time and a little more patience, the Yemeni president promised that he would take care of it. "The tribes in these areas are very difficult," he offered. "But I will do it."

"Good," Bush replied. "This fight is going to define the relationship between our two countries and between us personally."

The tension in the room eased as the conversation moved on to other issues. In return for Yemen's help, the Americans were talking about a package of aid and loans worth around $400 million. For Salih, who had grown accustomed to doing without US aid, the increase was astronomical. Pleased with the staggering jump in funding, Salih ventured to offer the US a little more, telling President Bush that he could help mediate his dispute with Saddam Hussein. Warming to the topic, one of his favorites, Salih continued, "There is an Arab proverb that says, if you put a cat into a cage it can turn into a lion."

Slowly and tersely, Bush replied, "This cat has rabies. The only way to cure the cat is to cut off its head."

7

A New War

Winter 2001

In the luxury Hotel de Crillon just off the Champs Elysées in the heart of Paris, Salih and his security team put together a plan. After his meeting with Bush the day before in DC, Salih knew he needed to move quickly, but he wanted to give tribal diplomacy one more chance. Any military confrontation in Yemen's tribal territories could spin out of control. The CIA and Ghalib al-Qamish agreed that the top target, Abu Ali al-Harithi, was holed up in his compound in Shabwa, while his deputy, Muhammad al-Ahdal, was most likely in the restive central region of Marib. Yemeni intelligence reports from Marib narrowed this down further, suggesting that a local tribesman, Ghalib al-Zayadi, had promised Ahdal protection.

Shortly after he arrived back in Sanaa, the president summoned the tribesman to town for a meeting. Wary of the president's intentions, Zayadi brought along a handful of relatives and fellow clansmen for protection. Salih wasted little time in getting to the point of the meeting. "You have been charged with providing shelter to Ahdal," he told Zayadi.

"Yes," Zayadi responded carefully, "I met with him as an intermediary because he is a Muslim and I didn't know who he was affiliated with." Dressed in a dark blue blazer over a dazzling white robe, Zayadi was taller than most Yemenis. Round, wire-rimmed glasses set off by a carefully trimmed beard gave him an intellectual air, an impression backed up by dual degrees in Quranic studies and missionary work.

"I want you to do something for me," Salih said finally. "I need you to convince Abu Assam to turn himself in," he said, using Ahdal's jihadi nickname.

Zayadi slowly nodded his agreement as the president laid out his plan. Salih had a letter that he wanted Zayadi to deliver to the al-Qaeda deputy. Inside were all the conditions for his surrender and guarantees for his protection. This is very important, Salih stressed, as he handed the letter to Zayadi.

After the tribesmen left the palace, Salih met Edmund Hull, the US ambassador, in a gazebo across town at the Ministry of Defense. Relaxed and smiling, Salih reported that he was making progress on the CIA's list and that negotiations were underway for Ahdal's surrender. If they weren't successful in two days, Salih continued, he would order an attack. Two days later, when Salih's deadline passed without any action, Hull wasn't surprised. As a young diplomat in Cairo, he had memorized a dictum that he repeated to himself at times like these: "Any action will take twice as long as you expect, but you will also find that you have twice the time you thought you had to accomplish it."

Over the next few days, Salih kept up the pressure, but everyone had an excuse. Zayadi claimed Ahdal had simply vanished. "After our meeting, I never saw him again," he told Salih. The president suspected he was lying or at least covering for the fugitive. He wasn't. Ahdal had disappeared, but Harithi and and an Egyptian aide had moved into Marib. On December 17, more than a week after his meeting with Zayadi, Salih gave up on diplomacy and ordered an attack.

EARLY THE NEXT morning, military units descended on targets across Marib, Shabwa, and al-Jawf. Tanks and armored personnel carriers backed by fighter jets and helicopters moved into the tribal arc of sand and mountains, stretching from the Saudi border south to the Gulf of Aden. Beyond sporadic checkpoints manned by a few soldiers along major roads, everything in this region was left to the tribes, and the army usually informed local leaders before any major movement of troops. This time Salih didn't tell anyone. The surprise incursion sent ripples of alarm through the region. Locals passed along reports of troop progress faster than the soldiers could navigate the rough terrain.

In Marib, however, the soldiers caught a break. East of Sanaa, the mountains of northern Yemen flatten into a wide-open desert of rolling dunes and gravelly plains that dip south into Shabwa before turning north and yielding to the Empty Quarter, a massive desert the size of Texas in the heart of the Arabian peninsula. On the sandy fringes of the Empty Quarter sits the village of al-Husn. Built on the site of an ancient market and tribal meeting place, the village has been led for generations by the Al Jalal family. It was also, according to Salih's sources on the ground, where a pair of al-Qaeda figures were hiding. Later it emerged that the two men were Harithi and an Egyptian aide.

Unhampered by the uneven mountains and narrow trails that slowed their colleagues further south, the soldiers in Marib reached al-Husn without tipping anyone off. The tanks and personnel carriers rattled to a stop in the hard sand just outside the cluster of mud huts as the soldiers spread out around the village in a loose circle. Overhead, a respectful distance away, a helicopter hovered, waiting for a signal. The plan was for an overwhelming show of military force that would intimidate the villagers. But the villagers were members of the Abidah tribe, a fiercely independent collection of clans and sub-tribes that had sent several fighters to Afghanistan in the 1980s. Led by Hamad bin Ali Jalal, a dashing young shaykh who was still settling into his leadership role after the death of his father three years earlier, a cluster of men moved out to meet the military.

The officers explained that they had no problem with any of the villagers; they only wanted the al-Qaeda suspects. A tribesman from Shabwa, Harithi was skilled at taking advantage of *'urf*, the tribal and customary code of law that held sway across much of Yemen, stressing his shared heritage in appealing for refuge. Once the pledge was given, the tribe was honor-bound to protect him. Jalal, the shaykh in charge of al-Husn, was caught between centuries of tribal precedent and the government's demands. He wanted to help the military, he explained to the soldiers, but they knew the rules. Yards behind the young shaykh, facing out from their mud-brick homes, which were built like small citadels with gun slits to withstand a siege, several tribesmen stood with Kalashnikovs and an assortment of older, well-worn rifles in defense of their shaykh and guests. Most of the tribesmen knew Harithi and his aide personally. The two men had been living with them for weeks and in that time they had shown themselves to be pious men, individuals who followed the local laws and conducted themselves with honor.

As the standoff between the cluster of gesticulating tribal elders and officers dragged on, the soldiers began to fidget and squirm in their winter uniforms. The heavy wool was uncomfortable in the sun. Suddenly, a massive boom shattered the morning stillness. The tribesmen opened fire on the soldiers spread out around the village. Overhead, the Yemeni fighter jet that had just shattered the sound barrier faded from sight. Convinced they were under attack, the villagers scrambled back inside the thick-walled mud structures, pulling out missile launchers and rocket-propelled grenades from private arsenals. The barrage was unrelenting, and the tribesmen managed to destroy several military vehicles before the rest scurried out of range. Falling back from the firefight, some of the soldiers tried to return fire, but there were no targets. The tribesmen were under cover behind the mud-brick walls. One group of soldiers, caught in the open and surrounded by tribesmen, quickly threw down their weapons and surrendered. Within minutes the battle was over. Scattered around the burning personnel carriers lay the bodies of nineteen dead soldiers. Nearly two dozen others were bleeding from shrapnel wounds, and thirty-five more had been captured.

The remainder of the military unit regrouped and assembled a mediation team to negotiate for the release of the captives. In the confusion of the fight, Harithi and the Egyptian had snuck out of the village and disappeared.

AROUND THE SAME time that winter, nearly 2,000 miles away in the mountains of eastern Afghanistan, hundreds of other al-Qaeda fighters were making their own escape. Al-Qaeda had been under attack for weeks, pushed east by an unrelenting bombing campaign that had destroyed their homes and shattered their caves. Near the Pakistani border, the men fell back into a six-square-mile patch of mountains and peaks known as Tora Bora. Here, 14,000 feet above sea level in a series of dank and musty caves and shallow trenches, al-Qaeda dug in. This, bin Laden told his men in early December, would be their last stand.

Weeks earlier, on October 7, the US had launched a well-coordinated air assault on al-Qaeda and Taliban positions across Afghanistan. The meager infrastructure that the Taliban, a black-turbaned Islamic militia that controlled much of Afghanistan, had managed to cobble together in their few years of rule was crushed almost overnight. The rudimentary air defense system was knocked out of commission within hours and Taliban training camps were pounded into kindling. Still the Taliban's lines held as eager new recruits arrived from Pakistan. A week after the bombing campaign began, US Special Forces linked up with the Northern Alliance near the city of Mazar-i-Sharif, on the border with Uzbekistan near where the last Soviet troops had exited more than a decade earlier. This ragtag group of Tajik tribesmen and other ethnic minorities had been on the verge of defeat only a month earlier, when al-Qaeda operatives assassinated their leader, Ahmad Shah Massoud, two days before 9/11. The same guerrilla leader Abdullah Azzam had befriended shortly before his own death more than a decade earlier, Massoud had spent the intervening years waging a lonely war against the Taliban takeover of his country. With him gone, US fortunes in Afghanistan depended on the loose union of anti-Taliban forces he had left behind.

Throughout October, US Special Forces operatives on the ground used lasers to paint Taliban positions for pinpoint missile strikes from bombers flying high above Afghanistan's needle-nosed peaks. By early November, constant shelling had softened the Taliban enough to allow for a frontal assault. Hundreds of Northern Alliance fighters rushed across the narrow Pul-i-Imam Bukhri bridge and into Mazar-i-Sharif. Nearly 200 miles southeast of the battle, in Kabul, bin Laden had breakfast with Hamid Mir, a Pakistani journalist he had known for years. Muslims, bin Laden told the shorter man, had the right to attack America. Then the al-Qaeda leader was on the move again, traveling east along the highway toward Jalalabad. Behind him, Kabul fell to Northern Alliance forces.

Several al-Qaeda members fought a rearguard action on the heels of their commander's eastern retreat, falling back from village to village until they reached Jalalabad, only 45 miles from the Pakistani border. Few of them had been with bin Laden during his siege of the city twelve years earlier. Bin Laden's new fighters were better trained and equipped than the ones he had led a decade earlier, but they were still no match for a sustained aerial assault. Bin Laden met the men as they poured into Jalalabad, wild-eyed and disheveled after weeks of bombings. Their clothes were ripped and stained and their beards were speckled with flakes of dried mud.

Bin Laden tried to keep their spirits up with speeches and prayers, but he knew the city wouldn't hold.

Bin Laden had been planning for this day for years, telling his sons and visitors that he only felt truly secure in the mountains. In 1987, at the height of the jihad against the Soviets, he had built a road that snaked north out of Pakistan up through the passes at Tora Bora before descending to Jalalabad. The natural caves just north of the border had caught his eye at the time, and he had spent months expanding them into a series of interlocking armories for weapons storage. When he returned to Afghanistan in 1996, he had deepened the caves and expanded the armories. Now, on the run from US bombers, bin Laden directed his men to regroup at Tora Bora.

On a good day, the 30-mile trip from Jalalabad along the narrow, winding road took three hours, but in the cold and short of food, the men didn't come close to top speed as they made their way south. Scattered across Tora Bora's rocky slopes was all that remained of bin Laden's organization in Afghanistan. One of the men, Jabir al-Fayfi, a twenty-six-year-old Saudi with a receding hairline, had only been in Afghanistan for nine months. After wasting most of his youth on drugs and laziness, Fayfi had hoped Afghanistan would serve as penance for his sins. The reality was nothing like he had expected. He hadn't cut his hair or shaved his beard since he arrived, and both were long and knotted with dirt and grime. He was always hungry and cold—hardships he had never considered when he sold his car to finance his jihad—and now it looked as if he would die in the mountains of Tora Bora.

Local al-Qaeda commanders grouped the men according to nationality so they could more easily understand the various dialects of Arabic once the shooting started. Besides the Yemenis and Saudis, there were units of Egyptians, Moroccans, and Algerians. Everyone had a role. Even green recruits like Salman al-Rabi'i, Fawaz's teenage brother, had been pressed into service, and somewhere down the mountain bin Laden's undersized personal secretary, Nasir al-Wihayshi, huddled in a dirt bunker with a handful of other Yemenis. Moving among the men, bin Laden and Zawahiri directed the last-minute preparations.

THE ATTACK NEVER came—at least, not the way bin Laden expected. The Arabs and their Afghan allies chipped away at the frozen earth for the first two weeks of Ramadan as they prepared for an American ground assault. Instead, the US ringed the area with nearly 2,000 Afghan mercenaries and fired more than 1,100 missiles into the mountains. None of it worked.

The Afghan mercenaries were under the command of two competing warlords, Hazarat Ali and Haji Zaman Ghamsharik. Ali had a fourth-grade education and a sketchy reputation, while Ghamsharik was a known drug smuggler who had been living in exile in France until the CIA convinced him to return to Afghanistan in exchange for a suitcase full of cash. The two men hated each other and refused to coordinate their plan. To US operatives on the ground, the idea of outsourcing the war to these two and their poorly trained followers was a catastrophic blunder. Both Gary Berntsen, the CIA commander in Kabul, and Dalton Fury,* the head of the Delta Force team at Tora Bora, repeatedly requested additional US troops. With fewer than 100 US Special Forces in the area, they worried the US was walking into a disaster of its own making. "We need US soldiers on the ground," Berntsen pleaded into his satellite phone during conversations with war planners in the US. "The opportunity to get bin Laden and his men is slipping away."

On the other end of the line, General Tommy Franks, the commander of the Afghanistan operation, overruled his frantic operatives on the ground. He wanted to maintain what the Pentagon called a "light footprint." The US wasn't going to repeat the mis-

*Dalton Fury is a pseudonym adopted by the commander at Tora Bora.

takes of the Soviet Union and find itself stuck in Afghanistan for a decade.

Early on December 3, the bombing of Tora Bora began in earnest. US warplanes, guided by Fury's men on the ground, pounded al-Qaeda targets strung out across the frozen slopes. Over the next four days, in a series of near-continuous bombing runs, the US dropped 700,000 pounds of munitions into the six-square-mile combat zone. The Arab fighters had never seen anything like it. The caves offered little cover from the heavy bombs raining down on them. Smoke and dust settled over everything, giving the men an ashen look. They couldn't fire back at the planes thousands of feet above them, and with few targets on the ground the trapped al-Qaeda fighters had no choice but to endure the onslaught. During the day, the Afghan mercenaries under Hazarat Ali and Ghamsharik drove them higher into the mountains, further limiting their options. The only reprieve came in the evening. Every night, as soon as the sun set, the Afghan mercenaries headed back down the mountains to break their Ramadan fast. Their own food long since gone, al-Qaeda members like Fayfi watched jealously, gnawing on whatever they could find.

Six days into the battle, on December 9, the US deployed an immense 15,000-pound bomb the size of a Volkswagen Beetle. Known in the military as a Daisy Cutter, the bomb had originally been designed to clear "instant" helicopter landing zones in the dense jungles of Vietnam. For most of the past decade it had been mothballed, but the Pentagon thought it might be commandeered as a "cave-buster." Too big to be strapped to a jet, airmen rolled it out the back of a C-130 cargo plane.

The explosion shook the mountains for miles and kicked up a huge cloud of smoke and dust that made it impossible for pilots to assess the damage it inflicted. On the ground, however, there was no doubt. Several men inside one cave had been incinerated in the blast and stories of the massive bomb flew through the lines, causing a panic as al-Qaeda's local allies started to desert their one-time friends and local villagers turned on the Arabs in an effort to drive them out of the mountains.

Through it all bin Laden stayed on the move, changing his position every few hours, but late in the afternoon of December 10 the Delta team thought they had a real-time read on him a little over a mile away. Fury sat on the information for a few minutes, silently wrestling with the decision. Hazarat Ali had already retreated for the evening and Fury was under direct orders not to take the lead in the fighting. The American commander hesitated as he assessed the situation: three of his men were tied down in a firefight and night was falling. Finally, remembering his instructions, Fury gave the order to retreat. It would be ten years before the US got another shot at bin Laden.

Two days later, as the bombs continued to rain down on al-Qaeda positions, Ghamsharik, the drug smuggler now allied with the US, provided al-Qaeda with an out. US forces had earlier overheard a radio transmission of bin Laden giving his men permission to surrender. I'm sorry for getting us trapped, bin Laden had lamented through the static.

Ghamsharik now told Fury that a large group of al-Qaeda fighters wanted to surrender that afternoon around 4 p.m. Fury was doubtful, but with so few men on the ground he had little choice but to defer to the Afghan mercenaries. Reluctantly he agreed to a short ceasefire. Al-Qaeda never showed. Instead, they radioed back to Ghamsharik, explaining that they needed more time to gather everyone and make their way down the mountain. They suggested 8 a.m. the next morning, December 13, for the new surrender meeting. Already frustrated by the ceasefire, Fury lost his temper when he heard about the extension. Al-Qaeda wasn't going to surrender; they were just playing for time. Convinced he had just been duped, Fury requested new US air strikes. But on the ground he couldn't do much without the support of the Afghan fighters, who were observing the ceasefire their leader had agreed to. That night, 800 al-Qaeda fighters slipped out of the mountains and into Pakistan.

Bin Laden and hundreds of others stayed behind. The al-Qaeda commander tried to rally his remaining fighters, telling them to "arm their women and children," but inside he must have feared this was the end. For days, as the fighting raged around him, he had been drafting a last will and testament. On December 14, the final day of Ramadan, he finished. He implored his wives not to remarry, and begged his children for forgiveness. "I advise you not to work with al-Qaeda," he concluded.

Later that day, depressed and possibly wounded, bin Laden and a few guards struggled down the mountains and out of Tora Bora. From their hideouts in the quartz and feldspar caves, the rest of his men did the same. By the time Fury's team cautiously made their way up the mountains on December 17, the caves were empty and al-Qaeda was gone.

AFTER TORA BORA, bin Laden, one son, and a few guards moved southeast toward Pakistan's tribal territories just over the border before doubling back into Afghanistan, while Zawahiri, one of bin Laden's other sons, and a few others took a different route out of the mountains. The rest of the men escaped as best they could. Wihayshi's small group of fighters took off southwest, hugging the Pakistani border and scrambling through the mountains until they reached the desert plain beyond Kandahar days later. Eventually they turned east toward Iran. Fayfi and a column of 300 Saudis and Yemenis who had stayed behind to cover bin Laden's retreat made their way out of Tora Bora on the first day of the traditional three-day feast that marks the end of Ramadan. Weak with hunger and poorly prepared for winter at high elevation, the men stumbled along, strung out in a single line among the pine trees. The temperature continued to drop as they trudged eastward, squinting through snow flurries. One of the leaders of the group thought he had a deal with the Pakistani army to let them over the border unharmed. When they reached the crossing on December 19, the guards said they could enter the country, but they would have to give up their weapons. Exhausted and starving, the men reluctantly agreed. The army moved them to a large mosque in a nearby village. You will be safe here, the Pakistanis assured the fleeing Arabs.

For weeks, as the bombs had fallen inside Afghanistan, the US had been putting pressure on Pakistan to seize Arabs coming across the border. The Pakistani Army and several freelance bounty hunters, attracted by promises of reward, descended on the border region to round up Arabs and other "foreigners," whom they later sold to the US.

Shortly after the Pakistani soldiers dumped Fayfi's group of Arabs at the mosque, they moved them again, this time unloading them inside a large walled compound.

"Where are we?" Fayfi asked one of the soldiers. "What is this place?"

"It's a prison," the man grinned back.

Eventually some Americans took custody of the prisoners and shipped them back across the border into Afghanistan. Two weeks later, Fayfi and the rest of the men landed at the military airstrip at Guantánamo Bay, Cuba. Blindfolded and shackled, the men had no idea where they were. "It was three months before I even realized I was in Cuba," Fayfi remembered.

Along with Fayfi's group, Pakistan had turned over dozens of other heavily bearded Saudis to the US, including a man named Said al-Shihri. Within months, the US had hundreds of men in custody at Guantánamo Bay.

IN MARCH 2002, four months after Yemen's failed operation in Marib, Salih summoned Ghalib al-Zayadi, the tribesman he had asked for help with al-Qaeda, for a second meeting. This time, Zayadi traveled to Sanaa alone. "I need your help again," Salih told him. "I want you to work with us to capture or kill Ahdal."

In exchange, Salih continued, "I will give you an official position, five million riyals, and a car." An official position meant a monthly salary without the hassle of having to show up for work—what Yemen's donors called ghost employees—and the five million riyals translated into just over $25,000, on top of the salary. What would be requird of Zayadi, Salih continued, might be as little as feeding the government information about Ahdal's whereabouts until he could be captured.

Zayadi sat silently processing the offer while Salih waited for his response. "But I don't know anything," the tribesman finally muttered weakly.

Salih frowned and exclaimed, "How often I have been disappointed with you." Then he added, "I am not happy if that is indeed your position." Zayadi replied that it was.

Before Zayadi could walk out the front gate, guards corralled him and threw him in the back of car for the short trip to Central Security headquarters. Led by the president's nephew Yahya, who in the tangled thicket of palace politics was also his son-in-law, the Central Security Forces were an armed wing of the Ministry of the Interior. Yahya's agents worked on Zayadi, alternating between threats and promises of cash if he would only cooperate. The tribesman was incensed. "I came to Sanaa for discussions," he said, alluding to the tribal code of honor and respect. "I never expected to be treated this way." After two days, Yahya turned him over to Ghalib al-Qamish and the PSO.

Instead of a Central Security interrogation room, Zayadi soon found himself deep underground, in the bowels of one of Yemen's secret prisons. Officers locked him in heavy leg irons and helped him waddle down a dank, musty corridor. Ignoring his protestations of innocence, the guards shoved him into a tiny, dark cell barely big enough for a single man.

In the cell next to him were five Cameroonians, three Muslims and two Christians, who had all been in the dungeon for eleven years. None of them had been charged with a crime or even seen the inside of a courtroom. The guards laughed at Zayadi's pleas for more food and shrugged off his requests to see a doctor. You have to understand, one of his captors finally told him, this is Political Security. "We don't have laws or human rights here. Think of yourself as sheep, and we're the shepherds." Zayadi sank back, convinced that he was never getting out.

8

Attrition

2002

In the years before 9/11, ensconced in exile thousands of miles from the Arab world and surrounded by followers who rarely questioned his vision for the future, Osama bin Laden convinced himself that the US and its Arab allies were as weak as the Soviets had been in the 1980s. The small cells he sent back to Saudi Arabia and Yemen in the summer of 2001 were supposed to shape and direct the revolutions he believed would follow the strikes on New York and Washington. But instead of rallying around al-Qaeda's black banner, Muslims around the world were horrified by the violence bin Laden unleashed in the name of Islam. His failure to convey his simple, seemingly self-evident message to Muslims back in the Middle East weighed heavily on him. Writing his will during the assault on Tora Bora, he reflected bitterly on the lack of popular support. In his moment of greatest need, even the Taliban had deserted him.

In Yemen, Fawaz al-Rabi'i, the cell commander bin Laden had sent back to Yemen in August 2001, finally understood the shaykh's parting instructions. Rabi'i met up with Abu Ali al-Harithi, al-Qaeda's commander in Yemen, and offered the older man his allegiance. Only twenty-two years old, Rabi'i had let his hair grow in

Afghanistan and its shiny black waves now reached past his shoulders, in marked contrast to Harithi's short hair and trimmed beard. But the two men, separated by twenty-four years, found they had much in common. Over meals in the desert, they shared stories of Afghanistan and discussed potential operations. Harithi wanted to bring in Abd al-Rahim Nashiri, the al-Qaeda operative who had orchestrated the attack on the USS *Cole* two years earlier. After that attack, insurance rates at Aden's port had skyrocketed and ships stayed away. But 400 miles east along the Gulf of Aden, near the city of al-Mukalla, one of Yemen's main oil terminals was vulnerable. Nashiri was familiar with the city from his work casing the *Cole*, and in February 2002 he sent Harithi $40,000 for the operation.

In a replay of preparations for the *Cole* attack, Harithi's men bought a small boat in the Red Sea port city of Hudaydah and then transported it hundreds of miles across the country to Yemen's southern coast. In al-Mukalla the al-Qaeda team rented a house with a view of the harbor, just as they had in Aden two years earlier.

At the same time, in the deserts northwest of al-Mukalla, the US put its own post-September 11 strategy into action. Days after the al-Qaeda team bought the boat, Ambassador Edmund Hull traveled to Marib. One of his first trips outside the fortified compound in Sanaa, Hull wanted to see for himself what the US would confront in Yemen's tribal territory. This was the same region where Harithi and Ahdal had found refuge in the days after September 11, and, in meetings with government officials and local shaykhs along his route east, the first-time ambassador tried to get a feel for the personalities involved. Hull was particularly impressed with Shaykh Rubaysh, a balding tribal elder with a bushy white beard who led a small village just off the main highway in Marib. In a late meeting on the way back to Sanaa, the gap-toothed shaykh took the ambassador by the hand and led him around the village with dozens of tribesmen in tow.

Pulling him forward, he showed the US ambassador a dilapidated one-room mud hut with a couple of boarded-up windows. Letters scrawled above the door read "hospital." This is what we need, the shaykh pleaded. Sensing an opportunity to make a new friend in a region where the US had few, Hull did some quick calculations. A new hospital and living accommodations for a permanent staff could easily be paid for with a surplus of funds the embassy had managed to save under Bodine.

"I promise," Hull told the shaykh and the trailing crowd of tribesmen, "that the US will build you a new hospital."

Back in Sanaa, Hull explained his reasoning to his staff. "You need to strengthen the government presence in these remote areas," he said. He wanted to use development and aid to counter al-Qaeda's appeal. The terrorist organization offered its members nothing but hardship and death, and Hull was convinced that if the US could put forward a more positive narrative it could slowly weaken al-Qaeda's support in the tribal territories. A $250,000 hospital, he told Washington, was a cheap price to pay for loyalty.

RABI'I LIKED NASHIRI'S plan for a *Cole*-like attack, but planning took time and Yemeni security forces had just arrested his father in an attempt to force Rabi'i to surrender. With Harithi's blessing, Rabi'i recruited his older brother, Abu Bakr, and another friend, Hizam Mujali, for a separate bombing campaign. In early March 2002, working out of a safe house on the outskirts of Sanaa, the three men constructed a handful of crude bombs. Shortly before dawn on March 16, they attacked the civil aviation building in downtown Sanaa. Two days later, they planted another timed explosive outside the house of Muhammad al-Surmi, the burly PSO officer who had turned al-Qaeda's traitor over to Abd al-Salam al-Hilah four years earlier. They also struck the homes of two other PSO officers in Sanaa, hiding the explosives in dusty piles of garbage. On April 4, they hit the PSO headquarters in

Sanaa, scorching the stone wall surrounding the building but doing little real damage. None of the bombs were intended to kill. They were a warning: al-Qaeda knew where Yemeni officials lived and worked.

One week after the attack on PSO headquarters, the three drove around Sanaa in the predawn light, dropping hundreds of leaflets out of their car. Their message was simple and direct: they wanted the release of 173 prisoners, including Fawaz and Abu Bakr's father. If the men weren't freed, the statement warned, the next bomb would claim lives, first PSO officers and then politicians. The government had thirty days. They signed the leaflets "Sympathizers of al-Qaeda."

THE MAY 10 deadline passed, but the threatened attacks never materialized. Al-Qaeda didn't have the infrastructure or the numbers to make good on the threats. The camps Harithi built in the early 1990s had all been destroyed or abandoned in the years after the 1994 civil war. In Marib, Ahdal was still on the run, and the rest of al-Qaeda's organization in Yemen consisted of the few cells bin Laden had dispatched prior to the September 11 attacks. Harithi had been as surprised as everyone else by the attacks, and when bin Laden's predicted uprisings failed to take hold he had to readjust and reorganize on the run. Following the assault on al-Husn in December 2001, he had begun to take extra security precautions. Harithi avoided speaking on the phone, preferring to meet his men in person, which made planning difficult. President Salih had also asked Harithi's tribe to hand him over to the state. The tribe refused, but the al-Qaeda commander heard rumors that the government had put a bounty on his head.

From the outside, things looked different. The bombings in March and April gave a distorted impression of al-Qaeda's true strength, exaggerating it far beyond reality. Sanaa went on high alert and visiting American officials treated the country like a war zone, landing in tight, corkscrew spirals for brief meetings at the airport before taking off again under tight security. When Vice President Dick Cheney came to town he used a dummy plane, distracting any would-be attackers with evasive maneuvers on a C-17 outfitted with anti-missile technology, instead of *Air Force Two*.

Tensions rose throughout the summer as the government continued to arrest men it worried might harbor sympathy for al-Qaeda or bin Laden. Like the roundup after the *Cole* attack, some were guilty but many were not. Hundreds of men were thrown into secret prisons scattered across the country. There were several small bombings and gun attacks, but it was nearly impossible to distinguish between al-Qaeda attacks and expressions of tribal frustration with the government's aggressive counterterrorism operations. In July, gunfire clipped the helicopter of Ali Muhammad Salih, a relative of the president and the military's deputy chief of staff, who was on an aerial tour of outposts near the Saudi border. Most media outlets reported the incident as an al-Qaeda attack, but it was impossible to know for sure.

Security officials at the US embassy were also on high alert. In Afghanistan, Ali Soufan, the FBI agent who had first linked 9/11 to bin Laden, had uncovered the outlines of Nashiri's maritime plot in Yemen during an interrogation of an al-Qaeda suspect whom the US had in custody. Soufan dutifully wrote up his report on the prisoner, whom the CIA had designated for rendition in the hopes that foreign agents, unconstrained by US law, could get more information out of him. Soufan, who believed the man was cooperating, asked the CIA for more time, but the agent in charge refused, claiming that the prisoner was deliberately misleading the FBI. The old turf wars that had done so much to derail US attempts to counter al-Qaeda in the years before 9/11 were still being waged. "There is nothing you or the FBI can do," the CIA official stormed. "You can't stop this rendition." Convinced he was right and that something was about to happen, Soufan distributed his memo warning of an impending attack on an oil tanker in Yemen to several government agencies.

IN SANAA, HARITHI and Rabi'i had come up with another plan while they waited for Nashiri's permission for the al-Mukalla team. Outside the US embassy, downhill from the Sheraton, a few al-Qaeda operatives mixed with the foot traffic and eyed their next target. For several days they took turns casing the embassy, noting patterns and studying its defenses. None of the men had been involved in the embassy bombings in Kenya and Tanzania in 1998, but they all knew how al-Qaeda had used truck bombs to kill more than 200 people in the coordinated strikes. That approach didn't seem possible here. Low, set back from the road, and built on an incline, the embassy was a hard target. A direct assault was out. Instead, the men recommended a rocket attack.

Once again, al-Qaeda fell back on old patterns. As they had with the *Cole*, the men bought the explosives at the wild Suq al-Talh arms market near the Saudi border. Harithi handled the shopping himself, selecting two rockets, more than 700 pounds of the plastic explosive Semtex, and several rocket-propelled grenades. The men packed the explosives carefully in plastic cartons, scattering a few bags of pomegranates across the top. It wasn't much camouflage, but it was enough to get through the checkpoints around Sanaa. The team settled on Monday, August 13, the first day of the Western work week, for the assault. Even though the US embassy held to a Yemeni schedule, operating Saturday through Wednesday, the men figured more Americans would be present on a Monday.

In preparation for the strike, the team holed up in a building on the outskirts of Sanaa. On Thursday evening, four days before the attack, Rabi'i and his older brother, Abu Bakr, slipped off to a small side room to get some rest while the other two men fiddled with the rockets. Shortly after they drifted off, a massive blast shook them awake. Rushing next door in their pajamas, the Rabi'i brothers stared at the scene in front of them. Static electricity had caused one of the rockets to misfire just as Walid al-Shibh walked in front of it. The shell had hit him square in the chest. Rabi'i didn't even need to check; the man was dead. Shibh's blood was all over the floor and most of his chest cavity was gone. In the corner, the second man, Samir al-Hada, was howling in pain and clutching the bloody stump where his hand had once been. Blinking through the acrid smoke, Rabi'i made a quick decision. They had to get out of the building, and the wounded man needed a doctor. The floor was already streaked with bloody footprints; the attack was off.

DAYS LATER, ACROSS the Persian Gulf in southern Pakistan, the US caught another break. After Tora Bora, hundreds of al-Qaeda fighters had slipped into Pakistan. Many of them had been arrested and shipped to Guantánamo, but several top commanders had escaped the dragnet. US operatives had been tracking these men for months as they moved between safe houses, and on September 11, 2002, they caught one.

Early that morning, Pakistani police surrounded a multistory apartment building in the impoverished port city of Karachi. They were after Ramzi bin al-Shibh, a Yemeni member of al-Qaeda and one of facilitators of the September 11 attacks. At 8:30 a.m., Pakistani officers moved into the building. They tried to keep the noise down, but they had to detain two men as they went up the stairs, and the scuffle tipped off the militants a few flights up. Peering out of their windows, the al-Qaeda operatives saw the police cordon in the streets below. The men decided to fight their way out and for the next four hours they lobbed grenades and fired off thousands of rounds, all the while screaming "Allahu Akbar." Police and military sharpshooters surrounded the building, tearing up the outside walls with heavy-caliber bullets and picking off two of the men. Finally, shortly after noon, exhausted and running out of ammunition, the remaining eight al-Qaeda members surrendered. Police bound and blindfolded the men before marching them down the stairs. As he was led out of the building, Shibh screamed out, "Allahu Akbar" one final time. Three days later, Pakistan handed him over to the US.

THE SAME WEEK the US received Shibh from Pakistan, US officials authorized an operation to partner with Egyptian intelligence agents and abduct a suspected al-Qaeda operative in Cairo.

In the months since the attacks, intelligence analysts had gone back over years of reports searching for anything they had missed the first time. It was depressing, time-consuming work. Among the things they uncovered were the Italian tapes that recorded Abd al-Salam al-Hilah, the Yemeni PSO officer, talking about "airplanes" and an upcoming attack. Along with that recording there was the one of Hilah's brother discussing a failed attempt to enter the US. In November 2001, the *Wall Street Journal* handed the CIA a secondhand computer one of its reporters had purchased at a market in Kabul. Stored on the computer's hard drive were nearly a thousand text documents, including one that detailed Hilah's role in double-crossing the traitor in Zawahiri's organization in early 1998. The retrospective evidence seemed damning. If Hilah wasn't an al-Qaeda member, he was certainly a sympathizer with potentially actionable intelligence. Given Hilah's position as an agent in Yemen's top intelligence agency, kidnapping him in Cairo might be the CIA's only chance.

In addition to his job with the Political Security Organization, Hilah also served as the Yemeni representative of the Arab Contractors Company, Egypt's largest construction company. In the fall of 2002, the head office in Cairo told him it needed to go over the accounts and get answers to some questions about his recent commissions. Hilah didn't think much of the summons. He traveled to Egypt often and even kept an Egyptian cell phone. Still, just to make sure, he checked with a contact at the Egyptian embassy in Sanaa. The officer told him not to worry. His name wasn't on any watch list.

After meeting his Egyptian contact, Hilah booked a flight for September 19. The trip shouldn't take long, he told his brother. Hilah reserved a room at the Intercontinental Semiramis, a massive five-star luxury hotel on the banks of the Nile in downtown Cairo. For the first few days, everything went as planned. He went to his meetings and kept in regular contact with his family back in Sanaa, calling them several times a day to confer with his brother. Then, on September 24, he didn't call. His family tried both his Egyptian and Yemeni cell phones, but there was no answer.

The next day, Hilah finally returned their calls, getting his younger brother, Abd al-Wahhab. "I've been invited to a meeting with some people," he told him hesitantly. Abd al-Wahhab pressed him but Hilah wouldn't elaborate. Abd al-Wahhab had never heard his brother so evasive and nervous. Hilah was a colonel in the PSO and a seasoned intelligence officer, but he was clearly spooked. "The atmosphere is cloudy and dark over here," he told his brother opaquely before hanging up.

Hours after that call, a small team of highly trained Egyptian agents pushed Hilah into the back of a waiting car. Driving him to a secret prison across town, the men held the Yemeni intelligence official for three days. The Egyptian agents left Hilah's phones on so they could track who tried to call him. Nearly all of the missed calls were from his family back in Sanaa. On September 28, the Egyptians turned Hilah over to their counterparts in the CIA, who put him on board a private plane at Cairo's International Airport for the two-and-a-half-hour flight to Baku, Azerbaijan. Shortly before takeoff, someone switched Hilah's two cell phones off.

WHILE THE CIA was working with the Egyptians on Hilah's abduction in Cairo, it got some more good news from its station in Sanaa. The building where al-Qaeda had planned the aborted embassy attack had finally yielded some clues. After the premature rocket explosion, officers from the Central Security Forces, under the command of the president's nephew Yahya, had taken over the investigation. Now they thought they had uncovered another al-Qaeda safe house in a northern suburb.

Moving quickly, a unit of troops surrounded the house. Late that night, an officer pounded on the front door while everyone else prepared to rush the house. "Abu Sayf," he shouted in an attempt to draw the suspect out, "open the door." For seconds there was no reply, then a burst of machine-gun fire erupted out of the house, wounding one of the soldiers in the leg. The rest of the men fell back, dragging the injured soldier with them. Unwilling to rush the well-fortified house, one of the officers ordered his men to switch to tear gas. Minutes later, as the house began to fill with the burning fumes, the back door opened and a suspect tumbled out. Several soldiers opened fire simultaneously, killing the man within feet of the door. The dead man was Yahya Mujali, the older brother of Hizam Mujali, who had been involved in the March and April bombings.

IN THE COASTAL city of al-Mukalla, the al-Qaeda team followed the news out of Sanaa with growing frustration. In the eight months since Nashiri had sent them the seed money for their operation, they had maintained a low profile and avoided detection. In March, a few weeks after they moved in, President Salih had arrived in town for a meeting with Ambassador Hull only minutes from their safe house. Even after Soufan's memo, the US had focused almost exclusively on attacks at Yemen's other two ports, Aden and Hudaydah, while Salih seemed mostly concerned with his own security.

Most of the men had returned to Yemen as part of Rabi'i's cell more than a year earlier, and they were tired of waiting. The boat was ready and the bomb was built. Nashiri and Harithi listened to their complaints, but both men counseled patience. The team grumbled but followed their orders. Then, in late September, they heard the news about Yahya Mujali and the shootout in Sanaa. They all knew Yahya and his two younger brothers, Hizam and Arif. The men had grown up with Yemen's uncompromising tribal code and they brought the same desire for revenge with them to al-Qaeda. The organization was their tribe now, and Yahya was one of their own. His death demanded a response.

Nashiri and Harithi understood what the men were going through, crammed together in the safe house waiting for orders. Shortly after Yahya's death, in early October, Nashiri gave the "go" order. The attack team had been set for weeks. As with the *Cole*, the boat would be steered by a pair of suicide bombers: Hasan al-Badawi and Nasir al-Kindi. Both men had volunteered for the operation. Kindi, a stocky, slightly cross-eyed figure who had grown up near al-Mukalla, had been dreaming about this day for years. It was the reason he gave up his commission in the army and traveled to Afghanistan, and why he returned to Yemen. Martyrdom would free him from guilt for his years of service in Ali Abdullah Salih's army.

Shortly after 9 a.m. on October 6, the pair shoved off. The weather was cloudless and balmy, a beautiful, still day off Yemen's southern coast. Several hundred yards away their target, a massive rust-and-gray oil tanker, sat nearly motionless in the water. The boat slowly picked up speed as they moved away from shore, and by the time they neared the tanker the only thing a junior officer on board saw was a "fast approaching" small craft.

The boat hit at 9:15 a.m. and the explosion penetrated eight yards through both hulls and into the cargo hold full of crude oil. The blast echoed back across the ocean, sparking a fire in the hold and blowing boat fragments dozens of feet in the air. The MV *Limburg*, a French-flagged tanker carrying nearly 400,000 barrels of oil, was on fire, and one of the crew was missing. In the confusion of the attack, a thirty-eight-year-old Bulgarian fitter, Atanas Atanasov, had panicked and jumped overboard. Struggling to swim in his clothes and shoes, he drowned only feet from the ship. The rest of the tanker's twenty-five-man crew, unaware of his fate, spent the next three hours battling the fire. At noon, Captain Peter Raes gave the order for the crew to abandon ship. Helicopters airlifted them back to shore as rescue teams worked to put out the fire and stop the oil spill.

By a strange coincidence, Ali Soufan was back in Yemen to witness the attack he had predicted months earlier in the report which would soon become known as the "crystal ball memo." Shortly after Badawi and Kindi slammed into the oil tanker, Soufan's phone at the Sanaa Sheraton rang. "Switch on your TV," the Marine colonel on the other end of the line said.

"What's wrong?"

"They did it," the colonel continued. "An oil tanker is on fire off the coast of al-Mukalla."

9

Victory

2002–2003

Shortly after the MV *Limburg* bombing, Edmund Hull asked his staff to coordinate a second trip to Marib. The ambassador, who hadn't faltered in his private assessment, still believed the US was making progress. In Dubai, police had arrested Abd al-Rahim al-Nashiri, the man who had financed the attack, and Yemen had stepped up its cooperation with the US. Unmanned Predator drones flying from an air base in Djibouti were now crisscrossing Yemen looking for targets. In Marib, where the new US-funded clinic had just opened, Shaykh Rubaysh declared his village a terrorist-free zone. Hull told a staff meeting at the embassy in Sanaa that the US was "in the red zone." But those last twenty yards, he cautioned, are often the most difficult. With Abu Ali al-Harithi still at large, Hull wanted another look at the desert province he believed was the key to victory. The embassy scheduled the visit for Sunday, November 3.

SOMEHOW, WORD OF Hull's trip leaked. Fawaz al-Rabi'i didn't have all the details, but he knew enough to plan an ambush. Assuming that Hull would travel by helicopter to Marib, Rabi'i organized a six-man team. He stationed one man in a building inside the airport, with instructions to call when the helicopter took off. Everyone else hid in a sandy depression east of the airport, directly below the helicopter's flight path. By 6 a.m. on November 3, just as the sun was starting to peek over the mountains east of Sanaa, the attackers were in place. The plan called for Rabi'i to fire a Russian-made surface-to-air missile at the helicopter, while Hizam and Arif Mujali followed suit with a pair of AK–47s. Both men were still mourning the loss of their older brother Yahya, who had been killed weeks earlier, and this ambush would be their revenge. Rabi'i's own older brother, Abu Bakr, would film the operation. The final member of the group, Muhammad al-Daylami, sat in the driver's seat of one of the vehicles in case they needed to make a quick getaway.

At 6:45 a.m. the call came from the airport lookout. Minutes later, the helicopter whirled into sight, thumping gently over the scrubland. Rabi'i steadied the cylindrical tube that held the missile against his shoulder and pulled the trigger. Instead of an explosion, Rabi'i watched the missile buzz past the helicopter, leaving a thin contrail in its wake. Next to him, the Mujali brothers sprayed the air with bullets. None of the men on the ground could tell if they had hit anything, but the helicopter banked sharply and retreated to the airport. There had barely been anything for Abu Bakr to film, only a single errant missile and a burst of machine-gun fire.

In his hurry to leave the scene, Arif Mujali tossed his gun under the front seat as he scrambled into the second car next to his brother. As the vehicles bounced over the stones and hard-packed sand on their way out of the depression, the AK–47, which Arif had neglected to lock, went off and a bullet hit him in the foot. Screaming in pain, the teenager tumbled out of the car as his brother slowed to a stop. The men soon discovered the gun under the seat and helped Arif hobble back to the car. Lying behind them in the sand as they drove away was a single bloody sandal.

FOR ALL OF al-Qaeda's preparation, Hull hadn't even been on the helicopter. Still, two of the bullets had penetrated the helicopter's cabin, slightly injuring a pair of Hunt Oil employees. Security officers at the US embassy gave Hull a briefing over the telephone as he drove east toward Marib in a convoy of vehicles. Hours later, the security team was back on the phone with a developing situation.

For more than a year, the NSA at Fort Meade, Maryland, had been monitoring a series of phone numbers it had linked to Harithi. Most of the time there was nothing to hear. After the December 2001 raid in Marib and the takedown of an al-Qaeda communications hub in Sanaa, Harithi had avoided talking on the phone. Instead he relied on couriers and face-to-face meetings, moving around the country to talk to his men. When he wasn't on the phone he was invisible to the US tracking team. For months the NSA had heard nothing. Then, on November 3, one of the numbers they were following clicked into use.

The phone, analysts at Fort Meade quickly determined, was somewhere in Marib. A separate US–Yemeni task force in Sanaa confirmed the location, and they relayed the information to a CIA team across the Red Sea at the drone base in Djibouti.

Harithi had called the Marib meeting to check in with his men. Around noon, the small cluster of men lined up for prayers in the middle of the desert, kneeling and rising in unison. Then they squatted around a few shared dishes for lunch. As always, Harithi hardly touched food. Like bin Laden, he ate only the bare minimum, believing his self-discipline brought him closer to God. The small group of al-Qaeda fighters lounged and chatted through the heat of the afternoon until someone gave the call for afternoon prayers.

Harithi had been in a wistful mood all day, mentioning that he wanted to die a martyr. After prayers, he returned to the subject. None of this was unusual for al-Qaeda members, who often tried to inspire one another by talking about their desire to give their life for God in violent jihad. But Harithi wouldn't let it go. Finally, tiring of their leader's morbid conversation, some of the men urged him to be patient and wait for God to choose the time. "The greatest martyrdom is to be killed in the path of God," Harithi responded, using a euphemism for jihad. The men nodded, but they were ready to talk about something else.

Harithi and six other men broke camp shortly after prayers. As they were piling into a pair of vehicles, one of Harithi's phones rang. Instinctively, the forty-six-year-old al-Qaeda commander switched it on and accepted the call.

It took the US less than four hours from the moment Harithi accepted the call to get a Predator drone armed with two Hellfire missiles locked onto the car as it drove through the trackless desert of dunes and sand hours east of Sanaa. The CIA in Langley and CENTCOM in Tampa had already signed off on the strike, and the drone operator could fire as soon as the car was isolated. Jockeying with the controls, the pilot brought the 36-foot-long drone into position and fired. The first missile slammed into the sand beside the car and exploded harmlessly.

Inside the car, Harithi immediately realized his mistake. He threw the phone out the window and screamed at everyone to get out. But there was nowhere to go. They were in the middle of the desert miles from cover. The pilot, who was controlling the drone from thousands of miles away in the US, waited a couple of beats before pushing the button for his second missile. He only had one shot left, and if he missed Harithi might escape before the US could put another drone in the area.

He fired a second time and waited. The screen in front of him flashed briefly as the car exploded into flames. He twisted the controls and circled the wreckage to make sure there were no survivors. There weren't, or at least he didn't see any. It later turned out that one of the men, Rauf Nassib, had survived the strike. But Harithi and five of his companions, including Kamal Darwish, a native of Yemen with US citizenship, were dead. After a few more passes, the remote-controlled drone vacated the area as an inbound Yemeni team arrived by helicopter to secure the scene.

President Salih had allowed the strike on the condition that it remained secret, and to do that Yemen needed to clean up the site and control the story. Within hours the BBC and the Associated Press, citing official sources in the Yemeni government, reported that a bomb the militants were transporting had exploded, killing them all. The US, however, couldn't keep silent about the operation. Part of it was pride in how well the first drone strike outside Afghanistan had gone, but there was also an element of political calculation. The strike took place on November 3, 2002, two days before US midterm elections, and the Bush administration, desperate for a visible victory in the war on terror, wanted to publicize the success as quickly as possible in an effort to help Republicans in close congressional races.

Shortly after the kills were confirmed, Paul Wolfowitz, the deputy secretary of defense, went on CNN to take credit for the strike. "We've just got to keep the pressure on everywhere we're able and we've got to deny the sanctuaries," he told the news channel. "The Hellfire strike was a very successful tactical operation." Yemeni officials in Sanaa watched in frustration as the boyish deputy unmasked the secret operation live on their televisions. The political points Wolfowitz was scoring at home came at their expense.

"This is why it is so difficult to make deals with the United States," Yahya al-Mutawakkil, the deputy secretary general of Salih's ruling party, fumed to the *Christian Science Monitor* days later. "This is why we are reluctant to work closely with them. They don't consider the internal circumstances in Yemen. In security matters, you don't want to alert the enemy."

AS HULL DEALT with the fallout over the drone strike, an FBI team at the embassy in Sanaa was busy pursuing its own leads. In the weeks after 9/11, with the crater at Ground Zero still smoldering a few blocks away, a short, light-skinned Arab man with curly hair walked into an FBI office in New York and offered himself up as an informant. The man, Muhammad al-Ansi, was in his late forties and part of the Yemeni community that had sprung up along Atlantic Avenue in Brooklyn. Although he had been in the US less than a year at the time, Ansi was already struggling to make a living. First he had tried tourism, renting space along Court Street in Brooklyn for a company he called Marib Travel. When that didn't work, Ansi went into business with a friend acting as an agent for Yemenis, who didn't trust banks and frequently did not have the proper documentation, to send money home. Operating on a tight budget, the pair often tucked the cash inside shipments of honey to avoid taxes and international restrictions.

Ansi started off slow with the FBI. He informed on his former partner in the money transfer business and later, as that case ended, on dozens of other Yemenis he knew in Brooklyn. His record in those first few months after September 11, when the FBI, which had been largely focused on organized crime since its founding in 1908, was desperate for leads on al-Qaeda, won him several admirers within the agency. Ansi gave what Special Agent Robert Fuller later testified was a stellar performance. In barely three months, he contributed to investigations that led to the arrests of twenty people and the seizure of over $1 million. Soon Ansi was tantalizing his handlers with the prospect of an even bigger case. He knew someone, he told agents, who was close to bin Laden. But, Ansi warned, he would need more money and a greater commitment from the FBI. The New York office gave him both.

Ansi had some idea how the game was played. He had worked for the US government before. In 1979, the embassy in Sanaa had hired him as a travel coordinator, only to fire him soon afterward. US diplomats gave him a second chance in 1984, but were forced to fire him a second time. Money troubles in Yemen, where he had two separate warrants out for his arrest, had forced him to move to the US in 2000. But how much the FBI knew about Ansi's background when agents agreed to his proposal is unclear. Still, even in Brooklyn, he had developed a reputation as a fraud. To some, he wove complicated stories of heart problems and medical bills. Others he convinced with tales of a family crisis. But the FBI agents, who benefited from the information he supplied, formed a much different picture of the man one Yemeni colleague described as "untrustworthy." With the exception of Ali Soufan and a handful of others, few of the agents knew anything about counterterrorism. In this confusing new world of radical jihad, Ansi became their guide.

After the meeting in December 2001, when Ansi told agents that the shaykh of his old mosque in Yemen was providing money and men to al-Qaeda, the FBI agreed to finance a trip to Yemen. Agents instructed Ansi to see if the shaykh, Muhammad al-Muayyad, was still active in al-Qaeda. Ansi's cover story for the exploratory meetings, which the FBI had hurriedly concocted, was that he was the front man for a wealthy former Black Panther who wanted to donate money to jihad.

MUHAMMAD AL-MUAYYAD was hardly the most obvious target. When the FBI informed the embassy in Sanaa that it was investigating him, Hull had to scramble to find out who they were talking about. A short, pudgy cleric with a bushy white beard, Muayyad looked like Father Christmas with Coke-bottle glasses and a cell phone. Orphaned at an early age, he found solace in religion and eventually graduated with a degree in Islamic studies. In the late 1970s, when Muayyad moved to a new, poverty-stricken district in southern Sanaa, the first thing he did was open a mosque. "Even before we had a house, my father was working for the poor and the orphans at the mosque," his oldest son, Ibrahim, remembered.

The mosque Muayyad built grew into a community center for

the poor that provided classes, bread, and blankets for the neighborhood's residents. By the 1990s, the charity center was serving some 9,000 people a day, earning Muayyad the local title "Father of Orphans." Like nearly every other Yemeni religious figure, he had recruited Yemenis for the jihad in Afghanistan during the late 1980s. And like the rest of them, Muayyad actively supported Hamas, a Palestinian militia group that was bent on the destruction of Israel. But so did nearly everyone in Yemen, where support for the Palestinian cause was a mark of a person's Islamic faith. The embassy's local contacts in Sanaa doubted that Muayyad had anything to do with al-Qaeda. The only thing that set him apart from other clerics in the city was the fact that Ansi knew him.

In January 2002, Ansi returned to New York and informed the FBI that Muayyad was guilty. He's purchasing weapons for al-Qaeda and sending them fighters, Ansi reported during a debriefing session. He also told agents that Muayyad had bragged about personally handing bin Laden $20 million. Worried about what such a large sum of money could do, agents pressed for more details. But Ansi hadn't recorded any of his conversations with Muayyad and, in the end, the FBI had to trust his word.

Over the next several months, the FBI sent Ansi—who is identified as CI1, or Confidential Informant One, in court documents—to Yemen two more times to prepare the trap for Muayyad. Ansi met with the shaykh several times, pressing him to accept money from the former Black Panther he claimed to represent. Muayyad hesitated at first, apparently trying to square the small-time crook he remembered with Ansi's new role as a powerful intermediary. But as the two spent more time together, Muayyad started to treat Ansi with more respect. In September 2002, he invited Ansi to be his guest at a mass wedding he had helped organize. The FBI informant happily accepted, even asking if he could bring a video camera and record the festivities for his "friend" back in the US.

The wedding dragged on as each of the sponsors addressed the crowd and the long line of white-robed grooms in plastic chairs. A common form of political patronage in Yemen, mass weddings are popular with the country's poor, who find the cost of an individual ceremony prohibitively expensive. Muayyad spoke early in the proceedings, delivering a dry sermon on God and charity. A parade of other heavily bearded clerics took a similarly bland line until Muhammad Siyam, a Hamas representative in Yemen, appeared on the stage. He had breaking news to share with the audience.

There has been a "Hamas operation in Tel Aviv," he announced to the crowd. Six Jews had been killed and more than sixty wounded in a bus bombing they would read about "tomorrow in the newspapers." Cries of "Allahu Akbar" rang out under the tent as Siyam smiled and held up his hands for silence.

"They held the wedding here to coincide with the wedding there," he added, using a common jihadi euphemism for a suicide attack. Once again the tent erupted in cheers. Standing off to one side, Ansi recorded the entire thing.

FOUR MONTHS LATER, in January 2003, Muayyad agreed to meet Ansi's American backer. The two had settled on Germany, and on January 5, Muayyad and an aide flew to Frankfurt. Three days later, the pair met Ansi and an undercover FBI agent posing as the former Black Panther in a hotel room near the airport. Working with their counterparts in German law enforcement, the FBI had bugged the room and set up a hidden camera. Before Muayyad and his aide met the American, Ansi cautioned them to agree with everything he said. The important thing is that "we get his assistance," Ansi reminded them.

Ansi introduced the men and acted as a translator for the undercover agent, who didn't speak Arabic. Almost immediately the agent, in his role as a former Black Panther looking to weaken the US, pressed Muayyad for details of any upcoming al-Qaeda attacks. Muayyad appeared nervous and responded with cryptic answers about his charity work. At one point the undercover agent asked directly whether the next attack would be against Israel or the US. Muayyad mumbled another vague answer, but Ansi pressed for a firm response. "So do you have any plans for that?"

"For now no," Muayyad answered. "We want to rearrange our papers."

Ansi translated this exchange back to the undercover agent as "They will start planning where it's going to be."

The meeting continued the next day. The FBI wanted to push Muayyad to confess something on tape but not so much it would cause him to bolt, while Muayyad sought to placate a wealthy donor. In the center of it all was Ansi.

Muayyad denied any foreknowledge of 9/11, but when Ansi grew animated about blessing Osama bin Laden, Yasir Arafat, and their "efforts against the Jews," Muayyad went along with him. "We ask God for that," the shaykh concurred. He was much more open about his work with the Palestinian organization, saying that he could "call Hamas and arrange things." But the US didn't want to hear about Hamas; it was interested in his ties to bin Laden, and especially the $20 million from Ansi's original report. How did he deliver it? When did he send it? What was it for? But those questions went unanswered. Muayyad talked about bin Laden in the past tense, referencing their time in the Afghanistan jihad of the 1980s. He didn't know anything about him now, and there was no mention of any money.

ON JANUARY 10, the FBI made its move. Muayyad still hadn't talked and his plane was scheduled to leave in a few hours. The agents had two options: arrest the shaykh and his aide now and hope for the best in court, or let them return to Yemen and risk letting Muayyad reconnect with bin Laden. It wasn't even a choice. Armed German agents, who had been standing by, burst into Muayyad's room and handcuffed the elderly shaykh and his twenty-nine-year-old assistant.

Two months later, in testimony before the Senate Judiciary Committee, Attorney General John Ashcroft went public with the arrests. Ansi's most damning allegation, the one the FBI never corroborated on tape, somehow found its way into Ashcroft's prepared remarks. Sitting behind the slender black microphone, Ashcroft told the senators on the committee that an "FBI undercover operation developed information that Muayyad personally handed Osama bin Laden $20 million from his terrorist fundraising network."

The US government's entire case rested on the shaky account of a single informant who had pocketed more than $100,000 for his work.

WHILE THE FBI was chasing ghosts in Germany, the real al-Qaeda was meeting in Yemen to figure out the next step. Harithi's death had been a major blow. Bin Laden's man in Yemen since the beginning, Harithi had established al-Qaeda's first training camps in the country and turned scores of young recruits into seasoned fighters. Neither Muhammad al-Ahdal nor Fawaz al-Rabi'i, his top two lieutenants, were ready to succeed him. Ahdal was more of a financial secretary than a commander, and he was still hiding from Salih with the tribes in Marib. Rabi'i might make a good commander someday, but at the moment he was too young and inexperienced. The last attack he had planned, on the Hunt Oil helicopter, had ended when Yemeni security services used the bloody sandal and a tip from a local citizen to track the injured Arif Mujali to a hospital in Sanaa.

But someone had to take over the scattered fragments of al-Qaeda's Yemen network. When the men met to decide how to respond to Harithi's assassination, Rabi'i took the lead. The US, he explained, his face framed by the long dark hair he refused to cut, had killed al-Qaeda's leader in Yemen. To get revenge, al-Qaeda needed to kill America's top official in Yemen.

For weeks in the late winter and early spring of 2003, a trio of al-Qaeda operatives shadowed Hull's motorcade whenever it left the embassy. Despite all the security precautions, convoys exiting the embassy had only two choices. They could turn right and head toward a traffic circle or left toward another circle. Both were choke points that Rabi'i believed would work perfectly for an ambush. But before he could put his latest plan into action, Yemeni intelligence stumbled onto the safe house in the Madhbah neighborhood in northwest Sanaa. Security forces raided the house in early March, but a communication error meant that they failed to adequately cordon off the building. Fighting their way free behind a wall of machine-gun fire and grenades, Rabi'i and Hizam Mujali were able to escape. The pair made it hundreds of miles south in their car before an officer stopped them at a checkpoint along the Gulf of Aden coastal highway in Abyan. Suspicious of Rabi'i's claim that he'd forgotten his ID card, the soldier climbed into the vehicle with the two men and directed them to drive the 30 miles west to Aden, where he could check their stories. As soon as they were out of earshot of the security checkpoint, Rabi'i and Mujali wrestled the soldier's gun away and shot him. Dumping his body along the road, the two reversed direction and headed for Marib, hoping to find refuge among the tribes. But the noose was tightening and al-Qaeda was running out of options as Salih continued his campaign of arrests. Two weeks after they killed the soldier, Yemeni forces captured Rabi'i and Mujali in Marib.

Hull barely had time to congratulate Salih on the arrests before another security incident threatened to derail the relationship again. On April 11, ten prisoners escaped from the PSO prison in Aden by drilling a hole in a bathroom wall. Among the escapees were Jamal al-Badawi and Fahd al-Qusa, al-Qaeda members who had both played supporting roles in the USS *Cole* attack.

"We had not even been told of their transfer to Aden," Hull told Washington, explaining that the embassy had thought the prisoners were still in Sanaa.

WEEKS AFTER THE prison break, FBI director Robert Mueller touched down in Sanaa for a meeting with President Salih. Upset that two men with US blood on their hands were once again free, the FBI director's message was direct and blunt. Salih had to recapture these men.

Five months later, Mueller squeezed in a return trip to Sanaa to personally check on the manhunt. Nothing seemed to have changed. Badawi and Qusa were still at large and the Yemenis didn't seem particularly concerned. The country was in the middle of Ramadan, and during the day Sanaa looked like a ghost town. Offices were closed and officials spent much of the day napping and waiting for sundown, when they could break their fast. The lack of activity rankled Mueller. Once again, he delivered a forceful and undiplomatic message to President Salih.

The Minister of the Interior, Rashid al-Alimi, tried to smooth over the differences by inviting both Mueller and Salih to his home for the evening feast. Mueller turned him down cold. Both Salih and his minister were insulted by Mueller's behavior and especially by his refusal to share a meal, a slight that carried significant weight in the Arab world. On the drive back to the airport, Hull, who was forced to act as a go-between Salih and Mueller, lost his temper and laid into the FBI director about US shortcomings while explaining that Yemenis were actually making progress in the war against al-Qaeda.

And they were. Shortly after Mueller left town, Yemeni agents got a tip on the whereabouts of Muhammad al-Ahdal. The intelligence said he was coming to Sanaa for a wedding. After Harithi's assassination and Rabi'i's arrest, Ahdal was the last major al-Qaeda leader in the country. If Yemen could get him, the terrorist organization's leadership structure would be eliminated and the list of names that Bush had presented as a litmus test two years earlier would be taken care of.

The worries of US-based analysts aside, al-Qaeda in Yemen was in complete disarray. The drone strike a year earlier had destroyed the organization's infrastructure in Yemen. Without Harithi, al-Qaeda in Yemen could not function. Scores of operatives had been arrested and those that were still at large, such as Badawi and Qusa, were compromised and on the run. Like a general without an army, Ahdal found his movements increasingly constrained by raids and security leaks. Instead of planning new attacks, he was consumed with staying a step ahead of Yemeni intelligence. When Salih's men finally tracked him down at a wedding party in Sanaa, Ahdal knew it was the end. He would die rather than be taken alive, he told his last few followers as he barricaded himself inside the house.

President Salih, eager to avoid a shootout in the capital, dispatched a trusted adviser to the scene. The negotiator spent hours talking to Ahdal, laying out Salih's deal and explaining the consequences of noncompliance. The details of the deal, which were not disclosed at the time, included a three-year prison sentence for Ahdal in exchange for his promise not to return to jihad, at least not in Yemen. It was either jail or the Americans, Salih's envoy said. Bowing his head, al-Qaeda's last leader in Yemen hobbled out of the house on his prosthetic leg and into a car that drove him across to town to the PSO prison.

II

FORGETTING

10

Rehab

2002–2004

More than a year before Ahdal's surrender, President Ali Abdullah Salih had come to a decision that would have far-reaching consequences for the fight against al-Qaeda. By late August 2002, the problem was clear to the Yemeni president. Months of arrests and cooperation with the US had done little but fill his prisons and alienate his domestic base. The tribal shaykhs, whose support he needed to maintain stability in the country, grumbled about the seizures. The president was taking too many of their young men, they complained. Salih was stuck; he couldn't just release the prisoners and he couldn't keep them in jail. He needed an out.

On August 24, 2002, Salih called Abd al-Majid Zindani and Abd al-Wahhab al-Daylami, the two hennaed clerics who had recruited so heavily for the jihad in Afghanistan, and invited them and several other preachers to the presidential palace. Six days later, after their Friday sermons, thirty heavily bearded men in long robes and open-toed sandals shuffled into one of Salih's reception halls to listen to his proposal.

Everyone knows the situation, Salih opened. Rows of clerics stared back at him. Few of the men in the room had supported

Salih's alliance with the US or the massive internal crackdown that followed. Salih had ignored their counsel then, and many of them suspected the only reason he wanted advice now was to give him religious cover with the tribes.

Over the next several minutes, Salih laid out what he had come to see as an elegant solution to the prisoner problem. Most of the men in jail, he acknowledged, had been arrested merely on the suspicion that they sympathized with al-Qaeda and few, if any, could actually be prosecuted. Instead of putting them on trial, Salih wanted to work with the clerics and create a program to reintegrate them back into society. Let's reeducate them and release them, he concluded.

As soon as Salih finished speaking, the criticism began. Leaning forward on their canes, some of the older scholars cited the case of Muhammad al-Dhahabi, an Egyptian cleric and former minister who had been assassinated by an extremist group in 1977 after heading a similar program in Cairo. Others expressed concern that they might be labeled American stooges for agreeing to the president's proposal. Salih could see where this was headed, and he quickly cut off discussion before the clerics could form a consensus against the plan. Take a few days and think about it, Salih told them, and then decide what it should look like. It was not a request.

For their part, US officials hated Salih's idea. They worried that what Salih called rehabilitation might create a revolving door. What was the good of sharing intelligence and helping Yemen arrest these guys, analysts wondered, if it was just going to release them months later? But Salih was adamant. His plan could work.

Three days after Salih laid out his proposal, the group of thirty clerics met again, this time without the president. None of them had changed their minds. The only holdout was a junior cleric who, by his own admission, was one of the youngest and least qualified scholars in the room. When they held their final meeting on September 4, Hamud al-Hitar, a soft-spoken district court judge, explained that he couldn't side with his colleagues. Instead, he asked their permission to submit a separate, minority report in support of the president's plan.

An hour later, before the judge had even started writing, Salih was on the phone asking how the meeting went.

"Not well," Hitar conceded.

"Yes, but what about you, what did you say?" the president pressed.

"I expressed my objection to the decision and said that I would undertake the dialogue, even if I have to do it on my own," Hitar answered.

"Well done," the president said. He had his man. Salih asked if Hitar had a team in mind.

"There are three colleagues I would like to work with," the forty-seven-year-old judge replied. That was all that the president needed to hear. The logistics and the rest of details were up to Hitar.

The sessions, or "dialogues" as the judge preferred to call them, started the next day.

SHORT WITH CLOSELY cropped hair and a beard the color of speckled steel wool, Hitar has the quiet, reserved air of a college professor. As a descendant of the Prophet Muhammad's family, he is a member of Yemen's upper class. But Hitar's aristocratic lineage masks a deep contrarian streak. When he split with his colleagues and agreed to champion Salih's idea for a religious dialogue with al-Qaeda suspects, it wasn't the first time he had broken from the pack.

In 1985, one year after being named chairman of Sanaa's Penal Primary Court, a rare honor for a young judge, Hitar made national headlines by handing down death sentences for two Muslims who had murdered a Jew. Although technically a protected minority, along with Christians, Jews in Yemen were often treated like second-class citizens. During the nineteenth and twentieth centuries, the Imams passed laws limiting the size of Jewish homes and styles of clothing. Other rulers prohibited Jews from riding animals in the presence of Muslims, on the grounds that riding allowed them to look down on their betters. Hitar's ruling provoked a great deal of anger and confusion.

It shouldn't have, he explained with a frustrated sigh. Yes, he had ignored all contemporary legal and scholarly precedents, but that was because they were wrong. He went back to the roots of the issue—in this case, the Quran and Sunnah, or traditions of the Prophet Muhammad. These sources, he argued, do not differentiate between Muslims and non-Muslims in instances of murder. He simply applied this understanding to the case before him. The public outcry, Hitar asserted, was the result of a general misunderstanding and misapplication of Islamic law over the years.

Hitar envisioned doing something similar with the al-Qaeda suspects in prisons. He could strip away years of mistaken scholarship and poor religious practice and explain to them what the Quran actually said. The program, he often told journalists, was a "labor of love."

AROUND 10 A.M. on September 5, 2002, Hitar and his handpicked team of scholars walked into a prison in downtown Sanaa for their first session. Dressed in his customary pillbox hat and robe, Hitar carried with him copies of the Quran and the Yemeni constitution, his two source documents. Before they entered the room, one of the guards asked Hitar to remove his *jambiya*, the large curved dagger most north Yemeni men wear tucked into their belts.

"Why?" the judge demanded.

"Security," the soldier said.

Hitar laughed him off and walked into the room. Sitting around the table were a handful of men in blue prison jumpsuits. Hitar walked past the prisoners to the front of the room and laid the Quran and constitution on the table. Only then did he look up and begin to speak. In short, crisp sentences he outlined the program. The Quran and the constitution will govern us, he explained. For Hitar, there was no legal difference between the two documents. Article 3 of the constitution stated: "Islamic law is the source of all legislation," and Hitar set out to prove to the prisoners that everything in it was in agreement with the Quran. To underline his point, Hitar picked up his copy of the constitution. "If you find anything in here that goes against God's word, tell me and I will change it. But if you don't find anything then you must agree to obey the constitution."

Hitar wanted to be clear from the start. "If you are right, we will follow you. But if we are right, you must follow us." The prisoners, many of whom had yet to be charged, were wary. They had been lied to and abused for years. What could one judge do?

"The president appointed me to this program, and I'm undertaking it on behalf of God and his prophet," Hitar continued.

For the next ten weeks, Hitar and his team met with 104 prisoners in an attempt to convince the men that their understanding of Islam had been distorted and perverted by power-hungry outcasts like bin Laden and Zawahiri. The young men he saw were well-intentioned, but misguided and poorly educated. Hitar believed they were overwhelmed by the linguistic and grammatical complexities of the Quran. These men are "not Quranic scholars and therefore they make a number of mistakes in reading the Quran," he observed in his reports. "Often there are passages that they take out of context or simply misinterpret because they do not put the proper stress on a certain syllable in a particular word."

Hitar's scholarly condescension grated on some of the prisoners.

They might not have his training, but they had studied the Quran and they respected bin Laden. The al-Qaeda commander, as many of them knew from personal experience, had turned his back on worldly pleasures and lived out God's toughest injunctions. Bin Laden fasted for days on end, often doing without water, and in Afghanistan he had even chosen a dilapidated farm for his home. Could Hitar do that? Bin Laden treated his men with respect, talking to them like equals and not confused schoolboys. The prisoners didn't need a lesson on the Quran. They already knew the book by heart. The judge, they told one another in late-night discussions, was willing to say and legitimize whatever Salih wanted. He's a puppet, they argued, twisting Islam beyond recognition.

Hitar had outlined eleven different subjects for debate, but the men spent most of the time listening to his lectures on the compatibility of the modern state and Islam. Who had authority to speak for Islam? Bin Laden and al-Qaeda, or Hitar and the Yemeni state?

The answer to that question would determine the success of the program, which is why Hitar was so insistent on pairing the Quran with the constitution. If he could convince the prisoners that civil law flowed out of Quranic mandates, as it claimed, then he thought he might be able to defuse the men he privately called "ticking time bombs." Hitar's argument, however, forced him into uncharted intellectual territory and ultimately led him to create a parallel world of positions and power that had little grounding in Islamic legal theory.

Everything in Islam, he told his prison audiences, was mirrored in the modern Yemeni state. In Hitar's parallel world, the presidency, like the caliphate of early Islam, was both a political and a religious office, the highest authority in the land. This meant that Salih was president and what Hitar called *wali al-amr*, a religious term of responsibility. The implications of this argument were enormous. If the prisoners accepted Hitar's premise, then Yemeni law, not an al-Qaeda oath, would determine their actions. To follow the Quran meant obeying the state. Most importantly for the prisoners, this meant that only Salih could authorize jihad. No one else—not bin Laden, Zawahiri, or any other cleric—possessed the Quranic authority to do so.

Hitar's innovative reading of Islamic legal theory made citizenship the single most significant factor in a person's religious life. Warming to the intellectual challenges of the theory, Hitar expounded on his argument. Every action the state takes is based on a valid Islamic precedent from the life of Muhammad, he boldly claimed in sessions with the glassy-eyed prisoners. Take the UN charter, for example. Yemen's membership in the modern organization is permitted by the fact that Muhammad signed the Treaty of Medina in 622, which in its own time acted as a sort of league for tribes that lived largely independent of one another. The same rationale could be applied to any treaty Yemen signed, he added.

It was like watching a brilliant mathematician work out complex theorems on a blackboard: vaguely entertaining, mostly confusing, and not at all clear how it related to real life. No matter how Hitar explained his theory, embellishing it with precedents and examples, everything rested on the assumed Islamic legitimacy of the state and the ruler. The prisoners who finally grasped the core of Hitar's argument had a difficult time imagining the poorly educated Salih, who had a reputation for whisky and women, as a religious authority. But that was the deal: acknowledge Salih's supremacy and sign a waiver pledging to abstain from violence, or stick to your beliefs and remain in jail.

On November 11, 2002, a week into Ramadan, Hitar completed his final session. He recommended that thirty-six of the 104 prisoners be released as a test group. At the end of the month, Salih freed the men as part of an amnesty program to mark the Islamic holy month. As a condition of their release, the men were required to check in with security officers once a month.

HITAR STARTED THE next round in the spring of 2003. But this time there was something new to deal with. That March the US had invaded Iraq, and everything changed.

Salih wasn't surprised. Ever since his Oval Office exchange with Bush in November 2001, Salih had known this day was coming. Still, the Yemeni president did everything he could to warn the US against another war. It is going to cause "great problems," he repeatedly told Ambassador Edmund Hull. Every American who came to Yemen heard the same message. Vice President Cheney, General Tommy Franks, and handfuls of assistant secretaries and military officers all had to listen to Salih's take. Hull faithfully reiterated the president's concerns in cables back to Washington. None of them made any difference.

Iraq shattered Hitar's parallel world of Islamic precedents for modern actions. In December 2003, one year after the first release, Hitar recommended that another ninety-two converted militants be set free. The test group, he told the president, had honored their pledge to give up violence and extremism. After that things moved much faster.

Yemen publicized the program in the Arabic press and portrayed Hitar as the moderate face of Islam, someone who could debate bin Laden. "Any place, any time," the judge would joke with journalists. Hitar took to the road, traveling to different governorates to peddle his program. He no longer held the small, intimate debates that characterized the program's first year. Now Hitar preached to dozens of inmates at a time.

Nasir al-Bahri, bin Laden's former bodyguard, then in his second year of custody, took part in the program. The prisoners, he explained, saw the judge as the "key to their release." He came to talk, Bahri said, but "there was no dialogue." The judge talked; "we listened and then we were released. He didn't change anyone's mind"

Hitar was their get-out-of-jail-free card. The men swore to

one another that while they might recant with their mouths, their hearts would never change. The more radical prisoners reassured uncertain inmates that Islamic law permitted their signature on Hitar's document even if they had no intention of abiding by its terms. The ends, they said, justified the means.

By early 2004 the flaws in Hitar's program were starting to show. Several released prisoners rejoined the fight, and headed to Iraq, where the war acted like a giant magnet for Yemen's jihadis. With no al-Qaeda leadership at home and a Western army in the heart of the Muslim world, the logic was clear. Iraq in 2003 and 2004 was the same as Afghanistan in the 1980s. The only difference was that the Yemeni state had supported one and not the other. The prisoners still in jail quickly spotted the contradiction.

Publicly, Hitar maintained that Iraq was "not a subject of the dialogue." But inside Yemen's prisons, he couldn't escape the war. For most Yemenis, the presence of US combat troops in Iraq clearly invoked the Quranic principle of defensive jihad. It was a simple case: non-Muslim troops attacking Muslims in a Muslim country. Fighting the US wasn't simply permitted; it was required.

Hitar tried to get around the problem by arguing that Iraq wasn't the issue. Fighting in Iraq isn't unjustified, he told roomfuls of prisoners. It is simply unsanctioned. Only President Salih could legitimately declare jihad. If he did, fighting would be allowed. If he didn't, the men couldn't participate. The evasion didn't take. Prisoners pushed back, arguing that if Salih didn't declare jihad in such an obvious case then he clearly wasn't a true Islamic leader. For men who had seen bin Laden's uncompromising stand in action, it was simple. Bin Laden followed the Quran no matter the consequences. Salih and Hitar did not.

DESPITE THE DIFFICULTIES, Hitar's rehab program sputtered on. Prisoners continued to sign on the dotted line, promising to behave if released. Hitar soon gave up trying to transform their ideological outlook, and the program evolved into a sort of tacit nonaggression pact between the government and the militants. Prisoners no longer had to disavow violent jihad; they only had to agree not to carry out attacks in Yemen. The state struck a dangerous compromise: don't attack us and we won't attack you.

It worked, at least for a while. After Ahdal's arrest in late 2003, al-Qaeda in Yemen disappeared. Its leaders were either dead or in jail, and those that weren't had moved on to Iraq. Yemen appeared calm. Hitar felt vindicated, pointing to the end of al-Qaeda in Yemen when pressed about the hundreds of prisoners he released. "The proof is in the results," he said. "Since we released the first group of prisoners there has not been one terrorist attack in Yemen," he proudly stated.

Throughout 2004, as Yemen's al-Qaeda threat seemingly evaporated, Hitar adapted his work to meet the state's newest challenge. For the past two years, there had been growing discontent in the far north of the country. This time, the threat came not from a Sunni extremist group like al-Qaeda but from a band of Zaydi rebels, who adhered to Shi'a Islam but were doctrinally distinct from the "twelver" Shi'ism practiced in Iran.* The two challenges were not so much separate as they were different manifestations of the same problem: the increasing radicalization of the country's religious landscape. Much as the two groups hated to admit it, the Sunnis and Shi'as in Yemen were inexorably linked. The rise of the former led to the reaction of the latter.

The problems had begun in 2002, months before Hitar started his rehabilitation program, in the governorate of Sadah near the Saudi border. Early that year, on January 17, a small group of frustrated farmers and students started chanting outside a local mosque

*Named after the first twelve imams, "twelver" Shi'ism has historically been at odds with Sunni Islam, unlike the "fiver" Shi'ism the Huthis adhered to, which is quite close to Sunni Islam.

in Sadah's provincial capital of the same name. Their voices rang out in the still mountain air. "God is Great! Death to America! Death to Israel! Curse upon the Jews! Victory for Islam!"

At the front of the group, dressed in a long white robe offset by a dark sports jacket, stood their leader, Husayn al-Huthi. Stocky and dark with a full beard and soft eyes, he had a commanding presence. Our community is under attack, he told his audience. Soon the Zaydis will be no more.

The men in the square knew what he was talking about. For centuries, families like the Huthis had been local royalty, supplying the Imams who ruled northern Yemen. The Zaydis took their name from Muhammad's great-great-grandson Zayd bin Ali, who in 740 AD had been brutally murdered by a Sunni tyrant, only to have his corpse unearthed and decapitated a few years later. Adopting the flexibility of marginalized groups, Zaydis charted a sort of middle course between Sunni and Shi'a. They were "fivers," the unofficial fifth school of Sunni Islam and followers of the fifth imam in Shi'a Islam. In Yemen, they were almost indistinguishable from their lowland Sunni neighbors, save for the fact that Zaydis had an extra line in their call to prayer and held their hands differently. The two groups intermarried and prayed in each other's mosques. Then came the revolution and civil war that overthrew the Imam in Sanaa and destroyed the Zaydi state.

By the time the eight-year civil war ended in 1970, Yemen had changed. The Zaydi imamate had been abolished in favor of a republic. Instead of an Imam, Yemen had a president and the ruling class of *sayyids*, or descendants of the Prophet, who for more than 1,000 years had been the only people eligible for the state's top office, suddenly found themselves powerless. It was a confusing time for *sayyid* families like the Huthis. Abdullah al-Sallal, the first president of the republic, came from a low-class butcher family. A man the Huthis considered beneath them now headed the state.

The Zaydis' political and religious enemies took advantage of their fall. Proselytizing Wahhabis from Saudi Arabia, who considered Zaydis infidels, sent money and teachers south, building schools and funding religious institutes in what they viewed as territory ripe for conversion. In 1979, Muqbil al-Wadi'i, a former Zaydi tribesman whom *sayyid* families like the Huthis had once mocked for his low-class background, returned from the kingdom. Ready for revenge after a childhood of bruises and insults, Wadi'i built a small school and started to attract a following among other Zaydi converts who had traditionally been abused by the ruling *sayyids*. Wadi'i's message of equality and Sunni Islam appealed to hundreds of young men frustrated with an antiquated social hierarchy that prevented them from marrying into the *sayyid* class.

Much like the jihadis who had destroyed Aden's graveyards following the 1994 civil war, Wadi'i, who was influenced by the same Wahhabi theology, singled out the Zaydis' shrine-like tombs as a particularly egregious sin that led people to worship men instead of God. The Zaydis posted armed guards around their cemeteries, but Wadi'i's young followers still found ways to slip in and smash the tombstones. Sadah was also where al-Qaeda had set up some of its first training camps in the early 1990s and where it bought the explosives for the USS *Cole* and MV *Limburg* attacks. Families like the Huthis saw themselves as the target of a two-pronged alliance bent on their destruction.

The men Husayn al-Huthi was addressing that day in the square knew the history. They had lived it. Huthi reminded them of Salih's broken promises to build hospitals and expand the electrical grid to Sadah. Zaydis were being targeted because of their religion.

In early 2003, a year after Husayn al-Huthi had organized his first protest, Salih passed through Sadah on his way to Saudi Arabia. Stopping for prayers, Huthi's men greeted him with more of their chants. In the calls for victory over America and the Jews, Salih heard a coded criticism of his rule. The president knew Husayn al-Huthi personally from when the Zaydi leader had been a member of parliament in the mid-1990s. Salih had even subsidized Huthi's master's degree in Sudan after he refused to run for reelection in 1997. The patronage had been part of what Salih called his snake dance. At the time, Salih had been strengthening the Zaydis at the expense of their Islamist rivals. In fact, Huthi had only returned home to Sadah in 2000, when Salih's calculations had changed and the Zaydis once again fell out of favor and the presidential funding came to an end.

Huthi's eloquent, deeply religious speeches had tapped into a current of discontent in Yemen. A massively corrupt government, rising food prices, and high unemployment pushed people to action, and not just in Sadah. Every Friday after prayers, Zaydi activists inspired by Huthi and his followers chanted outside the Great Mosque in Sanaa. Tucked deep inside the old city, Sanaa's oldest mosque, built by a companion of the Prophet, had become a symbol of the resistance. By June 2004, security forces had arrested 800 protesters in Sanaa alone. And the movement was spreading fast. Throughout the mountain towns of north Yemen—across al-Jawf, Amran, and Hajjah—men were repeating the chants.

11

A Revolt in the North

2004–2005

Shortly after noon on Friday, June 18, 2004, dozens of men streamed out of the wide wooden doors at the Great Mosque in downtown Sanaa. Within minutes, the narrow stone alleyways of the old city echoed with the now familiar chants: "God is Great! Death to America! Death to Israel! Curse upon the Jews! Victory for Islam!" But this time, Salih's men were ready. Plainclothes security officers and dozens of uniformed police beat back the protesters with clubs and sticks as they made several arrests.

About 150 miles to the north, in Sadah's mud-brick old city, Husayn al-Huthi's followers were involved in their own skirmish. Taking over a state mosque, they expelled the preacher who was on the government's payroll and pushed the caretaker into the street. After today, they proclaimed over the mosque's loudspeakers, there will be no more government lies emanating from this location.

Salih monitored the reports throughout the afternoon, but it was clear that the weekly clashes had reached a crisis point. Once again, the Yemeni president turned to his boyhood friend Ali Muhsin al-Ahmar for help. The gap-toothed general had been instrumental in defeating the southern Socialists in the civil war a decade earlier, and now Salih needed him in the north.

Troops from Ali Muhsin's First Armored Division rumbled out of their base in Sadah, moving toward Huthi's home nearly 30 miles away. The sudden military incursion triggered an immediate reaction. Huthi's well-armed tribal supporters, who were scattered throughout the mountains above the road, opened fire on the military. The soldiers shot back. Hundreds of miles north of the fighting, in a hospital in Riyadh where he was undergoing treatment for cancer, Shaykh Abdullah al-Ahmar, the powerful tribal leader, listened to reports of the unraveling situation.* Worried about the prospect of war just miles from his home in Amran, the elderly shaykh asked Salih to grant Huthi a delay. Give him a chance to travel to Sanaa and turn himself in, the shaykh pleaded. Reluctantly, Salih agreed. Twenty-four hours, that's it, the president said.

But Salih's ultimatum was never delivered. Twice General Yahya al-Amri, the military-appointed governor of Sadah, attempted to reach Huthi's farm, but each time he was turned back by gun-wielding men. The second time, on June 20, the governor traveled with a large detachment of troops. A gunfight erupted, as Huthi's well-armed followers again refused to let the soldiers pass. This inconclusive firefight in north Yemen's terraced cliffs would prove to be the opening battle of an eight-year rebellion, which would push the country to the verge of bankruptcy and distract it from the fight against al-Qaeda. The Huthi wars had begun.

ONE WEEK AFTER the fighting started, with the phone lines to his farm cut, Husayn al-Huthi sat down to write the president a letter. He was confused, he admitted. Why was Salih so upset with him? "I am certain that I have done nothing that would lead to such a feeling. I do not work against you," he scrawled in cramped, slanting lines. "I am by your side, so do not listen to hypocrites and

*Shaykh Abdullah al-Ahmar and Ali Muhsin al-Ahmar, despite being from the same Hashid tribal confederation, are not related.

provocateurs and trust that I am more sincere and honest with you than they are." Huthi concluded the one-page letter optimistically. He still believed they could work out their differences. "When we meet, if God is willing, I will talk to you about matters that are of great concern to you."

Still smarting from Huthi's public challenges, Salih refused direct contact with the forty-eight-year-old rebel commander. Instead, he sent a mediation team north into the mountains. Among the negotiators were Huthi's younger brother, Yahya, who was a member of parliament for Salih's ruling party, and their tiny, frail-looking seventy-eight-year-old father. Control your son, Salih told the Huthi patriarch, leaving the implicit threat to the family unspoken. The family tried, but every time they engineered a ceasefire, Ali Muhsin used the mediation team as cover to attack rebel positions with helicopter gunships.

High above the arid mountains, military jets from Sanaa flew bombing raids against suspected Huthi positions. The government estimated that Huthi had 3,000 supporters out of a population of nearly 700,000 scattered on farms and homesteads across an area nearly the size of New Jersey. But simple arithmetic was misleading. North Yemen's rugged geography, with peaks as high as a mile and a half above sea level, acted like a force multiplier, while deep, roomy caves provided shelter from the heavy aerial bombardment. Foreign minister Abu Bakr al-Qirbi described the region as "Yemen's Tora Bora."

Indiscriminate shelling compounded the problem. Air force bombs plowed into farmers' fields, destroying a year's worth of planting and investment and driving entire families into debt. Off the farms, the security forces that had been hunting al-Qaeda for the past two and a half years moved north to fight the Huthis. They brought the same tactics of mass arrests and property seizures to their new war. The fighters' elderly fathers, younger sisters, and a smattering of cousins were arrested in house searches across Sadah.

Zaydis, like suspected jihadis, were guilty until proven innocent. The government controlled most of the urban areas in Sadah, but to defeat the Huthis it needed to pacify the countryside. Working from village to village proved messy, slow, and corrosive. The army's collective reprisals pushed hundreds of neutral tribesmen into Huthi's camp.

In early July 2004, Salih asked Hamud al-Hitar, the judge who was busy rehabilitating al-Qaeda prisoners, to adjust his program to deal with the Huthi fighters the government had captured.

Can't be done, Hitar reported back after a couple of weeks of sessions. "The difference between al-Qaeda and the Huthis," he explained to the president, "is that al-Qaeda follows the book. This means that when you show an al-Qaeda fighter something from the Quran that contradicts what they have been told, they believe you." It is different with a Huthi fighter, Hitar continued. "He follows a man, not a book, and it is much more difficult to combat this."

WEEKS LATER, THE military's chief of staff, Major General Muhammad Ali al-Qasimi, met with journalists in Sadah to deliver some good news. "We are in the mop-up phase," he announced. The war, he claimed, should be finished within twenty-four hours.

Throughout the summer, as various mediation and rehabilitation efforts sputtered on, the army flooded the area with soldiers, pushing Huthi's supporters deeper into the mountains. Heavy shelling had destroyed much of the region, and early estimates suggested it would be years before Sadah recovered. On August 5, the army had killed more than 140 Huthi supporters in a pitched battle. "That is all over now," Qasimi proudly stated. "The rebellion is weak and confined."

The general, who like many in the upper ranks of the military was a member of Salih's Sanhan tribe, explained that the Huthi fighters were restricted to two districts, roughly 30 miles apart.

West of the provincial capital, Husayn al-Huthi and several dozen followers continued to hold out, while north of the city his top deputy, Abdullah al-Ruzami, another former member of parliament, led the second group. The conflict would come down to this pair of last stands, Qasimi boldly predicted.

But the rebels wouldn't give up. They were defending the same mountains they had played in as children. During the day government forces, backed by tribal militias who saw an opportunity to weaken their rivals among Huthi's supporters, fought their way forward into the mountains, only to be forced back at night. Natural guerrilla fighters, the Huthis' hit-and-run style of assault took a toll on Yemen's cumbersome military of tanks and heavy machinery.

Two weeks after Qasimi's press conference prediction, a group of Huthi fighters ambushed a military patrol and killed dozens of soldiers. Among the dead was Abd al-Alim al-Hitar, a thirty-five-year-old colonel in the army and Hamud al-Hitar's younger brother. Air force jets hit back in retaliation, increasing their bombing runs from Sanaa. But the pilots were still working without much in the way of actionable intelligence. All they could do was drop more bombs and hope some of them hit the right targets.

Amazingly, in the jagged mountains and miles of territory, one of them did. A lucky strike destroyed the intricate water system Huthi had built in his cave hideout west of Sadah city. Trapped inside by the roaming bands of soldiers and tribesmen who had swarmed the mountains inspired by a $55,000 reward, Huthi and some family members waited in the dark.

On September 10, three days after the water ran out, Huthi sent two of his wives, one of whom was nursing a small child, out of the cave and into the daylight in a play for time. Dressed in rags and smudged with dirt after days in the dark, the women looked like refugees. Government soldiers quickly located the women and ordered Huthi to come out with his hands up. "I want to talk to the president," he shouted back. "I will only surrender to him."

The only demand he'd made since the fighting started was still a nonstarter. Slowly, the beaten man shuffled toward the cave's entrance. As he passed into the light, one of the soldiers thought he saw him reach for his pocket. Opening fire, the soldiers hit him several times in the chest. The dirty figure crumpled back toward the mouth of the cave. Huthi died minutes later, unable to utter another word as the dust around him darkened to mud.

We don't know what he was thinking, one of the soldiers at the scene later admitted. "We don't know if Huthi was going to attack or if he wanted to surrender." Searching his body, the soldiers found a pistol stuffed in his pocket.

THE MONTHS OF guerrilla war in the north had taken a heavy toll on Yemen's military. The army estimated its losses at 473 dead and 2,588 wounded, although independent estimates put the numbers much higher. Equipment and armaments losses alone reached into the millions of dollars. The Huthis were judged to have fared worse in the war, but the costs to both sides were dwarfed by the civilian casualties and economic damage brought on by three months of war. Yemen's economy, which had never been secure, was now in serious trouble.

In early September, shortly before Huthi was killed, US Assistant Secretary of State Lincoln Bloomfield Jr. arrived in Sanaa to meet with Salih and other top military commanders. Concerned that surface-to-air missiles known as man-portable air-defense systems, or MANPADS, might fall into al-Qaeda hands and threaten civilian airliners, the US had initiated a global buyback program. Yemen had nearly 1,500 of the devices in storage, and there were reports of dozens more in the hands of arms traders around the country.

A distinguished fifty-year-old diplomat who vaguely resembled Ronald Reagan, Bloomfield was worried about leakage from Yemen's armories. Al-Qaeda had already used one of the weapons systems, when Fawaz al-Rabi'i barely missed bringing down the Hunt Oil helicopter two years earlier, and even though most of the organization was in prison Bloomfield wanted to avoid a repeat performance. He told Salih that the US would buy all of Yemen's MANPADS.

Salih was also worried about the surface-to-air missiles, but it was the Huthis that kept him up at night. For Salih, al-Qaeda was a minor nuisance in a messy country, but the Huthis were an existential threat. A bloody rebellion in the Zaydi heartland had the potential to challenge Salih's rule in a way al-Qaeda never could. And the rebels had used the MANPADS to devastating effect during the three-month war, taking out helicopters and planes. Allowing them to get their hands on the weapons, which they purchased from arms dealers in Sadah, was "a big mistake," Salih conceded to Bloomfield.

"Rest assured, Yemen will not have such weapons anymore," the president continued. "But everything has a price. You will have to pay," he paused, drawing out the number. "One million dollars for each."

After a few moments of awkward silence, Salih laughed. The Yemeni translator turned to Bloomfield and nervously whispered, "I feel it is my duty to make sure you understand this is a joke." Bloomfield nodded his understanding, but he couldn't help wondering how much of a markup the smiling president was going to charge on the $2,000 weapon.

The amount the US will pay, he reiterated to Salih, is "fixed but well above what we believe to be the market price."

Salih wasn't alone in wanting more out of the US. The day before, Bloomfield had given military chief of staff Muhammad al-Qasimi a licensing agreement for the C-130 cargo plane, which allowed for the US to help with repairs. "These few parts to a transport plane represent the biggest step forward in our military-to-military cooperation in years," the general remarked sarcastically as he signed the document.

Yemen had expected a lot more in return for defeating al-Qaeda. Salih wanted tanks and jets, not spare parts. "We need our F–5s in Sadah," he complained. The Huthis were on the run in the north, but Salih knew the war was far from over.

AFTER HUTHI'S DEATH, the fighting in the north dissolved into a tentative ceasefire as government forces slowly receded back to the cities, leaving armed fighters in control of some districts. Wary of provoking more clashes and, potentially, another round of fighting, the military stayed on base and left the Huthis alone. The government still had hundreds of prisoners locked up around the country, and Salih thought he could trade them for a permanent ceasefire.

In January 2005, Badr al-Din al-Huthi, the seventy-eight-year-old patriarch of the family, came down from the mountains to oversee the postwar negotiations. Now that his son was dead, it fell to the aging and ill Badr al-Din to protect the men who had fought for his family. Shorter than most Yemenis, the hunched-over cleric had an unruly white beard and was hardly the best choice for a negotiator. Scholarly and short-tempered, he was uncomfortable among contemporary politicians and their diplomatic niceties.

Badr al-Din brought his wives and most of his family with him to Sanaa, and the whole entourage moved into the cramped apartment which his son Yahya kept in the capital. A part-time residence, Yahya only used the decrepit and leaky flat when parliament was in session, sleeping there for a few nights at a time before returning home. As the days stretched into weeks and still no meeting with the president materialized, tempers grew short in the overcrowded space. The Huthi women, who were often divided by domestic jealousies, complained of getting wet when it rained and muttered that living under a riverbank would be better. The tiny apartment was a far cry from the castle-like homes they were used to in Sadah.

But the family was stuck. Fearful of government reprisals and unsure of what was acceptable, no one in Sanaa would rent to a Huthi. Finally a fellow Zaydi scholar, who had made public his opposition to Husayn al-Huthi's political stance, took pity on the family and offered them the use of one of his houses in the city. When Salih heard about Badr al-Din's difficult living situation, he sensed an opportunity. Offer him a house in Sanaa, he ordered an aide, something big enough to accommodate all his women.

It wasn't the first time a government had tried to bribe the Huthi patriarch. In 1979, just as the skirmishes between the Zaydis and Muqbil al-Wadi'i were getting underway in Sadah, Badr al-Din wrote a book ridiculing Saudi Arabia's chief cleric, Abd al-Aziz bin Baz. The blind cleric, who served as a mentor to Osama bin Laden, took the attack personally and ordered a hit on his rival.

Fleeing the Saudi assassins, Badr al-Din left Yemen for a circuitous exile that would last for years before finally ending in Iran. Fresh off its Islamic Revolution, Iranian clerics tried to convert the Yemeni from "fiver" Shi'ism to the "twelver" Shi'ism they practiced. Badr al-Din refused and turned down the ayatollahs' offer of a "beautiful house." He was, as a fellow Zaydi put it, "incorruptible." Badr al-Din told the Iranians that he had his own beliefs. In 2005, Salih's intermediary heard the same message. Badr al-Din didn't want a house. He wanted a meeting with the president and the return of his son's body.

Increasingly upset with the slow progress he was making in Sanaa, Badr al-Din lost his temper. In early March, he spoke out in a rare interview with a Sanaa-based paper. Pressed on the state of negotiations for the prisoners and whether he had met with the president, Huthi cut the question short. "I have not met with him."

"Ever?" the interviewer pushed.

Like his son before him, Badr al-Din never got his meeting. The interview was his final overture, but even before it was published he left Sanaa to return home.

ON MARCH 19, 2005, the same day that Badr al-Din's interview was published, the second Huthi war began. The fighting started just outside Sadah city in the sprawling weapons bazaar of Suq al-Talh, where al-Qaeda had purchased the munitions for the USS *Cole* and MV *Limburg* attacks. Halfway down one of the narrow, garbage-strewn lanes, a knot of tribesmen had gathered in front of a tiny shack, sounding out a few soldiers about trading some weapons. The back-and-forth of impromptu deals was common in the arms market, where soldiers often unloaded government equipment for cash, later claiming it had been lost or stolen. Somehow the deal went bad and the argument turned deadly. One of the soldiers opened fire, killing two of the tribesmen, who also happened to be Huthi supporters. The soldiers fled the market, dragging a wounded colleague with them.

Across the governorate battle lines were hastily redrawn. Many of the rural regions that the government had neglected to pacify in the months after Huthi's death took up arms once more. In early April, President Salih made a halfhearted attempt at deescalation, announcing a new opportunity for the Huthis to turn themselves in. But Salih's brinkmanship, which had served him so well in nearly three decades of rule, was beginning to falter. In Sanaa, people speculated that Salih either wanted war or was losing his touch. But Salih was just as confused as everyone else. He had no idea what the Huthis wanted or how to get them to stop fighting. "They are surrounded but continue to fight like donkeys," he vented to political officers from the US embassy.

Early on April 8, Huthi snipers slipped past military checkpoints and into Sadah. The well-coordinated assault took the army by surprise. Convinced he needed to avoid an urban war, General Ali

Muhsin ordered reinforcements into the heart of Sadah's labyrinthine old city. It took the army two days to clear the maze of narrow alleys and dusty streets. Tired, sweaty young men went from building to building, poking their heads into dark rooms looking for snipers. By April 10, the exhausted soldiers had completed the sweep and were ready to hit back. Troops loyal to Ali Muhsin descended on Badr al-Din's home district outside the city. The elderly cleric wasn't home, having escaped ahead of them to a small village on the Saudi border. It would be the last time anyone outside the Huthis saw the weakened, ill cleric. Unable to exact their revenge on the man, the soldiers destroyed his house. That was the plan. What came next was not.

Watching the walls crumble must have seemed strangely cathartic after the long hours of fear and frustration the exhausted young recruits had spent hunting for snipers in shadowy buildings. When Huthi's house fell, the soldiers turned to his neighbor's house, and then the house after that. Hours of frenzied destruction later, the Yemeni military had created enemies where none had existed before.

The army, the primary source of Salih's power, looked undisciplined and incompetent. Worried about the public perception of its ineptitude, the government hurriedly announced the end of the second war on April 13, 2005. The fighting fell off as both sides regrouped. Small incidents—a grenade attack in Sanaa in late April and an assassination attempt on an army officer in early May—kept the military on its toes. But by mid-May the battles were replaced by a tense stalemate.

Privately, Salih directed intermediaries to negotiate with Abd al-Malik al-Huthi, the youthful successor to his father and older brother. The talks sputtered on throughout the summer with little progress. Just like his father before him, the twenty-five-year-old Abd al-Malik quickly grew frustrated with the process. Offers were made and details discussed, but there was still no meeting with Salih, who seemed determined not to cave in to the family's demand. Without the president's personal involvement, the issue was caught in a strange bureaucratic limbo.

In August, Abd al-Malik went public with the talks, telling the same paper his father had spoken to five months earlier that he was cutting off all negotiations with the government. "I am doing this," he told the paper, "because the government is torturing prisoners in Sadah and Sanaa." The allegations were impossible to prove, but after months of talks and no change, there was nothing to keep him at the negotiating table.

More importantly, the successive Huthi wars created a rift within Yemeni society. Worried that the Huthis wanted to revive the imamate and challenge him for control of the state, Salih overreacted. Instead of targeting only the Huthis, he began a process of marginalizing powerful Zaydi families, who formed the backbone of the state. In time, the fighting that started in the north would grow into a contest between Yemen's powerful Zaydis and its more numerous Sunnis, weakening Salih and his military while encouraging groups like al-Qaeda.

12

Prison Cells

2004–2005

Fifteen months after the PSO threw Ghalib al-Zayadi into solitary confinement, they came for him again. The guards in Sanaa pulled the tribesman who had refused to help Salih capture al-Qaeda fighters out of the hole and marched him back up the dank hallway. He had survived. The months of no visitors, the constant fear, and the cramped uncertainty had taken their toll, but he hadn't succumbed to the darkness.

Zayadi didn't know if Salih had forgiven him or if pressure from his tribe had finally paid off. In either case, he was out of solitary. The guards helped the blinking prisoner shuffle his way across the compound to the main prison.

Built on the outskirts of Sanaa in the 1970s, the PSO prison is dwarfed by the white stone cliffs that mark the city's western edge. At the center of the compound is a long multistory building with a cylindrical body and two angled wings. Inside, the main prison population lived on top of one another, up to twenty men crammed together inside five-by-four-meter cells about the size of a master bedroom. The sweaty cages were perfect incubators for the bacteria and illness that often swept through the building, decimating weakened prisoners who ate only what their families brought them. Poor medical care compounded the problem. Bribes sometimes helped get an outside doctor past the guards, but only Yemen's strong tribal system made any lasting difference. Afraid of what Yemenis call *tha'r*, revenge killing, guards avoided the tribesmen. Instead they focused on the easy prey, unaffiliated Yemenis and foreigners. These were the men who found themselves dragged down to the stained cement rooms deep inside the prison, where they were burned with electric rods and hung by their arms until they passed out.

Thin and disoriented from the months underground, Zayadi struggled to make sense of his new world: hundreds of unwashed men in prison jumpsuits who moved and prayed. After the otherworldly silence of solitary, the sounds overwhelmed him. Life came back to him in pieces; eating with others, praying as a part of a group, all the things he had forgotten during his fifteen months of darkness. Some of the men helped. Over dinner one night, he met Fawaz al-Rabi'i, the dashing young al-Qaeda commander, who introduced him around the prison. The men looked at their incarceration as a trial, something to be endured. "We will be stronger for this," they told him.

RABI'I HADN'T WASTED any time. Shortly after his arrest in Marib in late 2003, he had been transferred to the PSO prison in Sanaa, and it was in his cell that he began the long process of rebuilding what Salih and the US had destroyed. Qasim al-Raymi and Hamza al-Quayti, two friends from Afghanistan who were now fellow prisoners, helped with recruiting. All three men had spent time under bin Laden's tutelage—Quayti had run a guesthouse and Raymi had been an instructor at a training camp—and they saw themselves as al-Qaeda's natural leaders in Yemen. Locked away in Yemen's most notorious prison, the three started over. Small snatches of conversation in the hallway turned into whispers late at night in their cells. They organized clandestine study circles and directed a growing number of recruits, teaching them how to use the Quran as a guide to contemporary politics.

Inside the prison, al-Qaeda's message resonated with the many prisoners who had never been charged. Raymi gave a sermon every Friday in the cell, angrily denouncing the lack of justice and what he called the "Zionist–Crusader alliance." That is who put us here, he breathed as the men crowded around, the Jews and their agents. The accusations seemed to fly out of the twenty-six-year-old's jet-black beard. He put George W. Bush and Ali Abdullah Salih in the same camp. If anything, the Yemeni president was worse, since he claimed to be a Muslim while actually working with the Americans. Who put you here? Raymi asked in a fierce whisper. What crime did you commit?

Raymi talked about Afghanistan and his time on the front lines, always bringing the discussion back to God and the Prophet. Quranic study, he said, led to jihad. Before he left for Afghanistan in the late 1990s, Raymi had memorized all 114 chapters of the Quran, and now he encouraged others to do the same. In private conversations the stocky prisoner probed even further, asking younger prisoners if it was wrong to work for the establishment of God's law. What did you do but try to follow the Quran? If you are guilty, why haven't they charged you? More than mere explanation, Raymi and the rest of al-Qaeda's prison network offered a political program, a way to redress wrongs and shape the future. Even those who didn't agree with their message respected their piety. "I differed with them on some points," Zayadi said. But "they have a burning desire to fight for their religion." It is men like these, he continued, "who will one day establish an Islamic state."

Rabi'i, Raymi, and the others often fasted during the day while they walked confused prisoners through complicated points of theology. When they did eat, they shared their meager meals with the weak and took time to pray with the sick as al-Qaeda's prison network bonded into a community. "I found them to be humble, pious men," Zayadi recalled. "They were reasonable and wise."

Nearly a decade older than both Rabi'i and Raymi, Hamza al-Quayti assumed the role of elder statesman. The balding thirty-four-year-old dealt with the small complaints and daily gripes of prison life. Like most Yemeni members of al-Qaeda, like bin Laden himself, Quayti had been born in Saudi Arabia to a Yemeni father. The kingdom and its conservative theology had formed his early outlook and put him on the path to jihad and Afghanistan. In his cell in Sanaa, Quayti used the anger and despair he found to help shape al-Qaeda's next generation, the fighters who would one day replace him.

A few months after Zayadi arrived from solitary, the al-Qaeda trio reconnected with Nasir al-Wihayshi, another old friend from Afghanistan. Wihayshi, the slight young Yemeni whom bin Laden had made his personal secretary, had changed in the years since 9/11. In Afghanistan he had been bin Laden's shadow, following him everywhere; now he seemed calmer and more self-assured. In his soft-spoken way, Wihayshi told them about the horror of Tora Bora. After his escape in December 2001, he went south, eventually crossing the border into Iran, where he was arrested. Two years in Iranian prisons had given him plenty of time to reflect and plan. The 9/11 attacks had succeeded beyond anything al-Qaeda could have imagined, but since then the organization had made too many mistakes. These have to be corrected, Wihayshi said. And he had a plan.

Wihayshi's four years with bin Laden had been a hands-on tutorial in building a terrorist network. He commended the initial work Rabi'i and the rest had done in the prison. Now it was time to take the next step. The men stayed up nights plotting and planning, dissecting the mistakes of the past in Yemen and Afghanistan and debating how to avoid them in the future.

OUTSIDE THE PRISON, hundreds of miles away in Iraq, resistance to the US invasion was growing. In much the same way Yemenis had gone off to Afghanistan in the 1980s, a new generation of fighters went to Iraq. By early 2004, smuggling networks had sprung up across Yemen to help recruits travel north to Jordan and Syria, where they could sneak across the border into Iraq. Pressed by the US, Salih announced a new law forbidding Yemenis under the age of thirty-five from traveling to Jordan or Syria without prior approval from the government. Soon Salih's men were arresting hundreds of young Yemenis at airports and border crossings. Once again, the Yemeni president had little choice but to throw the suspected fighters in prison. Security services dumped these frustrated, angry young men into increasingly overcrowded cells, unwittingly delivering them into the heart of al-Qaeda's fledgling prison network.

Every day Wihayshi sat with the new prisoners, many of whom were in jail for the first time, laying out a worldview that explained everything from the US invasion of Iraq to their own incarceration. The recruits found solace and comfort in Wihayshi's words. They listened as the al-Qaeda veteran told them they were part of a global war. It's the Americans, Wihayshi confided. They and their Jewish backers are to blame. It was his version of Raymi's Zionist–Crusader alliance, the ultimate cause of all strife in the world. Like Raymi, Wihayshi had memorized the Quran during his time at a religious institute in southern Yemen, and he supported his arguments with carefully selected verses. His recall and casual references to private conversations with Osama bin Laden impressed the younger men. In prisons around the country, other jihadi veterans replicated Wihayshi's network. While Salih focused on the Huthi rebellion in the north and the US poured money and men into Iraq, al-Qaeda grew in the shadows.

THE MEN THAT Wihayshi found needed direction. They were eager but uneducated, dedicated but inexperienced. Uthman al-Sulawi, a twenty-something high school dropout from the central highlands region around Taizz, was one such prisoner. During the late 1990s, he had spent time studying at a religious institute in Sanaa. But after a couple of years, he lost interest and quit his studies. He returned to the institute after September 11, reenergized and full of questions. For the next two years, under the guidance of a local shaykh, Sulawi studied the Quran and Islamic jurisprudence.

One day, a friend at the institute introduced him to a returning fighter from Iraq, who talked to him about the science of jihad. It's more than just fighting, the man explained on walks in the rocky ravines outside Sanaa. It's about a lifestyle of devotion and sacrifice.

Sulawi joined a group of student who were preparing to go to Iraq. They contributed what little money they had to a common fund and spent hours dreaming of the operations they would carry out against US forces. One of the cell members, a man Sulawi considered his mentor, made it to Iraq first and carried out a suicide attack on US forces in Baghdad. Back in Sanaa, the men listened to the reports of his attack with smiles and cries of "Allahu Akbar." But before they could smuggle themselves out of the country, Yemeni forces raided the mosque and arrested the entire cell.

Initially despondent, Sulawi came to see his arrest as the hand of God. Prison brought him into contact with al-Qaeda and taught him to be patient. Wihayshi and Rabi'i re-created with scraps of paper and imagination what bin Laden and Zawahiri had built with books and computers in Afghanistan. This training camp of the mind turned raw products like Sulawi into finished fighters.

TWO CONTINENTS AWAY, on the southeastern tip of Cuba, in America's newest detention facility, another set of al-Qaeda veterans initiated their own prison program. More constrained than the prisoners in Yemen, the detainees at Guantánamo Bay still found a way.

Soon after the prison was completed in early 2002, prisoners such as Jabir al-Fayfi, the balding Saudi from Tora Bora, started landing at the tiny airstrip. Hooded and shackled, with earplugs that blocked all sound, Fayfi had no idea where he was. Rough arms pulled him off the plane, wrenching him forward as he stumbled and tried to keep up. Eventually, the arms jerked him to a stop and twisted him down. For the first time in days there was stillness, no vibrating airplane walls and no pushing guards. Fayfi shifted his legs gently, feeling the rough edges of the concrete through his thin pants. It was his only point of contact with the world.

One by one the guards pulled the prisoners to their feet, walking them to a processing tent for fingerprinting. Inside, one of the men removed Fayfi's hood and earplugs and put paper and pencil on the table in front of him. "Why don't you write a letter," he instructed.

Fayfi, who hadn't been in touch with his family for months, sat down and started writing. He had barely finished the traditional opening—"In the name of God the most merciful, the most compassionate"—when the guard ripped the letter out of his hands. "They only wanted a sample of my handwriting," Fayfi remembered.

The rules at Guantánamo took some getting used to. Prisoners couldn't put their hands outside their blankets, speaking was forbidden, and, most frustrating of all for the detainees, the public call to prayer was banned. Silent, unblinking guards refused every request. They wouldn't engage with the detainees, as the White House had started calling the prisoners. "We only want to know the direction to pray," a few of the men complained in English.

The US wanted the men as confused and disoriented as possible, and high-ranking officials at the Pentagon were passing around copies of a 1970s sociology text called *The Arab Mind*. In sweeping generalizations, the book argues that Arabs only understand power. Anything that was familiar or a marker of normal life, such as the beards most of the men wore, had to be removed until the detainees lost their bearings and, the CIA hoped, their defenses. Bathroom habits and sleep patterns were altered in a shocking new course of what psychologists called "learned helplessness," which was designed to break the detainees' spirits and make them easier to control and interrogate.

The untested treatments, many of them the work of a pair of outside consultants, James Mitchell and Bruce Jensen, who reverse-engineered a US Army training manual on surviving torture, took a heavy toll on the prisoners. Several of the men slowly went crazy, locked in rooms where female interrogators sprayed their naked bodies with ice water or assaulted them with high-pitched sounds, refusing to let them sleep. Others who had arrived at Guantánamo with preexisting mental problems deteriorated further. One Yemeni, who claimed to have traveled to Pakistan in search of cheap medical care for a brain injury before being swept up in the post-September 11 bounty hunt, never seemed to grasp the charges against him, confusing al-Qaeda the terrorist organization with a city of the same name in the Yemeni highlands.

"I am from Urday city in Yemen, not a city in al-Qaeda," he told the military tribunal that had been established to determine if he had been properly classified as an enemy combatant. "My city is very far from the city of al-Qaeda."

The officer walked him through the charges a second time, explaining through a translator that al-Qaeda was an organization, not a city.

"Whether it is a city or an organization, I am not from al-Qaeda," the confused prisoner repeated. "I am from Urday city."

Fayfi struggled in his own way. He sat for Guantánamo's barber, silently furious as the American scraped away at his knotted beard. Across the camp, in specially constructed rooms, he repeated his story for a changing cast of interrogators. Every four months, new ones appeared and he had to start the process over. It wasn't until midway through the first round of questions that the translator even let slip that they were in Cuba. Slowly, as the reality of his incarceration sank in, Fayfi started to change. Prison authorities relaxed the early ban on talking, and hardcore detainees took to lecturing from their bunks. Every evening their voices floated into neighboring cells, soothing the lonely and broken prisoners with familiar Arabic.

Like the al-Qaeda operatives in Yemeni prisons, the ones in Guantánamo explained away their detention as a trial. They were at war with the US, and their own governments back home had abandoned Islamic law and sided with the Americans. Some of the countries, like Saudi Arabia, even sent investigators to help the US evaluate the prisoners—proof, the prison ideologues argued, that this was a war on two fronts: at home and abroad. Absent competing narratives and faced with periodic bouts of what the Bush administration referred to as "enhanced interrogations," detainees clung to the voices down the cellblock, imbibing their harsh, uncompromising message as truth.

"That was the first time I was really affected by *takfiri* ideology," Fayfi recalled of his time in Guantánamo, using the loaded term for excommunicating fellow Muslims. The same idea that bin Laden and Zawahiri had used to justify attacks against Muslim leaders, *takfir* held that any person who failed to work for the establishment of Islamic law could not be considered properly Muslim and as a result—in a world that was divided between good and evil—was a legitimate target.

"In Afghanistan the thinking wasn't really extreme. We were just fighting," Fayfi added. But in Guantánamo, those ideas festered. As Fayfi's beliefs evolved, so did his behavior. One internal report noted that he had become "increasingly non-compliant and hostile to the guard force and staff." Fayfi routinely participated in block disturbances and even threw urine in the face of a guard.

Guantánamo transformed him from a recovering drug addict to a hardened jihadi.

At its peak in 2003, Guantanamo held 680 detainees, including the younger brothers of Fawaz al-Rabi'i and Qasim al-Raymi. A year later, in September 2004, Abd al-Salam al-Hilah, the Yemeni PSO agent the US had kidnapped in Egypt, arrived after two years at various CIA black sites around the world. Guantánamo Bay also held Said al-Shihri, the thirty-one-year-old Saudi who had left home for Afghanistan shortly after September 11. Shihri had been a *takfiri* for years, seeing the world in black and white. Guantánamo only convinced him of the righteousness of his path.

Shihri didn't cause disturbances or lead uprisings, but still officials worried that the quiet man with gray-flecked hair might be a "negative leader." Saudi evaluators put him on a list of the thirty-seven most dangerous prisoners, and the US believed he had been trained to resist interrogation. For years his story had stayed the same, plausible but full of too many nagging unknowns. Unable to crack his cover, officers issued reports every few months recommending him for continued detention. Silent and outwardly compliant, Shihri waited for the day he would get out.

EVEN WHEN THE US did try to work through the domestic court system, it had difficulties. In September 2003, after months of diplomatic wrangling, the US received Muhammad al-Muayyad, the Yemeni cleric the FBI had arrested in Germany months earlier. In order to secure the extradition of Muayyad and his aide from Germany, the US had promised not to seek the death penalty or send the pair to Guantánamo. As Justice Department lawyers prepared for trial in New York, FBI investigators found they had an issue. Their star informant, Muhammad al-Ansi, the man the FBI had paid more than $100,000 for his work in the case, was causing problems. Quietly, the agency started investigating him.

In months of luxurious living, Ansi had raced through the FBI's money, leaving $100 tips at steakhouses and investing in several questionable business schemes. The big blow had been a $68,000 dry cleaning business he bought in upstate New York. When his cash ran out, he simply stopped making payments. He bounced checks across the state and left a slew of angry creditors in his wake. Ansi tried soliciting help from Yemeni expatriates around Brooklyn, but with his record of failure and work with the FBI, few were willing to help. Looking for a fresh start, he moved south to Falls Church, Virginia, just outside Washington DC.

In Virginia, the Yemeni con man started pouring out his troubles to a new set of strangers. He convinced a housekeeping manager at a hotel to lend him $3,800, which he never repaid. "He literally cried about his troubles," she said. "I believed him because he seemed like a successful man who was having just a little bit of bad luck."

Ansi's bad luck soon got worse. In May 2004, the FBI charged him with bank fraud, which meant the government was now prosecuting its star witness. Ansi was the only person who had heard Muayyad brag about handing bin Laden $20 million. If he didn't testify, that evidence would be inadmissible.

Ansi told FBI agents that he desperately needed money. When that didn't work, he said he was sick and needed help paying for his diabetes medicine and emergency surgery. Next he offered to testify in the Muayyad case in exchange for a trip back to Yemen to visit his wife, who he claimed was sick. Each time the agents came back with the same answer: the $100,000 he had already been paid was all the government was going to give him. But Ansi remembered an early conversation with an agent who told him he would be a millionaire, and he wanted the FBI to follow through on that promise.

Around the same time, Ansi's name and role in the Frankfurt sting leaked. When a Yemeni paper picked up the story, his family back in Sanaa started receiving threatening phone calls. For Ansi this was yet one more sign that the FBI had failed to live up to its original agreement. Agents had failed to protect his identity, they wouldn't give him permanent residency in the US, and they still refused to give him any more money. "It is my big mistake that I have cooperated with the FBI," he told outsiders. "I am not crazy to destroy my life and my family's life to get $100,000."

In the fall of 2004, in debt and desperate, Ansi turned to the *Washington Post* for help. He thought the prospect of a newspaper article about his plight might pressure the FBI into providing more cash. When this latest plan failed, Ansi settled on an even more public spectacle. Early on November 15, Ansi sat down in his rented Virginia apartment and wrote a pair of rambling, distraught letters. The first he addressed to Robert Fuller, his handler at the FBI, who had testified years earlier that Ansi was a "stellar" informant.

"Today Monday 11/15/04, I will **SUICIDE** myself," the frustrated Yemeni wrote in stilted English, underling the bolded, all-caps word with two lines. "I will **BURN** myself at unexpected place and be sure I will call you before 15 minutes," he continued, later penciling in the phrase "in NY" to the sentence in an apparent attempt to throw the FBI off his trail. Ansi couldn't resist a final shot at the man he had come to blame for all his troubles. "Please be sure to send my body to my family in Yemen along with my personal effects (lugages are packed) in my apartment. ((I hope you will be happy))."

The second letter he addressed to Caryle Murphy, one of the reporters he had cooperated with at the *Post*, repeating the threats of suicide and warning her that he would call her ten minutes before his planned immolation. Ansi faxed Fuller's letter to the FBI office in New York and copies of both to the *Washington Post*. Later that day, Ansi followed up his fax with a phone call to the *Post*, repeating his threat to burn his body at an unexpected place. He called the newspaper two more times, and the final time, just after 2 p.m., he told reporters that he had already doused himself with gasoline and would "be setting himself on fire in two minutes, not ten, and it would take place near the White House."

After he hung up the phone, Ansi walked up to the White House's northwest guardhouse on Pennsylvania Avenue and asked one of the security officers to deliver a personal note to President Bush. When the officer refused, Ansi retreated 15 feet, took a lighter out of his pocket, and lit a corner of his jacket on fire. Secret Service officers responded immediately, wrestling him to the ground and extinguishing the flames before he burned to death.

Doctors later found that Ansi had burns on 30 percent of his body, and while he recuperated under armed guard his role as a confidential informant came under scrutiny in lengthy articles by the *New York Times* and the *Washington Post.* Journalists at both newspapers questioned how a suicidal and clearly unstable figure had managed to convince the FBI, on seemingly little evidence, to go after Muhammad al-Muayyad.

ON JANUARY 28, 2005, barely two months after Ansi's attempted suicide, the trial of Muayyad and his assistant got underway in a Brooklyn courtroom. With Ansi still in the hospital, the US government prosecutors elected not to call him as a witness. His absence meant that much of the case for Muayyad being a member of al-Qaeda had to be discarded. Instead, they focused on the Yemeni cleric's connections to Hamas, which was designated a terrorist organization under US law, and decided to build much of their case around the video of the mass wedding that Ansi had shot back in September 2002. The tape clearly showed the Hamas official announcing a suicide attack in Israel, and the prosecution planned to argue that Muayyad's role as an organizer of the wedding meant he would have had foreknowledge of the bombing. The judge ruled that he would allow the tape, but only if Ansi took the stand. Worried about their witness's credibility after his suicide attempt, the government declined and instead focused on the victims of the suicide attack in Israel.

Gideon Black, a Scottish law student and survivor of the bombing, talked about his younger cousin, who died in the explosion. In emotional and at times tearful testimony, the twenty-one-year-old re-created the day, describing for jurors the moment of detonation. There was "glass, metal, and shrapnel flying in all directions particularly towards the back of the bus." After the explosion, he continued, "there was an eerie silence for a few moments and then sirens, screaming, panic."

Four weeks into the trial, after the prosecution rested, Muayyad's court-appointed lawyers gambled and called Ansi to the stand as a hostile witness. They wanted to paint the Yemeni informant as a deranged man with a grudge. The risky strategy meant that the government could now charge Muayyad with being a member of al-Qaeda, and the wedding video would get a full airing on a big-screen television that was wheeled into the courtroom. On paper Ansi might have been an unbalanced con man, but in person he could still captivate. And in the course of his testimony he displayed the same charm and theatrics he had used his entire life.

Ansi alleged that as a "dangerous man," Muayyad always traveled with an armed guard. Apparently unaware that armed guards customarily surround political and religious figures in Yemen, one of the defense attorneys, Howard Jacobs, seized on the accusation. "If they were real," he asked Ansi, "where were those guards on the wedding tape?" As the jury watched, Ansi asked Jacobs to rewind the wedding tape and play it a second time.

"Stop," he cried, pointing at the screen. There, in the fuzzy still frame, stood a man with a machine gun.

On March 10, after five days of deliberation, the jury returned guilty verdicts for both men. It acquitted them of supporting al-Qaeda, which the prosecution had never been able to prove, but convicted them of material support for Hamas. The judge sentenced Muayyad to seventy-five years in the Supermax prison in Florence, Colorado, and fined him $1.25 million.

IN YEMEN, PEOPLE followed the Muayyad case as it moved toward its conclusion. Few could understand how a man they knew as the "father of orphans" could even be tried in a US court for aiding Hamas. Muayyad was a Yemeni who had never traveled to the US prior to his extradition, and fundraising for Hamas was legal and even encouraged in Yemen. In the PSO prison, Wihayshi and the rest of al-Qaeda's leadership lectured on the case, pointing to it as one more example of US aggression. It shows their "great arrogance," the al-Qaeda commander told his fellow prisoners, advising them to pray for the shaykh's release.

Early that spring, just as Muayyad's case was coming to its conclusion in Brooklyn, one of the prisoners had an idea. Hizam Mujali, the al-Qaeda operative who had been part of the assault on the Hunt Oil helicopter three years earlier, had heard about a daring attempt by prisoners in Iraq to tunnel out of the US-run prison at Abu Ghraib. The attempt had been discovered, but the twenty-six-year-old liked their approach. "Why can't we do that here," he asked fellow prisoners.

"Impossible," one of them replied. "That's not a way of out here."

The discussion ended, but over the next few days several of the men reported dreams about a tunnel full of crawling prisoners. Due to overcrowding brought on by the Iraq war roundups, the PSO had moved several al-Qaeda suspects out of the main prison building and into an annex near the southern wall. One of their bathrooms even looked out onto the street and a neighboring mosque. That mosque was the goal, the men decided. They estimated they would have to dig about 50 yards to reach it. Using metal spoons their families had included with their food, the men pried up the floor tiles and began to dig.

Just as they were getting started, a Yemeni court announced that it would uphold the death sentence of Ali al-Sawani, an Islamist who had been convicted of murdering a local Socialist politician in late 2002. None of them knew Sawani personally, but they all applauded his actions and were outraged by the court's decision. A trio of prisoners led by Qasim al-Raymi, the firebrand preacher who had been an instructor at one of bin Laden's camps in Afghanistan, asked to see the prison director.

"You've already sacrificed enough to the Crusaders," Raymi railed at the director in defense of the condemned man. "Men like Abu Ali al-Harithi," he screamed. "It's enough. They don't need more of our sons."

Shaking with fury as he shouted, Raymi argued that Yemen shouldn't kill Sawani just to please its foreign masters. "But if you do," Raymi threatened, "then we will respond in kind."

When Ghalib al-Qamish, the leathery head of the PSO who had once worked with Ali Soufan, heard about Raymi's threats, he ordered the three men shackled and thrown into solitary. Then he took six more prisoners from Raymi's cell, including Wihayshi and Fawaz al-Rabi'i, and gave them the same punishment—decapitating the group's leadership and delaying the escape attempt.

The whole thing was a mistake, Wihayshi later wrote. "We never should have gotten involved in the Sawani affair." It would be another nine months before al-Qaeda could try again.

13

Policy Shift

2005

On July 17, 2005, President Ali Abdullah Salih invited dignitaries to the presidential palace in Sanaa for a celebration. Twenty-seven years earlier, following the brutal assassinations of his two immediate predecessors, Salih had been sworn in as president. The yearly gathering often served as Salih's state of the union address, which he typically delivered in the coarse, clipped barracks Arabic he had acquired as a soldier. As tribal shaykhs in long robes mixed with Western ambassadors in expensive suits in the polished reception room, Salih discreetly stepped onto the raised platform aides had placed behind the podium and began to speak.

He talked about the "peaceful transfer of power" that led to his selection as president, before discussing the challenges the state had overcome during the past three decades. Pausing periodically to consult his notes, Salih went down the list: tribal violence and revenge killings had given way to a civil war and threats to the union, but through it all the state endured. None of these successes, he reiterated, would have been possible without the help of patriotic Yemenis both in his ruling party and in the opposition. Then, as his speech built toward its conclusion, Salih made a stunning announcement: "I am not, nor will I put myself forward as, a candidate in the upcoming presidential elections." Staring straight into the cameras, Salih announced his retirement. He would not seek reelection in 2006. "The homeland wants new blood," he said.

Throughout his speech, Salih had used the second person plural pronoun, speaking of common struggles and shared victories, but now he abruptly switched to the first person singular. Looking out across a sea of shocked faces, Salih called on all parties to search within their ranks for qualified replacements. "The time has come for another peaceful transition of power."

WITHIN DAYS OF Salih's announcement, just as Yemenis were beginning to talk about a true democracy and real choices, the speech was unmasked as political theater. Salih's pledge had been designed to deflect criticism prior to an unpopular decision to ease government subsidies on diesel and gas.

Over the previous decade, Salih had balked at lifting the subsidies on three separate occasions, telling advisers from the World Bank and the International Monetary Fund that the move would spark riots. But with Yemen's economy struggling to stay solvent after two rounds of war against the Huthis in the north, the donors were in agreement: the subsidies had to go. Salih listened to proposals from international organizations, but he knew their advice to eliminate them in a gradual, transparent process would be a political disaster. Key allies would turn on him as soon as the price of food, which relied on cheap diesel and gas for transport to market, spiked. Lifting the subsidies would affect every segment of Yemen's economy.

Late in the evening on July 19, two days after Salih's speech, state television announced that as of midnight all fuel subsidies would be removed. Within hours, people were hoarding fuel as prices doubled and then tripled across the country. The next morning, the riots Salih had predicted began, as armed gangs marched through the streets chanting and looting. By promising not to seek reelection, Salih had shifted the blame for the decision onto his aging prime minister, Abd al-Qadir Bajammal, who was little more than a figurehead. While the crowds attacked banks and international institutions, which they held partially to blame, Salih secretly negotiated what he would later term a "compromise" solution. He knew any lifting of subsidies, no matter how slight, would spark riots, and so he directed government officials to announce a complete removal that he could later scale back to the percentage that the international donors had originally requested. After three days of rioting that left nearly fifty dead across the country, Salih did just that, telling the public that he had commanded the government to restore a partial subsidy while simultaneously slashing the sales tax in half and increasing the salaries of government employees by 10 percent. Salih, state media declared, was the nation's savior. The script was familiar to most Yemenis. In 1995, the last time the government had significantly reduced fuel subsidies, Salih had used a similar move. That was just how he played politics: solving one crisis by creating another.

Watching Salih's political theater play out against a backdrop of riots and burning cars, US officials at the embassy in Sanaa doubted the president had ever been serious about his pledge not to run for reelection. Every year the State Department gamed out potential successors to Salih, and every year it came up empty. That might be precisely the point, one diplomatic cable speculated. When it came to the presidency, Salih was "the only game in town." Neither of Yemen's two most powerful players—Shaykh Abdullah al-Ahmar or General Ali Muhsin al-Ahmar—had any desire for the office. Both men were older than Salih and they liked their roles as kingmakers.

When Salih refused to recant on his pledge after the riots, a handful of Yemenis chose to act as if he had been serious about stepping down and declared themselves candidates for the presidency. Almost immediately, the president's network of supporters sprang into action. One candidate, Nasir Sabr, a member of Salih's own party, withdrew his name after a hand grenade was thrown at his car while he was meeting with officials at the US embassy. Newspapers reported that another candidate, who lived in Cairo and had been involved in a coup attempt years earlier, would be arrested if he returned to Yemen. Other exiles were similarly handicapped. One of them, Ahmad Numan, the brother of Yemen's deputy foreign minister, announced his candidacy from Europe. "Are you going to leave to manage his campaign," Salih joked with his deputy. Numan took the hint, and his brother's campaign disappeared overnight. The message was clear: if Salih wasn't running, neither was anyone else.

AFTER SALIH'S OVAL Office meeting with President Bush in November 2001, the US had poured millions of dollars in money and military equipment into Yemen. Most of it benefited Salih's relatives and allies in the military, greasing the system of patronage that kept his regime intact. A steady trickle of US military advisers rotated through the training sites that American taxpayer dollars built just outside Sanaa. Heavily bearded men in dark sunglasses, identified only by first names, worked with Salih's eldest son, Ahmad, who commanded the country's Republican Guards as well as Yemen's Special Forces. Following one training session, Ahmad pulled aside the American officer and said he wanted to be qualified as a Navy SEAL.

"Do you swim?" the man asked.

"No, but you could teach me," Ahmad said.

"Well, we'll see," the American responded evasively. Privately, he worried that Salih's heir apparent had been watching too many action movies. Hopefully, he told his supervisors, the request was just one of Ahmad's passing whims.

Other trainers worked with the counterterrorism unit in the

Central Security Forces, under the command of Yahya Salih, the president's nephew. There were also new scanners and computers for border control units at airports in Sanaa and Aden. The US even built Salih a Coast Guard from scratch, supplying everything from the boats and the funding to the training and the computers.

When President Bush won reelection in 2004, Salih informed the new US ambassador to Sanaa, Thomas Krajeski, that he wanted to be among the first foreign leaders to visit Washington and personally offer his congratulations. There are things that can only be discussed face-to-face, Salih added as an incentive.

The US held off. With al-Qaeda seemingly in check, there was none of the urgency there had been three years earlier. It isn't the right time for a visit, Krajeski wrote from Sanaa.

TALL, WITH A salt-and-pepper beard, Krajeski was a career foreign service officer. Born in Groveland, Massachusetts, just off the Merrimack River forty-five minutes north of Boston, Krajeski had stayed close to home for college, attending the University of Massachusetts at Amherst. Originally a Russian specialist, he retooled himself as an Arabist when the Cold War ended. Prior to arriving in Sanaa, Krajeski had spent two years in Iraq as a political adviser to Paul Bremer. From the Green Zone in Baghdad, he watched firsthand as the country descended into chaos and sectarian warfare. Temperamentally at odds with the more cerebral and reserved Hull, who had stayed on to help with the transition, Krajeski tried to overcome the gap in their personalities by asking the older man for guidance. He had never served anywhere like Yemen. Eastern Europe and the city-states of the Persian Gulf were poor tutorials for the country's labyrinthine tribal system. Even Iraq and its messy war seemed somehow less complicated than the swarm of names and power centers coming at him now.

Hull gave him a crash course in Sanaa politics, introducing him around the capital and urging him to make the economy and economic reform his top priority. Shortly before he left the country, Hull summed up the days of conversation with a final piece of advice: "Qualify Yemen for the Millennium Challenge." A bilateral foreign aid agency which the Bush administration had founded in 2004, the Millennium Challenge Corporation, known to diplomats by its acronym MCC, was guided by the idea that countries would develop more effectively if the US tied aid to good governance and economic freedom.

Krajeski spent much of his first year following Hull's advice, but almost as soon as he got Yemen provisionally qualified in early 2005, its performance in the three areas of assessment—ruling justly, investing in people, and economic freedom—started to slip. Salih wanted the money, not the reforms. Throughout the spring, Krajeski warned Salih that he needed to deliver. The ambassador made it clear that international donors wouldn't be satisfied with words; they needed action. But while Salih nodded his understanding in meetings, worrying reports continued to filter into the embassy.

In late May, a high-placed Yemeni informant told US officials that Salih was more greedy and paranoid than ever, describing him as "unrealistically and stupidly confident." Two weeks later, Krajeski tested the informant's conclusions in a private conversation with Salih, congratulating him on the decision to develop the port at Aden with international investment. "Dubai Ports International is an excellent and experienced company with an international reputation," Krajeski offered. "It is the right choice to develop the huge potential of Aden Port and the Aden Free Zone."

"I picked them myself," the president smiled.

Towering more than a foot above the Yemeni president, Krajeski listened to Salih's self-congratulatory explanation. The US liked the selection of Dubai Ports, but it was more interested in how the decision had been made. Krajeski tempered his criticism in an internal cable, but everything, he concluded, "is still ultimately decided according to the president's whims."

IN NOVEMBER 2005, nearly one year after Salih's initial request, the US finally agreed to a state visit. For months that summer, in cables between its embassy in Sanaa and headquarters in DC, the State Department had tried to figure out how best to deal with the Yemeni president. He's an enigma, analysts at the State's Bureau of Intelligence and Research admitted as they struggled to write his profile. As with the Egyptian jihadis of the 1990s, the Americans found that Salih blew hot and cold. He was engaging and conciliatory in private but all too often combative in public. Which was the real Salih? Was there a real Salih? Paid informants with inside access to the president continued to peddle stories of Salih joking about his ability to pull the wool over the eyes of the Americans.

Krajeski's top aide, Deputy Chief of Mission Nabeel Khoury, a native Arabic speaker, suggested the US act tough when Salih got to Washington. His "feet must be held to the fire on what has thus far been mere lip service," he wrote. "MCC membership serves as both a carrot and stick in this regard." It is a delicate balance, Khoury continued. "Salih must be reassured of the tangible benefits from his partnership with the US, but must not be allowed to leave Washington thinking that he can maintain US friendship with a business as usual approach."

Something needed to change; that much, at least, was clear. Krajeski's private warnings to the Yemeni president hadn't done any good. The US ambassador repeated them and Salih nodded, but there never seemed to be any action. Corruption had spiraled out of control as military officers bought diesel at the subsidized rate before smuggling it out of the country to sell at a premium. Individuals in the National Security Bureau, the new intelligence agency the US had pushed for in 2002, hoping that it would replace the jihadi-riddled PSO, were just as deeply involved in diesel smuggling as their counterparts in the PSO. So too were Yahya Salih and his officers in the Central Security Forces, which also received US funding and training.

Corruption had been a problem in Yemen for decades, as Salih's family and inner circle seized land across the country for their various business interests. But the old generation of careful crooks, the men who had come up with Salih, had given way to spoiled youngsters who believed they were entitled to whatever they took. Yahya Salih had large commercial farms in the south and industries spread throughout the country, while his three brothers pocketed millions from black-market diesel. Other family members made out even better, raking in kickbacks and sweetheart contracts from foreign investors. Saudi Arabia, Yemen's biggest donor, warned the US against putting cash into the country, saying it usually ended up in Swiss bank accounts.

In early October, a month before Salih's trip to the US, Krajeski went public with his criticisms and told an opposition newspaper that democratic reform in Yemen had "stopped." If the rookie ambassador was looking for a response, he didn't have long to wait. The next day, Yemen's stable of official columnists and journalists tore into him in newspapers and on state television, warning Krajeski against interfering in Yemen's internal affairs. The concentrated effort and near unanimous message suggested a directive from the top. The US, it seemed, finally had Salih's attention. Still, Krajeski hadn't expected such a sharp reaction. Dutifully he backtracked, claiming that his true sentiments had been lost in translation. He had given the interview in English, he explained, and someone had translated it into Arabic.

Four days later, as embassy staffers continued to slog their way through columns and articles condemning Krajeski's remarks, the ambassador asked the English-language *Yemen Observer* if he could try again. Published by Faris Sanabani, a slick, young Westernized Yemeni who doubled as Salih's press secretary and spokesman, the *Yemen Observer* was firmly in Salih's camp. In the interview, Krajeski explained that he had meant to say that democracy in Yemen had "stalled" or "slowed down," which had been translated as "stopped." That was it, the ambassador said: a simple mistake.

Salih never quite got Krajeski's message. For all his signaling and attempts at subtlety, Krajeski apparently failed to communicate the shift in US policy to the man who mattered most. When Salih left for Washington in early November, he expected to be rewarded as a close and indispensable ally. After all, in the four years since his first visit with Bush, he had done everything the US wanted. The list of names the CIA had given him had all been eliminated. Harithi was dead. Ahdal and Rabi'i were in jail, and there hadn't been an al-Qaeda attack since the MV *Limburg* bombing three years earlier. Every time a security threat popped up, he dealt with it. Earlier in 2005, when a blustery cell of militants emerged, threatening the US embassy in Sanaa and forcing it to shut down briefly, Salih's troops had arrested the men responsible within days. "I respond to you immediately when you need something," Salih told the embassy.

The calculating Yemeni president had several ideas as to how Bush could repay him for his vigilance and quick action. In Salih's mind, the Washington trip was a shopping spree, and he landed in DC with a wish list. Another war against the Huthis—the third—was just getting underway in Sadah, and the president needed to replenish his armory. He had helped the US with al-Qaeda and now he wanted help with his own terrorists.

On the first day of his three-day trip, Salih got a taste of just how much things had changed. Secretary of State Condoleezza Rice informed him that Yemen was being suspended from the Millennium Challenge Corporation. The cut would cost Yemen $20 million in aid. Ill prepared for the meeting, the Yemeni president could only sputter in frustration as Rice "rapped him over the knuckles" on corruption and lack of reform. If nothing changed,

Rice continued, the US would not view Salih as a legitimate candidate in the 2006 presidential election. Krajeski had been saying the same thing for months, but Salih had never quite believed the US was serious. Seemingly overnight, the US had changed its rationale for foreign aid. Al-Qaeda, the US explained, was yesterday's problem.

The next day, Salih had a meeting at World Bank headquarters, just a couple of blocks from the White House on Pennsylvania Avenue. Headed by Paul Wolfowitz, the same person who had deliberately leaked the details of the drone strike that killed Harithi in 2002, Salih didn't expect much. World Bank officials wasted little time. Yemen, they said, had regressed significantly on key indicators. As a result, the World Bank would be slashing aid to the country from $420 million to $280 million. Just like Rice, they cited widespread government corruption as the deciding factor.

Two days later, on the flight home, Salih finally lost it, screaming at aides and firing his entire team of economic advisers within minutes of takeoff. The group of young, Western-educated English speakers couldn't wait to get back to Sanaa and away from their fuming boss. "It was horrible," one later recalled. "The longest plane ride of my entire life."

Weeks later, when Salih had calmed down, he rehired most of them. "Do you really think that if Freedom House and the rest changed our ratings, it would make any difference?" he asked one of the young men, who, in the messy world of family politics, was related to Salih's newest wife.

"Of course," the nervous aide responded. "That was the reason they cut it in the first place."

Salih smiled and shook his head. "The Americans give money to who they want when they want."

The trip was a turning point in US–Yemeni relations. The money that had been flowing into the country since September 11 started to dry up. By the beginning of 2006—as US security aid dipped to a new low of $4.6 million—the US decided that al-Qaeda in Yemen was no longer a threat and it could put its money and resources elsewhere. Without al-Qaeda, Yemen was just one more poor country.

ONE MONTH AFTER Salih's visit to the US, Hamud al-Hitar, the judge who ran Yemen's rehabilitation program, followed him to Washington. Over the past year, the US government had silently dropped much of its opposition to his program and had even hosted Hitar for a Ramadan meal at the embassy in Sanaa. Like officials in Yemen, the US realized that it could no longer keep hundreds of suspects indefinitely detained. For Salih, it had been tribal pressure and domestic concerns; for the Bush administration, it was Guantánamo Bay and the court system. Several junior officials at the State Department thought Hitar's rehab program offered a potential solution for some of the Yemeni detainees in Guantánamo. Hitar had already talked to European diplomats in Paris and London, but this was his first trip to the US.

On December 10, a few days into his trip, *al-Quds al-Arabi*, a pan-Arab paper published in London, ran a front-page story alleging that at least three of Hitar's Yemeni graduates had carried out suicide attacks against US forces in Iraq. Hitar read the article in his Washington hotel room with a sense of disbelief; someone was trying to sabotage him.

That night he called Khaled al-Hammadi, the Yemeni journalist who wrote the story. "You know what I am trying to do here," Hitar demanded. "How could you do this to me?"

Hammadi shrugged into the phone. He was doing his job, reporting what his sources gave him. But both men knew the program was dead.

"There were two camps in the ministry at that time," Hitar recalled later. "One supported my work and one did not."

Hitar's detractors in the Ministry of the Interior had tried a similar tactic months earlier, leaking a similar story of released prisoners fighting in Iraq to the Associated Press. When that didn't work, Hitar's enemies waited for his arrival in the US and the eve of his big meeting. US officials kept the meeting, but they could never recommend Hitar's program if prisoners he released had gone on to kill US soldiers in Iraq.

Others in the Bush administration, who had always been wary of Hitar and his claims, used the article as a final piece of leverage and pressured Salih to end the program. By the time Hitar returned to Yemen, rehab was over.

III

THE NEXT GENERATION

14

The Great Escape

2006

The day after Hitar's rehabilitation program died on the front page of the newspaper, al-Qaeda's prison network got a second chance. Nasir al-Wihayshi and the rest of the leaders had served their time in solitary and were now back in the two-room communal cell. That night after prayers, the men revived their original plan to tunnel to the mosque they could see from their window in the annex along the prison's southern wall. As the men talked that evening, Fawaz al-Rabi'i, the charismatic cell leader whom bin Laden had dispatched back to Yemen prior to 9/11 and who was now entering his second year in prison, moved into the interior room and started prying up tiles. It was December 11, 2005.

Falling back on security precautions many of the men had learned at the camps in Afghanistan, they pledged to keep a low profile. No one outside of the cell could know about the plan. After they pulled up the floor tiles, the men found a layer of dirt that they scraped at with the spoons and metal plates they had bent into modified hand shovels. The cell's interior door blocked the view of the guards in the hallway while in the larger, outer room the prisoners who weren't digging took turns reciting the Quran in an effort to mask the sounds from inside the cell. "We tried to be as loud as possible," Wihayshi said.

Digging started every morning after the dawn call to prayer and ended only when the prisoners heard the fifth and final call of the day crackle through the loudspeakers. Initially it was slow going. After a few inches of dirt the men hit a layer of poorly mixed concrete. Sharpening their plates on the uprooted floor tiles, the men fashioned them into crude picks that they used to chip through the concrete. In three weeks of work, they progressed only a foot. After they made it through the concrete, they were back up against their most persistent problem: what to do with the dirt? At one point, some of the prisoners tried pouring it down the drain, but the cheap pipes clogged and flooded the bathroom just off the cell. One of the men then suggested using the squat toilets. Little more than a ceramic basin with footrests around a hole in the ground, squat toilets are common in Yemen; the man thought they could mix the dirt with water and pour it down the hole. That worked for a while, but in time the toilet backed up as well. Next they tried hiding the dirt under their prison-issue mattresses that sat on the floor along the walls. Eventually the men started packing the dirt in the cheap plastic bags that often came with their food and storing it in the bathroom, out of sight of the passing guards.

In early January 2006, as Yemen continued to struggle with prison overcrowding, the PSO transferred five more inmates into the cell. There were now twenty-three men in two tiny rooms. One of the new men, Jamal al-Badawi, had been involved in the USS *Cole* attack and had escaped from a PSO prison in Aden in 2003. In his mid-forties, Badawi had hard amber eyes and a full beard that was just beginning to gray. Stoic and given to quiet reflection, he rarely smiled, preferring to hide a row of crooked and yellowing teeth. Badawi's time in prison had sapped his desire for jihad and he wanted no part of Wihayshi's plan. The last time he escaped, a Yemen judge had ordered his execution by firing squad. An appeals court eventually overturned the death sentence, but Badawi had no desire to risk a second conviction. Wihayshi sat with the older man, reminding him of the al-Qaeda oath many of the men had taken. They had all been part of the same struggle, bin Laden's former secretary explained; surely Badawi would not abandon his friends when they needed him most. Their conversation lasted for hours, and when it ended Badawi had agreed to help.

Besides the spoons, plates, and a couple of deflated soccer balls cut in half to move the dirt, the prisoners didn't have much equipment. Wires from a cannibalized fan powered an improvised miner's light, while a water jug was pressed into service as a bucket and strips of braided clothes functioned as a makeshift rope. Later, one of them found a metal rod buried in the dirt beneath the prison. One day, when the men had dug most of the 50 yards, a soldier entered their cell with orders to fix a broken door. Worried that the soldier would see the dirt that had spilled out of the inner room and was visible below the door separating the two rooms, one of the prisoners started an argument in an attempt to distract the guard. The soldier finished his measurements and left without ever opening the door. "It was like there was a veil over his eyes so that he couldn't see the dirt," Wihayshi recalled.

At the beginning of February 2006, they caught another break. Prison officials had ordered another round of repairs to their cell and the men worried that this time they would not be able to hide the dirt. Convinced they had to escape before the repairmen started their work on Saturday, the first day of the Yemeni work week, Qasim al-Raymi led a four-man team down the narrow tunnel on Thursday evening for a final push. The men scraped away the last few inches of dirt beneath the mosque floor. Raymi jammed the metal rod against the floor tiles as hard as he could. The sharp crack of the metal hitting tile resounded in the quiet night air, echoing through the empty mosque and back over the prison wall 15 yards away. Startled by the sound, one of the guards in the watchtower fired his gun, later telling his supervisor that he had heard a grenade explode. In the tunnel the prisoners froze, waiting for a second shot. The minutes crept by as the men received whispered updates from the prisoners back in the cell above. When it became clear that no one was coming to investigate, Raymi cautiously went back to work. Hours later, aching and sore from their efforts with the metal rod, the four men punched through the final tile and into the mosque. Fresh air rushed into the hole as the men smiled and whispered "Allahu Akbar" in one another's ears.

The prisoners had hoped to come up in the mosque's mortuary, but as they poked their heads through the broken tiles they realized they were in the women's bathroom, the least-used room in the mosque. Satisfied that the building was deserted, the four crawled back to the cell to share the good news.

Already after midnight, the men decided to wait for dawn prayers to make their escape. This way the prisoners could use the early morning worshippers at the mosque as cover for their escape. Plus, it would allow them to say their first prayers as free men in the shadow of the prison where they had been held for so long. Shortly after 3 a.m., the prisoners dipped into the hole one final time.

Inside the women's bathroom in the mosque, the men knocked the dust off their clothes and hugged one another in silence as they waited for the call to prayer. In order not to arouse suspicion, they decided to perform their prayers in the walled-off room reserved for women, which was rarely occupied. When prayers finished around 5:30 that morning, the men walked out the front door in twos and threes, mixing with the rest of the sleepy worshippers in the predawn shadows. Shuffling away from the mosque, they watched as the neighborhood men peeled off down side streets and alleyways for a couple more hours of sleep. It was Friday morning, February 3, 2006, and al-Qaeda was back.

THE US QUICKLY concluded that the twenty-three prisoners must have had inside help. The odds of them digging 50 yards blind from a prison cell to the women's bathroom of a neighboring mosque were simply too great. The prison, after all, was run by the PSO, the same organization that had produced Abd al-Salam al-Hilah, the Guantánamo Bay detainee who had once tipped bin Laden and Zawahiri off to a traitor within their ranks. Analysts at the CIA and FBI could only guess at the extent of the conspiracy. We don't know "how many people were involved," one official admitted. Some in Washington suggested that the prison break might be Salih's response to the aid cuts four months earlier. Others speculated that sympathetic guards had simply ignored evidence of digging.

Two of the escapees, Jamal al-Badawi and Jabir al-Banna, were on the FBI's most wanted list, Badawi for his role in the USS *Cole* attack, and Banna for his involvement in the 2002 Lackawanna Six case in Buffalo, New York, in which six Yemeni–Americans had been charged with providing material support to al-Qaeda based on a trip they took to Afghanistan in the summer of 2001. Salih tried to blunt the criticism, pledging a $25,000 reward for each suspect. But the Yemeni president had other things to contend with. In the north, Yemen's third war against the Huthis was going poorly. Nothing Salih's generals tried—blockades, a troop surge, even a scorched earth campaign—made any difference. Yemen was bogged down in its own costly insurgency. Salih also had reelection to think about. Even though he reiterated his pledge not to run every few weeks, almost no one in Yemen believed him. Two months earlier, at his party's nominating conference in Aden, Salih had hinted that he might actually be persuaded to stand for another term—but only if the "young blood" couldn't be found in time, he qualified.

In late February, weeks after the prison break, Salih announced that secret back-channel talks with the Huthis had produced a breakthrough. As part of the deal, Salih replaced the governor of Sadah with a more neutral figure, and released 500 Huthi prisoners. In an interview that same month, Salih announced that he was in contact with some of the prisoners and that they would be back in custody soon. Privately, Salih reached out to shaykhs across the country, informing them that he would be willing to cut a deal with the fugitives. Most of the men could not be charged with a crime, and if they agreed not to carry out any attacks in Yemen, Salih promised he would pardon them.

NORTH OF THE border in Saudi Arabia, the kingdom was cleaning up the remnants of its own al-Qaeda problem. In January 2002, shortly after his escape from Tora Bora, bin Laden had sent dozens of Saudi fighters back to the kingdom. After losing hundreds of men to the bounty hunt in Pakistan, he wanted to preserve enough of a following to regroup and plan more attacks. The exhausted jihadis had made their way home as best they could that winter, smuggling themselves through Pakistan and Iran as they trickled back into Saudi Arabia. Almost as soon as his men were in place, bin Laden had started pressing them to carry out attacks. Local cell leaders countered that they needed more time. Worried that his men were being cautious when they needed to be bold, bin Laden had overruled his lieutenants on the ground and ordered them to strike.

On May 12, 2003, nearly two months after the US invasion of Iraq, the Saudi branch carried out its first attack. Shortly after 11 p.m. that evening, four vehicles carrying explosives and men slipped through the streets of the Saudi capital of Riyadh. Despite their concerns about the lack of preparation time, the men had planned well. In near-simultaneous bombings, they hit three housing compounds in eastern Riyadh that catered to Westerners. At two of the compounds, they fought their way past the outer guards and exploded their car bombs on quiet residential roads inside. The blasts sheared giant slabs of concrete off nearby apartment buildings, and when the survivors stumbled out into the street, the al-Qaeda gunmen opened fire. The synchronized attacks left more than thirty people dead, including nine Americans. Hundreds more were wounded in the carnage that would take weeks to sift through.

In a speech the following day at the Indiana State Fairgrounds, President George W. Bush called the attack "ruthless murder," and Saudi Arabia vowed to crack down on those responsible. Prince Nayif, the seventy-year-old Minister of the Interior who had once discounted bin Laden's role in the 9/11 attacks, directed his son and deputy, Muhammad bin Nayif, to take the lead in investigating the bombings. Throughout the summer, bin Nayif's troops arrested dozens of suspects and killed Yusuf al-Uyayri, bin Laden's top commander in the country. But on November 8, al-Qaeda struck again.

Disguised as police officers, al-Qaeda operatives attacked the al-Muhaya housing compound on the western edge of Riyadh, less than half a mile from one of Nayif's private homes. The massive car bomb shook the windows of the prince's palace. But without Uyayri to guide them, al-Qaeda had badly miscalculated. Instead of Americans and other Westerners, the compound housed mostly foreign Arabs who worked in the kingdom. Among the seventeen dead were five Muslim children, and the pictures of those corpses, which were shown on television and published in newspapers, shocked conservative Saudi society. For the first time, clerics in the kingdom's mosques delivered sermons condemning al-Qaeda and its bloody ways. The organization had become a killing machine that struck wildly in all directions. "Before, people could find excuses," one Saudi professor told a Western reporter in the days after the attack. "It is getting so irrational that you cannot explain it, you cannot defend it, you cannot understand it."

After the Muhaya bombing, domestic support for the organization evaporated as members complained that even their own families had turned against them. What Saudis had once overlooked as the violent actions of a few had become something that targeted them all. They could not tolerate the mass murder of Muslims on their doorsteps. With a shrinking number of safe houses and little money, bin Laden's young followers lashed out against Saudi security forces. That campaign of lightning strikes gave way to a series of abductions and videotaped beheadings. But it was too late. Few in Saudi Arabia understood what the fighters were doing. If al-Qaeda wanted to kill Americans, they wondered, why didn't they go to Iraq?

In early April 2005, Saudi soldiers surrounded a farm near the town of al-Rass in the center of the country. The gun battle lasted for three days. When it was over, fourteen senior operatives lay dead, and the Ministry of the Interior announced that the al-Qaeda cell in Saudi Arabia had been defeated.

ON THE MARGINS of those operations stood a pair of young Saudi brothers named Ibrahim and Abdullah Asiri. Neither had been part of al-Qaeda's organization inside the kingdom; they had wanted to fight in Iraq, not Saudi Arabia. Their father, Hasan, a member of Saudi Arabia's armed forces, had raised the boys in a strict and conservative home. A short, sinewy man, Hasan was bald with a short, snowy-white beard. He had not allowed any of his seven children—four sons and three daughters—to watch television or listen to music. Instead, he had encouraged his children to memorize the Quran and concentrate on their studies. All the boys tried to please their father, but only Abdullah had really excelled. "Ever since he was small, he was always the best," Ibrahim remembered. "His name was always at the top at the mosque and at school."

Five years older and much more attractive than his skinny younger brother, Ibrahim doted on Abdullah. After school the two usually joined a group of neighborhood boys for soccer, before dinner and prayers. Sensitive and frail, Abdullah was always looking to correct the everyday injustices he saw all around him. Powerless on his own, he relied on Ibrahim to enforce his uncompromising verdicts.

In 2002, months after the September 11 attacks, Abdullah turned sixteen and for the first time started to question the assumptions that had guided his life. Ibrahim was busy with his chemistry studies at King Saud University across town, and Abdullah soon started spending most of his free time at a neighborhood mosque. The clerics liked the quiet, shy boy who hung on their every word, and they often asked him to give the public call to prayer; Abdullah's teenage voice singing out through the mosque's loudspeakers and inviting the neighborhood to come and pray. As Abdullah's outward piety grew, so did his desire for answers. Saudi Arabia prided itself on being an Islamic nation. In 1986, the same year Abdullah was born, the king had changed his official title. The office, a royal decree stated, would now be known simply as the "protector of the two holy places," a reference to the cities of Mecca and Medina, the Prophet Muhammad's hometown and the city that had once provided him refuge. From the beginning, Saudi's legal system had been based on Shariah law and its flag featured the *shahada*, the Islamic profession of faith, on a field of green above a sword. Al-Qaeda, which claimed it only wanted to uphold Shariah law—through the sword if need be—later adopted something similar for its own flag: a black banner with the *shahada* emblazoned in white script. For all of the kingdom's outward professions of faith, what Abdullah saw didn't match what he read in the Quran. Saudi society, the teenager believed, had become a nation of hypocrites, casually ignoring God's clear instructions. Every weekend men spent the morning praying in the mosques before speeding across the causeway to nearby Bahrain for an evening in bars and discos that were forbidden in the kingdom. At home, Qurans were tossed around like any other book, stacked on the floor and handled carelessly. Abdullah believed people should treat God's word with the respect it deserved, and when they didn't he lost his temper. The sensitive boy from the soccer field had grown into a sixteen-year-old fanatic lecturing men decades older on the shamefulness of shaving their beards.

One day, as he and Ibrahim were driving past a school, Abdullah spotted a box of trash filled with old newspapers. Pulling the car to the side of the road, Abdullah nearly broke down in tears. Those papers might have some of the ninety-nine names of God written on them, he told his brother. "They should be properly disposed of, not mixed in with the other trash or used to wrap food." For the next hour, the two brothers pulled the dirty, sodden papers out of the box. "He didn't stop until he had removed every scrap of newsprint," Ibrahim remembered.

After September 11, Saudi Arabia had sided with the US and supported the wars in Afghanistan and Iraq. How could this be, Abdullah asked himself. In the 1980s and 1990s, the Saudis had supported the jihads in Afghanistan and Chechnya. What had changed?

For most of his life, Abdullah had taken the opinions of the state's religious scholars as God's truth, but now, as his questions shifted from social concerns to politics, he started to doubt their cautious answers. Muslims were still protecting their lands and fighting non-Muslims, just as they had in the 1980s and 1990s. The difference was the royal family. Instead of supporting the jihad, they were putting their financial security and comfortable lives ahead of their duties as Muslim leaders.

IN 2004, WITH the war in Iraq descending into brutal cycles of violence, Abdullah and Ibrahim joined a group of young Saudis preparing to travel across the border. As the recruits poured in the cell split, leaving one brother in each group. Shortly before

Ibrahim, who had dropped out of college to focus on training, was scheduled to leave Riyadh, Saudi security forces raided their safe house and arrested the entire cell. "Up until that point I didn't know that the Saudi government was in the service of the crusaders," Ibrahim later remarked.

Abdullah visited his older brother in prison, listening as Ibrahim complained about his treatment at the hands of the security services. "They are infidels wrapped in the clothing of God's religion," Ibrahim warned.

His time in prison radicalized both brothers and convinced them that Saudi Arabia's rulers could no longer be considered true Muslims. Now they understood why al-Qaeda had attacked targets within Saudi Arabia. The royal family had made its choice, to stand with the US and the Jews instead of with the weak and oppressed. When Ibrahim was released months later, the brothers gravitated toward other frustrated young Saudis looking to restart al-Qaeda's domestic campaign. Though poorly organized and amateurish, several of these cells had popped up all over the country in late 2005.

On February 24, 2006, one of the cells attempted to drive two car bombs into the Abqaiq oil refinery in Saudi Arabia's eastern province. The world's largest oil processing plant, Abqaiq handled nearly two-thirds of Saudi Arabia's daily exports, which alone accounted for more than 10 percent of global output. The brazen mid-afternoon attack failed, but the shock caused oil prices to jump by $2 a barrel.

At the Ministry of the Interior in Riyadh, Prince Nayif's son Muhammad was furious. He thought he had eliminated al-Qaeda's Saudi network nearly a year earlier, at al-Rass. The forty-six-year-old prince promised an unrelenting campaign. His troops quickly took down several cells, and in late June they hit an al-Qaeda safe house in northern Riyadh. Listening to the fragmented reports of the raid that afternoon, Ibrahim suggested they flee. "We should go to Yemen," he said. Abdullah hesitated. Angry at the arrest of their friends, he wanted to stay and fight, not run. Finally, after a heated discussion, he gave in to his brother's pleading; it was time to escape.

Their father had been born in Asir, a mountainous province on the Yemeni border, and some of his family still lived there. Staying off the main roads, the brothers cautiously worked their way south. Saudi border patrols crisscrossed the desert routes, looking for the economic refugees and smugglers that crossed the border from Yemen. Camping rough in the sparsely populated desert with only a small pistol between them, the brothers moved slowly. Each time they saw one of the shimmering SUVs the Saudi border guards drove, they scrambled behind cover and waited. Dirty and sweaty in the July heat, the pair trudged through the low mountains toward Yemen.

As they neared the border the patrols increased. One day, convinced they had been seen, Abdullah directed his brother to hide behind one boulder while he ducked behind a second. "When they come through here, you shoot them with the pistol," Abdullah instructed. "Then we'll take their weapons."

Ibrahim looked at his brother's twenty-year-old, sweat-streaked face and started to laugh. The plan was just like Abdullah, hope and optimism over reality. They were two men with one small pistol against a heavily armed Saudi patrol. "We only have three bullets," Ibrahim reminded his brother. They waited, but the soldiers never came. A few days later, on August 1—five weeks after they had left Riyadh—the two crossed the border into Yemen.

AFTER THE STIFLING environment in Riyadh, where bin Nayif's men were constantly raiding their safe houses, the Asiri brothers found Yemen's lax security a welcome change. Fighting in the north, near where Ibrahim and Abdullah crossed the border, had fallen off as the Huthis strengthened their control over the countryside. In Sanaa, following three days of what state newspapers had dubbed "spontaneous demonstrations" by state workers and schoolchildren, President Salih had finally agreed to stand for reelection. The US was similarly preoccupied with elections. Congressional Democrats were campaigning hard against the Iraq war and appeared poised to win a majority in both houses for the first time in years. The worse the war went, the better they polled. Even an air strike that had killed Abu Musab al-Zarqawi in June 2006 did little to ease the public's growing concern. In August, opposition to the war in Iraq hit a new high. More than 61 percent of respondents told a CNN poll that they disagreed with the war, while 57 percent disapproved of Bush's overall performance.

There were other, less quantifiable consequences to the war. Iraq acted like a giant black hole, sucking in government resources and expertise until hardly anyone was left to cover the rest of the region. The remaining skeleton crews at the CIA and other intelligence agencies, full of inexperienced officers with limited language skills, didn't have the time or training to track twenty-three escaped prisoners in Yemen.

AFTER THE PRISON break six months earlier, in February 2006, the escapees had vanished. Moving in twos and threes, the men found shelter wherever they could. Nasir al-Wihayshi and Fawaz al-Rabi'i had split off from Qasim al-Raymi that first morning. Worried the PSO would be watching their families and friends in Sanaa, the two had focused on casual acquaintances, but none of the men they approached would help. Everyone was too scared. Late that morning, just as the pair was growing desperate, an elderly woman in downtown Sanaa agreed to hide them. She lived less than a mile from a security headquarters and there were officers patrolling her neighborhood, but she never hesitated, Wihayshi later wrote admiringly. The old woman's kindness that first morning was the only thing that saved the two men who would resurrect al-Qaeda's Yemen branch.

As he had in the aftermath of his father's arrest in 2002, Rabi'i wanted to arrange an immediate attack. Wihayshi counseled patience, but as Salih's quiet tribal negotiations took a toll the men started to put together a plan. Within weeks, four escapees had surrendered in exchange for commuted sentences, and in April Yemeni forces arrested another fugitive in a raid on a Sanaa apartment building. There were other distractions as well. That summer Rabi'i's elderly father had fallen ill. After learning of his father's hospitalization, Rabi'i had disguised himself as a patient and snuck into the hospital for a visit. Sitting next to his father's sickbed in hospital pajamas, Rabi'i filled him in on the months since the escape. He had gotten engaged, the twenty-six-year-old told his father. It was the happiest his father had ever seen him. The girl came from a good family, Rabi'i explained. Her father, Yahya Mujali, had been the al-Qaeda operative killed by Yemeni forces in late 2002. Rabi'i was close to Mujali's two brothers, Hizam and Arif, who had become the girl's guardians, and in prison the three men had worked out the details of the marriage that they believed would unite two of Yemen's great jihadi families. Rabi'i's father listened as his son explained his dreams for marriage and the family he hoped to have. For the next four hours, the two chatted in whispers as Yahya al-Rabi'i told his son how much he admired him. It would be the last time the two spoke.

After the failure of the Saudi campaign in 2003 and 2004, bin Laden had repeatedly issued taped audio messages calling for attacks on the oil industry in the Persian Gulf. The failed Abqaiq attack in February 2006 had been one response, and that fall Rabi'i put together a similar plan for Yemen. Together with some of other escaped prisoners and with Wihayshi's blessing, Rabi'i decided to attack an oil port in Hadramawt, along Yemen's southern coast, and a refinery in the desert east of Sanaa.

On September 15, 2006, five days before Yemen's presidential elections, Rabi'i gave the order. He had organized a pair of two-man suicide teams; each would be led by an escapee and assisted by a younger recruit in a separate car. The plan was essentially a vehicular one-two punch. The first car would take out the security at the gate so the second suicide bomber could drive unobstructed toward the target inside the compound. Early on the morning of the attack, the men said their prayers and loaded the four vehicles with the TNT-rigged gas canisters. Dressed as an oil worker and a soldier, the first team hit the Duba port in Hadramawt at 5:15 a.m. Neither car managed to breach the gate, exploding under a barrage of gunfire near the gate. Thirty-five minutes later, at 5:50 a.m., the second pair of attackers drove their cars toward the security perimeter around the Marib refinery east of Sanaa. Spooked by the speeding vehicles, guards opened fire, detonating both before they could breach the gate.

In his last will and testament, written five days before the attack, Umar Jarallah, the lead bomber in the Marib attack, had advised his fellow fighters not to give up, no matter the results: "This road is full of danger, difficulties, problems, and hardships."

15

Resurrecting al-Qaeda

2006–2007

Less than a week after the failed bombings, Salih cruised to a reelection victory with nearly 80 percent of the vote. Then he went after al-Qaeda. On October 1, Yemeni forces surrounded a tiny two-story house on the outskirts of Sanaa, where they believed Fawaz al-Rabi'i and another escapee, Muhammad al-Daylami, were hiding. The narrow mud-brick building was set back from the road on a slight incline and nestled snugly between a construction site and a six-foot mud wall, which combined to form a tight alleyway leading up to the house. Around 10 a.m. that morning, soldiers took up positions in the shadows of the half-constructed building next door while others crouched behind the wall. Weeks earlier, they had taken down another al-Qaeda safe house in Sanaa, their second since the prison break. Both times the escapees had surrendered without a shot, but this time the soldiers had been briefed to expect something different. Rabi'i might fight. Secretly, some of the men hoped he would. Rabi'i had already escaped them once, years before, and during his weeks on the run following that raid in 2003, he had murdered a soldier outside a checkpoint in Abyan.

Shouting for the people inside to come out, the soldiers took a deep breath and waited. For a minute there was no response. Then a single shot rang out. Following orders, the soldiers opened up on the house, concentrating their fire on the two second-story windows. The barrage tore up the outside walls and kicked chunks of mud and cement into the air. From inside the house the men returned fire, lobbing grenades and sticks of dynamite out the narrow windows. One of the soldiers' bullets hit Daylami almost exactly between the eyes, killing him instantly. As the echoes from the automatic weapons faded, the soldiers heard Rabi'i shouting from inside the house. He was ready to surrender. The battle had lasted only a few minutes.

Peeking out from behind the ground-floor door next to the garage, Rabi'i tossed his gun into the dirt. Framed by the mud wall on his right and the half-constructed building on his left, Rabi'i lifted up his shirt to show he didn't have a bomb strapped to his chest, and then started to inch his way down the tight alleyway. From somewhere ahead of him, one of the soldiers sighted down the barrel and squeezed the trigger. The bullet hit Rabi'i in the chest. The last of the original al-Qaeda commanders in Yemen, and bin Laden's handpicked lieutenant, died feet from the door. State media later claimed that both Daylami and Rabi'i had been killed in the shootout. But within the jihadi community the word spread: Rabi'i had been murdered. The message was clear: if al-Qaeda killed soldiers, the military would respond in kind.

Rabi'i's father, Yahya, never believed the official story. As he received condolences days later in a bereavement tent across town, his mind wandered to the fate of his four sons. Fawaz was dead. Abu Bakr, who had also fought for al-Qaeda, was in prison. His youngest son, Salman, whom he hadn't seen in five years, was in Guantánamo. And Hasan, the oldest, wouldn't even talk to him after years of being arrested every time the government wanted to pressure his brothers. One way or another, all his sons were gone. Yahya Rabi'i sat at his son's wake by himself. Still, as he told the men who came by to touch his hand and whisper in his ear, he could take pride in Fawaz's death. "My son lived as a lion, and he died as a lion."

THE DEATH OF Rabi'i opened the way for Nasir al-Wihayshi to take full control of rebuilding al-Qaeda. Throughout the winter, bin Laden's former secretary put his personal stamp on the group, making it more methodical and patient. Using the blueprint he had seen bin Laden perfect in Afghanistan, Wihayshi built a network that would last. He knew what had happened in Yemen the first time, when Harithi's death had crippled the network, and he had seen the failures in Iraq and Saudi Arabia. Al-Qaeda had to learn from its mistakes.

Moving in a giant arc, Wihayshi worked his way east out of Sanaa toward the deserts of Marib and then north into the wastelands of al-Jawf before turning back south for the mountains of Shabwa and Abyan where he had been born. He recruited locally, attracting men the same way he had in prison. Even though he had been away from Yemen for nearly a decade, he still understood how the society functioned, and the importance of tribal and clan ties. Along with Qasim al-Raymi, Wihayshi laid the groundwork for a durable organization, appointing local *amirs*, or commanders, who would direct al-Qaeda's operations in their home districts. The two Afghan veterans prioritized major tribes and prominent families. Wihayshi wanted his men to be tied by blood and tribe to the power structure in their area. This was his insurance against the pressure that would inevitably come.

During the hard winter months when Yemen turned brittle with cold, Wihayshi sat in crowded councils throughout his arc of influence, making plans and listening to suggestions. Early in 2007, one of these councils elected Wihayshi head of al-Qaeda in Yemen. Just like his mentor bin Laden, Wihayshi required each man to swear the oath of allegiance known as the *bay'a*. Nine years earlier, he had sworn a similar oath to bin Laden, promising to obey the al-Qaeda commander he idolized. Now recruits who had never traveled to Afghanistan were doing the same thing to him as they became part of bin Laden's circle, disciples of his disciple. Wihayshi connected them to the 1980s and the glory days of the jihad in Afghanistan.

Some of the Saudi recruits, men like Abdullah Asiri, later swore a second oath, promising to carry out a suicide attack whenever Wihayshi commanded. As al-Qaeda took root in Yemen, Wihayshi built his hierarchy. At the center of his arc, almost directly east of Sanaa in the governorate of Marib, Wihayshi named Ali Doha, a baby-faced tribesman with just a shadow of a mustache, his commander for the region. Described by a fellow al-Qaeda member as a "precious pearl," Doha was one of al-Qaeda's prison recruits. He was young, easily impressed by Wihayshi's time and experience in Afghanistan, and, most importantly, a member of the powerful Abidah tribe.

Doha quickly organized a few other former prisoners into a cell. Marib was the site of the drone strike that had killed Harithi and helped to destroy al-Qaeda's initial network in Yemen. After their escape from prison, Wihayshi and his new lieutenants had compiled a list of names for assassination. They focused on two groups of Yemeni officers: those who tortured al-Qaeda members and those who worked closely with the US. They called them "the guilty ones." Near the top of their list was a forty-three-year-old colonel and criminal investigator named Ali Mahmud Qasaylah. Wihayshi believed the chubby police detective had been a local contact for the US in its 2002 strike on Harithi. And since Qasaylah was an outsider in Marib, there would be no tribal blowback after his death.

As bin Laden had taught him, Wihayshi left the details up to his men on the ground: centralization of decision, decentralization of execution. Doha and his three-man cell had little trouble planning the assassination. Tribal and family contacts could keep the men abreast of the detective's movements. Doha's cell knew the local geography, all the hidden depressions and dry riverbeds known as wadis that crisscrossed the region.

Late in the evening on March 29, the men sprung their ambush on a road outside the city of Marib. Rising up from the shadows around a dune, the three men strafed Qasaylah's car with bullets and left the detective's lifeless body slumped in its seat as they faded away. The government gave Qasaylah a state burial in Sanaa, but with no witnesses and no suspects the investigation into his death stalled. Al-Qaeda's first successful attack in Yemen in years had barely registered in Sanaa.

IN MAY, AN article in the pan-Arab daily *al-Hayat*, citing sources in Marib, suggested that al-Qaeda had been behind the ambush. The article revived the flagging investigation as officials at the Ministry of the Interior took out a half-page ad announcing a $25,000 reward for information leading to the arrest of the cell responsible. But while the government played catch-up, al-Qaeda was busy tightening its ranks.

Even among Yemenis who had fought in Iraq or Afghanistan, a local jihad was controversial. Many of the veteran fighters pushed back against Wihayshi's idea of rebuilding al-Qaeda in Yemen. Why here, they asked the eager young emissaries Wihayshi sent them. They didn't understand the need for a jihad at home. They had gone to Iraq and Afghanistan because of the US invasions, which had triggered the idea of defensive jihad and compelled their participation. To defend Muslim lands, they had to fight. But was that really the case in Yemen? The US hadn't invaded, and no matter what al-Qaeda claimed, Salih was still nominally a Muslim. If the escaped prisoners wanted to fight so badly, the men said, they should go to Iraq or Afghanistan where they could take on the Americans directly.

Wihayshi listened to their criticism. He understood what they were saying. After all, he had left Yemen in 1998 to fight abroad. But the men didn't seem to grasp how much things had changed. After 9/11, he argued, there were no longer any neutral parties. Yemen had sided with the US. Besides, Wihayshi pressed, they only had to look around them to see that Yemen too was under Western military attack. Patiently, the soft-spoken commander walked the doubters through the evidence: the drone strike that killed Harithi, the targeting of jihadis in Yemen who hadn't committed any crimes, and the government's decision to forbid travel to Iraq. All of this had been done at the behest of the US. But any examination led to one conclusion: just like Iraq and Afghanistan, he continued, Yemen was a legitimate theater of jihad.

Few of the veterans were persuaded. They had done their fighting, and jihad was a young man's game. But Wihayshi warned them that his fighters were uncompromising. You were either for them or against them.

On May 22, the debate turned bloody. At 7:30 that morning, Faris al-Raymi, Qasim's younger brother, told his mother he was leaving for the day. Only twenty-three years old, Faris had already fought in Iraq and Afghanistan, and he was tired. As the older woman peeked out the window, watching her son leave, she caught a glimpse of a man she didn't know waiting in the street. Her son greeted the man, kissing his cheek and grabbing his hand. Then the two moved out of sight.

Zakariya al-Yafai, the man in the street, had been one of the first escapees to surrender and take advantage of Salih's offer of a commuted sentence. But he had maintained contact with other escapees who were still on the run, and he had promised to guide Faris to the safe house where his brother was hiding. At least, that is what Yafai said. Al-Qaeda had been pressuring Faris for months, begging him to carry out an attack in Yemen. He turned them down each time. His jihad was over, he told them. He only wanted to see his brother.

Around 10:30 a.m., three hours after Faris told his mother goodbye, a passerby noticed an unusual lump sticking out of the dirt and garbage piled in a narrow Sanaa side street. As the man approached, he saw the blood and then the body. Faris had seven bullet wounds in his chest and head. An ambulance rushed him to the hospital, but he never regained consciousness and died a week later.

Qasim called his parents, explaining to them that a "gang" killed his brother. "I had nothing to do with it," he swore to his father. One month later, however, Qasim al-Raymi would publicly espouse the same type of uncompromising jihad that had led to his brother's death.

ON JUNE 21, Raymi released a twenty-one-minute audiotape directed at al-Qaeda's old guard in Yemen, the men he and Wihayshi had been trying unsuccessfully to recruit for the past year. It was time for them to pick a side, he declared.

In the first public announcement of al-Qaeda's return to Yemen, Raymi said that the group had selected Nasir al-Wihayshi as their leader. But most of his recorded message was an extended appeal. In his deep voice, Raymi warned of the dangers of negotiating with Salih's government. The arrangements this president offers you are nothing more than a "treasonous alliance with tyrants," he said. Jihad could not be paused for any reason, no matter how noble. There could be no negotiations and no deals—not even in exchange for the release of al-Qaeda prisoners in Salih's prisons. "If they are killed they end up as martyrs," Raymi explained. "So how can jihad stop for the sake of prisoners? Return to your senses."

Six days later, al-Qaeda released a second statement. This time, al-Qaeda spoke directly to the government, publishing its call in a local paper. The group had four demands: Salih should release all al-Qaeda members from prison, lift restrictions on travel to Iraq, stop cooperating with the enemies of Islam, especially the US, and return to Shariah law. If Salih failed to meet any of their demands, the statement warned, al-Qaeda was prepared to act.

That same month, as if to underscore the growing threat the escaped prisoners posed, the USS *Chafee*, a 508-foot guided missile destroyer patrolling in the Gulf of Aden, fired several missiles at a meeting of Islamists in northern Somalia. Among the dead was Mansur al-Bayhani, one of the escaped prisoners who had turned himself in to the authorities in exchange for a commuted sentence. At the time, Bayhani had promised he would not carry out any attacks in Yemen, and while he had kept his part of the agreement—fighting in Somalia instead of Yemen—it was clear that Salih's private deals were not a solution.

DAYS AFTER BAYHANI'S death, al-Qaeda made good on its threat to act in Yemen. On July 2, less than a week after the published statement, Doha's Marib cell struck again.

After the Qasaylah assassination, the three tribesmen had pressed for another opportunity. Operatives in Sanaa sent them a young Yemeni named Abdu Muhammad al-Ruhayqah, whom they had recruited as a suicide bomber. The twenty-one-year-old had grown up in the squalor of Sanaa's overcrowded Musayk neighborhood, just blocks from the US embassy. This time, the plan was to attack one of the tourist convoys that often visited Marib.

Centuries earlier, near the end of his life, Muhammad had instructed his followers to "expel the infidels from the Arabian peninsula." Bin Laden had invoked the prophetic injunction fifteen years earlier for al-Qaeda's first attack on the hotel in Aden, and both Wihayshi and Raymi continued to take it seriously. The two used the command to construct a theory of jihad that justified every attack they ordered. For al-Qaeda, tourists weren't innocent civilians; they were non-Muslims in the Prophet's peninsula and as such legitimate targets.

Yemen didn't get many tourists. But those who did come often made a day trip to Marib to visit the two temples of the legendary Queen of Sheba, whom the Bible mentions as a contemporary of King Solomon. The poorly maintained archeological sites were little more than a pair of fenced-off patches of sand with stone pillars at the center. For al-Qaeda, however, they were perfect, a confined space with a single exit.

Doha's plan called for Ruhayqah to drive a car bomb into a tourist convoy as it pulled out of the temple grounds. Their speed would be down and the vehicles vulnerable and exposed as they turned back onto the main road. Plus, when the convoy exited the site the vehicles would be bunched together, which gave al-Qaeda the best chance to maximize casualties. There was only one problem: Ruhayqah didn't know how to drive. For weeks, the men had taken him out into the desert, teaching him steering and acceleration in the region's hard-packed wadis. Finally, Doha passed along word: the youngster was ready.

In the days leading up to the strike, an al-Qaeda cameraman shadowed Ruhayqah, recording his last will and testament and filming hours of footage for future recruiting videos. On the eve of the attack, he caught the soon-to-be suicide bomber napping in a grove of fruit trees. Lying on top of a thin blanket with his hair curling around his ears, Ruhayqah looked like a child. The camera zoomed in on his face, soft and relaxed in sleep, staying there for several seconds before panning away to the trees and the desert beyond. "The martyr resting before the operation," the video caption later read.

Early the next afternoon, as the rest of the country settled in for the daily qat chew, Ruhayqah moved his vehicle into position. Behind him on the backseat and strewn across the floor of the 1982 Toyota Land Cruiser were the explosives al-Qaeda technicians had built for the operation. Several hundred yards away, over a couple of low ridges and out of sight, the cameraman turned on his equipment and waited. Ruhayqah could see the tourists snapping some final photographs as they piled back into their own dusty Toyota Land Cruisers. As the first vehicle pulled out of the site, turning onto the main road back to town, he gunned the engine and headed for the middle of the convoy.

The explosion nearly obliterated one of the tourists' Land Cruisers, spraying bits of metal and human flesh across the blacktop and out into the sand. The crumpled chassis of another came to rest feet off the road, where it would burn for hours.

Several hundred yards away, al-Qaeda's cameraman heard the blast before he saw it, a muffled boom above the wind whistling through his microphone. Holding the camera with his hand, he panned the barren landscape, greedily zooming in on the plume of black smoke rising above the dunes. He held the shot for minutes, silently watching the smoke tumble upward like a raised fist before dissipating and eventually dispersing. In the video al-Qaeda later released there is no commentary, only the mute pictures of sand and smoke.

Investigators spent days combing through the sand, painstakingly collecting body parts of the seven Spanish tourists and two Yemeni drivers Ruhayqah had killed. An eighth tourist later died at the hospital.

ALMOST IMMEDIATELY, THE government went on autopilot. Worried about the fallout, President Salih called a press conference and blamed non-Yemeni Arabs for the deaths. As he had with the USS *Cole* and MV *Limburg* attacks years earlier, Salih tried to present his country as a victim instead of part of the problem. This is an outside virus that harms the nation, he told journalists.

The next night, July 5, Salih made another attempt to pin the attack on outsiders. Around 10 p.m., government counterterrorism forces surrounded an apartment in western Sanaa where Ahmad Duwaydar, a stout and balding fifty-year-old Egyptian, lived with his Yemeni wife and children. A former jihadi in Afghanistan, Duwaydar had moved to Sanaa with the wave of Egyptian exiles in the mid-1990s. Convicted in absentia as part of a massive terrorism trial by an Egyptian court in 1999, Duwaydar couldn't leave Yemen for fear of being arrested. Salih's security agents had watched the retired jihadi for more than a decade, noting his struggles to support his family as a part-time electrician, and now they had found a use for him.

After a round of warning shots, soldiers allowed Duwaydar's wife and children to leave the apartment. But he had to stay inside. The next morning, official newspapers reported that he had been killed resisting arrest.

Salih believed a quick reaction to the Marib bombing would buy him time with the international community. But he knew the problem was worse than he had admitted in the press conference. On August 5, more than a month after the suicide attack, Salih left Sanaa for a series of meetings with tribal leaders in Marib. Their support for al-Qaeda had to stop, Salih warned. The days of giving refuge to fugitives and criminals were over. Abidah, the president explained, needed to think about its future. There were no explicit threats, but Salih's message was clear. Almost immediately, the shaykhs produced some intelligence, telling security officials about an al-Qaeda safe house. Three days later, soldiers backed by tanks and helicopters moved in on the one-story dirt building. The early morning raid was over almost before it began. Surprised and surrounded, the four al-Qaeda fighters inside didn't stand a chance. Three of them, including Ali Doha, died within minutes. One of the tribesmen made it out the door, firing his gun wildly as he tried to sprint for cover in his ankle-length robe. Aiming from behind a dune, a sniper dropped the weaving figure with a careful shot.

The bloody mess of clothes and limbs inside the mud hut took some time to sort out and piece back together. Doha's nose had been blasted away and his mouth was a mushy mess of teeth and pulp. Initially, the soldiers believed they had killed Qasim al-Raymi, whom the shaykhs had suggested might be hiding at the safe house, but the al-Qaeda commander wasn't there. Instead, they had destroyed Ali Doha's Marib cell, killing all three tribesmen and an eighteen-year-old the government believed was Ruhayqah's replacement, a suicide bomber in training.

WIHAYSHI HAD PLANNED for exactly this type of setback. He knew there would be losses. That is why he had insisted each cell be self-contained and isolated from the rest of the network. Wihayshi kept recruiting and planning and Raymi continued to run his mobile training camps in the desert, imparting the skills he had learned in Afghanistan to a new generation of fighters.

In Sanaa, Salih pushed ahead with his strategy of private deals. On October 16, Yemen announced that Jamal al-Badawi, who had helped organize the USS *Cole* attack, had surrendered to local authorities and agreed to give up jihad in exchange for his freedom.

Shocked that Yemen would release someone who had killed American sailors and was on the FBI's most wanted list, President Bush dispatched his top counterterrorism adviser, Frances Townsend, to Yemen. The bouncy forty-five-year-old former prosecutor shared her boss's frustration. John O'Neill, the lead investigator on the *Cole* attack, had been a close friend. On September 11, the former FBI agent had sent her a reassuring text message only minutes before he was crushed to death as the first tower fell. Townsend wanted to finish what O'Neill had started.

In a meeting at his winter residence in Aden, Salih tried to reassure Townsend. Don't worry about Badawi, he told her. "He is under my microscope." Over lunch, Salih explained that he had been communicating with Badawi for months—information he had not previously shared with his American allies. Two weeks ago, Salih continued, he had personally met with the fugitive for a frank discussion. "Badawi promised to give up terrorism and I told him that his actions damaged Yemen and its image," Salih said. "He began to understand."

Townsend listened tight-lipped as Salih described the deal as a sort of house arrest. Yes, Badawi was living and working on his farm outside Aden, but the government was monitoring him closely. He won't commit any more crimes, Salih pledged.

There wasn't much for Townsend to say; the president had made his decision. Struggling to get something useful out of the trip, she tried another angle, asking if US officials could interrogate Badawi. Sure, the president said, just coordinate with the Political Security Organization.

Sensing Salih's growing impatience, Townsend tried to move on, asking about Yemen's effort to combat weapons trafficking. But before she could finish, the president interrupted her. He had another guest he wanted her to meet. Faris al-Manaa, the northern tribesman the Huthis had tried to assassinate and one of Yemen's biggest arms dealers, walked into the room.

"Hey FBI," Salih called to the embassy's assistant legal attaché, "if he does not behave properly you can take him back to Washington in Townsend's plane or to Guantánamo." As the waitstaff brought a chair for Manaa, Salih added that the government had recently confiscated one of his arms shipments, keeping them for military use.

"He can be considered a patriot now," Townsend joked.

"No," Salih laughed. "He is a double agent. He also gave weapons to the Huthi rebels."

In an embassy cable written a week after the lunch, Stephen Seche, the new US ambassador, tried to make sense of Salih's bizarre performance. His comments and Manaa's presence at the palace, the ambassador wrote with diplomatic understatement, raised "serious questions about the president's commitment to stopping weapons trafficking."

Still, Seche noted, there was reason for optimism. On November 1, after its two-year suspension, Yemen was scheduled be reinstated to the Millennium Challenge Corporation, the organization the Bush administration had established to link aid to political and economic reforms. "Overall," Seche concluded, this meeting was more constructive than some observers would have expected."

The ambassador's optimism was short-lived. Back home on the campaign trail, Republican presidential hopeful and former New York City mayor Rudolph Giuliani seized on Badawi's release and began calling for Yemen to stop siding with terrorists: "As a first step, I urge the US government to cancel the more than $20 million in aid scheduled to be delivered to Yemen." Days later the US did just that, suspending Yemen from the MCC a second time.

16

Echoes of Battles

2008

At the end of 2007, a young Saudi member of al-Qaeda named Nayif al-Qahtani approached Wihayshi with an idea. He wanted to start a magazine. Years earlier, al-Qaeda's Saudi branch had done something similar, publishing an online journal of commentary and religious justification for their attacks in the kingdom, and Qahtani thought something similar might help recruitment in Yemen.

Qahtani's background and limited education made him an unlikely choice to head up the project. Only nineteen years old, he had arrived Yemen a year earlier, fleeing a rocky marriage and a pregnant wife. The youngest of several boys, he had been raised almost entirely by his oldest brother, who had looked after him following the death of their father more than a decade earlier. "He possesses no leadership qualities," his brother later told reporters, describing Qahtani as quiet and shy. But Wihayshi liked the teenager's earnest attitude and told him to go ahead.

For weeks the young Saudi sat in front of his laptop, downloading material and typing articles. He wrote about the arrest of Yemeni fighters by Ali Abdullah Salih's troops, about the situation in Palestine, and of course about the war in Iraq. He even profiled himself in a two-part interview that was described in the magazine as a conversation between the editors and "one of Saudi's most wanted militants." Success, the new editor intuitively grasped, bred success.

Shortly after he finished work on the magazine he called *Sada al-Malahim*, or "The Echo of Battles," Qahtani met up with several other fighters at one of the mobile training camps in northern Yemen. As the men relaxed one evening after drills, they started talking about their dreams for jihad. Abdullah Asiri, the skinny young Saudi fugitive who had fled to Yemen with his older brother, said his greatest wish was to carry out what he called a "martyrdom operation" in Saudi Arabia. There were nods and smiles from the circle.

"I want to establish a media foundation," Qahtani confessed quietly when it came his turn to talk. The teenager outlined his vision for a publishing empire that would build on the new magazine, releasing everything from audio and video recordings to collections of poetry and jihadi anthems. He even mentioned the possibility of a blog. Wihayshi encouraged the big talk, and by early January 2008, he had finished tinkering with Qahtani's draft of the journal. Al-Qaeda's leadership had added a statement threatening the Yemeni government with more attacks if it didn't release the al-Qaeda prisoners it held. On January 13, 2008, the first issue of *Sada al-Malahim* was posted to several jihadi Internet forums. Five days later, al-Qaeda struck.

MORE THAN 300 miles east of Sanaa, in the magnificent desert wadi of Hadramawt, Hamza al-Quayti, the balding elder statesman who had helped settle disputes in prison, readied his men. Hadramawt, which means "death has come" in Arabic, is a bleached land of sand and stones where almost nothing grows. Roughly the size of South Dakota, Hadramawt stretches from the Gulf of Aden to the Saudi border, and at nearly 75,000 square miles it is Yemen's largest governorate. From the air it looks just as barren as its name implies, miles of angular white cliffs bisected by a 125-mile-long canyon-like wadi that is more than nine miles across at its widest point. The lack of vegetation and extreme heat gave rise, centuries ago, to a myth that the gates of hell could be found in one of the region's many caves.

A trio of ancient walled cities cuts down the center of the wadi at the center of the governorate, giving the region a narrow ribbon of green. Everywhere else, brown dominates, and it was here, along one of the side roads, that Quayti set his ambush. Parking his pickup on the shoulder, he squatted in its shade with three other men, waiting for the tourist convoy they knew would be coming. Bedouins in Yemen often parked their trucks on the edge of the road as they scrambled off for prayers or a bathroom break, and Quayti was hoping that the seemingly unoccupied truck would attract little attention from a passing line of Land Cruisers. He was right. It wasn't until the gunmen slid around the front of the pickup, firing short, steady bursts from their assault rifles, that the tourists realized they were in danger. The masked men followed up their initial volley by rushing the four vehicles, screaming "Allahu Akbar" and shooting into them one final time.

Quayti's gunmen escaped as easily as they had arrived, leaving the pockmarked Land Cruisers strung out on the road behind them. As the panicked screams inside the vehicles faded into traumatized sobbing, the fifteen survivors wiped away the blood and the glass to assess the situation. Two Belgian tourists and two Yemeni drivers were dead. Al-Qaeda would use this type of lightning strike to great effect throughout 2008, a steady accumulation of attacks that eventually paralyzed Yemen's tourist industry and exacerbated the country's economic decline.

THE US GOVERNMENT noted the growing number of attacks in its travel warnings for Yemen, but its primary focus continued to be Jamal al-Badawi and Jabir al-Banna, the two prison escapees on the FBI's most wanted list. After Giuliani's October 2007 outburst and the suspension of aid money, Yemen claimed it had returned Badawi to prison. Salih even arranged for US officials to tour the prison in Aden where he was being held. But as soon as the US delegation left, guards smuggled Badawi out the back. The whole thing was an elaborate shell game, a ploy by Salih to get US money while keeping his promise to Badawi.

At least the embassy had an idea where Badawi was. No one knew anything about Banna. After the escape he had simply disappeared. For two years there was nothing, no sightings and no rumors, not even a nibble on the State Department's terrorist hotline. Then, on February 23, he resurfaced.

Early that afternoon, a stocky, bearded man in a white robe and jacket with a decorative shawl draped over his shoulders walked into a crowded courtroom in downtown Sanaa, pushed his way to the front, and announced that he was Jabir al-Banna. The judge and the prosecutor stared at the man in shock. Jabir al-Banna was a wanted terrorist with a $5 million bounty on his head. Banna produced his identity card and started to speak.

"I've been sentenced to ten years in this case, and three years in another," he said. "But it's wrong. I haven't committed any crimes in this country or the United States." Standing in the middle of the court he'd interrupted, Banna added that he was free as part of a private deal with President Salih. Then, as the cameras clicked around him, he turned and walked out of the room. None of the guards moved to stop him.

President Bush was furious. Banna was an American citizen and a wanted terrorist whom the US had indicted for his role in the Lackawanna Six case. What was Salih, ostensibly a US ally, doing making a deal with him? Frances Townsend had already taken her shot with the enigmatic Yemeni president and since retired. This time, Bush asked Robert Mueller to press Salih.

The graying, square-jawed FBI director landed in Sanaa in early April for his meeting with Salih. He wanted Badawi and Banna, but there was much more to discuss. On March 13, al-Qaeda had released the second issue of *Sada al-Malahim*. Five days later, like clockwork, the organization struck again, firing five modified missiles at the US embassy compound.

None of the missiles found their mark, falling short of the embassy and striking a girls' school instead, killing one guard and injuring a number of students. Al-Qaeda put out a public statement praying for the quick recovery of the female students, while reiterating its previous warnings for Muslims to avoid getting too close to government and foreign offices. "We have told you that we will be targeting these places, so please don't go near them," the statement concluded.

The US had ordered its nonessential embassy staff out of the country after the failed attack, and Mueller wanted to ensure the safety of those who remained. Salih reassured him that his security forces were up to the task. But on Badawi and Banna, the president was evasive. When Mueller pressed him about possible extradition, Salih countered with demands for the return of Muhammad al-Muayyad, the Yemeni cleric the US had lured to Germany back in 2003 and who was now serving a seventy-five-year sentence.

The normally reserved director couldn't believe what he was hearing. The Yemeni president was making deals with terrorists while US diplomats were being shelled, and now he wanted to spring another one. Barely keeping his temper in check, Mueller ended the meeting.

IN THE FIRST week of July 2008, the British government hosted a conference in London to discuss the growing threat of al-Qaeda in Yemen. One French analyst told the assembled Whitehall officials that the attacks were nothing more than "loud firecrackers." Throughout the spring and early summer, Wihayshi's men had attacked army checkpoints, security patrols, oil installations, the presidential palace in Sanaa, the Italian embassy, and a housing compound where a number of US diplomats lived. The attacks made a lot of noise and broke a few windows, but that was it, the analyst concluded with a dismissive wave of his hand.

Two weeks later, the war of firecrackers turned more deadly. On July 23, Hamza al-Quayti released a short video threatening Yemen with more attacks if the government didn't stop torturing the al-Qaeda members it held in prison. Dressed in a gray robe and a mask, Quayti spoke directly into the camera. Most of his message was directed at Ghalib al-Qamish, the head of the PSO and the man who had once thrown him into solitary. "O, you Sharon of Yemen," he said in a reference to former Israeli prime minister Ariel Sharon. "You plunderer, you piece of garbage, you will see, God willing, how our brothers will come out of your prisons."

After the recording, aides shuffled into the room carrying suicide jackets and machine guns, which they placed around the makeshift set like props. Then they allowed a young Yemeni to take his place next to Quayti for a round of photos.

Two days later, that same young man, Ahmad al-Mashjari, made good on Quayti's threat and drove a car packed with explosives into a military compound in Hadramawt, killing three and wounding nearly two dozen. A twenty-three-year-old medical student from a nearby town, Mashjari had wanted to go to Iraq, but other fighters had encouraged him to stay home and wait for an opportunity in Yemen. Quayti's men posted pictures of the two, along with a statement of responsibility, on the Internet. "The blood of Muslims is not free," they cried, naming five fighters the suicide attack avenged.

Al-Qaeda's justification rang hollow with most Yemenis. Outraged at the loss of Muslim lives, preachers in mosques around the country condemned the attack. Mashjari hadn't even killed soldiers; most of the dead and wounded were civilians, cleaning ladies and small children. Much like the Saudis, following the November 2003 strike on a compound of Arab workers in Riyadh, Yemenis around the country cursed the terrorists and wondered why the organization was so intent on destruction and violence. In the face of this groundswell of emotion and public outrage, the Yemeni government released a single, tepid statement condemning the attack. For years it had been trying to get the upper hand in the fight against al-Qaeda, and now, when the group had finally overreached and alienated society, the government failed to act. Unlike the Saudi government, which had waged a massive campaign of front-page profiles and television ads following the November 2003 attack, the Yemeni government was shockingly silent.

IN A TRIO of safe houses just down the road from the damaged military compound, Quayti's cell waited out the uproar. Like bin Laden, his family was originally from Hadramawt, and after the prison break he'd come home to build his cell. He eventually settled in the dusty, decaying city of Tarim, more than 300 miles east of Sanaa. Even though the city boasted 365 mosques, one for every day of the year, Quayti knew it was still a small town. Everybody knew everybody else's business, and the sight of several unattached bearded men wandering between the three rental properties would not go unnoticed by local gossips. To get around this, Quayti required all of his men to disguise themselves as women whenever they went outside. The full veils hid their beards while the enveloping black cloaks blurred their figures. But Quayti had not anticipated that a house full of women could present as much of a problem as a house full of single men.

One of their neighbors had been watching the house for months. What kind of house doesn't have any men, she wondered to friends. Worried that a bad element might be taking root, she decided to see for herself. Instead of the woman she expected, a bearded man opened the door. "The women aren't here right now," he said brusquely. The elderly busybody's mind immediately jumped from prostitution to drugs. As soon as she got home, she called the police.

When the police patrol arrived at the house hours later, they quickly realized they had stumbled upon something much bigger than a drug ring. The young man who opened the door to the outer courtyard slammed it in their faces as soon as he saw their uniforms and scrambled back through the walled-off yard to alert the others. Fearing they had been discovered, the seven men inside the house opened fire. Unprepared to deal with the rocket-propelled grenades and machine guns the suspects had trained on them, the police established a security perimeter and called for backup. The standoff lasted throughout the night of August 10, as both sides prepared for the battle they knew was coming.

In the morning, the counterterrorism unit which had relieved the overmatched policemen brought in two tanks and tried to rush the squat cinderblock house. The tanks couldn't get close enough in the narrow maze of buildings, and the unit lost two men in the frontal assault before it fell back. Sensing a momentary advantage, Quayti ordered his men to try to make it to one of the other safe houses beyond the security perimeter. The six left Abdullah Batis, a young militant from the small Hadrami village of al-Qatn, behind to cover their retreat.

Surrounded by a cache of grenades and several machine guns, Batis fought for hours in the summer heat, rotating guns and screaming "Allahu Akbar" to keep his courage up as he moved among the bare concrete rooms. Outside, in the sweltering jumble of one-lane roads and unpaved alleys, the rest of the cell was in trouble. Yemeni sharpshooters picked them off as soon as they broke cover. More an extermination than a battle, the whole thing took most of the afternoon to complete. When it was finished, one of the soldiers snapped a photo of Quayti's corpse sprawled in a crumpled Z shape in the dust. Of the seven-man cell, five were dead and two, Ali al-Akbari and Muhammad Bawaydhan, were in government custody.

In the aftermath of the shootout, the Yemeni government claimed that Quayti had masterminded all the al-Qaeda violence that had plagued the country since the February 2006 prison break. Inexplicably, the US and the UK accepted the narrative of a single, hyperactive cell, and both countries used the raid as justification to relax travel warnings to Yemen. Overlooked in the congratulatory phone calls and messages was the localized nature of Quayti's cell. Five of the men were from the same city, and only one of them came from outside Hadramawt. Like the Marib cell, Quayti's was one among many.

Nine days after the battle, al-Qaeda eulogized the dead fighters in an Internet statement and warned of a retaliatory strike. "The proof," the message concluded, "will be in what you see and not in what you hear." Few in the US embassy paid any attention as the ambassador filed a request to allow employees who had left in the spring to return.

PEGGED TO THE movement of the moon, the Islamic year lasts 354 days, eleven days fewer than the calendar used in the West. For Muslims this means that Ramadan, the holy month of fasting and abstinence, falls at a different time every year, sometimes coming in the summer and sometimes in the winter. In 2008 it began on September 1, and US officials worried that al-Qaeda operatives might try to take advantage of Ramadan, which is traditionally a time of self-reflection and introspection for the more than one billion Muslims worldwide, to launch an attack on the US to mark the anniversary of 9/11.

A spike in Internet chatter during the first few days of September, much of it concentrated on the jihadi forum al-Ikhlas (Arabic for "faithfulness"), raised concerns even higher. One of the banner ads on the site teased an upcoming message from Osama bin Laden. For years the al-Qaeda leader had been deliberately tipping his hand, toying with his adversaries in intelligence agencies around the world by leaving tantalizing clues to his next attack hidden in his public statements. Most of these were subtle and hard to read, but they were there. In 2000, before the USS *Cole* attack, bin Laden had worn the curved Yemeni dagger known as a *jambiya* tucked into his belt when he appeared in a video calling for more attacks. Agents also wondered if bin Laden might be communicating with key lieutenants through some hidden subtext in these messages, perhaps giving a final order or putting a plot in motion.

Late in the evening of September 10, hours before bin Laden's tape was due to be released, al-Ikhlas was knocked offline. The cyberattack sent shockwaves through the jihadi community, who in the years since 9/11 had come to view the Internet as an untouchable haven. Site administrators scrambled to fix the problem as users trickled into other, more minor forums looking for the bin Laden tape. But there was no tape and al-Ikhlas, which had been al Qaeda's main distribution center for years, was permanently disabled.

Over the next few days, many in the intelligence community gradually started to breathe a little more easily. With the forum down and September 11 behind them, they believed the US had escaped the threat.

CENTURIES EARLIER, IN 624 AD, which corresponded to the second year of the Islamic calendar, Muhammad had led a small group of supporters on a raid against a much larger army of polytheist Arabs at the wells of Badr, a watering station on the road the road between Mecca and Medina. At the time, the fifty-four-year-old commander was still just a political upstart with few followers. Overmatched and outnumbered, the tiny band of Muslims—backed, the Quran says, by legions of angels who descended to earth to support the believers—thrashed their opponents on the seventeenth day of Ramadan. Muhammad's first major military victory, the battle of Badr, set the stage for the sweeping conquests that would follow. And it was this anniversary that al-Qaeda chose for its most daring raid in Yemen yet.

Downhill from the Sheraton in eastern Sanaa, the US embassy compound occupies several blocks along the western edge of a residential road. In order to reach the main gate, one has to pass through two checkpoints, an outer one at the southern corner of the compound and then a second one nearly 150 yards down the road shortly before the main gate. At 9:15 a.m. on September 17, seven attackers in two modified Suzuki jeeps equipped with homemade armor sped toward the first checkpoint. Five gunmen dressed as soldiers jumped out of the first jeep and opened fire, sending the Yemeni guards scrambling for cover and clearing a driving lane for the second, explosive-laden car. Screaming "Allahu Akbar" as they fired, the five men sprinted down the street trailing the second car. With houses on their right as they ran and the embassy wall on their left, the plan was for the two suicide bombers to crash their Suzuki into the main gate and then for the five gunmen to pour through the breach and into the compound.

As the jeep neared the embassy's main gate, a local security contractor pressed a button to engage a secondary metal drop bar, the only barrier that remained between the speeding vehicle and the embassy's black metal gates. Just as the thick metal bar lowered in front of the Suzuki and its two suicide bombers, the Yemeni contractor took a bullet in the chest from one of the attackers running down the street. His quick thinking in the moments before he died caused the jeep to crash into the drop bar and explode yards from the main gate, near a line of Yemenis waiting to enter the embassy. The two suicide bombers died in the explosion and trapped the five remaining gunmen on the street in front of the embassy nearly

150 yards from their own Suzuki. The men had never expected to survive the attack and none of them tried to fight their way back to the vehicle. Instead, they took up defensive positions behind a series of yellow-and-black-striped cement barriers that ran parallel to the embassy's outer wall—only now they were fighting Yemeni soldiers instead of American diplomats, who were locked down and safe behind the embassy's thick walls. For the next hour and a half, amid the smoke and wailing sirens of the shattered street, the five held out until soldiers from the Central Security Forces surrounded and killed them.

The deadliest attack on a US embassy since al-Qaeda's 1998 synchronized assault on the embassies in Kenya and Tanzania, the bombing left more than a dozen people dead, most of them civilians who had been in the embassy line. The only American killed in the attack was Susan al-Banna, an eighteen-year-old Yemeni–American who was in line to process paperwork for her new husband. The newly married woman was Jabir al-Banna's cousin.

Three of the embassy attackers had been released through Hitar's rehabilitation program, and all of the men had attended the same mosque in the Red Sea port city of Hudaydah. The US had been worried about Marib and the arc of tribal territories to the east; now it seemed as though al-Qaeda was coming at it from every direction. In the US, the Democratic nominee for president, Barack Obama, noted the attack with alarm. "We must do more," he told reporters. If the polls were right and he won, Yemen would soon be his problem. Weeks after it had asked its regular employees to return, the embassy went on lockdown once again.

Around the same time, an appeals court overturned the conviction of Muhammad al-Muayyad, the Yemeni cleric the US had arrested in Germany, and took the unusual step of ordering a new judge to retry the case. Within months, both Muayyad and his aide were free and back in Yemen.

THAT FALL SAUDI ARABIA released Said al-Shihri, the former Guantánamo Bay detainee the US had once labeled a "negative leader." After the US transferred him home in late 2007, Saudi Arabia had put him through months of religious rehabilitation. A better-funded, more organized version of Hitar's program, the Saudis thought they could succeed where the Yemenis had failed. The good food and gentle atmosphere helped Shihri regain much of the weight he had lost in Guantánamo, and when he finished the state offered to find the thirty-five-year-old a wife and a job. He declined.

Later that fall, he invited several of the men he had met in rehab to a banquet in the temperate mountain city of Taif. In the mountains just south of Mecca along Saudi's western coast, Taif was the country's unofficial summer capital. After the food was cleared, Shihri got to the point. He had asked them here, he explained, because they had unfinished business. Many of the men knew Shihri from Guantánamo and they all respected him, but they were still shocked at what he proposed. Shihri wanted them to rejoin al-Qaeda.

Listening to Shihri's well-rehearsed arguments, Jabir al-Fayfi, the recovering drug addict who had fought at Tora Bora, found his thoughts drifting to his life at the moment. After Guantánamo and his stint in Saudi Arabia's rehabilitation program, he had accepted the state's offer of a wife and now he had a daughter. Did he really want to give that up for a life on the run? Hadn't he done enough?

Shihri ended his pitch with a call to arms. It was time to finish what God commanded them to do.

In the discussion that followed, Fayfi didn't say much, but his mind was already made up. His life was in Saudi Arabia with his family. He was done with al-Qaeda. The meeting broke up later that night. The few Shihri had managed to convince stayed for more discussions and further instructions. Eventually, those men would move south to Yemen with their new leader. Fayfi went home to Riyadh.

FIVE WEEKS AFTER the attack on the embassy, al-Qaeda in Yemen tried a more targeted attack. Ever since Shaykh Rubaysh had met with Edmund Hull six years earlier, swearing to keep his village "terrorist-free" in exchange for a new US-funded hospital, al-Qaeda had been watching the family. In August 2007, one of Shaykh Rubaysh's sons, Muhammad, a bullish middle-aged security officer, had taken part in the raid that destroyed the cell responsible for the suicide attack against the Spanish tourists in Marib. There is only one punishment for "selling out your religion," Wihayshi explained when Rubaysh's role in the raid was confirmed. "The loss of your life."

As a security officer, Muhammad Rubaysh often traveled with a security detail, and al-Qaeda's planners worried that they wouldn't be able to get close enough to shoot him. Instead, the military committee proposed a bomb. Wihayshi liked the idea. When he had been with bin Laden in Afghanistan, the al-Qaeda commander had authorized just such an operation to assassinate the Northern Alliance commander Ahmad Shah Massoud, another difficult target, in the days leading up to 9/11.

One of al-Qaeda's explosives experts put together a simple parcel bomb with a pressure switch set to detonate when the cover was lifted. On the outside of the book-sized package he pasted a photo of an American attack helicopter, a symbol of Rubaysh's betrayal, and then wrapped the whole thing in newspaper photos of President Salih. A local member of al-Qaeda dropped the package off at a Marib gas station, a typical way of delivering mail in a region with limited postal service and no official addresses.

Three days later, on the morning of October 20, al-Qaeda made its move. One of the men put in a call to Rubaysh and told him there was a package waiting for him at the gas station. When the security chief picked it up later that afternoon, the explosion was powerful enough to rip off a large part of his face and wound soldiers standing yards away. Rubaysh died minutes later, in an ambulance on the way to the hospital.

Weeks later, in the sixth issue of *Sada al-Malahim*, al-Qaeda took credit for the assassination. "Anyone whose hands are stained with the blood of the mujahidin or who cooperates with the secular infidels will suffer the same fate."

17

The Merger

2009

In early January 2009, Nasir al-Wihayshi asked several operatives to arrange an interview for him with a local journalist. Weeks earlier, Said al-Shihri, the former Guantánamo Bay detainee, had crossed the border into Yemen with the Saudis he had recruited at the banquet in Taif. The influx of men presented Wihayshi with the opportunity he had been looking for. There had always been plenty of Saudis within al-Qaeda in Yemen—men like Ibrahim and Abdullah Asiri—but none of them had Shihri's presence or experience. The former Guantánamo Bay detainee quickly came to an agreement with Wihayshi. In much the same way as Osama bin Laden and Ayman al-Zawahiri had united their own organizations years earlier in Afghanistan, Wihayshi and Shihri would announce a merger between the Yemeni and Saudi branches of al-Qaeda. The new group would be called al-Qaeda in the Arabian Peninsula, or AQAP as intelligence agencies came to know it.

Al-Qaeda agents in Sanaa approached several local journalists, dangling the possibility of an exclusive interview, before settling on Abdalilah Shaya, an urbane young Yemeni who favored designer glasses and a slicked-back hairstyle. Qasim al-Raymi, who had been named a military commander in the new organization, vetted the agents' choice in a Sanaa safe house. As Raymi finished his background check, he informed Shaya that al-Qaeda would need a list of his questions in advance.

Soon after Shaya submitted his questions, word came back that al-Qaeda was ready. The journalist was not allowed to bring his laptop, cell phone, or anything electronic that intelligence agencies could use to pinpoint their location. Al-Qaeda would take care of everything. Armed guards patted Shaya down and blindfolded him before putting him in the car al-Qaeda had sent. When the men removed the blindfold, Shaya was standing in the middle of a bare room surrounded by several young men. In front of him, sitting on a small table, was an open laptop al-Qaeda had arranged for his use. A slim man in a black-checked headdress with a gray-flecked beard motioned for Shaya to sit next to him. Greeting him in a Saudi accent, the man showed Shaya the green vest he was wearing. "Do you know what this is?" he asked.

Looking into the stranger's face, Shaya sensed he was being teased. "I don't know," he stuttered. "Some sort of a pack."

"It's a suicide vest," the man said, taking the straps off his shoulders and draping them over Shaya. "Don't be scared," he whispered.

Shaya had never seen a suicide vest in person, and he froze as the Saudi eased the heavy pack down onto his chest. "There are enough explosives in here to take out two floors," the man bragged. Slowly, as Shaya struggled to control his breathing, the Saudi demonstrated how the bomb worked, showing him the deep pockets for explosives and the small detonator switch that triggered everything. "I'm never apart from this," the man breathed, gently running his hand over the rough green fabric. Seeing the discomfort on Shaya's face, the Saudi prodded him. "Go ahead, feel it for yourself," he instructed. "Run your hand over the top."

Shaya blanched and tried to move, but his hand wouldn't respond. "Stop," the man barked. "Don't touch that. You'll set the bomb off."

No one in the room moved. Slowly, the man's face crinkled into a smile. It was a joke. Chuckling softly, the Saudi lifted the vest off Shaya's chest and introduced himself as Said al-Shihri, a former detainee at Guantánamo Bay.

Shaya tried to calm himself and remember his questions during the round of introductions that followed. Minutes later, a throng of masked gunmen slipped into the room, signaling Wihayshi's arrival. Stealing yet another page from bin Laden's playbook, the young al-Qaeda commander wanted to make the sort of dramatic appearance his hero had perfected in Afghanistan. Shaya watched as the others greeted the little man in the light blue robe and white turban. He had seen Wihayshi's mug shot, but in person the al-Qaeda commander seemed even smaller, his sharp nose and sunken cheeks masked by the tufts of facial hair that jutted out from his face. Soon it was Shaya's turn. The shaykh was standing right in front of him. Wihayshi shook the journalist's hand and embraced him with a gentle smile. "Welcome," he said. "Sit here beside me."

Shaya wanted to start the interview, but Wihayshi shook his head. "We have certain obligations," he said as aides brought out tea and cold drinks. A few minutes later, several plates of food appeared. Shaya's face registered surprise. He hadn't expected hospitality from terrorists. Wihayshi noted his reaction, but instead of commenting the al-Qaeda leader merely raised his eyebrows politely. As he finished the food hospitality dictated he consume, Shaya realized he had no idea who these men were. This wasn't the al-Qaeda he had read about.

For the next ninety minutes, Wihayshi tried to educate him, walking the young journalist through the religious justification for al-Qaeda's past actions and laying out their plan to "cleanse the Arabian peninsula." The soft-spoken al-Qaeda commander politely evaded questions about the death of innocent Muslims like Susan al-Banna, who had been killed in the attack on the US embassy months earlier, and laughed off Shaya's attempts to portray

Ali Abdullah Salih as a legitimate ruler. "What elections?" Wihayshi protested.

At the end of the interview, Wihayshi stood up to escort Shaya to the door. Remember, he cautioned, the interview is embargoed until we let you know. The al-Qaeda leader had one more surprise.

AT THE SAME time Wihayshi was giving his interview, Jabir al-Fayfi, the balding fighter from Tora Bora, was watching the latest war between the Israelis and the Palestinians play out on his television in Riyadh.

Shortly after sunset on January 3, 2009, Israeli troops had crossed over the border into Gaza. Their orders were to put an end to the rocket attacks that Hamas had been launching from the ever-growing shantytowns under their control. For the next three weeks, Israeli jets pounded the cramped 140-square-mile strip of land along the Mediterranean coast. By the time the Israeli ground troops withdrew on January 21, more than 1,100 Palestinians lay dead behind them.

Fayfi watched the weeks of war on al-Jazeera. His eyes took in the smoke and eerie flashes of light that jumped across the screen as he thought about his own daughter. What about the Palestinian children in Gaza, he wondered. Didn't they deserve what his daughter took for granted?

From somewhere deep in his mind, Shihri's words from the banquet in Taif echoed back to him. Fayfi could still hear the passion and determination in the slim Saudi's voice when he spoke about their unfinished duty. He'd been wrong. His daughter wasn't a reason to give up the jihad; she was why he had to fight. He was going to Yemen.

MORE THAN 6,000 miles away, Barack Obama was coming to his own decision. On January 22, 2009, his second full day in office, the newly elected president signed the executive order that he had promised during his campaign. Seated at a table in the West Wing in front of a phalanx of retired military officers, Obama promised to close Guantánamo Bay and "restore the standards of due process and the core constitutional values that made this country great even in the midst of war."

The next day Wihayshi released his surprise. Along with the Shaya interview, the al-Qaeda commander had put together a short video featuring himself, Shihri, Raymi, and Muhammad al-Awfi, another former Guantánamo Bay detainee. The four represented AQAP's new leadership: two Yemenis and two Saudis.

Wihayshi's nineteen-minute video put a face on the worst fears of some in the US government: men the US once had in custody were free and threatening to kill Americans. "By God, we are coming," AQAP's new leaders swore into the camera. "We will bring delight to the eyes of our mothers in Palestine and Gaza," they promised. "Either we will come to them with the flags of Jihad waving above steeds of war with the determination of our forefathers, or we will die in this cause." As bin Laden had years earlier, AQAP left no doubt. It was targeting the US.

In Saudi Arabia, Shihri and Awfi's appearance in the video set off a desperate scramble for information. Saudi intelligence hadn't even been aware the pair had left the country; they thought the men were home with their families. Muhammad bin Nayif, the prince in charge of the Ministry of the Interior, ordered an immediate review of the kingdom's rehab program. In early February, Saudi Arabia released the results: eighty-three men, including eleven former Guantánamo Bay detainees, had relapsed and rejoined al-Qaeda. Many of these men, Saudi intelligence claimed, had fled to Yemen.

Near the top of Saudi Arabia's wanted list was Jabir al-Fayfi. Days earlier, the balding thirty-four-year-old had made good on his silent pledge and left home for Yemen. For years, weapons and drug smugglers had been slipping across the porous Saudi–Yemeni border, and al-Qaeda had adapted those same networks for recruits coming south. In mid-January, shortly before Wihayshi released his video, Fayfi and a handful of other Saudis met their Yemeni guides in the mountainous wasteland north of the border. The smugglers guided Fayfi's band through the rocky shrub brush of southern Saudi Arabia before depositing them just over the border in a tiny Yemeni village. Eventually, after the group had passed through several hands, an al-Qaeda member arrived to collect them. The man gave each of the Saudis a weapon and warned them to expect trouble.

The men had to travel through Huthi territory to reach the next hideout. For the next four hours the small convoy of cars picked its way down narrow mountain roads, avoiding tribal checkpoints and potential ambushes. At one point, the al-Qaeda guide told Fayfi and the rest of the Saudis to switch cars and then they moved out again. None of the Yemenis would explain what was going on and the Saudis were getting worried. "This is chaos," Fayfi mumbled to himself as he stared out the window, his gun clutched firmly in his hands. Finally, somewhere in northern Sadah, the cars pulled off the dirt road and rolled to a stop in front of a small house.

Inside was Nasir al-Wihayshi and the rest of AQAP's leadership. This, the al-Qaeda commander softly explained to the exhausted Saudis, was their swearing-in ceremony. In the corner, one of Wihayshi's aides had set up a camera to film the event. Another man read the oath out loud as the Saudis repeated it after him, reciting the *bay'a* and pledging to obey Wihayshi. As their words faded into the still air, the rest of the room rushed in to greet Fayfi and the other Saudis with smiles and words of welcome. They were now members of AQAP.

LESS THAN A month after the swearing-in ceremony, Muhammad al-Awfi, the former Guantánamo detainee who had appeared in Wihayshi's video, went missing. At first Wihayshi told his men that a tribe had betrayed the Saudi commander. But soon word filtered in that Saudi Arabia had announced a general amnesty for any al-Qaeda fighters who wanted to surrender. Awfi, the Saudis claimed, had taken advantage of the offer and was already home with his family.

In order to make sure the Saudis—foreigners who didn't always understand Yemen—stayed out of trouble, Wihayshi had housed them with local families and limited their movement around the country. After Awfi's defection, the restrictions became more severe. "This is nothing like Afghanistan," Fayfi complained to fellow fighters. "There I could travel anywhere. But here it is like being in a prison of your own choice."

The Saudi recruits who had come south with Fayfi spent most days out of sight in tiny shack-like safe houses in the northern mountains close to where they had sworn their oath of loyalty. Often the houses, which they had to share with the families who hosted them, didn't have running water or electricity. Fayfi wasn't allowed to call his wife or daughter. Each time he requested a transfer to another region so he could take part in an operation, Wihayshi told him to be patient.

IN EARLY MARCH, Wihayshi dispatched one of the teenagers from his corps of suicide-bombers-in-waiting to Shibam, in the eastern desert of Hadramawt. A UNESCO World Heritage Site known as the "Manhattan of the desert," Shibam is a breathtaking city of 500 mud-brick tower houses that rises more than 100 feet from the valley floor. The city dates back to the time of Christ and is one of Yemen's few legitimate tourist attractions. Wihayshi's men instructed the eighteen-year-old bomber to stake out the hill overlooking the city where tourists often stopped for photos.

Al-Qaeda left the ultimate target up to the teenager, but they told him they wanted a lot of casualties. They decided against giving the bomber a suicide vest, which AQAP's leadership worried might give him away or prove too hot in early summer. Instead, an al-Qaeda bomb-maker designed a rectangular, four-inch-deep metal box in which they could place the explosives. To disguise his handiwork, the technician bolted a large framed print over the top of the box.

Shortly after lunch on March 15, the al-Qaeda operative climbed the hill and waited for the tourists to come to him. Throughout the afternoon, a few solitary individuals made it to the top. The teenage bomber joked with the foreigners in broken English and even posed for a picture. Just as the sun was starting to dip behind the western mountains, a sweaty group of South Koreans crested the hill—the large group he had been waiting for. He scrambled to get into position as the sun started to dip behind the mud skyscrapers. As the tourists fumbled with their cameras, the suicide bomber walked toward them, clutching the heavy metal box to his chest. The explosion ripped through the group, killing four South Korean tourists and their Yemeni guide, who had moved forward to greet his countryman.

Four days later, al-Qaeda tried again. A South Korean security delegation had flown to Yemen to investigate the bombing in Shibam, and Wihayshi had somehow discovered when their flight would be leaving. This time he selected a twenty-year-old Yemeni named Khalid al-Dhayani.

The evening before the attack, Dhayani recorded his last will and testament. Lifting a silver boom box in front of his chest, he shook it at the camera. "This is my suicide vest," he screeched, his voice breaking with youth, "a cassette player on which we will both listen to the tunes of explosives." The camera cut away to show how the bomb had been prepared. Inside the speakers, nestled behind its plastic front, al-Qaeda had packed hundreds of nails. For the next twenty minutes, Dhayani ranted through his final statement before finally addressing his parents and then just his mother. "This is better for me than life in their prisons," he told her, his voice breaking once more. "Don't listen to anyone who speaks ill of us."

The next morning, Dhayani took his explosive-filled boom box and scouted out a position on the airport road. His handlers had briefed him well and he knew exactly what the cars in the South Korean convoy looked like. He didn't have to wait long. As soon as Dhayani saw the vehicles, he shouldered his boom-box bomb and walked between the first two cars. The nails shattered the windows in both cars, but miraculously no one except Dhayani died; his mangled body splattered across a scorch mark that would remain for months.

DURING THE SUMMER, al-Qaeda made its case to the Yemeni public as it attempted to justify the two suicide bombings. Ignoring the Yemeni guide it had killed, AQAP instead focused on the South Korean tourists. One of the group's in-house clerics, Abu Amr al-Faruq, published a nineteen-page booklet. "We warned them," he wrote, pointing to months of public statements before explaining the theology behind the strikes, once again falling back on the Prophet's command to "expel the infidels from the Arabian peninsula."

At the same time, Qasim al-Raymi, who was still easing into his new role as AQAP's military commander, met with Said al-Shihri in Marib. Ever since the Awfi defection in February, Raymi had been looking for a way to strike back at the Saudis and Muhammad bin Nayif. The Saudi prince had become al-Qaeda's top target. He was the individual responsible for destroying al-Qaeda's network in Saudi Arabia in 2003 and again in 2006, and there was evidence that bin Nayif was cultivating his own network of informants and spies inside Yemen. The standing offer of amnesty was only his latest attempt to weaken al-Qaeda.

Raymi explained that he wanted to send a Yemeni across the

border under the pretense of coordinating the surrender of Saudis. This way, he continued, al-Qaeda could use bin Nayif's success with Awfi against him. As Raymi and Shihri continued to talk, it became clear that the bomber would need to be a Saudi. A Yemeni national would not be able to get close enough to the prince. The bomber had to be someone who knew Saudi Arabia and its customs. Shihri suggested Abdullah Asiri, the young Saudi who once said his biggest dream was to carry out a suicide attack in Saudi Arabia. Drawing on his background in chemistry, Ibrahim Asiri had emerged as one of al-Qaeda's top bomb-makers, and he offered to build the bomb his brother would use. Both brothers wanted revenge on the man they blamed for Ibrahim's arrest and their flight from their homeland.

ON JULY 26, General David Petraeus, the head of US Central Command, responsible for all US military actions in the Middle East, North Africa, and central Asia, landed in Sanaa for a meeting with President Salih. Petraeus's first visit to Yemen, eight months earlier, had been tense. Airport guards had attempted to impound his luggage and the general had informed Salih that in future such treatment would mean that Yemen was not a friend who wanted assistance from the US. This time around, Salih was on his best behavior. Meeting Petraeus in a pair of dark sunglasses that masked an ugly bruise under his left eye from a mountain biking accident, Salih pledged full counterterrorism support. "Without restrictions or conditions," he offered. AQAP is "a dangerous poison."

Five days after that meeting, Salih demonstrated his new commitment to counterterrorism by putting his troops in the field. Almost immediately, things went wrong. One of the military trucks, filled with weapons and chests of money to buy off the tribal shaykhs in Marib, took a wrong turn down a desert wadi and got lost. Other tanks and soldiers arrived at the correct village in Marib, but bombed the wrong house. Heavy tank shells punched through the mud walls of village homes as the tribesmen returned fire. Next door, Aidh al-Shabwani, the al-Qaeda suspect who was the target of the raid, joined his tribal neighbors in fighting off the military's assault. The battle of Marib, as the fight came to be known in al-Qaeda propaganda, lasted more than six hours. Late in the day, a small band of al-Qaeda fighters led by Qasim al-Raymi outflanked the military, which was now fighting most of the village. Firing rocket-propelled grenades from nearby orange groves, the al-Qaeda reinforcements destroyed five tanks before the military retreated. None of the al-Qaeda targets were killed.

As the fight drew to a close in the village, a second contingent of al-Qaeda fighters who were speeding through the desert to reach the village came upon the lost military cargo truck. The men quickly captured the seven soldiers guarding the truck and seized the weapons and money. Driving their loot back to the village, they turned everything over to Raymi, who was the ranking al-Qaeda official at the scene. Lining the soldiers up against a cinderblock wall, Raymi made a quick decision. Instead of executing the men, he asked them to publicly repent for targeting God's warriors. Al-Qaeda, Raymi explained, didn't have a problem with the enlisted men, only with Salih and the Americans. An al-Qaeda technician quickly set up a video camera as each of the seven soldiers paraded past, confessing that he had been wrong to believe Ali Abdullah Salih's lies. Before he let them go, Raymi made each man swear on the Quran that he would never again take up arms against al-Qaeda.

IN SANAA, WHILE people speculated about the government's latest embarrassment in Marib, a thirty-eight-year-old Yemeni–American cleric with a bushy black beard and wire-rimmed glasses took to the Internet to dissect the operation on his blog. The son of a Yemeni minister, Anwar al-Awlaki had been born in the US in 1971 while his father studied agriculture at New Mexico State University as a Fulbright Scholar. The family moved back to Yemen in 1978, where Awlaki spent most of his childhood before returning to the US in 1991 to attend Colorado State University.

On September 11, Awlaki was an imam at a popular mosque in Virginia, and in the fear-filled days after the attacks he often found himself called on to explain Islam to Americans. He answered questions for the *Washington Post* in an online chat and even attended a prayer breakfast at the Pentagon. But in late 2002, citing a climate of fear and intimidation, Awlaki left for Britain. His London lectures quickly won him a wide following among Western Muslims, who respected him as someone who could present traditional Muslim values in a modern way. By the time he left London two years later, in 2004, people were again asking questions about his past. He had met two of the September 11 hijackers in San Diego and the 9/11 Commission had never been able to determine the exact nature of the relationship. "He was a 9/11 loose end," the commission's executive director later acknowledged.

In Yemen, Awlaki was arrested in a murky case that was never fully publicized. The last the US heard, Yemen released him in December 2007, citing a lack of evidence. Now Awlaki was coming out in favor of the al-Qaeda fighters in Marib and asking his followers to pray for their success in the war against Salih and the US.

Around the time Awlaki was writing about the battle of Marib on his website, Michelle Shephard, a stylish blonde national security reporter for the *Toronto Star*, was in Yemen trying to track him down. Awlaki's online lectures had popped up in a terrorism case she had covered back in Toronto, and she wanted to hear what the cleric thought of his words being used to justify violence. A local contact had given her the phone number of the Awlaki family home in Sanaa, but the English-speaking female who answered swore Awlaki was out of the country. Unconvinced, Shephard asked the woman to pass along a message to Awlaki. The cleric never called back.

Shephard wasn't the only one looking for Awlaki that summer. In August 2009, Umar Farouk Abdu Mutallab, a twenty-two-year-old Nigerian graduate student with short black hair and a winning smile, had arrived in Yemen on a break from his studies in Dubai. Mutallab had studied Arabic in Yemen previously, and he quickly reestablished himself as a language student at an institute in downtown Sanaa. But instead of focusing on Arabic classes, Mutallab spent his time visiting Sanaa's mosques in the hope of meeting someone who could put him in touch with Awlaki. The young Nigerian believed the cleric was the key to his future. He had recently decided to join the jihad and, as a fan of Awlaki's increasingly radical Internet sermons, Mutallab wanted the cleric's guidance. At one mosque, a man who claimed he knew how to get in touch with Awlaki took down Mutallab's contact information. Within days Mutallab received a text message from Awlaki, giving him a number to call. During their short conversation, Awlaki instructed the young graduate student to write an essay explaining his desire to join jihad.

Mutallab spent days on the essay before sending it to Awlaki, who was hiding among tribal allies in southern Yemen. Don't worry, the cleric responded after reading Mutallab's response. He would find a way for the Nigerian to join the jihad.

IN SOUTHERN YEMEN, Qasim al-Raymi was touring AQAP's safe houses and showing off the suicide belt Ibrahim Asiri had built for his brother. "Pray for the one who will wear this belt that he may complete his operation," Raymi told operatives in Abyan and Shabwa. The men could sense something big was in the offing. Raymi had never asked them to pray over a suicide belt before. But when the men asked about the operation, Raymi only smiled and said, God willing, they would hear about it soon.

A few weeks later, Abdullah Asiri left Marib for the long journey to the Saudi border. His brother Ibrahim, who had built the bomb he was wearing, had agreed to drive him most of the way. The few who knew the purpose of his trip wished the brothers well. Abdullah had always been a popular member of the organization, often volunteering for laundry duty and cooking for the other men. No task was below the skinny twenty-three-year-old, who spent his off days fasting and reading the Quran. Shortly before they arrived at the border, Ibrahim stopped the vehicle in a cluster of sand dunes and nodded to his brother. It was time. The two men hugged one final time, as Ibrahim whispered in his brother's ear. Then al-Qaeda's bomb-maker watched his little brother, the boy who had once made him dig through garbage to make sure God's name was properly disposed of, disappear over the sand toward Saudi Arabia.

At the border crossing, Asiri approached the Saudi guards, explaining that he needed to speak to Muhammad bin Nayif. He had a letter from Said al-Shihri's wife and stepson, who had fled south with the fugitives, and he would only talk to the prince.

"Peace and blessings upon you, brother Abdullah," the prince said once the guards had set up the call. "How are you?"

Bin Nayif had been briefed that Asiri claimed to be an emissary for a number of Saudis in Yemen, all of whom wanted to turn themselves in.

"How is your brother Ibrahim?" the prince asked. "I hope he is well."

"He is good, thanks be to God," Abdullah murmured into the phone.

"I bring you good news," bin Nayif continued. "Both your mother and father are doing well." The subtle dig was intended to remind Abdullah that while he and his brother had fled Saudi Arabia, their loved ones had not. Bin Nayif had looked after them, but he could have just as easily imprisoned them.

Eventually, as the pleasantries trailed off, bin Nayif asked the youngster what he wanted.

"I want to meet with you," Abdullah said, adding that some of the Saudis were afraid and wanted to hear from bin Nayif himself that they wouldn't be jailed if they came home. "Can you send a plane?" Abdullah asked. "If I talk to them in your presence then, by the power of God, they will be reassured."

Bin Nayif agreed and said he would send his private plane to Najran to collect the al-Qaeda operative for a meeting.

SHORTLY BEFORE 7 a.m. on Thursday, August 27, the prince's plane returned to the coastal Saudi city of Jeddah, landing at King Abd al-Aziz International Airport north of town. One of bin Nayif's assistants escorted Abdullah to a rented flat across town, where he could nap and relax for the rest of the day before meeting the prince that evening after they broke their Ramadan fast. Bin Nayif didn't want anything spooking Asiri and he told his men to give the al-Qaeda suspect his space.

That evening, Abdullah made his way to the prince's palace, easing past the light security and into the main room where bin Nayif was receiving visitors. Bin Nayif greeted the skinny young man with a hug, kissing his cheeks and once again inquiring after his health. Abdullah held up his cell phone, explaining that he wanted to put in a call to Yemen so the prince could personally assure the renegades that they would be welcomed back.

Of course, bin Nayif agreed.

Back in Yemen, several al-Qaeda fighters crowded around the phone, waiting to hear the explosion they knew was coming. "Speak up," they told Abdullah. Everyone wanted to hear.

"Okay," Abdullah said, handing the phone to bin Nayif, "here is the prince."

"Peace and blessing be upon you," bin Nayif said into the cell phone. "I am your brother and I hope you are well." Continuing with the traditional greeting, bin Nayif added, "I'm so happy to hear your voice and the voices of all your brothers." Just as he started his next sentence, an explosion ripped through the room and cut the line.

While Nayif was distracted with the phone, Abdullah had slipped his hand inside his robe and detonated the bomb he had inserted up his rectum in order to bypass security. Abdullah's body absorbed most of the blast as the explosion went straight up, separating his head from his body and blowing a blood-spattered hole in the roof. Somehow bin Nayif, who had been standing less than a yard away from Abdullah, survived the blast.

The next day, Saudi state television showed King Abdullah meeting with bin Nayif at the hospital. "It was a mistake," bin Nayif told the king, confessing that he hadn't had the bomber searched. The only sign of injury was some white medical tape wrapped around the middle finger of the prince's left hand.

18

Targets

2009–2010

On December 14, 2009, almost four years after Nasir al-Wihayshi and Qasim al-Raymi escaped from prison, US secretary of state Hillary Clinton designated Al-Qaeda in the Arabian Peninsula a terrorist organization. Two days later, the military gave a hurried forty-five-minute briefing to an interagency team of officials and lawyers, laying out their plans for what they called Operation Copper Dune. The military wanted to kill three men—codenamed Akron, Toledo, and Cleveland—whom it had located in southern Yemen. Akron, the main target of the raid, was a man named Muhammad al-Kazami, who US analysts believed was responsible for the 2007 suicide attack on the Spanish tourists in Marib and was now thought to be planning an operation against the US embassy in Sanaa.

Listening to the military's clipped presentation that afternoon on a secure conference call, Jeh Johnson, the Pentagon's top lawyer, felt unprepared for the decision he was being called on to make. The military needed to know if it could legally hit the three targets, and Johnson had spent less than an hour with the evidence. Ultimately, he authorized the strikes on Akron and Toledo, but scratched Cleveland. The possibility of civilian casualties, he felt, was simply too great. With the paperwork in place and Johnson's permission, the military put Operation Copper Dune into motion.

Halfway around the world, in the predawn darkness of December 17, a US Navy ship in the waters off the coast of Yemen opened fire. The target was a small encampment several miles inland, which US intelligence believed to be the al-Qaeda training camp where Kazami was living. Nestled in the low, rocky foothills of southern Abyan, near the village of al-Majalla, the site was nearly inaccessible by road. From the air the only thing US targeters could see was a handful of brush lean-tos scattered among stunted trees and, at night, tiny pinpricks of light that suggested campfires.

Minutes after they left the ship, the cruise missiles equipped with cluster bombs sliced through the darkness to explode among the tents. In Washington, Johnson watched a real-time feed of the attack on what some in the military had dubbed Kill TV. The grainy figures he had seen moving around a moment earlier were gone, obliterated in a series of silent flashes. Inside the camp, the ground rolled and bucked under the force of the blasts, which shattered trees and flung rocks into the air. The cluster bombs, designed to eject smaller submunitions, spewed more explosives into the air as shrapnel tore through flesh and fabric. The bombs that failed to detonate buried themselves in the hard ground, where they formed a minefield of unexploded ordnance. Across the gravel shelf, where a few minutes earlier families had been spread out beneath tattered blue tarps, there was now only pulsating bursts of light and screams of terror. One tribesman who arrived on the scene later recounted the aftermath. "You see goats and sheep all over," he said. "You see the heads of those who were killed here and there; you see children. And you cannot tell if this meat belongs to animals or human beings."

In one of the flimsy structures a US missile killed Muhammad al-Kazami as well as his wife and children, who were sleeping next to him. Most of the other victims, however, were local bedouins who lived off the animals they raised in this neglected mountain valley in southern Yemen. Instead of an al-Qaeda training site, the US had attacked a bedouin camp. Kazami had been their guest, not the other way around.

After watching the destruction on Kill TV, Johnson told a friend, "If I were Catholic, I'd have to go to confession." He felt much like another government lawyer, who had once compared attempting to stop a targeted killing to "pulling a lever to stop a massive freight train barreling down the tracks." Johnson and the other government lawyers were the ones who were supposed to pull the lever, but in the face of military certainity they often felt powerless to do so.

Al-Qaeda would later claim that fifty-eight people, including a number of women and children, were killed in the raid.* Survivors spent much of the rest of the day washing the corpses that were still intact and preparing them for burial. Some men walked across the scorched gravel pulling spent shell canisters out of thorn bushes and untangling scraps of clothing from trees, wondering what the bedouins had done to invite such wrath.

More than 150 miles north of the carnage at al-Majalla, Yemen upheld its part of the coordinated strikes. As US cruise missiles were on their way toward the bedouin camp, Yemeni counterterrorism units surrounded a two-story stone house just north of Sanaa, where they believed Qasim al-Raymi was hiding. In the early morning shootout, Yemeni forces killed a former Guantánamo Bay detainee, Hani Shalan, who had disappeared months earlier, and made several arrests, but there was no sign of Raymi.

---

*Amnesty International eventually put the number of dead at fifty-five, including fourteen AQAP operatives and forty-one local residents, of whom thirty-five were women and children. The discrepancy is most likely due to the fact that three people died days later after stepping on unexploded ordnance.

THREE DAYS LATER, on the evening of December 20, Salih bin Farid, a wealthy shaykh of the al-Awaliq tribe with a graying goatee and wrinkled pouches under his eyes, called an intertribal meeting at his home just over 60 miles from al-Majalla. Earlier that day he had toured the bomb site, and been shocked at what he had seen. Instead of the al-Qaeda training camp the news was reporting, Farid found a bedouin encampment littered with shattered corpses. The powerful tribal leader, whose family had once ruled for the British as sultans, spoke fluent English, and he saw several shell fragments with the words "made in the USA" stenciled across them. Those shells, he quickly realized, disproved the Yemeni government's claim of having carried out the strike.

Angered at the loss of life and government lies, Farid organized a massive protest of several thousand tribesmen that he scheduled for December 21. The night before the planned protest, close to 150 tribal leaders met at Farid's mansion-like house to agree on a set of ground rules. Several of the tribes were involved in long-standing feuds, which would need to be set aside for such a large gathering. Around 9:30 that evening, as Farid and his guests were feasting and talking, one of his guards slipped in and said that there were five or six young men outside who wanted to talk to him.

"Ask them to come up," Farid instructed.

"But they are heavily loaded with machine guns, with hand grenades, with rocket launchers."

"Doesn't matter," Farid replied. "We are equipped the same."

The young men, who turned out to be surprisingly clean and well dressed for the impoverished region, declined Farid's offer of food. The elderly shaykh knew most of their families and tribes, but as the young men spoke, Farid noticed something was not quite right. The men were clearly well off, but they had no jobs. Some people say "that we are al-Qaeda," they laughed.

"Are you?" Farid pressed.

The men admitted they were and asked if they could attend the protest the next morning. Farid was wary. His rally was about showing the world that the US had attacked a bedouin village, not an al-Qaeda training camp, but the men in front of him were tribesmen as well and they had a right to attend. "If you are coming tomorrow as ordinary tribesmen you are welcome," Farid said, but he wouldn't allow them to attend as al-Qaeda.

"Okay," the men said when Farid finished his lecture, "we will not come." Still, something about the men bothered Farid, and he warned them a second time against coming to the protest as al-Qaeda. "If you do come," he repeated in his gravelly voice, "shave my beard if you survive three days." A customary tribal oath in Yemen, where to publicly shave someone's beard is considered an irredeemable insult, Farid was telling the men that if they broke their agreement he would have them killed within three days. The al-Qaeda operatives assured Farid that they wouldn't attend the protest.

The next morning they came anyway. As the young al-Qaeda operatives pulled up to the meeting site, they could see thousands of tribesmen milling about, discussing the strikes. Muhammad al-Kilwi, a tall man with a hennaed beard that was just starting to grow out and expose its black roots, stepped out of the car with a microphone. Dressed in a green military jacket and a *futa*, the patterned cloth skirt southern Yemeni men often wear, he climbed on top of the car and started to speak.

"Al-Qaeda's war in Yemen is against the United States," he said, "not against the Yemeni military."

As Kilwi's voiced echoed across the plain, dozens of tribesmen wandered over to hear what he had to say, recording his message on cameras and cell phones. "Soldiers, you should know that there is no problem between us and you," he continued as two men stood guard, clutching their rifles and scanning the crowd for threats. "Our issue is with the Americans and their lackeys." Pausing for breath, he continued, "I warn you to remove yourself from the ranks of the Americans, and know that the victory in this is for God's community."

One of Farid's men recognized Kilwi and the other men as the al-Qaeda fighters from the night before and hurried to find his shaykh, who was relaxing under a canopy of several large tents that been set up for tribal dignitaries. "I warned them," Farid snarled, snatching a machine gun from the ground beside him. "Either they will kill me or I will kill them," he huffed as he struggled to his feet. Several of his guards restrained their elderly leader and promised him they would take care of the problem. But when they made it back to the other side of the rally, the car full of al-Qaeda fighters was already driving away.

Just as Farid had feared, Kilwi's short speech distracted from the purpose of his rally. Later that evening, al-Jazeera broadcast handheld footage of Kilwi, whom it correctly identified as an al-Qaeda operative.

Two days later, on Christmas Eve, the US staged a second cruise missile raid. The $600,000 missile soared over the sea and coastal mountains before crashing through the roof of a small stone house near the tiny village of Rafdh. The explosion killed the four men inside and shook the valley awake. More than two hours from the nearest paved road in Shabwa, Rafdh was a world unto itself, a place where villagers eked out an existence without running water or electricity, and a single schoolhouse offered the only sign of a government. For years the building had stood empty. But in early 2009, shortly after he was released from prison, Fahd al-Qusa, al-Qaeda's slender screw-up who had overslept and missed filming the *Cole* attack nine years earlier, arrived with an offer to supply the village with teachers. Within weeks, Qusa returned with a handful of young men, who started teaching the kids how to read the Quran as well as a subject they called "religious sciences." What the Yemeni government had failed to provide for years, al-Qaeda delivered in days.

Along with the villagers, Qusa gathered around the shattered remains of the stone hut early on December 24 to survey the damage. He knew all the victims personally. One of the mangled bodies belonged to Muhammad al-Kilwi. Just as Farid had predicted, the men hadn't survived three days.

BY THE TIME the US launched its Christmas Eve attack, AQAP's latest plot was already underway. Months earlier, Umar Farouk Abdu Mutallab, the young Nigerian student who had sent Anwar al-Awlaki an essay explaining why he wanted to join the jihad, had left Sanaa for the southern province of Shabwa. In October, Mutallab sent his father a series of brief text messages, informing him that he would no longer be in touch.

"Forgive me for any wrongdoing," Mutallab typed. "I am no longer your child." After his final text, the twenty-two-year-old disassembled his phone and destroyed the SIM card.

Worried and unable to get in touch with his son, Umaru Mutallab, a prominent bank executive, met with US officials at the embassy in the Nigerian capital of Abuja and warned them of his son's radicalization. The officers duly noted Mutallab's suspicions, writing in their report that Umar Farouk was in Yemen and possibly in contact with AQAP. CIA officials added the Nigerian's name to a database of more than half a million names housed at the National Counterterrorism Center. But the vaguely worded notice failed to trigger any alarms and Umar Farouk's name was never passed along to the FBI, which maintained its own separate watch list that acted as a feeder for the Department of Homeland Security's no-fly list. Nor had anyone in any of the overlapping bureaucracies that had been established in the eight years since September 11 thought to revoke the US visa Mutallab had received more than a year earlier. The system failed miserably, Secretary of Homeland Security Janet Napolitano later admitted.

While his father sounded the alarm in Nigeria, Umar Farouk

was swearing the *bay'a* and agreeing to carry out a martyrdom operation. Once again, AQAP asked Ibrahim Asiri to build the bomb. The attack on bin Nayif had failed because the bomber had hid the bomb in his rectum and his body absorbed most of the blast. This also explained why the Saudi prince had escaped with only superficial injuries even though he had been standing so close to his attacker. To avoid this problem with his new bomb, Asiri had to find a way to conceal an explosive on Mutallab's body that was strong enough to down an airplane yet small enough to pass through security undetected. Asiri used the plastic explosive PETN, as he had for the bin Nayif attack, but this time, instead of building a cavity bomb, he sewed the explosive into specially made underwear.

Umar Farouk bought a ticket to Ethiopia for December 7. Before he left Yemen, an al-Qaeda cameraman recorded footage of him firing weapons at one of AQAP's mobile training camps. Then the smiling youngster had sat down to record his last will and testament.

After a brief stay in Ethiopia, Mutallab flew on to Ghana. On December 22, his twenty-third birthday, Mutallab was in the Ghanaian capital of Accra. That same day President Obama was meeting in the White House with officials from the CIA, FBI, and Homeland Security to review possible plots against the US. Just down the hall from Obama's meeting, John Brennan chaired a second meeting devoted to Yemen and threats from AQAP. But no one in the administration put the two together.

Two days later, as the US launched the Christmas Eve strike that killed Kilwi and three other al-Qaeda operatives, Umar Farouk flew to Lagos, Nigeria, and from there to Amsterdam, where he boarded Northwest Airlines flight 253 early on Christmas morning. Seated in 19A on the Airbus A330, directly above the fuel tanks and next to the airplane's internal wall, the young Nigerian waited until the plane neared Detroit before retreating to the bathroom.

Twenty minutes later, he returned to his seat. Complaining of an upset stomach, he pulled a blanket over his lap. Underneath the blanket, he grasped the syringe that would spark a chemical reaction and trigger the bomb, but when he plunged it down there was only a loud pop and some sparks as his pants caught on fire. Apparently shocked that there was no explosion, Mutallab remained in his seat staring at the small fire and the smoking, partially melted syringe that he still held in his hand.

Several seats away Jasper Schuringa, a Dutch filmmaker, saw the sparks and rushed across to tackle the now burning figure. Along with flight attendants and other passengers, Schuringa put out the flames and dragged Umar Farouk into the business class section, where he was handcuffed. Minutes later, the plane landed at the metro airport in Detroit.

JOHN BRENNAN WAS at home cooking Christmas dinner when he got the call from the White House situation room. The voice on the phone informed him that somebody on a plane landing in Detroit had "a bit of an issue." Nearly 5,000 miles away in Hawaii, where he was spending the holidays, President Obama received a similar message.

Days later, during a press conference that followed a hurried review of the intelligence system, Brennan explained that AQAP had caught the US by surprise. The US, Brennan told reporters, knew that AQAP had the aspiration to attack the US, "but we didn't know they had progressed to the point of actually launching individuals here." Nearly a decade after September 11, the US had once again underestimated al-Qaeda.

In fact, the US seemed confused as to the exact nature of AQAP. Brennan described it as "an extension of al-Qaeda core coming out of Pakistan," while the State Department more accurately treated it as a distinct terrorist group with its own hierarchy and decision-making apparatus. In private, Obama was furious with the security failure. "We dodged a bullet, but just barely," he told officials when he returned from vacation in early January. In a tense White House meeting with his deputies, Obama asked them to imagine if the bomber had succeeded. "He could have gotten it right and we'd all be sitting here with an airplane that blew up and killed over a hundred people."

Unsure of what Obama would order after the near-miss in the skies over Detroit, General Petraeus had already returned to Yemen for another meeting with Salih. The CENTCOM commander wanted to present Obama with as many options as possible. Petraeus asked Salih to allow US Special Forces to conduct raids inside Yemen. "You cannot enter the operations area," Salih said, arguing that US soldiers would only further inflame the situation. Already, Salih continued, the US had killed far too many civilians in the al-Majalla strike on December 17.

Interrupting the president, Petraeus pushed back, arguing that the only civilians killed in the al-Majalla bombing were Muhammad Kazami's wife and two children. Salih turned to his aides for confirmation, but none of the Yemenis seemed convinced by Petraeus's claim of three civilian casualties. They had all seen the photos of mangled corpses: women and children stacked up next to the road awaiting burial. Part of the disconnect between Petraeus's count and the images on Yemeni television was the White House's new way of classifying casualties. Unless there was explicit intelligence exonerating specific individuals, the US counted all males of military age at a strike site as combatants.

Still, Salih did offer Petraeus something. The US no longer had to rely solely on missile attacks from warships patrolling offshore; it could now put military planes into Yemeni airspace to attack al-Qaeda targets inside the country. "We'll continue saying the bombs are ours, not yours," Salih promised. Behind him, Deputy Prime Minister Rashad al-Alimi joked that he had just "lied" to parliament, telling them that the bombs in the al-Majalla strike had been American-made but deployed by Yemenis.

Two weeks after Salih gave Petraeus permission to expand the war in Yemen, US jets struck a car near the Saudi border which they believed was carrying a number of al-Qaeda fighters including Qasim al-Raymi. The missiles destroyed the car but missed the fighters, who were tucked beneath a rock overhang resting when the bombs fell. A single piece of shrapnel grazed Raymi, cutting across his stomach. Everyone else escaped without a scratch.

IN LATE JANUARY, as US aircraft scoured the Yemeni countryside for targets, Abdalilah Shaya, the wavy-haired journalist, traveled south to Shabwa for his second interview with Anwar al-Awlaki. The fugitive cleric, who was being sheltered by his tribe, had grown his beard out in the weeks since Shaya had last seen him. The wiry hair on his face now reached well below the collar of his robe. During their first interview, in late November, Shaya had wanted to know about Awlaki's links to Major Nidal Hasan, the army psychiatrist who gunned down thirteen people at Fort Hood, Texas, on November 5, 2009, the worst shooting to ever take place at a US military base.

Awlaki admitted to having exchanged e-mails with Hasan for nearly a year prior to the shooting and praised him as a hero, but stopped just short of saying he had given the order for the attack. "I didn't put Nidal Hasan into action," he told Shaya at the time. "Rather it was America's crimes and oppression that forced him to act."

This time Shaya asked about Umar Farouk and the attempted Christmas Day bombing. Did Awlaki have anything to do with this latest attack? Did he know Umar Farouk?

"I had communications with him," Awlaki said, choosing his words carefully. "He was one of my students."

When Shaya pressed him further, Awlaki denied having any part in the planning or execution of the plot. But the cautious cleric wouldn't say whether he knew of the attack in advance. "I did not tell him to do this operation, but I support it," Awlaki added cryptically.

US investigators doubted Awlaki's public claims. Under interrogation in Michigan, Umar Farouk had admitted that a man, whom the government later identified as Awlaki, had recruited him and instructed him on the mission. Those conclusions meshed with what John Brennan and his team had found during their review of the US intelligence system. Until late 2009, the investigators discovered, AQAP had been focused on attacks inside Yemen. This raised a key question: why the sudden shift to targeting the US? The answer, many believed, was Anwar al-Awlaki. Their theory was that as Awlaki advanced up the ranks of AQAP, he had rechanneled the energies of a skilled subset of operatives into plots against the US.

This theory oversimplified a complex organization. Al-Qaeda in Yemen had been growing and evolving since 2006, moving from small-scale attacks in Yemen to larger ones in Saudi Arabia and the US. More than the brainchild of a single man, the Christmas Day attempt was the natural outgrowth of an increasingly ambitious group that had several former Guantánamo Bay detainees in its ranks.

Nevertheless, Brennan's Awlaki-centered view prevailed, and the White House's Office of Legal Counsel started work on a memo that would provide the legal framework for the Obama administration to kill an American citizen without ever charging him in court. Basing their memo on what the intelligence agencies concluded about Awlaki's role within AQAP, White House lawyers eventually argued that the US was legally within its rights to kill the fugitive cleric if he couldn't be captured. This, the memo argued, would get around the long-established presidential ban on assassination as well as the Bill of Rights, which in the Fifth Amendment guarantees that the government may not deprive a citizen of life "without due process of law." Attorney General Eric Holder would later argue that "due process" and "judicial process" are not one and the same. "The Constitution guarantees due process, not judicial process," he said. In his opinion, and that of other administration lawyers, the White House's internal interagency review satisfied constitutional requirements. Holder refused to explain how the review process worked or how the administration decided who should be targeted for killing, but he did say that Americans should be "assured that actions taken in their defense are consistent with their values and their laws."

Even before the memo was completed, the Office of Legal Counsel gave oral approval for placing Awlaki on the CIA's list of targets. Within weeks of Umar Farouk's attempt to down the Northwest airliner, the decision to kill Anwar al-Awlaki had become official US policy.

EACH WEEK DURING the early part of 2010, Brennan and National Security Adviser Tom Donilon chaired separate meetings on the situation in Yemen. After the Christmas day attempt, David Axelrod, Obama's top political adviser, began attending the sessions that were known as "Terror Tuesday" within the White House, where defense officials selected which targets to strike. Obama, however, denied the military and CIA permission to carry out "signature strikes" in Yemen, which would have allowed the US to target suspicious individuals even when it didn't know their names. "We are not going to war with Yemen," Obama warned. Instead, the US relied on what Brennan called a "scalpel" approach; a series of missile and drone strikes on which Obama had to sign off individually. One of these attacks killed Nayif al-Qahtani, the young Saudi behind *Sada al-Malahim*, and in March another one took out Jamil al-Anbari, a key al-Qaeda figure who had fought in Iraq. But these were midlevel commanders who were easily replaced, not the group's top leaders who had authorized the attack on the US.

Despite the strikes, life in al-Qaeda's mobile training camps continued much as it had before. Small groups of men dressed in T-shirts and jeans or robes and headscarves met at prearranged sites in the desert for training sessions before scattering in different directions, only to reassemble later. Often these sessions consisted of little more than firing rocket-propelled grenades at a cluster of trees or a few rounds of target practice on an assortment of machine guns. Qasim al-Raymi, AQAP's military commander, moved around the country, supervising the training and recruiting more fighters. The US strikes, like the one in al-Majalla that had killed so many civilians, often enraged local tribesmen who lost friends or relatives in the bombings. Many of these angry young men found their way to al-Qaeda, which promised them a chance for revenge. After the al-Majalla attack at the end of 2009, Abu Bakr al-Qirbi, Yemen's foreign minister, estimated there were 300 members of AQAP in Yemen. Within three years, that estimate would triple to more than 1,000. "The US sees al-Qaeda as terrorism," one tribal leader explained, "and we consider the drones terrorism."

On May 25, after weeks of drone flights, the US thought it had a lock on Aidh al-Shabwani, the al-Qaeda fighter who had been the target of the battle of Marib a year earlier. The tip, like most the US used to carry out its strikes, came from allies within Yemeni intelligence. But instead of Aidh al-Shabwani, the US missile killed Jabir al-Shabwani, the deputy governor of Marib, and four bodyguards. A distant relative of the al-Qaeda fighter, Shabwani had been tasked with arranging meetings with al-Qaeda members in an effort to get them to surrender.

"How could this have happened?" Obama asked when it became clear that the US had killed the wrong man. The answer that came back was not reassuring to a president who was being asked to authorize strikes based on the intelligence his military presented to him. "We think we got played," one administration official admitted, explaining that some analysts believed Salih had used the US to eliminate a political rival.

The killing highlighted a serious flaw in the US approach to fighting AQAP; it was wholly dependent on Salih. Without its own intelligence assets, the US could only pursue the targets Salih offered. Joint Special Operations Command, which oversees the Special Forces units within the US military, "wasn't as up to speed as they should have been," a US intelligence official involved in the strike later said. The US had little idea what was happening on the ground in Yemen.

IN JULY 2010, Abdalilah Shaya, the journalist who had interviewed most of AQAP's top leaders, went grocery shopping with his friend Kamal Sharaf, a political cartoonist who often poked fun at President Salih. Outside a local supermarket, Shaya waited in the car while Sharaf ran inside. When Sharaf walked out of the store a few minutes later, he saw "armed men grabbing [Shaya] and taking him to a car." Months earlier, in the days after the al-Majalla attack, Shaya had traveled to Abyan to document the results of the raid for al-Jazeera and a handful of other news outlets. His impassioned stories of civilian casualties and pictures of shell fragments stamped with the words "made in the USA" had quickly found their way into the US press, where they helped to discredit the official story of a unilateral Yemeni strike.

The Yemeni security agents who abducted Shaya that day in July wanted to send the journalist a message. "We will destroy your life if you keep on talking about this issue," one of them warned before dumping him on the street in the middle of the night.

One month later, on August 6, the security agents returned. It was the beginning of Ramadan, the month-long celebration of daylight fasting and abstinence, and Shaya refused to come out of the house. In the ensuing scuffle one of his teeth was broken and he was badly bruised. The agents left him in an underground cell for a month before transferring him to the Political Security Organization prison where al-Qaeda had staged its great escape four years earlier. In prison, Shaya reconnected with his friend Sharaf, who had also been detained. The PSO offered Sharaf a deal: stop making fun of the president and go free. Sharaf agreed, but Shaya refused to stop his reporting.

DURING THE SUMMER of 2010, AQAP had picked up the pace of its attacks, assassinating dozens of Yemeni security officials in drive-by shootings across the south. But it hadn't lost sight of the US. Nearly every public statement the organization made threatened revenge for the attack on al-Majalla.

In Shabwa, top al-Qaeda leaders met to discuss the possibility of acquiring ricin, a highly toxic poison. Even a speck of the white powder could kill if inhaled. A year earlier, Raymi had suggested packing toxins around the bomb al-Qaeda used in its attempted assassination of Muhammad bin Nayif, and now the organization started to look for ways to manufacture the poison. Eventually the men discarded the poison bomb idea as too difficult, but they quickly developed a second plan to hit back at the US.

As al-Qaeda's latest plot developed, Jabir al-Fayfi came to a momentous decision. For the second time in as many years, the balding Saudi changed his mind about jihad. Ever since the Awfi defection more than a year earlier, Fayfi had been chafing under what he considered Wihayshi's overbearing leadership style, which allowed for only minimal contact with his wife and daughter. Convinced he needed something to trade for his safe return to Saudi Arabia, especially after AQAP's attempt on bin Nayif's life, Fayfi collected as much information as he could on future plots and then took off for the border. Following a hurried debriefing,

Saudi Arabia passed several pressing tips along to its Western allies. French intelligence received one of the first calls.

Two weeks after the Saudis warned the French, a woman dressed in an abaya, the all-enveloping black cloak, and a full facial veil walked into a UPS office in an upscale Sanaa neighborhood and dropped off a package for Chicago. Several minutes later, another package for the US was left at the Federal Express office just down the road.

Within hours, Muhammad bin Nayif was on the phone to John Brennan, a longtime friend who had once served as the CIA station chief in Riyadh. Nayif warned him about a pair of bombs on cargo planes headed for the US. Along with Fayfi's information, Saudi Arabia had drawn on several other sources to piece together the information bin Nayif was now sharing with the US. Weeks earlier, al-Qaeda had carried out a dry run, sending several packages to different addresses in the US. Officials in the US had intercepted those packages, but this time the bombs were live. The US issued an international alert and asked its allies in the Middle East and Europe for help. Officials in Dubai discovered the first package, a PETN bomb—the same type of plastic explosive AQAP had used in the bin Nayif and Christmas Day attacks—hidden in a computer printer, while agents in central England eventually uncovered the second one.

THAT SAME MONTH, Abdalilah Shaya, the journalist Yemeni intelligence agents had abducted in August, appeared in a state security court locked in the white metal cage reserved for defendants. His wavy hair had been shorn down to a buzz cut, and as the judge read out the charges against him he paced slowly around the cell, "smiling and shaking his head in disbelief." Besides being labeled AQAP's "media man," Shaya had also been charged with recruiting for al-Qaeda and inciting the organization to assassinate President Salih and his eldest son, Ahmad.

After the judge finished reading the list of charges, Shaya addressed the court and his fellow journalists who had come to observe. “When they hid murderers of children and women in Abyan, when I revealed the locations and camps of nomads and civilians in Abyan, Shabwa, and Arhab when they were going to be hit by cruise missiles, it was on that day they decided to arrest me,” he shouted referring to his reporting on the al-Majalla bombing. Before the guards pulled Shaya out of the cage and back to prison, he yelled out one final sentence: “Yemen, this is a place where, when a young journalist becomes successful, he is viewed with suspicion.”

19

Out of the Shadows

2011–2012

In January 2011, Yemen's state security court sentenced Shaya to five years on charges of belonging to al-Qaeda. Almost immediately, prominent tribal shaykhs petitioned Salih to overturn the verdict, and by the end of the month the president announced that he was prepared to pardon the journalist. Days later, on February 2, President Obama phoned Salih. With the collapse of the regime in Tunisia and protests spreading across Egypt, Salih had just announced a series of reforms. "Yemen is not Tunisia or Egypt," government ministers told journalists. Once again, just as in 2005, Salih promised not seek reelection. His current term, which was scheduled to end in 2013, would be his last. But already, inspired by what they were seeing in North Africa, protesters had taken to the streets to call for the end of Salih's thirty-three-year rule.

Obama told Salih that while he welcomed the reforms, Yemeni security forces must "show restraint and refrain from violence against Yemeni demonstrators who are exercising their right to free association, assembly, and speech." Near the end of the call Obama brought up the case of Abdalilah Shaya. According to a White House statement, Obama "expressed concern over the release." The next day Salih backed away from his pledge to pardon the journalist, and Shaya remained in jail.

On February 11, barely a week after Obama's call, Hosni Mubarak resigned as president of Egypt, ending a thirty-year dictatorship and making him the second Arab leader to fall in less than a month. In Yemen, protesters set up camp in front of Sanaa University and dubbed the grubby traffic roundabout the Square of Change. "The people want the fall of the regime," they chanted in unison, their voices rippling through Sanaa's narrow streets. From his presidential palace across town, Salih watched the tent city grow. Throughout January and February, aides had traveled the country distributing bags of cash and new cars to tribal shaykhs who promised to remain loyal. Those payments now seemed insufficient in the face of so much public anger.

Both sides knew there was a reckoning coming, and on Friday, March 18, two months into the protests, it arrived. Hundreds of demonstrators who had been hunched over in congregational prayers across the cement square stood and once again began the chant against Salih. High above them, snipers who had taken up positions on the roofs of neighboring buildings opened fire. Caught in a crossfire as the bullets shrieked past them, the men in the square rushed for cover, skittering across the cardboard and newspapers they had been using as prayer rugs moments earlier. As the bodies fell, men stripped off their jackets and shirts to ferry the wounded down the street to a mosque. By the end of the day fifty-two men were dead and more than 300 were injured.

Shocked by a massacre which many of them had followed on al-Jazeera's live feed, Salih's allies started to desert him. He fired his cabinet that night, and three days later, on his sixty-ninth birthday, Ali Muhsin al-Ahmar, the general Salih had enlisted to defeat the Socialists in the 1994 civil war and turned to again in 2004 for the fight against the Huthis, abandoned him. Ali Muhsin announced his defection live on television, saying that his soldiers in the First

Armored Division would now protect the protesters. Within minutes, several other top army commanders had joined the nascent rebellion. By the end of the day Yemen's military had split. Half followed Ali Muhsin into revolt while the rest—many of whom were commanded by Salih's sons and nephews—reaffirmed their loyalty to the president.

Hundreds of miles south, in the sand and gravel foothills of Abyan, confused soldiers who hadn't been paid in weeks abandoned their post outside a munitions factory near the village of Jaar. In their wake masked men, whom villagers later described as al-Qaeda fighters, streamed into the one-story cement hangar looking for ammunition. Shortly after the masked men disappeared, an explosion ripped through the building, blowing off the roof and killing more than 120 looters who were scavenging for scrap metal.

From their hideouts in Abyan and Shabwa, Wihayshi and the rest of AQAP's leadership reassessed the possibility of establishing an Islamic state in the south. Months earlier, Wihayshi had written to Osama bin Laden in Pakistan and asked permission to seize and hold territory in Yemen. It's not "the right time," bin Laden had responded in a series of courier-carried letters on USB flash drives. There's not "enough steel," bin Laden said, referring to AQAP's lack of popular support on the ground. But with Salih's government and military collapsing, Wihayshi saw an opening.

In April, Adil al-Abab recorded an audio session for an online jihadi forum. Abab, al-Qaeda's chief cleric, claimed that the organization had already made great progress in the days since the massacre in Sanaa. "Today we control Jaar," he said, referring to the small, impoverished city a few miles north of the provincial capital of Zanjubar. "The largest problem that we face here is the lack of public services such as sewage and water, and we are trying to find solutions."

Al-Qaeda, Abab explained to his listeners, was not the nihilistic organization so often portrayed in the media. "We have, here in

Jaar, full plans for projects we want to achieve for the people," he continued. "We want to make contracts with investors so as to arrange these affairs." He acknowledged that mistakes al-Qaeda had made elsewhere had hurt the group's recruiting efforts, but they were fixing that in Yemen by using a different name that was free of the baggage of death and destruction that many had come to associate with al-Qaeda. Instead, he said, Ansar al-Shariah, or the Supporters of Islamic Law, is the name "we use to introduce ourselves."

For the first time since Osama bin Laden had founded al-Qaeda nearly two decades earlier, the organization was talking about more than just attacking the West. It wanted to provide social services and govern. AQAP was entering a new phase and it was on the move, acquiring as much territory as it could hold. "First Zanjubar then Aden," Abab predicted boldly.

AROUND THE SAME time Abab recorded his remarks in Yemen, a team of US Navy SEALs was training in Nevada's high desert for a mission to Pakistan. Weeks earlier, President Obama had authorized a raid on a three-story compound in Abbottabad, Pakistan, where CIA analysts believed Osama bin Laden was hiding. By Thursday, April 28, training was complete and the SEALs were in Jalalabad, the same city in eastern Afghanistan that bin Laden and his Arab fighters had besieged more than two decades earlier, in 1989. The SEALs preferred to operate on dark nights, when their infrared goggles and superior technology gave them the greatest advantage. The next few nights—the end of April and the beginning of May—represented their best chance for optimal conditions. Obama met with his national security team that same evening for a final discussion. Leon Panetta, the head of the CIA, thought the intelligence was the best the US was likely to get, but Michael Leiter, who ran the National Counterterrorism Center, wanted more confirmation. Obama listened to the back-and-forth but said little. Just after 7 p.m. he ended the meeting, saying he wanted to sleep on the decision.

The next morning, April 29, he gave his answer: the mission was a go. Saturday afternoon, Vice Admiral Willian McRaven, the head of Joint Special Operations Command who had designed the raid, spoke to Obama one final time and told him it would take place the next evening, Sunday, May 1. "Godspeed to you and your forces," Obama signed off as he dressed for the annual White House correspondents dinner.

Barely twenty-four hours later, the SEALs were in motion, flying east toward Abbottabad in two modified MH-60 Black Hawk helicopters. The ninety-minute flight went off without a hitch as the Black Hawks easily avoided Pakistan's air defense system. But as soon as they neared Abbottabad, the SEALs ran into problems. Instead of hovering as the SEALs had planned, one of the Black Hawks got caught in its own rotor wash as it descended and was forced to land hard in the corner of the compound. Outside the gate, the second Black Hawk touched down and waited. Both had full teams on board; twelve SEALs in the first helicopter, eleven and a translator in the second. In the White House, President Obama, Vice President Joe Biden, and a host of other top officials crowded into a small office off the White House situation room. Staring at a small computer, their only link to the men on the ground, the officials waited impatiently for an update from the silent machine. Secretary of State Hillary Clinton later said the small group of officials could only "hope and pray that the men who were carrying it out would do so successfully and safely." After what seemed like an eternity to the officials in the room, a voice broke the silence and announced that the SEAL team on the ground was safe and ready to proceed with the mission.

Moving quickly, the SEALs made their way toward the center of the compound, breaking into teams of three as they ran. One group headed for the guesthouse, while the other teams used

C-4 explosive to blast their way into the inner courtyard. In the main house, three SEALs stormed up the stairs, killing one of bin Laden's sons on their way to the top. On the third floor they saw their target peeking out from behind a door. Pushing their way into the room, one SEAL gathered two of bin Laden's wives in a massive bear hug while a second lowered his weapon and fired.

Eighteen minutes after the SEALs had crash-landed in the compound, Osama bin Laden was dead. Twenty minutes after that, at 1:10 a.m. local time on May 2, the SEALs were on their way back across the border with bin Laden's body and bags of intelligence.

In Yemen, Wihayshi mourned the loss of the man he called his shaykh, writing, "God decided to take you, leaving me only sorrow." The head of al-Qaeda's most dangerous branch was also determined to strike back. "Don't delude your foolish people that since you killed Osama that this war will end," he warned Obama. "What is coming will be worse." But for all of Wihayshi's threats, it was the US that struck next.

THREE DAYS AFTER President Obama's dramatic late-evening announcement that the SEAL team had killed Osama bin Laden, the US got another break. Anwar al-Awlaki had been spotted in Yemen. After bin Laden, Obama believed Awlaki represented the greatest threat to the US. He even told officials that Awlaki was a higher priority than Ayman al-Zawahiri, who would soon replace bin Laden as the head of al-Qaeda. Obama had been clear with his national security team. "I want Awlaki," the president said. "Don't let up on him."

Unlike other strikes, where the president preferred to avoid civilian casualties at all costs, Obama didn't want to rule anything out when it came to Awlaki. "Bring it to me and let me decide in the reality of the moment rather than in the abstract," he told Brennan and others.

That morning, the American-born cleric was traveling in a

pickup in southern Shabwa. It was just before dawn in Yemen, but the US quickly put several aircraft in the sky over the mountainous province. A special operations aircraft, backed by Harrier jets and Predator drones, soon located the truck, but none of them could get a missile lock. Waiting for a clear shot, the small American squadron continued to track the pickup as it weaved through the darkened landscape of rocks and dirt thousands of feet below. Minutes later everything—the equipment, the weather, and the terrain—came together and the special operations team got a lock. Firing a short-range Griffin missile, the team waited for the explosion. There was a brief flash of light below, but the pickup never stopped. They'd missed.

Inside the truck, the force of the explosion shattered the windows. Thinking they were under attack from someone on the ground, Awlaki shouted at the driver, "Speed up." He wanted to pass through the danger zone as quickly as possible. None of the men in the truck had been hurt, but Awlaki was worried about the drums of gasoline the men were carrying in the back. As the truck picked up speed, US forces fired a second missile. This time the pickup disappeared in a fireball. Seconds later it reappeared, accelerating out of the explosion.

With the second missile, Awlaki and the rest of the al-Qaeda fighters quickly grasped the situation. They all knew what had happened to Abu Ali al-Harithi during the first US drone strike in Yemen nearly a decade earlier. That time the US had missed its target once, but killed him with a second missile. Already Awlaki and the men in the truck had escaped twice in short succession. Their luck couldn't hold forever. Using a cell phone, the forty-year-old cleric called for help. Within minutes, as the US aircraft tracked them overhead, two local al-Qaeda operatives, Abdullah and Musad al-Harad, caught up to Awlaki in a rocky depression with another truck.

Meanwhile, the US had a new problem. The Harrier jets were

almost out of fuel. Dipping their wings, they turned back. The drones kept up the chase, shadowing the pickup as they fought through early morning cloud cover. Somehow the US operators missed al-Qaeda's brief rendezvous on the ground. Awlaki and the others jumped out of the first truck, trading places with the Harad brothers. By the time the clouds cleared and the equipment refocused, Awlaki was heading one way while the Harad brothers moved off in the opposite direction in the original pickup. The US aircraft stayed with that first pickup. Locking onto the truck, they fired again. Another fireball lit up the gravelly landscape. This time the truck didn't reappear.

From a cave where he had taken refuge, Awlaki saw the explosion that killed the Harad brothers. Then he curled up on the ground and went to sleep. His narrow escape, he later told friends, "increased my certainty that no human being will die until they complete their livelihood and appointed time."

EAST OVER THE mountains from where the US had missed Awlaki, al-Qaeda made its move. On May 27, hundreds of fighters left their stronghold in Jaar and slipped the eight and a half miles south through the mountains to Zanjubar, Abyan's coastal capital. The offensive Adil al-Abab, al-Qaeda's chief cleric, had predicted a month earlier was underway. Al-Qaeda quickly overran a Central Security Forces base on the eastern edge of the city. Salih had established the force in 1980 on the heels of several failed coups as a way to protect the regime. But over the years its mission had evolved, and after September 11 it had received millions in aid and training from the US. As the soldiers fled that day much of the US-purchased equipment, including heavy artillery, tanks, and armored transports, fell into al-Qaeda's hands, along with stores of chemicals the group would soon use to replenish its bomb-making laboratory. Most of the soldiers—save for fifty stragglers captured by al-Qaeda—made it out and raced south across an open patch of soft desert toward the Twenty-Fifth Mechanized Brigade base.

After a short break to regroup and distribute the looted equipment, the al-Qaeda fighters attacked the Twenty-Fifth Mechanized Brigade base. Muhammad al-Sumali, the general in command of the brigade, was as unprepared for the al-Qaeda advance as the Central Security Forces had been. A short, heavy-set man with sagging jowls and a mustache just starting to gray, Sumali later told journalists that the governor and most local officials had fled to Aden and safety as the militants poured into the city. As Sumali's forces fought off the assault, stringy-haired fighters quickly secured the governor's palace across town, raising al-Qaeda's black flag over the white stone buildings. Inside the governor's private office, one al-Qaeda fighter videotaped another as he pulled a framed picture of Salih off the wall and stomped on it with his sandals.

When soldiers at a small Republican Guard outpost, the third and final military installation in Zanjubar, failed to reply to Sumali's calls for help, the general radioed Ali Muhsin in Sanaa. The two military men had known each other for years, and Sumali had previously served under Ali Muhsin. But dynamics in the capital had changed. Yemen's army was still divided, and if Sumali wanted Ali Muhsin's support he would have to publicly back the renegade general. If not, Sumali was told, he could call Salih and ask him for help. But the president had few troops loyal to him in the area and both men knew it. The next closest unit, the 119th, eight miles west of Zanjubar, took its orders from Ali Muhsin. Protesting that he was a soldier, not a politician, Sumali declined to take sides.

Sumali's decision to remain neutral in the contest of wills between Salih and Ali Muhsin in Sanaa had immediate consequences. Outside the city, but close enough to hear the fighting, the 119th stayed put. Sumali and his men were on their own. If they fell, al-Qaeda could advance unimpeded toward Aden, 32 miles west along the highway, and complete the final piece of Abab's predicted offensive.

Over the next several days, as Sumali's men were under siege in their base, al-Qaeda fighters secured the area and established checkpoints on the three highways out of the city. Manned by young fighters who searched passing cars for fleeing soldiers, the crude stations often consisted of little more than a tattered desk chair next to a fifty-five-gallon drum that anchored a hand-painted banner for Ansar al-Shariah, the name AQAP had adopted months earlier as part of its rebranding process. The well-armed men dressed like locals, in long robes and *futa*-type skirts, and all carried a green canvas pouch that held bullets, grenades, and the pocket-sized copy of the Quran the men were never without. Over the next few weeks, most of the city's 20,000 inhabitants fled their homes. Abyan's capital was now in al-Qaeda's hands.

IN SANAA, SALIH listened to the reports coming out of Abyan, but there wasn't much he could do. On May 22, days before the al-Qaeda takeover of Zanjubar, he had reneged for the third time on his pledge to sign a deal that would have seen him step down from power in exchange for immunity. Backed by the US and the UN and sponsored by Yemen's six neighbors in the Gulf Cooperation Council, the deal guaranteed that Salih would not be prosecuted for any crimes he might have committed as president. Salih's last-minute refusal to sign sparked a two-week street war in Sanaa that only ended when a bomb ripped through a private mosque inside the presidential palace. Severely burned in the attack, Salih had to be flown to Saudi Arabia for emergency surgery.

With Salih out of the country, Yemen continued its drift toward fragmentation. In the far north, near the Saudi border, the Huthis consolidated their control over Sadah, while elsewhere tribal shaykhs and militias of uncertain origin pressed for as much territory as they could hold. In Abyan and parts of Shabwa, Wihayshi's al-Qaeda fighters set up courts and started to implement their version of Shariah law. Much like the early days of the Taliban in Afghanistan, when black-turbaned fighters cracked down on the crime and chaos around them, AQAP took an uncompromising approach to restoring security and order.

One day, residents in Jaar, which al-Qaeda had renamed Waqar, Arabic for "dignity," were summoned to a sandy clearing with trash lapping at its edges. The new police force al-Qaeda had established in town had caught two teenagers stealing electrical wire. A judge had ordered *hudud*, which under Shariah law is a fixed category of punishments for specific crimes; the penalty for theft is amputation. One of the boys protested, "I'm not a thief but conditions forced me to that." As the crowd watched, an al-Qaeda member lopped off the teenager's right hand with a sword. A judge later said that al-Qaeda eventually gave the boy 120,000 riyals (about $600) "to start a new life."

Al-Qaeda's other public actions, however, suggested that Wihayshi and the rest of the leadership were still conscious of bin Laden's warning that they didn't have enough public support. Throughout the summer, with temperatures in southern Abyan routinely topping 100, two small pickups drove around Jaar and parts of Zanjubar distributing water to families. Other groups of fighters fielded complaints and tracked down stolen property. In an area of Yemen that had been neglected for decades, first by the Socialists and then by Salih, the attention and effort was unprecedented. In Jaar, north of the vicious fighting in Zanjubar, AQAP dug water lines and strung electrical lines to houses that had never had either. "It is like a dream," one resident told an al-Qaeda cameraman as fighters connected his house to the electrical grid.

In Washington, US military commanders nervously watched al-Qaeda's territorial takeover. On June 10, General James Mattis, who had replaced Petraeus as the head of US Central Command, proposed an airstrike on a soccer stadium near the outskirts of Zanjubar, where al-Qaeda fighters had gathered to shell Sumali's base. Mattis, who had fought in both Iraq and Afghanistan, was worried that Yemen was becoming the next Afghanistan. Better to hit the militants hard now, the general reasoned, or else the US would be dealing with the threat for years to come.

Across the room, John Brennan listened to Mattis lay out his plan with growing concern. What the general was proposing would mark a dramatic shift in US policy. No longer would the US be engaged in targeted strikes against key leaders in Yemen; now it would be relaxing the rules and hitting every al-Qaeda target it could find, which ran the risk of greater civilian casualities and an extended war. As the meeting drew to a close, Brennan pushed back against the general's plan with a subtle bureaucratic maneuver, saying he couldn't take the proposal to the president until higher-level officials had signed off. The next day was Saturday, and Brennan chaired the emergency morning meeting to vet Mattis's attack plan. The deputies pared back the target list and later that evening Obama approved a greatly reduced version of the strike. The message to the military was clear: Obama was not going to give them free rein in Yemen.

Later that month, Obama was even more explicit. In one of the White House's "Terror Tuesday" meetings, an official referenced the "campaign" in Yemen. There is no "campaign" in Yemen, the president interrupted angrily. "We're not in Yemen to get involved in some domestic conflict. We're going to continue to stay focused on threats to the homeland—that's where the real priority is." There would be no "signature strikes" in Yemen. Instead, the US once again settled on the more limited option of surgical strikes aimed at AQAP's top leaders, the ones actively plotting against the US.

On the ground in Yemen, however, things continued to deteriorate as al-Qaeda gained more territory. On June 22, nearly 300 miles east of Jaar in the port city of al-Mukalla, sixty-two al-Qaeda suspects staged a massive prison break. Among the escapees were

Ali al-Akbari and Muhammad Bawaydhan, the final two members of Hamza al-Quayti's Tarim cell who had been arrested after the shootout in 2008. Within days most of the escapees had rejoined Wihayshi, and soon kiosks throughout Abyan were selling jihadi anthems and rhythmic poems that celebrated al-Qaeda's latest prison escape.

In Aden, Yemen's Southern Command sent convoys of men and supplies east along the desert highway to Zanjubar to relieve Sumali's beleaguered forces. Each time, al-Qaeda fighters managed to beat back the reinforcements in bloody battles near the narrow sand berms that bordered the highway. Confined to their base and surrounded by al-Qaeda fighters, the Twenty-Fifth Mechanized Brigade held out as best it could. Twice al-Qaeda snipers nearly assassinated Sumali as he directed his troops from the passenger seat of his armored Toyota Land Cruiser. Once the bullet hit the front windshield, sending a river of cracks down the glass directly in front of Sumali. Another time, the sniper hit the passenger-side window in line with the general's head.

On July 25, Sumali, who had let his beard grow during the siege, gave a pleading phone interview to a reporter from the pan-Arab daily *al-Sharq al-Awsat*. "Our soldiers' morale is high. We will not surrender to al-Qaeda," the general said as the sounds of battle echoed in the phone. "Our problem," he continued, "is water and food."

Obama was still wary of getting sucked into Yemen's internal fighting. But it didn't appear as though he had much of a choice. If the US didn't do something, Sumali's base might fall and AQAP could march on Aden. Already the organization controlled too many towns, space Obama worried it could use to launch attacks against the US.

Shortly after Sumali's desperate interview, the US airdropped supplies for his troops. Days later, Saudi Arabia cooperated with another US supply drop, and Saudi jets soon started flying bombing raids over Zanjubar in an attempt to relieve the pressure on Sumali's men. Much of the city had been destroyed during the two months of shelling between al-Qaeda and Sumali's men. Hospitals and schools had been reduced to rubble and the minarets that had once dominated the city's skyline crumbled and sagged under the pounding. The Saudis hit the few targets that were still standing. Outside the city, burned-out tanks littered the sandy wastes between the coastline and the desert highway. Corpses of dead soldiers lay scattered throughout the city where they had fallen, bloated and rotting in the summer sun.

Throughout August, as the US and Saudi air raids continued, most of the fighting on the ground took place at night, when the temperature cooled. During the day, the two sides stayed under cover and shouted at each other through loudspeakers. Al-Qaeda had no problems with the soldiers, they shouted. They only wanted to implement Shariah law.

Finally, on September 10, under enormous pressure from the US and Saudi Arabia, Yemen's military, including units loyal to General Ali Muhsin, bunched for a push on Zanjubar. The reinforcements rolling into the town later that day encountered only token resistance. Al-Qaeda, under orders from Qasim al-Raymi, melted away into the mountains near Jaar. The four-month siege was over.

Just over a week later, protests in Sanaa turned bloody once again when snipers still loyal to Salih and his family opened fire on the marchers, killing more than fifty in two days of fighting. In Saudi Arabia, state media showed a recovered Salih meeting with King Abdullah. Four days later, on September 23, Salih went to the airport under the guise of meeting a plane of visiting aides, but instead of returning to town the president boarded the plane and flew back to Yemen. "He tricked us and he tricked the Saudis," one US official said. "We're not happy at all."

EARLY ONE MORNING as the fighting was drawing to a close in Zanjubar, Anwar al-Awlaki's fifteen-year-old son Abd al-Rahman wrote his mother a short note and then, while everyone in the house was still sleeping, dropped out a second-story window at the family's compound in Sanaa. The ninth-grade student, who had curly hair and wore wire-rimmed glasses like his father, was so shy that his grandfather sometimes worried about him. "I am sorry for leaving in this kind of way," Abd al-Rahman wrote to his mother. "Forgive me. I miss my father and want to see if I can go and talk to him." The family's guard saw the teenager exit the front gate around 6:30 that morning. It was the last time anyone in the compound would see him.

Three weeks later, on September 30, his father and three other al-Qaeda operatives including Samir Khan, a young American, walked to their cars outside a small house in the northern region of al-Jawf. Far from his tribal sanctuary in Shabwa, Anwar al-Awlaki must have believed he would be safe in the wide desert near the Saudi border. But months earlier, the US had received intelligence about Awlaki from a Somali prisoner who had worked with the American cleric. The prisoner had provided the US with a broad-brush picture of Awlaki's world, and when a source in Yemeni intelligence delivered a key tip, the US was ready. Earlier that morning, US drones from Djibouti, as well as some from a secret drone base in the Arabian peninsula which had just come online, had taken off in pursuit of him.

Buzzing overhead, the fleet of armed drones waited until the men were outside the house and far from the children inside before firing a pair of missiles. Reports from the ground later confirmed what the cameras had captured from the air: Anwar al-Awlaki, Samir Khan, and the other two men were dead.

Speaking at Fort Myer, Virginia, later that day, President Obama praised the drone strike. "The death of Awlaki is a major blow to al Qaeda's most active operational affiliate," the president said. "Awlaki was the leader of external operations for Al-Qaeda in the Arabian Peninsula. In that role, he took the lead in planning and directing efforts to murder innocent Americans."

Two weeks later, Obama signed off on another strike in Yemen. The target that night was Ibrahim al-Banna, an Egyptian member of AQAP, who the US believed was plotting a new attack. The missile streaked down through the night air toward a cluster of figures huddled around a campfire on the outskirts of a town in the southern governorate of Shabwa. The first missile plowed into the fire, and seconds later another slammed into the ground yards away. But instead of killing Banna, the US had hit a group of teenagers who were eating dinner. Among the nine dead that night was Anwar al-Awlaki's American-born son, Abd al-Rahman, who had just turned sixteen.

WEEKS AFTER THAT strike, with protests still raging across Yemen and AQAP gaining more territory in Abyan and Shabwa, Salih flew back to Riyadh with a handful of aides. It was November 23, the day before Thanksgiving, and Salih announced that he was finally ready to sign the immunity agreement sponsored by the international community and Yemen's neighbors in the Gulf Cooperation Council. The sixty-nine-year-old president looked fit and in surprisingly good spirits as he launched into a rambling speech that accused the opposition in Yemen of executing a "coup against the constitution." Then with a quick smile and a chuckle, he signed the piece of paper in front of him. According to the terms of the deal, Salih would continue as president for three more months until his long-serving vice president, Abd Rabu Mansur Hadi, took over.

As the transition away from Salih's thirty-three years of rule began, Muhammad bin Nayif, the Saudi counterterrorism head AQAP had attempted to assassinate two years earlier, put in motion a daring, three-country intelligence operation. Along with MI6, Britain's foreign intelligence arm, and the CIA, bin Nayif devised a plan to target Ibrahim Asiri, AQAP's top bomb-maker. Asiri had built the device his brother used in the attack on bin Nayif, and his thumbprint had been found on the bomb Umar Farouk Abdu Mutallab was wearing on Christmas day, 2009. The CIA also suspected him of designing the two printer cartridge bombs in late 2010. And now, US intelligence believed that he was close to being able to surgically implant bombs inside of people. AQAP had already completed testing on animals and the intelligence analysts worried the group might soon dispatch a walking bomb. In the two months since the death of Anwar al-Awlaki, Ibrahim Asiri had emerged as the West's top target in AQAP.

Bin Nayif designed a simple sting operation to get Asiri. In much the same way al-Qaeda had used one of his successes in getting Muhammad al-Awfi to surrender in early 2009 as a blueprint for its assassination attempt on him later that year, bin Nayif played one of al-Qaeda's victories back against the group. Months earlier, MI5, the UK's domestic intelligence agency, had recruited a British citizen of Saudi origin and bin Nayif wanted to use him as bait.

When al-Qaeda overran Zanjubar in early 2011, it had obtained several canisters of chemicals from military laboratories. It later used these and other materials to "transform the modest lab" which had produced the 2009 underwear bomb and the 2010 cartridge bombs into a "modern" one. By early 2012, al-Qaeda had plenty of bombs; what it lacked was individuals with passports that would allow them to travel freely in the West. This, bin Nayif reasoned, must have been why Mutallab had been able to join and be deployed by al-Qaeda so quickly. Sticking to a similar script, bin Nayif instructed the new British recruit to make himself available to al-Qaeda by spending time in mosques and letting it be known that he was looking to join the group. His cover story, much like Mutallab's, was that he was an Arabic language student, looking to study his family's native tongue. Within weeks, al-Qaeda had taken the bait and operatives were vetting the undercover agent for a suicide mission.

That winter was a dangerous time to be working undercover inside al-Qaeda. In February 2012, Abd Rabu Mansur Hadi officially took over as Yemen's new president. Almost immediately, the portly sixty-six-year-old gave the US unfettered access to targets in Yemen. After years of Salih's double dealings and mood swings, Hadi's openness was a welcome change. With a limited base of support and many of Salih's relatives occupying key positions in the still divided military, Hadi needed strong US and international backing to make sure he survived in power. In exchange, Yemen's new president promised to make combating al-Qaeda his top priority.

That same month al-Qaeda announced that it had uncovered three spies—two Yemenis and a Saudi—who were working with Saudi and American intelligence. The men were accused of placing electronic tracking chips in cars used by al-Qaeda fighters for easier targeting by US planes and drones. Al-Qaeda convened a Shariah court in Jaar, which quickly found the trio guilty and sentenced them to death for their roles in a US airstrike in early 2012 that had killed ten al-Qaeda fighters. The death sentence al-Qaeda posted to the Internet was accompanied by videotaped confessions of all three.

As a warning to other would-be spies, al-Qaeda elected to make a public spectacle of the executions. They shipped the Saudi, Ramzi al-Ariqi, back to Shabwa, where he had been arrested, and sentenced the Yemeni who, according to al-Qaeda, had physically put the tracking chips in the cars to death by crucifixion. On the day of the execution in Shabwa, truckloads of heavily armed al-Qaeda fighters descended on the dusty city of Azzan to watch. The charges were read out over a loudspeaker as four masked men pulled a blindfolded Ariqi out of the back of a van and marched him through a crowd of jostling onlookers toward a dusty clearing they had marked off with green security tape. The men forced Ariqi to kneel on a faded blue tarp in the center of the clearing. Blinking into the bright sunlight as three men in white lab coats and surgical masks removed his blindfold, Ariqi repositioned himself and brought his hands toward his face for a final moment of prayer. The video al-Qaeda made of the execution goes dark and then, seconds later, a single shot rings out followed by a rough chorus of voices shouting "Allahu Akbar."

In Abyan, the executions were similarly well attended. One of the men killed in the US airstrike had left behind a young son named Salim, and al-Qaeda wanted the boy to witness the crucifixion. Dressed in a light blue robe with childish curls in his hair and most of his baby teeth still in place, Salim looked about six years old. On a bright early spring day, al-Qaeda fighters nailed the convicted spy to a rough cross of wooden beams reinforced with steel pipes, and then lashed him to a street post. As the crowd surged forward for a better view, one of the men picked Salim up and put him on his shoulders. "That's the traitor who killed my father," the boy said, pointing at the crucified man.

Weeks after the executions, in mid-April, an al-Qaeda operative handed the British undercover agent a bomb. More advanced than the one Ibrahim Asiri had designed for the 2009 Christmas day attempt, this one had two triggering mechanisms: one chemical and one manual, in case the initial one failed as it had on the airliner over Detroit. Like the one Mutallab had used, this latest bomb contained no metal and was once again sewn into a pair of specially made underwear. The undercover agent still hadn't met Asiri, the target of the operation, or any other of al-Qaeda's top leaders, but with the bomb in hand he no longer had an excuse to remain in Yemen.

Al-Qaeda had left the details of the operation up to the would-be bomber, instructing him only to transit through a Persian Gulf country on his way to Europe, where he could catch the US-bound flight he would bomb. This route, al-Qaeda's planners seemed to believe, would limit the attention someone coming from Yemen would attract from airport security. Instead, the undercover agent arranged a meeting in Yemen with his Saudi handler and handed over the bomb. The intelligence agent flew the bomb out of the country on a private plane and turned it over to US officials, who transported it back to the FBI laboratory in Quantico, Virginia, for further analysis. Meanwhile, the undercover agent kept up the pretense of the plot, leaving Sanaa on a flight to the United Arab Emirates.

Days after the British agent left Yemen and was debriefed, the US launched a drone strike on Fahd al-Qusa, the Yemeni operative who had once missed filming the *Cole* attack. The May 6 strike in southern Shabwa killed Qusa and another al-Qaeda operative who was in the car with him that evening. The attack was part of a missile surge that the US had instituted in early 2012 after Hadi assumed the presidency. After nearly three years of resisting calls for signature strikes in Yemen, Obama had finally relented and allowed the military greater freedom. The surgical approach Obama and Brennan favored no longer seemed to be working. The US kept killing al-Qaeda operatives in Yemen, but AQAP continued to grow. Instead of calling them "signature strikes," the Defense Department now referred to them as terrorist-attack-disruption strikes, or TADS.

Later that week, al-Qaeda released an obituary of Qusa that concluded with a chilling threat. "And to America, we remind them of what our Shaykh Fahd al-Qusa—may God have mercy on him—said to you: 'The war between us will not end and the coming days are bringing something new.' "

PRINCIPAL CHARACTERS

Muhammad al-Ahdal: al-Qaeda deputy and moneyman in Yemen until 2003, when he surrendered as part of a secret agreement. He was freed in 2006 and lives in Yemen.

Abdullah al-Ahmar: head shaykh of the powerful Hashid tribal confederation and Yemen's speaker of parliament from 1993 until his death in 2007. He also headed Islah, the Yemeni opposition party.

Ali Muhsin al-Ahmar: a contemporary and fellow tribesman of President Salih who commands the First Armored Division. He was President Salih's iron fist and led the war against the Socialists in 1994 and the Huthis in 2004. The general defected in early 2011 and continues to hold his position in the military under Yemen's new president.

Muhammad al-Ansi: Yemeni informant who convinced the FBI to go after Muhammad al-Muayyad. He attempted suicide outside the White House in 2005 when the FBI refused to increase his payment.

Abdullah Asiri: Saudi national who traveled to Yemen in 2006 to join al-Qaeda. He carried out a suicide attack in an attempt to assassinate Prince Muhammad bin Nayif of Saudi Arabia in 2009. The prince survived.

Ibrahim Asiri: Saudi national who traveled to Yemen in 2006 to join al-Qaeda. He has since emerged as one of AQAP's top explosives experts and built the bomb his brother used in the 2009 attempt on Muhammad bin Nayif, as well as those for the December 2009 "underwear bomber" plot and the 2010 parcel bomb plot. Currently at large, he is believed to be in Yemen.

Anwar al-Awlaki: US–Yemeni cleric who left the US following the September 11 attacks. He later claimed to have been radicalized in a Yemeni prison and had contact with Nidal Hasan, the Fort Hood shooter, and Umar Farouk Abdu Mutallab, who attempted to bring down a US airliner over Detroit on Christmas Day, 2009. He was killed in a US drone strike in September 2011.

Jamal al-Badawi: logistics director for the USS *Cole* attack. On the FBI's most wanted list, he escaped from prison in 2003 and again in 2006, and is currently free and living in Yemen as part of an agreement he made with then President Salih.

Nasir al-Bahri: Osama bin Laden's former bodyguard, often known by his nickname Abu Jandal. He is currently free and lives in Yemen.

Jabir al-Banna: US citizen who was involved in the Lackawanna Six case. On the FBI's most wanted list, he escaped from a Yemeni prison in 2006 and is currently free and living in Yemen as part of an agreement with then President Salih.

Tariq al-Fadhli: Osama bin Laden's deputy, who fought at the siege of Jalalabad in 1989. He led several veterans of Afghanistan back to Yemen in 1990, where they initiated a guerrilla war against the Socialists in Abyan. After the civil war in 1994, Fadhli abandoned jihad in favor of money and favors from then President Salih. He currently lives in Yemen.

Jabir al-Fayfi: Saudi former drug addict who traveled to Afghanistan to find redemption and a new life. He fought in the battle of Tora Bora and later ended up in Guantánamo Bay. After his release, he joined AQAP only to abandon the group and surrender to Saudi authorities. He is currently free and lives in Saudi Arabia.

Abu Ali al-Harithi: "Godfather" of al-Qaeda in Yemen, who built most of the group's infrastructure in the 1990s. The head of al-Qaeda in Yemen after September 11, he was killed in a US drone strike in November 2002.

Abd al-Salam al-Hilah: PSO agent who tipped off Osama bin Laden and Ayman al-Zawahiri to a traitor within their ranks. Kidnapped by Egyptian forces in 2003, he was later transferred to Guantánamo Bay, where he remains.

Edmund Hull: US ambassador to Yemen 2001–04. He was instrumental in defeating al-Qaeda's initial organization in Yemen. Now retired, he lives in the US.

Salih al-Khanabashi: Yemeni of Somali descent who took part in al-Qaeda's first terrorist attack in Aden in 1992. He later managed one of bin Laden's farms in Sudan. He currently lives in Yemen.

Muhammad al-Muayyad: Yemeni cleric arrested by the FBI in a sting operation in Germany in 2003. He was sentenced to seventy-five years in prison, but his conviction was overturned on appeal. He returned to Yemen in 2009. Currently free, he lives in Yemen.

Umar Farouk Abdu Mutallab: Nigerian student who attempted to bring down a US airliner over Detroit on December 25, 2009. He is currently in a US prison.

Muhammad bin Nayif: Saudi prince and deputy Minister of the Interior who was responsible for defeating al-Qaeda in Saudi Arabia in 2003–06. He survived an assassination attempt in 2009.

Ghalib al-Qamish: head of Yemen's top intelligence agency, the PSO. He worked closely with John O'Neill and Ali Soufan.

Fahd al-Qusa: cameraman who missed filming the USS *Cole* attack. He was later released from Yemeni prison and rejoined al-Qaeda. On the FBI's most wanted list, he was killed in a US drone strike in May 2012.

Fawaz al-Rabi'i: charismatic Yemeni fighter who was born in Saudi Arabia and later joined al-Qaeda in Afghanistan. Bin Laden sent him back to Yemen shortly before the September 11 attacks. He was arrested by Yemeni forces in 2003 and escaped prison in 2006, then was killed the same year after surrendering a second time. His younger brother is currently in Guantánamo Bay.

Qasim al-Raymi: Yemeni fighter who was a trainer at an al-Qaeda camp in Afghanistan. He escaped from prison in Yemen in 2006. The military commander of AQAP, he is at large and believed to be in Yemen. His younger brother is currently in Guantánamo Bay.

Ali Abdullah Salih: president of North Yemen 1978–90 and of unified Yemen 1990–2012. He currently lives in Sanaa, where many of his relatives continue to hold key posts in Yemen's military and intelligence agencies.

Abdalilah Shaya: Yemeni journalist who reported on the US strike at al-Majalla in December 2009 and interviewed several top AQAP leaders. He was abducted in 2010 and convicted of terrorism in January 2011. Following a call from President Obama to then President Salih in February 2011, his request for pardon was refused. He is currently in prison in Yemen.

Said al-Shihri: former Guantánamo Bay detainee from Saudi Arabia who rejoined al-Qaeda in 2009. The deputy commander of AQAP, he is currently at large and believed to be in Yemen.

Ali Soufan: FBI agent who was in Yemen on September 11, 2001. He provided key information linking bin Laden to the hijackers, and predicted the attack on the ship MV *Limburg* in 2002. Retired from the FBI, he currently lives in New York where he runs the Soufan Group, a private consulting company.

Nasir al-Wihayshi: Osama bin Laden's personal secretary, he fought in the battle of Tora Bora and escaped to Iran, where he was imprisoned. Extradited to Yemen in 2003, he escaped from prison in 2006 and was the individual most responsible for rebuilding al-Qaeda in Yemen. The head of AQAP, he is currently at large and believed to be in Yemen.

Ghalib al-Zayadi: Yemeni tribesman who refused to help President Salih track down Muhammad al-Ahdal in 2001. He was later detained and met many of AQAP's future leaders in prison. Currently free, he lives in Yemen.

Abd al-Majid al-Zindani: Yemeni cleric who recruited for the jihad in Afghanistan in the 1980s. He later became part of Yemen's presidential council and provided a fatwa permitting the killing of Socialists during the 1994 civil war. Although not a member of al-Qaeda, the US named him a "specially designated global terrorist" in 2004.

ACKNOWLEDGMENTS

This book has been a long time in the making. The idea was born during my time as a Peace Corps volunteer in Jordan in 2002, but it wasn't until November 2008 as I was browsing in Kramerbooks & Afterword Café in Washington DC that everything finally came together and I started writing.

Several people have contributed to the shaping of this book, but three individuals stand out. Without the help of Brian O'Neill, Michelle Shephard, and Levi Johnsen this book would never have been completed.

Ever since our time together as roommates during the spring of 2000 in Cairo, Brian O'Neill has been a close friend and my first editor. For more than a decade he has read nearly every word I've written and this book was no different. Brian read through several drafts with extraordinary patience and grace. This book owes much to his intelligence, generous nature, and friendship.

During the course of researching and writing this book I was fortunate enough to meet Michelle Shephard of the *Toronto Star* on one of her reporting trips to Yemen. An incredibly talented reporter and writer, Michelle has also become a dear friend, and she read and commented on the entire manuscript, shaping and sharpening it far beyond what I would have been capable of on my own. Her keen eye and uncompromising style have saved the book from numerous errors.

My brother, Levi, is one of the wisest men I know, and his calm words and steadying influence lightened the load during numerous overseas phone calls as I once again "revised" chapter one. This book would not have been possible without his advice and love.

In Yemen, I benefitted from the collective knowledge of several individuals who took the time to help me get to know their country. My first and best guides were a group of friends I chewed qat with on a daily basis. Ammar, Abd al-Hakim, Shaqib, and Amir all gave me a tutorial on Yemeni history and politics that I never could have found in books. I'm honored to call them friends. Christopher Edens, then resident director of the American Institute for Yemeni Studies, was as giving a mentor as I could have hoped for during my first year in Yemen. Muhammad al-Ahmadi and Khaled al-Hammadi, two of Yemen's best journalists, were kind enough to share with me many of their thoughts on al-Qaeda on numerous occasions. Nasser Arrabyee has also been a kind and considerate host in Yemen. Murad Zafir has been an entertaining chewing partner on many occasions in Sanaa. His unique perspective has often forced me to rethink my position. From Abu Bakr al-Qirbi and Abd al-Karim al-Iryani to Hamid al-Ahmar and Hamud al-Hitar, several prominent Yemeni politicians and tribal leaders have taken the time to talk with me and help me understand Yemen from their perspective.

In addition to the Yemenis, many of whom desire not to be named, I have also been aided by the considerable talents of Western scholars who study Yemen. Most notably, my supervisor at Princeton University, Bernard Haykel, has been the best adviser a young graduate student could have desired. He is both demanding and gracious. Several other scholars of Yemen have also freely given of their time and expertise in conversations. Paul Dresch willingly talked with me in Sanaa and his books have helped to shape my understanding of Yemen. Steven Caton, Robert Burrowes, and Thomas Stevenson all helped show me the ropes when I first arrived in Yemen as a young Fulbright student. Daniel Varisco and Charles Schmitz have similarly helped and challenged my assumptions on the country. The late Christopher Boucek was an exceedingly kind and humble man, and the spirit with which he approached his work has been an inspiration for me. Among the younger generation of scholars, I have been impressed and awed by the work of April Longley Alley, Stephen Day, Sarah Phillips, and Stacey Philbrick Yadav, all of whom have been kind and giving colleagues. Samuel Liebhaber, a brilliant young scholar and dear friend, helped lighten the load over several bags of qat during the first year of research for this book.

In the diplomatic world Barbara Bodine, Charles Dunbar, Edmund Hull, and James Larocco introduced me to the vast and complicated world ambassadors are forced to navigate. Any success I've had in portraying that side of the story owes much to their accumulated wisdom.

Every writer needs an editor and I have been blessed with several. Eric Marquardt of the *CTC Sentinel* at West Point's Combating Terrorism Center was the first editor to commission and publish my thoughts on al-Qaeda in Yemen. I owe much to his careful queries and thoughtful approach. Jonathan Shainin, once of the *National* and now of the *Caravan*, is a rare talent who makes every piece he touches better. At *Foreign Policy*, Blake Hounshell has been a gracious editor who has an unerring eye for what works in print. He has also been kind enough to commission pieces and allow me the freedom to pursue pieces that didn't always have immediate policy applications.

Thad Livingston and Donald Seaton at the *Hastings Tribune* gave me my first writing job as a college student with no credentials and Darren Fowler taught me how to tell a story. Hastings College was also where I was first exposed to Yemen and serious scholarship thanks to Robert Babcock, who gave up precious free time to tutor me. His course on the Greek and Roman World changed the course of my life. Bruce Cruikshank, then of the history department, took it upon himself to read drafts of every paper I wrote one year. His red pen made me want to be a better writer. Denny Storer continues to advise and guide as he has done faithfully since my undergraduate days.

In Princeton, I have been uplifted and supported by a close group of friends who have kept me grounded and encouraged during the struggles of four years of writing. Michael McKoy, David Hsu, Samuel Baker, Nate Johnson, Matt Escara, Sam Feng, and Thomas Dixon—your friendship and prayers have meant more than you could know. Matt Ristuccia has provided much needed guidance and advice. I was similarly sustained during a long year of writing in Cairo by Kristopher Achter's friendship. Jeff Taylor, another close friend, kindly agreed to lend his talents to the author photograph. Charles Roddie and his family graciously put me up in Oxford when I showed up on their doorstep in flight from the revolution in Egypt.

Andrew Nash, another friend from Cairo, provided the key piece of criticism halfway into the project that helped me reenvision the story I wanted to tell. This book would have been much different without his insight. Casper Oswald has been a close friend for more than a decade and I've lost count of the number of conversations we've had about Yemen. Thank you, Casper.

Will McCants has, in many ways, blazed the trail I am now following, first at Arizona and then at Princeton. His careful and conscientious scholarship has been a model that I have tried to replicate and he graciously agreed to read and comment on a chapter. Aaron Zelin of jihadology.net and now of the Washington Institute for Near East Policy has always been quick to supply al-Qaeda documents I have misplaced in moves.

Among Western journalists, Robert Worth and Jeremy Scahill, along with Michelle Shephard, are the gold standard of reporting on Yemen. All three have spent time on the ground in Yemen and their careful, finely textured reports show the depth of their knowledge. Both Robert and Jeremy graciously read and commented on chapters, strengthening the book greatly in the process. I am especially indebted to Jeremy for allowing me to use an interview he conducted in Yemen.

Additionally, I have benefited from the intrepid reporting of several young freelance journalists who have made Yemen their home in recent years. Laura Kasinof, Iona Craig, Adam Baron, Jeb Boone, and Tom Finn have all provided an invaluable window into a rapidly changing Yemen.

Mohammed al-Basha deserves special thanks for years of conversations and debates. We don't always agree on what is happening in Yemen but our sparring sessions have consistently deepened my understanding of the country he calls home. His comments on the draft manuscript saved me from more errors than I like to recall.

None of the people I have thanked here are responsible for the content of this book and some will disagree with part or all of what I have written. But I do hope they recognize the Yemen they know in these pages. Any remaining errors of fact, of course, remain my responsibility.

In the years that I have been living with this book I have received several grants and fellowships that made much of the research and writing possible. A Fulbright Fellowship first sent me to Yemen in 2003, while several fellowships from the American Institute for Yemeni Studies allowed me to return. The University of Arizona, through the Foreign Language and Area Studies fellowship, and Princeton University have both provided generous funding. A Fulbright-Hays Fellowship in 2010–2011 gave me more time in Cairo, where part of the writing was accomplished.

I have been blessed in having the type of agent I had heard about but worried no longer existed. Rick Broadhead believed in this project earlier than anyone else and he has been a tireless champion. The reason you hold this book in your hands today is because of Rick's work.

At W. W. Norton, Brendan Curry has been exactly the editor this book needed. In weeks of work he took an unruly manuscript and transformed it into a book. A deeply caring editor, Brendan has been patient and understanding through a long process. His line edits were incredibly perceptive and, at least to me, surprisingly funny. His assistant, Melanie Tortoroli, has been a joy to work with and has accomplished many of the thankless tasks necessary to seeing a book into print. Julia Druskin produced a wonderful map to accompany the book. Allegra Huston has been a tireless and conscientious copy editor and her attention to detail made the book much stronger than it would have otherwise been. In the UK, Robin Dennis of Oneworld has done much to see this book into print on a compressed schedule. Henry Rosenbloom of Scribe has been a great champion in Australia and New Zealand.

Finally, I would like to thank my father, Arthur Johnsen, for his love and support. Thanks as well as to Chuck Kutik for his patience and love. This book is dedicated to my mother, Karen Kutik.

A NOTE ON SOURCES AND TRANSLITERATION

In writing this book I have benefited from decades of work by several brave journalists writing in both Arabic and English. Covering al-Qaeda is often a risky undertaking and these men and women provide an invaluable service for those of us who come after them. I have also been aided by living in Yemen for extended periods of time during the last eight years. This has brought me into contact with viewpoints held by Yemenis that would otherwise not have been available to me. In all instances, I am grateful to the warm spirit and passionate nature of the individuals I spoke with. Several of these interviews are cited in the notes, but many more who either didn't want to be named or who were not immediately relevant to the story of al-Qaeda are not cited. Many of these interviews and conversations did, however, help to inform the background of this story. I am grateful to the Yemenis I have grown to know and trust over the last eight years of work on Yemen.

A third major source of information has been the documents, videos, and audio recordings al-Qaeda in Yemen and later al-Qaeda in the Arabian Peninsula have released. Since 2007 the group has released a great deal of material through jihadi forums on the Internet and later through its media wing, *al-Malahim*. Of course, judging the accuracy of this material is a difficult task, but thanks to journalists and defectors it has been possible to check and double-check much of what al-Qaeda has released. Unless otherwise noted, all translations from the Arabic are my own.

Students of Arabic will also notice that I have adhered to a modified version of the transliteration guide outlined by the *International Journal of Middle East Studies*. However, in cases of words that are already widely used in English—such as al-Qaeda, bin Laden, and al-Awlaki—I have used the more common spelling rather than a more rigid transliteration. For ease of reading I have often dropped the diacritcal marks for the Arabic letters ʻayn and hamza. I trust that those who notice the missing diacritics will forgive me their absence. What reads easily to Arabists can often be distracting to others. I have also dropped the "al" definite article that precedes many names in Arabic on second reference. However, each time the full name is used it is fully spelled out. For instance: Nasir al-Wihayshi becomes Wihayshi. Again, I hope that this decision, which was made for ease of reading, will not unduly frustrate purists.

NOTES

Chapter 1: A Far-Off Land

3 "Hisham has been martyred": Abdullah Azzam, "The martyr Hisham bin Abd al-Wahhab al-Daylami," available at: http://alfarooq.itgo.com/mjahideen/hisham_aldeleemy.htm

4 "My heart was sad": Ibid.

8 "The sermon that day": Mustafa Badi al-Lawjari, *Afghanistan: Occupation of Memory* (Arabic), NP: 2003, 16.

9 flight across the country: This section is drawn from Lawjari, *Afghanistan*.

12 "made me want to find": Abd al-Rahman al-Muhammadi, "Interview with the head of Osama bin Laden's farm in Sudan" (Arabic), *News Aden*, reprinted in *News Yemen*, January 11, 2011.

12 west out of Pakistan toward Kabul: Steve Coll, *Ghost Wars: The Secret History of the CIA, Afghanistan, and bin Laden, from the Soviet Invasion to September 10, 2001* (New York: Penguin, 2004), 190–92.

13 Tucked inside the city: Lawrence Wright, *The Looming Tower: Al-Qaeda and the Road to 9/11* (New York: Knopf, 2006), 138–39.

14 what to do after Afghanistan: Issam Abd al-Hakim, "Interview with Shaykh Abd al-Majid al-Zindani" (Arabic), *Jihad* 64 (February 1990), 24.

15 "There was just a little blood": Aryn Baker, "Who Killed Abdullah Azzam," *Time*, June 18, 2009.

15 "My destiny": Quoted ibid.

16 wounded in the fighting: Issam Diraz, *Osama bin Laden and the Battle of the Lion's Den* (Arabic) (Cairo: al-Manar al-Jadid, 1991), 50.

Chapter 2: The Next Afghanistan

21 wouldn't make it six months: Jim Hoagland, "North Yemen seen shaky despite US aid," *Washington Post*, April 11, 1979. I am indebted to Nicholas Schmidle for the reference.

24 liberating his father's homeland: Peter Bergen, *The Longest War: The Enduring Conflict Between America and al-Qaeda* (New York: Free Press, 2011), 19.

24 spent freely: Ibid.

24 called al-Qaeda: Wright, *The Looming Tower*, 131–34.

25 "There are no caves": Ibid., 157.

26 "This is like a summer storm": James A. Baker III, *The Politics of Diplomacy: Revolution, War & Peace, 1989–1992* (New York: Putnam, 1995), 318.

26 "This will be the most expensive": Ibid., 327.

28 "Women . . . defending Saudi men": Quoted in Bergen, *The Longest War*. 19.

29 opposition to the king: Wright, *The Looming Tower*, 162.

29 "relief operations in Somalia": UN Security Council Resolution 794, paragraph 10, available at: http://www.un.org/documents/sc/res/1992/scres92.htm.

30 "decentralization of execution": Khaled al-Hammadi, "Interview with Nasir al-Bahri," *al-Quds al-Arabi*, translated by Foreign Broadcast Information Service, August 3, 2004.

30 Nahdi laid out: Muhammadi, "Interview with the head of Osama bin Laden's farm in Sudan."

30 parked on the tarmac: Edward F. Mickolus with Susan L. Simmons, *Terrorism: 1992–1995* (London: Greenwood Press, 1997), 251.

31 "Absolutely": Muhammadi, "Interview with the head of Osama bin Laden's farm in Sudan."

32 When the two men reached the airport: Khanabashi later claimed to have carried out his portion of the attack, but the evidence that exists suggests that the security forces in Aden managed to force the two jihadis they'd arrested to disclose the location of the explosives.

32 where the explosives had been: Mickolus, *Terrorism*, 251.

32 nearly severing his hand: John F. Burns, "Yemen links to bin Laden gnaw at FBI in Cole inquiry," *New York Times*, November 26, 2000.

32 track down the jihadis: Brian Whitaker, *The Birth of Modern Yemen*, chapter 8, e-book available at: http://www.al-bab.com/yemen/birthofmodernyemen/default.htm.

33 Khanabashi had sought refuge: Muhammadi, "Interview with the head of Osama bin Laden's farm in Sudan."

34 Marib and Shabwa: "Biography of Abu Ali al-Harithi" (Arabic), posted to multiple jihadi websites, available at: http://www.muslm.net/vb/showthread.php?t=208626.

34 These things happen: Muhammadi, "Interview with the head of Osama bin Laden's farm in Sudan."

Chapter 3: The Dogs of War

35 Bin Laden immediately sent word: Muhammadi, "Interview with the head of Osama bin Laden's farm in Sudan."

36 one of bin Laden's farms: Ibid.; for more on bin Laden's life in Sudan, see Wright, *The Looming Tower*, 166–69.

36 "money and honor": Ibid.

36 declared him an infidel: Khaled al-Hammadi, "Interview with Nasir al-Bahri," part 3, *al-Quds al-Arabi*, March 28, 2005, translated by FBIS.

37 wound several others: Wright, *The Looming Tower*, 193.

37 Bin Laden had a house: Hammadi, "Interview with Nasir al-Bahri."

38 bullet in his thigh: "Biography of Abu Ali al-Harithi."

38 killed several other attackers: Wright, *The Looming Tower*, 193; Hammadi, "Interview with Nasir al-Bahri."

38 India for treatment: Muhammadi, "Interview with the head of Osama bin Laden's farm in Sudan."

38 Indian girl: Ibid.

38 Bid had bypassed: Whitaker, *The Birth of Modern Yemen*, chapter 10.

40 flight back to Sanaa: Muhammadi, "Interview with the head of Osama bin Laden's farm in Sudan."

40 "Take it": Quoted in Wright, *The Looming Tower*, 195.

42 fleeing the fighting: Christopher Walker, "North Yemenis accuse the south of Scud attack," *The Times* (London), May 7, 1994.

42 The Soviet-made missiles: Ibid.

42 a rough pair of crutches: Muhammadi, "Interview with the head of Osama bin Laden's farm in Sudan."

43 abandoned Aden for the port city of al-Mukalla: Whitaker, *The Birth of Modern Yemen*, chapter 13.

44 Bid went into exile: Ibid.

45 swarm of locusts: Khaled al-Hammadi, "International groups are requested to take decisions to protect the people of the south" (Arabic), *al-Quds al-Arabi*, April 17, 2009, reprinted in *Mareb Press*, April 17, 2009.

46 "Idiots": Author discussion with a Yemeni in Aden, March 2004. Name withheld by request.

Chapter 4: Faith and Wisdom

48 stepped off the plane in Sanaa: "Interview with Ibrahim al-Banna" (Arabic), part 1 of 2, *al-Jarida* (Kuwait), November 4, 2010.

49 influenced the younger Zawahiri: Wright, *The Looming Tower*, 125.

49 active role in the civil war: "Interview with Ibrahim al-Banna."

49 mountains of Amran: Ibid.

50 dictators' club: Wright, *The Looming Tower*, 214.

50 grenade launcher misfired: Ibid.

51 "Suddenly I found": Craig Turner, "Egyptian president survives assassination attempt," *Los Angeles Times*, June 27, 1995.

51 failed to kill him: Ayman al-Zawahiri, *Knights Under the Prophet's Banner* (Arabic), 2nd edition, 94.

51 Zawahiri left Sanaa: "Interview with Ibrahim al-Banna."

53 dereliction of duty: Mohammed al-Shafey, "Al-Qaeda's secret emails," part 2, *al-Sharq al-Awsat English*, June 13, 2005.

53 Zawahiri's men drove him: Andrew Higgins and Alan Cullison, "Friend or foe: the story of a traitor to al-Qaeda—murky loyalties in Yemen undo the betrayer, who finds himself betrayed—ominous words before 9/11," *Wall Street Journal*, December 20, 2002.

53 reconsider his resignation: Wright, *The Looming Tower*, 260–61.

54 Nasrallah's story: Higgins and Cullison, "Friend or foe."

55 PSO's point man on jihadis: Human Rights Watch, *Black Hole: The Fate of Islamists Rendered to Egypt*, March 2005, 34–39.

55 operatives seized Nasrallah: Higgins and Cullison, "Friend or foe."

57 600,000 graduates: Others put the number slightly higher. See, for instance, Paul Dresch, *A History of Modern Yemen* (New York: Cambridge University Press, 2000), 173.

57 Wihayshi could recite the Quran: Nayif al-Qahtani, "The wanted: between yesterday and today" (Arabic), *Sada al-Malahim* 8 (March 2010), 36.

58 "always together": Jabir al-Fayfi, "Interview on Homuna" (Arabic), Saudi Television, December 2010.

58 "I was in the highest authority": Robert Worth, "Ex-jihadist leader defies Yemeni president, easy labels," *New York Times*, February 26, 2010.

58 darkness and ignorance: Khaled al-Hammadi, "Interview with Tariq al-Fadhli" (Arabic), *al-Quds al-Arabi* 1999.

58 "You are fighting": Ibid.

58 "This is someone": Ibid.

60 seventh US military official: Brian Whitaker, "Abu Hamza and the

Islamic army," *al-Bab*, available at: http://www.al-bab.com/yemen/hamza/day.htm.

60 "a paradise": BBC Four Documentaries, "Sheikh Abu Hamza," aired April 26, 2003. Punctuation has been modified for grammar.

61 the way he drove at home: Brian Whitaker, "The Aden bomb plot," *al-Bab*, December 14, 1999.

61 police had arrested them all: Ibid.

62 four vehicles: Brian Whitaker, "The Abyan kidnapping: introduction," *al-Bab*, February 16, 1999.

62 butt of his gun: Brian Whitaker, "The Abyan kidnapping: witnesses," *al-Bab*, February 16, 1999.

62 "We've got the goods": Whitaker, "The Abyan kidnapping: introduction."

63 "higher contacts": Ibid.

63 fired his gun in warning: Whitaker, "The Abyan kidnapping: witnesses."

63 "Shariah law in Yemen": Whitaker, "The Abyan kidnapping: the trial so far," *al-Bab*, March 6, 1999.

64 Abu Ali al-Harithi: Brian Whitaker, "The Abyan kidnapping: statements attributed to the defendants," *al-Bab*, February 1999.

64 "Yes, three times yes": Whitaker, "The Abyan kidnapping: the trial so far."

Chapter 5: The Southern Job

66 sank just offshore: Federal Bureau of Investigation, *Terrorism 2000–2001*, 8, available at: http://www.fbi.gov/stats-services/publications/terror/terrorism-2000-2001#Terrorist%20Incidents.

66 he expected better: Hammadi, "Interview with Nasir al-Bahri," 2004.

66 it pained him to do so: Wright, *The Looming Tower*, 194.

66 local family in Yemen: Khaled al-Hammadi, "Interview with Nasir al-Bahri," *al-Quds al-Arabi*, translated by Foreign Broadcast Information Service, March 20, 2005.

66 local aristocracy: Ibrahim Ahmad al-Maqhafi, *The Yemeni Geographical and Tribal Dictionary* (Arabic), 2 vols. (Sanaa: Dar al-Kalimah, 2002), vol. 2, 759.

67 jihad in Bosnia: Hammadi, "Interview with Nasir al-Bahri," March 20, 2005.

67 "treacherous": Ibid.

68 "Every one of you": Ibid.

69 "no authority over me": Ibid.

70 telling Abu Salih about a madman: Higgins and Cullison, "Friend or foe."

70 "will never be forgotten": Sebastian Rotella and Josh Meyer, "Wiretaps may have foretold terror attacks," *Los Angeles Times*, May 29, 2002.

71 "waiting for the wind": Ibid.

72 kidnapping plot: Brian Whitaker, "Attack on the USS *Cole*: the suspects," *al-Bab*, http://www.al-bab.com/yemen/cole1.htm.

72 Master Chief James Parlier: Jeff Schogol, "Memories Strong Five Years After *Cole* Blast," *Stars and Stripes*, October 12, 2005.

73 secret code: US Department of Defense, al-Nashiri charge sheet, available at: www.defense.gov/news/nashirichargesheet.pdf.

73 start filming: Ali Soufan, *The Black Banners: The Inside Story of 9/11 and the War against al-Qaeda* (New York: Norton, 2011), 225–26.

73 pager on vibrate: Wright, *The Looming Tower*, 320.

74 swayed helplessly in the sea: Soufan, *The Black Banners,* 168.

74 "a hostile people": Barbara Bodine, "9/11 miniseries is bunk," *Los Angeles Times*, September 8, 2006.

74 "This is a country": Quoted in Wright, *The Looming Tower*, 323.

75 "It is my job": Bodine, "9/11 miniseries is bunk."

75 "I have tried everything": Interview with Clint Guenther, "The Man Who Knew," *Frontline*, PBS, aired June 28, 2002, available at: http://www.pbs.org/wgbh/pages/frontline/shows/knew/interviews/guenther.html.

75 "The realities": Bodine, "9/11 miniseries is bunk."

75 opening other doors: Interview with Mary Jo White, "The Man Who Knew," *Frontline*, PBS, aired May 2, 2002, available at: http://www.pbs.org/wgbh/pages/frontline/shows/knew/interviews/white.html.

76 O'Neill returned to the US: Wright, *The Looming Tower*, 329.

76 Qamish refused to take meetings: Interview with Barry Mawn, "The Man Who Knew," *Frontline*, PBS, aired May 17, 2002, available at: http://www.pbs.org/wgbh/pages/frontline/shows/knew/interviews/mawn.html.

77 let him back in the country: Interview with Clint Guenther, "The Man Who Knew."

77 "They decided": Interview with Barry Mawn, "The Man Who Knew."

77 wanted his father released: Abdalilah Haydar Shaya, "Interview with Fahd al-Qusa" (Arabic), al-Jazeera, December 26, 2009.

78 turned himself in to the PSO: Ibid.

78 "The Americans had": Ibid.

78 a member of parliament: Ibid.

79 "I heard you were going": Higgins and Cullison, "Friend or foe."

80 Saudi Arabia's morality police: Rashad al-Shar'abi, "From the house of Fawaz al-Rabi'i" (Arabic), *News Yemen*, October 9, 2006.

80 eventual September 11 hijackers: Nabil al-Sufi, "Yemen and al-Qaeda" (Arabic), *al-Hayat*, November 24, 2006.
80 "die a martyr": al-Shar'abi, "From the House of Fawaz al-Rabi'i."
80 twelve-man cell: Ibid.

Chapter 6: Allies

81 poverty was apparent: Soufan, *The Black Banners*, 162.
82 last official act: Wright, *The Looming Tower*, 352.
82 land in Yemen: Walter Pincus, "Yemen hears benefits of joining US fight," *Washington Post*, November 28, 2001.
82 report on the *Cole* attack: Steven Lee Myers, "Cohen says the blame for the *Cole* is collective," *New York Times*, January 20, 2001.
84 "We denied them": Quoted in Pincus, "Yemen hears benefits."
84 "Ali," he gasped: Soufan, *The Black Banners*, 284.
85 "Yemen is deemed unsafe": Ibid., 286.
85 "any means necessary": Wright, *The Looming Tower*, 362.
85 "I'm not talking": Quoted ibid., 363.
86 PSO headquarters: Ibid.
86 "You shouldn't even be": Shaya, "Interview with Fahd al-Qusa."
86 "Why is he in jail?": Wright, *The Looming Tower*, 364.
87 "We need to talk": Soufan, *The Black Banners*, 295.
87 responsible for him: Author interview with Nasir al-Bahri, Sanaa, July 2006.
87 arguing theology: Soufan, *The Black Banners*, 295.
87 "Look again": Ibid., 316.
87 "Are you claiming": Ibid., 317.
87 Soufan knew: Ibid.
88 tied the hijackers to al-Qaeda: This description of the interrogation is based on three sources. Lawrence Wright gives an excellent account in *The Looming Tower*, 361–67. Nasir al-Bahri shared his memories of Afghanistan and Yemen with me during an interview in Sanaa in July 2006. Al-Bahri also gave a series of illuminating interviews to Khaled al-Hammadi of *al-Quds al-Arabi* in 2004 and again in 2005.
88 "bomb it back to the Stone Age": The ally, of course, was Pakistan. The quote is attributed to then US Deputy Secretary of State Richard Armitage by Pakistani president Pervez Musharraf. See Pervez Musharraf, *In the Line of Fire: A Memoir* (New York: Free Press, 2006), 201.
88 Yemen was the next logical target: Nasir Muhammad Ali al-Tawil, *The Islamic Movement and the Political System in Yemen* (Arabic) (Sanaa: Khalid

bin Walid, 2009), 448. I use this source to give a sense of the mood in Yemen immediately after the September 11 attacks.

90 "chosen sides": Christopher Cooper, "Desert blues: in war on terrorism battlefields may look a lot like Yemen," *Wall Street Journal*, October 9, 2001.

90 slip out of the country: Raymond Bonner, "Long at odds with the US, Yemen is now cooperating to fight terror," *New York Times*, November 25, 2001.

91 This has to stop: Author interview with Yemeni government official, Sanaa, July 2004.

91 "nuts and bolts of terrorism": Quoted in Howard Schneider, "For Yemen a risk and an opportunity," *Washington Post*, January 2, 2002.

91 "Every nation": George W. Bush, "Freedom at War with Terror," speech given September 20, 2001, available at: http://georgewbush-whitehouse.archives.gov/news/releases/2001/09/20010920-8.html.

91 Bush–Salih meeting: Patrick Tyler, "Yemen, an uneasy ally, proves adept at playing off old rivals," *New York Times*, December 19, 2002.

92 $400 million: Pincus, "Yemen hears benefits."

92 "There is an Arab proverb . . . head": Tyler, "Yemen, an uneasy ally."

Chapter 7: A New War

93 The CIA and Ghalib al-Qamish agreed: Edmund Hull, *High Value Target: Countering al-Qaeda in Yemen* (Washington: Potomac Books, 2011), 29.

93 fellow clansmen for protection: "Interview with Ghalib al-Zayadi" (Arabic), *Mareb Press*, January 5, 2009.

93 Salih–Zayadi meeting: Ibid.

94 Ahdal's surrender: Hull, *High Value Target*, 29.

94 "Any action will take": Ibid.

95 Harithi and an Egyptian aide: Ibrahim al-Banna, "The Martyrdom of the Commander Abu Ayman," *Inspire* 8 (Fall 2011), 13–15.

95 Al Jalal family: al-Maqhafi, *The Yemeni Geographical and Tribal Dictionary*, vol. 1, 344.

96 faded from sight: Frank Gardner, "Yemen's al-Qaeda supporters," BBC.co.uk, August 3, 2002.

96 scurried out of range: Hull, *High Value Target*, 30.

97 thirty-five more had been captured: Ibid.

98 the right to attack America: Peter Bergen, "The Battle for Tora Bora: The Definitive Account," *New Republic*, December 22, 2009.

98 rearguard action: Turki al-Suhayl, "Jabir al-Fayfi: trained in al-Faruq camp" (Arabic), *al-Sharq al-Awsat*, December 22, 2010.

99 secure in the mountains: Quoted in Bergen, *The Longest War*, 69.

99 built a road: Ibid.

99 Local al-Qaeda commanders grouped the men: Suhayl, "Jabir al-Fayfi."

100 last-minute preparations: Bergen, "The Battle for Tora Bora."

100 1,100 missiles into the mountains: "Tora Bora Revisited: How We Failed to Get Bin Laden and Why It Matters Today," Report for Senate Committee on Foreign Relations, November 30, 2009, 11; Bergen, *The Longest War*, 72.

100 Hazarat Ali and Haji Zaman Ghamsharik: "Tora Bora Revisited," 11.

100 requested additional US troops: Bergen, *The Longest War*, 74.

100 "We need US soldiers": Gary Berntsen, *Jawbreaker: The Attack on Bin Laden and al-Qaeda: A Personal Account by the CIA's key Field Commander* (New York: Crown, 2005), 290.

100 "light footprint": Bergen, *The Longest War*, 73.

101 700,000 pounds of munitions: Bergen, "The Battle for Tora Bora."

101 whatever they could find: Suhayl, "Jabir al-Fayfi."

101 C-130 cargo plane: "Tora Bora Revisited," 2.

102 local villagers turned on the Arabs: Suhayl, "Jabir al-Fayfi."

102 gave the order to retreat: Dalton Fury, *Kill Bin Laden: A Delta Commander's Account of the Hunt for the World's Most Wanted Man* (New York: St. Martin's Press, 2008), 191.

102 I'm sorry for getting us trapped: "Tora Bora Revisited," 7.

102 Ghamsharik now told Fury: Bergen, *The Longest War*, 77.

102 playing for time: Fury, *Kill Bin Laden*, 210–28.

103 800 al-Qaeda fighters: "Tora Bora Revisited," 11.

103 feared this was the end: Bergen, *The Longest War*, 77.

103 "I advise you": Quoted ibid., 85.

103 out of Tora Bora: Ibid.

103 Zawahiri . . . took a different route: Ibid., 78.

103 Weak with hunger: Suhayl, "Jabir al-Fayfi."

104 "It was three months": Turki al-Suhayl, "I was influenced by takfiri ideology while I was detained at Guantánamo" (Arabic), *al-Sharq al-Awsat*, December 29, 2010.

105 Salih–Zayadi meeting: "Interview with Ghalib al-Zayadi."

Chapter 8: Attrition

107 as the Soviets had been in the 1980s: Soufan, *The Black Banners*, 343–45.
107 Taliban had deserted him: Wright, *The Looming Tower*, 371.
108 $40,000 for the operation: Soufan, *The Black Banners*, 349; Hull, *High Value Target*, 33.
109 "I promise": Hull, *High Value Target*, 46.
109 "You need to strengthen": Interview with Edmund Hull, "In Search of al-Qaeda," *Frontline*, PBS, aired October 6, 2002, available at: http://www.pbs.org/wgbh/pages/frontline/shows/search/interviews/hull.html.
109 to pay for loyalty: Hull, *High Value Target*, 46.
109 civil aviation building in downtown Sanaa: Ibid., 34.
110 release of 173 prisoners: "Al-Qaeda sympathizers claim bomb responsibility," *Yemen Times*, April 15–21, 2002.
110 If the men weren't freed: Hull, *High Value Target*, 34.
110 hand him over to the state: "Biography of Abu Ali al-Harithi."
111 *Air Force Two*: Hull, *High Value Target*, 37.
111 interrogation of an al-Qaeda suspect: Soufan, *The Black Banners*, 489–505; Susan Schmidt, "Yemen recovers huge cache of explosive from blast site," *Washington Post*, September 10, 2002.
111 "There is nothing": Soufan, *The Black Banners*, 500.
112 memo warning of an impending attack: Ibid., 502–3.
112 Harithi handled the shopping: Hull, *High Value Target*, 53.
112 checkpoints around Sanaa: Soufan, *The Black Banners*, 500.
112 Rushing next door: Arafat Madabish, "Yemeni security forces kill two of the most dangerous members of al-Qaeda" (Arabic), *al-Sharq al-Awsat*, October 2, 2006.
113 the attack was off: A slightly different version of this story is related in Soufan, *The Black Banners*, 504–5.
113 scuffle tipped off the militants: David Rohde, "Karachi raid provides hint of al-Qaeda rise in Pakistan," *New York Times*, September 14, 2002.
114 "Allahu Akbar": Ibid.
114 *Wall Street Journal*: Alan Cullison, "Inside al-Qaeda's Hard Drive," *Atlantic Monthly*, September 2004.
114 questions about his recent commissions: Human Rights Watch, *Black Hole*, 36.
115 watch list: Department of Defense, "JTF–Gitmo Detainee Assessment of Abd al-Salam al-Hilah," September 24, 2008. Released via Wikileaks.

115 The trip shouldn't take long: For an account of al-Hilah's abduction, see Human Rights Watch, *Black Hole*, 34–39.
116 "Abu Sayf": Karl Vick, "Yemen pursuing terror its own way; tactics, results vary, but target is Al Qaeda," *Washington Post*, October 17, 2002.
116 Yahya Mujali: Hull, *High Value Target*, 52.
116 safe house: Ibid., 36.
116 Aden and Hudaydah: Ibid., 51.
117 gave the "go" order: Hammadi, "Interview with Nasir al-Bahri," August 3, 2004.
117 Nasir al-Kindi: Abu Nasir al-Kathiri, "Martyr Biography of Nasir al-Kindi," translated by Flashpoint Partners, November 23, 2010.
117 "fast approaching": "Craft 'rammed' Yemen oil tanker," BBC.co.uk, October 6, 2002.
118 "crystal ball memo": Soufan, *The Black Banners*, 504.
118 "Switch on your TV": Ibid., 502–3.

Chapter 9: Victory

119 looking for targets: Neil MacFarquhar, "Unmanned US planes comb Arabian desert for suspects," *New York Times*, October 23, 2002.
119 terrorist-free zone: Hull, *High Value Target*, 92.
119 "in the red zone": Ibid., 59.
119 He stationed one man: Ibid., 60.
120 quick getaway: Ibid., 59.
120 tossed his gun: Soufan, *The Black Banners*, 506.
120 bloody sandal: Hull, *High Value Target*, 60.
121 Hunt Oil employees: Ibid.
121 avoided talking on the phone: "Biography of Abu Ali al-Harithi."
121 somewhere in Marib: James Bamford, "He's in the Backseat," *Atlantic Monthly*, April 2006.
121 hardly touched food: "Biography of Abu Ali al-Harithi."
122 "The greatest martyrdom": Ibid.
122 strike on Harithi: Ibid.
122 Nassib, had survived the strike: Hull, *High Value Target*, 98.
123 "This is why": Philip Smucker, "The Intrigue behind the Drone Strike," *Christian Science Monitor*, November 12, 2002.
124 Marib Travel: William Glaberson, "Terror case hinges on wobbly key player," *New York Times*, November 27, 2004.

124 fire him a second time: Glaberson, "Terror case."
125 "untrustworthy": Ibid.
125 finance a trip to Yemen: Ibid.
125 Hull had to scramble: Hull, *High Value Target*, 68–69.
125 "Even before we had a house": "Who is Shaykh al-Muayyad" (Arabic), available at: http://www.almoayad-zayed.net/view_news.asp?sub_no=1_2006_06_14_50030.
126 The embassy's local contacts: "Yemen General and Islah Party Reacts to Arrests," US diplomatic cable, January 14, 2003. Released via Wikileaks.
126 "friend" back in the US: William Glaberson, "Video, previously excluded, is shown at sheikh's terror-financing trial," *New York Times*, February 24, 2005.
126 The wedding: Ibid.
127 "the wedding here": Ibid.
127 "we get his assistance": Glaberson, "Terror case."
128 "So do you have any plans": Ibid.
129 "FBI undercover operation": John Ashcroft, "The Terrorist Threat: Working Together to Protect America," prepared remarks to Senate Judiciary Committee, March 4, 2003, available at: http://www.justice.gov/archive/ag/testimony/2003/030403senatejudiciaryhearing.htm.
129 $100,000 for his work: Glaberson, "Terror case."
129 Arif Mujali: Soufan, *The Black Banners*, 506.
130 America's top official in Yemen: Hull, *High Value Target*, 63.
130 shadowed Hull's motorcade: Ibid., 72.
130 able to escape: Ibid., 73.
130 wrestled the soldier's gun away: *Yemen Times*, April 7–13, 2004.
131 "We had not even been told": Hull, *High Value Target*, 84.
131 progress in the war against al-Qaeda: Ibid., 93.
132 He would rather die: "Interview with Ghalib al-Zayadi."
132 negotiator spent hours: Ibid.

Chapter 10: Rehab

136 Salih had ignored their counsel: Descriptions of the original meetings are based on the author's interviews with Hamud Abd al-Hamid al-Hitar on July 16, 2004, and August 10, 2005. Both interviews took place at Hitar's house in Sanaa. Nasser Arrabyee, a Yemeni journalist, was my translator.
136 Muhammad al-Dhahabi: Author interview with Hamud Abd al-Hamid al-Hitar, July 16, 2004. For more on al-Dhahabi, see Gilles Kepel, *Mus-*

lim Extremism in Egypt, translated by Jon Rothschild (Berkeley: University of California Press, 1986).

137 Salih was on the phone: Muhammad Maruf, "Yemeni judge on dialogue with al-Qa'ida supporters," *al-Quds al-Arabi*, translated by FBIS, December 18, 2004. The date of the original article in Arabic is not supplied.

138 It shouldn't have: Author interview with Hamud Abd al-Hamid al-Hitar, August 10, 2005.

139 "If you find . . . particular word": Author interview with Hamud Abd al-Hamid al-Hitar, July 16, 2004.

140 knew the book by heart: Hammadi, "Interview with Nasir al-Bahri," August 3, 2004.

140 "ticking time bombs": Author interview with Hamud Abd al-Hamid al-Hitar, July 16, 2004.

141 Treaty of Medina: R. B. Serjeant, "The Constitution of Medina," *Studies in Arabian History and Civilization* (London: Variorum Reprints, 1981), 12.

141 a test group: "Interview with Hamud al-Hitar" (Arabic), *26th of September*, November 11, 2004. The first dialogue session ran from September 5, 2002, to November 11, 2002.

142 "great problems": Hull, *High Value Target*, 70.

142 "key to their release": Tim Whewell, "Crossing Continents," BBC Radio, aired October 13, 2005.

142 "we listened": Author interview with Nasir al-Bahri, Sanaa, July 21, 2006 (conducted in Arabic).

143 rejoined the fight: Whewell, "Crossing Continents."

143 "not a subject of the dialogue": Ibid.

145 "fivers": J. Leigh Douglas, *The Free Yemeni Movement 1935–1962* (Beirut: American University of Beirut Press, 1987), 7.

145 an extra line . . . differently: Dresch, *A History of Modern Yemen*, 15.

146 Huthi's men greeted him: "President's speech in his meeting with some Zaydi ulama" (Arabic), *26th of September*, July 3, 2004. Reprinted in Adal al-Ahmadi, *The Flower and the Stone: The Shi'a Rebellion in Yemen* (Arabic) (Sanaa: Markaz 'Ubadi, 2004), 259.

147 800 protesters in Sanaa alone: "Interview with Hasan Zayd" (Arabic), *Elaph*, October 2, 2009.

Chapter 11: A Revolt in the North

148 pushed the caretaker into the street: Rashad al-Alimi, "Report from the Minister of the Interior to Parliament" (Arabic), *26th of September*, July 3, 2004. Reprinted in al-Ahmadi, *The Flower and the Stone*, 267.

149 soldiers shot back: Ibid.

149 Twenty-four hours: "Interview with Hasan Zayd."

149 A gunfight erupted: Iris Glosemeyer, "Local Conflict, Global Spin: An Uprising in the Yemeni Highlands," translated by Don Reneau, *Middle East Report*, Fall 2004, 44–46.

149 "I am certain": Muhammad bin Salam, "Al-Huthi Appeals," *Yemen Times*, June 28, 2004.

150 helicopter gunships: Muhammad bin Salam, "Interview with Yahya al-Huthi," *Yemen Times*, June 20, 2005.

150 "Yemen's Tora Bora": Lutfi Shatarah, "al-Qirbi: Our battle with al-Huthi resembles the battle of Tora Bora" (Arabic), *al-Sharq al-Awsat*, September 30, 2004.

151 "The difference . . . combat this": Author interview with Hamud Abd al-Hamid al-Hitar, July 16, 2004.

151 "We are in the mop-up phase": Husayn al-Jarabani, "Yemeni chief of staff: We are entering the final battle with al-Huthi" (Arabic), *al-Sharq al-Awsat*, August 8, 2004.

151 "That is all over now": Ibid.

152 Hitar's younger brother: Husayn al-Jarabani, "Yemen: tens killed, among them a brigade commander in an ambush prepared by supporters of al-Huthi" (Arabic), *al-Sharq al-Awsat*, August 24, 2004.

152 Huthi's last stand: Abd al-Rahman al-Mujahid, *The Shi'aization of Sa'dah, Vol. II: The Thought of the Believing Youth in Balance* (Arabic) (Sanaa: 2007), 129–31.

154 Salih–Bloomfield meeting: "President Saleh to A/S Bloomfield, 'No New MANPADS,'" US diplomatic cable, September 2, 2004. Released via Wikileaks.

155 The Huthi women: Muhammad al-Khamari, "Interview with Yahya Ali al-Imad" (Arabic), *al-Wasat*, August 11, 2005.

156 took pity on the family: Ibid.

156 accommodate all his women: Ibid.

156 a circuitous exile: Ibid.

156 "incorruptible": Ibid.

156 heard the same message: Ibid.

156 "I have not met with him": Jamal al-Amr, "Interview with Badr al-Din al-Huthi" (Arabic), *al-Wasat*, March 19, 2005.

157 The soldiers fled the market: Husayn al-Jarabani, "Yemen: two commanders from the Shabab al-Muminin were killed and four wounded in a clash with security forces in Sadah" (Arabic), *al-Sharq al-Awsat*, March 20, 2005.

157 a halfhearted attempt at deescalation: Husayn al-Jarabani, "Yemen: delay for supporters of al-Huthi the elder to surrender themselves" (Arabic), *al-Sharq al-Awsat*, April 3, 2005.

157 "They are surrounded": "Saleh Discusses Security Concerns with Ambassador," US diplomatic cable, April 10, 2005. Released via Wikileaks.

157 well-coordinated assault: Husayn al-Jarabani, "Yemen: al-Huthi's supporters enter into a street war with security forces in Sadah" (Arabic), *al-Sharq al-Awsat*, April 9, 2005.

158 the elderly cleric . . . border: Husayn al-Jarabani, "Yemen: al-Huthi the elder escaped" (Arabic), *al-Sharq al-Awsat*, April 12, 2005.

159 "I am doing this": "al-Huthi announces that he is cutting off his negotiations with the authorities" (Arabic), *al-Wasat*, August 3, 2005.

Chapter 12: Prison Cells

160 PSO prison: "Interview with Ghalib al-Zayadi."

165 Uthman al-Sulawi: "Uthman Ali Numan al-Sulawi" (Arabic), martyr biography, *Sada al-Malahim* 14 (2010), 67.

165 suicide attack on US forces: "Uthman Ali Numan al-Sulawi," 68.

166 Fayfi in Guantánamo: Suhayl, "Influenced by takfiri ideology."

166 *The Arab Mind*: Seymour Hersh, "The Gray Zone: How a Secret Pentagon Program Came to Abu Ghraib," *New Yorker*, May 24, 2004.

167 James Mitchell and Bruce Jensen: Scott Shane, "Two US architects of harsh tactics in 9/11's wake," *New York Times*, August 11, 2009.

167 "I am from Urday city": Allal Ab Aljallil Abd al Rahman, Combatant Status Review Tribunal Transcript, published by the *New York Times*, http://projects.nytimes.com/guantanamo/detainees/156-allal-ab-aljallil-abd-al-rahman/documents/4.

167 Guantánamo's barber: Suhayl, "Influenced by takfiri ideology."

168 "That was the first time": Ibid.

168 "In Afghanistan the thinking": "Jabir al-Fayfi relates his experience" (Arabic), *Hamumana*, Saudi Television, December 2010, available at: http://www.youtube.com/watch?v=5zj66sAeFec&feature=related.

168 "increasingly non-compliant": Department of Defense, "Jabir al-Fayfi: JTF GTMO Detainee Assessment," December 16, 2005. Released via Wikileaks.

169 "negative leader": Department of Defense, "Said Ali al-Shihri: JTF GTMO Detainee Assessment," April 13, 2007. Released via Wikileaks.

170 "He literally cried": Glaberson, "Terror case."

170 prosecuting its star witness: Ibid.

170 wanted the FBI to follow through: Caryle Murphy and Del Quentin Wilber, "Terror informant ignites himself near White House," *Washington Post*, November 16, 2004.

171 "It is my big mistake": Ibid.

171 "Today Monday": Muhammad al-Ansi, letter to Robert Fuller, reproduced in *Washington Post*, November 16, 2004.

172 "be setting himself on fire": Murphy and Wilber, "Terror informant."

173 Gideon Black: Glaberson, "Video, previously excluded."

173 "glass, metal . . . panic": *United States v. Al Moayad*, available at: http://caselaw.findlaw.com/us-2nd-circuit/1029782.html.

173 "If they were real": Glaberson, "Video, previously excluded"; *United States v. Al Moayad.*

173 man with a machine gun: Glaberson, "Video, previously excluded"; *United States v. Al Moayad.*

174 example of US aggression: Hamil al-Masik, "Three years to escape, part 1" (Arabic), *Sada al-Malahim* 7 (January 2009), 18.

174 "Why can't we do that": Ibid.

174 men reported dreams: Nasir al-Wihayshi, "The new leader of al-Qaeda in Yemen relates the details of the escape of al-Qaeda members from an intelligence prison" (Arabic), *al-Ghad*, June 25, 2007.

175 "You've already sacrificed": Ibid.

175 "We never should": Ibid.

Chapter 13: Policy Shift

176 "peaceful transfer . . . transition of power": Ali Abdullah Salih, speech, July 17, 2005 (Arabic), in *The Speeches and Interviews of President Ali Abdullah Salih for 2005* (Sanaa: Information Documentation Center, 2006), 39.

178 After three days of rioting: Gregory D. Johnsen, "Salih's Road to Reelection," *Middle East Report Online*, January 13, 2006.

178 potential successors to Salih: Laura Kasinof and Scott Shane, "Radical cleric demands ouster of Yemen leader," *New York Times,* March 1, 2011.

178 "the only game in town": US diplomatic cable 05SANAA2766, September 17, 2005. Released via Wikileaks.

179 a hand grenade was thrown: "Explosion near US Embassy targets potential presidential candidate in Yemen," *News Yemen*, November 11, 2005.

179 "Are you going to leave": US diplomatic cable 05SANAA2766.

179 "Do you swim?": Author interview with a US military official, Sanaa, August 2009. Name withheld by request.

180 Salih added as an incentive: "Yemen President Saleh Wants Washington Trip," US diplomatic cable, December 6, 2004. Released via Wikileaks.

180 Krajeski wrote from Sanaa: Ibid.

181 "Qualify Yemen for the Millennium Challenge": Hull, *High Value Target*, 112.

181 "unrealistically and stupidly confident": US diplomatic cable 05SANAA 1352, May 23, 2005. Released via Wikileaks.

181 "Dubai Ports International": "Good News for Yemen's Investment Climate: Dubai," US diplomatic cable, June 14, 2005. Released via Wikileaks.

182 "the president's whims": Ibid.

182 pull the wool over the eyes of the Americans: "Priorities for Washington Visit: Saleh Needs to be Part of the Solution," US diplomatic cable, June 28, 2005. Released via Wikileaks.

182 "feet must be held to the fire": Ibid.

182 diesel smuggling: US diplomatic cable 05SANAA1352, May 23, 2005. Released via Wikileaks.

183 Swiss bank accounts: Abeer Allam and Roula Khalaf, "Saudis prepare to abandon Yemen," *Financial Times*, March 22, 2011.

183 "stopped": Johnsen, "Salih's Road to Reelection."

184 "I respond to you immediately": "Saleh on Kanaan: We've Got Him," US diplomatic cable, April 13, 2005. Released via Wikileaks.

184 "rapped him over the knuckles": Quoted in Sarah Phillips, *Yemen and the Politics of Permanent Crisis* (New York: International Institute for Strategic Studies and Routledge, 2011), 42.

185 "It was horrible": Author interview with Yemeni diplomat, Sanaa, August 2009. Name withheld by request.

185 "Do you really think": Ibid.

186 *al-Quds al-Arabi*: Khaled al-Hammadi, "Yemeni sources report failure of dialogue," *al-Quds al-Arabi*, translated by FBIS, December 10, 2005.

186 "You know what": Author interview with Khaled al-Hammadi, Sanaa, July 7, 2006 (conducted in English).

186 "There were two camps": Author interview with Hamud Abd al-Hamid al-Hitar, August 5, 2009 (conducted in Arabic).

187 leaking a similar story: Paul Garwood, "Yemen said linked to guns in Saudi attack," Associated Press, October 11, 2005.

Chapter 14: The Great Escape

191 PSO prison break: This section draws heavily on Wihayshi, "The new leader of al-Qaeda relates details of the escape."

195 "how many people were involved": Hassan M. Fatah, "Some Yemenis back fugitive terror figures," *New York Times*, February 16, 2006.

195 $25,000 reward: Nasser Arrabyee, "Yemen announces reward for news on al-Qaeda fugitives," *Gulf News*, February 15, 2006.

196 "back in custody soon": Ghasan Shirbil, "Interview with President Salih" (Arabic), *al-Hayat*, February 26, 2006.

196 dozens of Saudi fighters: Thomas Hegghammer, "The Failure of Jihad in Saudi Arabia," West Point Combating Terrorism Center, February 25, 2010, 12.

196 ordered them to strike: Ibid., 13.

197 synchronized attacks: Ibid.

197 "ruthless murder": "US: More than 90 dead in Saudi blast," *Guardian*, May 13, 2003.

197 massive car bomb: Dominic Evans, "Suicide attack kills up to 30, injures about 100, in a Riyadh residential complex," Reuters, November 9, 2003.

197 "Before, people could find": Neil MacFarquhar, "Among the Saudis, attack has soured Qaeda supporters," *New York Times*, November 11, 2003.

198 turned against them: Quoted in Hegghammer, "The Failure of Jihad," 22.

198 why didn't they go to Iraq: MacFarquhar, "Among the Saudis."

198 watch television or listen to music: Salim al-Najdi, "The Biography of Abu al-Khayr, Abdullah Hasan Tali Asiri" (Arabic), *Sada al-Malahim* 11 (November 2009), 50.

198 "His name was always": Ibid.

199 The clerics liked: Abdullah al-Oreifij, "Suicide Bomber Named," *Saudi Gazette*, September 1, 2009; Nasir al-Haqabani and Faysal Mukrim, "Saudi Ibrahim Asiri constructed the two package bombs" (Arabic), *al-Hayat*, November 1, 2010.

200 "They should be properly": al-Najdi, "Biography of Abu al-Khayr," 51.

201 "Up until that point": Ibid., 52.

201 caused oil prices to jump: Khalid R. al-Rodhan, "The Impact of the Abqaiq Attack on Saudi Energy Security," Center of Strategic and International Studies, February 27, 2006.

201 "We should go to Yemen": al-Najdi, "Biography of Abu al-Khayr," 53.

202 "When they come through here": Ibid., 54.

203 CNN poll: "Poll: Opposition to war at all-time high," *CNN News*, August 21, 2006.

203 agreed to hide them: Abu Jana al-Qarshi, "The women of Yemen and the crusader's war" (Arabic), *Sada al-Malahim* 11 (November 2009), 22.

204 snuck into the hospital: al-Shar'abi, "From the house of Fawaz al-Rabi'i."

205 "This road is full of danger": Umar Jarallah, "The last will and testament of Umar Jarallah" (Arabic), *Sada al-Malahim* 10 (September 2009), 48.

Chapter 15: Resurrecting al-Qaeda

207 bullets hit Daylami: Murad Hashim, "Report from Sanaa" (Arabic), al-Jazeera, October 1, 2006.

207 hit Rabi'i in the chest: Author interview with Muhammad al-Ahmadi, Sanaa, August 2009.

207 State media: Arafat Madabish, "Yemeni security services kill two of the most dangerous members of al-Qaeda and arrest a third" (Arabic), *al-Sharq al-Awsat*, October 2, 2006.

208 "My son lived as a lion": Shar'abi, "From the house of Fawaz al-Rabi'i."

209 swore a second oath: Najdi, "Biography of Abu al-Khayr," 54.

209 Ali Doha: "Obituary of Abd al-Aziz Juradan" (Arabic), *Sada al-Malahim* 2 (March 2008), 20.

209 "precious pearl": "Interview with Nayif al-Qahtani" (Arabic), *Sada al-Malahim* 1 (January 2008), 8.

209 2002 strike on Harithi: Faysal Mukrim, "Yemen: al-Qaeda announces its responsibility for assassinating an officer and threatens others" (Arabic), *al-Hayat,* May 1, 2007.

210 the investigation into his death stalled: Abd al-Was'a al-Hamdi, "The funeral procession of the martyr Ali Qasaylah brings him to his final resting place in Martyr's Cemetery" (Arabic), *al-Thawra*, April 3, 2007.

210 al-Qaeda had been behind the ambush: Mukrim, "Yemen: al-Qaeda announces its responsibility."

210 half-page ad: Gregory D. Johnsen, "Is al-Qaeda in Yemen Regrouping?," *Terrorism Focus*, May 22, 2007.

211 Faris al-Raymi: Muhammad al-Ahmadi, "Details on the death of Faris al-Raymi" (Arabic), in *al-Ghad*, June 25, 2007.

212 "If they are killed": Gregory D. Johnsen and Brian O'Neill, "Yemen attack reveals struggle among al-Qaeda's ranks," *Terrorism Focus*, July 10, 2007.

213 return to Shariah law: *al-Shar'a* (Arabic), reprinted in *News Yemen*, July 2, 2007.

213 Among the dead was Mansur al-Bayhani: Muhammd al-Ahmadi, "al-Bayhani first Yemeni from al-Qaeda to be killed in US airstrike" (Arabic), *al-Ghad*, June 20, 2007.

214 teaching him steering and acceleration: "The Marib cell" (Arabic), *26th of September*, August 2, 2007.

214 "The martyr resting": The video was posted to the al-Ikhlas Web forum on March 29, 2008. See Gregory D. Johnsen, "al-Qa'ida in Yemen's 2008 Campaign," *CTC Sentinel*, April 2008.

215 mute pictures of sand and smoke: Ibid.

215 Salih called a press conference: Faysal Mukrim, "Ali Salih said that the suicide bomber was an Arab not a Yemeni" (Arabic), *al-Hayat*, July 4, 2007.

215 This is an outside virus: Abd al-Aziz al-Oudah, "Saleh: Suicide bomber might not be Yemeni," *Yemen Observer*, July 8, 2007.

216 he had to stay inside: "al-Wasat: Basaywani prevented from surrendering" (Arabic), *al-Wasat*, reprinted in *News Yemen*, July 12, 2007.

216 meetings with tribal leaders in Marib: Husayn al-Jarabani, "Yemeni president meets with Abida shaykhs" (Arabic), *al-Sharq al-Awsat*, August 6, 2007.

216 a sniper dropped the weaving figure: Al-Qaeda in the Arabian Peninsula, "Rubaysh: The Just Punishment" (Arabic), al-Malahim video, May 2009.

217 Qasim al-Raymi: "In a land and air attack between Marib and al-Jawf, Qasim al-Raymi and three others meet their death" (Arabic), *News Yemen*, August 8, 2007.

217 suicide bomber in training: "Interior Ministry: The terrorists who were killed in Marib were planning a new operation" (Arabic), *al-Mu'tamar*, August 9, 2007.

217 agreed to give up jihad: "Al-Qaeda militant surrenders after Yemen jailbreak," Reuters, October 16, 2007.

217 reassuring text message: Susan B. Glasser and Peter Baker, "An outsider's quick rise to Bush terror adviser," *Washington Post*, August 27, 2005.

217 Townsend–Salih meeting: "Townsend–Saleh meeting provides opening for additional CT cooperation," US diplomatic cable, October 30, 2007. Released via Wikileaks.

218 embassy cable: Ibid.

219 "As a first step": "Giuliani: Cut off aid to Yemen over release of bombing suspect," *CNN News*, October 26, 2007.

Chapter 16: Echoes of Battles

220 Nayif al-Qahtani: Abu Khalid Assiri, "#4 Martyr Bio," al-Malahim media, December 21, 2010; Fahd al-Ray'i, "Weak and Misled Militant not al-Qaeda Material," *Saudi Gazette*, July 19, 2010.

220 "He possesses no leadership qualities": al-Ray'i, "Weak and Misled Militant."

221 "one of Saudi's most wanted militants": "Interview with al-Qahtani" (Arabic), *Sada al-Malahim* 1 (January 2008), 8.

221 "I want to establish": Assiri, "#4 Martyr Bio."

222 attack on tourist convoy: Ahmad al-Haj, "2 Tourists killed in Yemen convoy attack," Associated Press, January 18, 2008.

223 tour the prison in Aden: "US says bomber of U.S. destroyer *Cole* still jailed," Reuters, October 29, 2007.

223 smuggled Badawi out the back: "Authorities free al-Badawi a second time" (Arabic), *al-Wasat*, December 5, 2007.

223 "I've been sentenced": Robert Worth, "Wanted by FBI, but walking out of a Yemen hearing," *New York Times*, March 1, 2008.

224 "We have told you": Soldiers' Brigades of Yemen, statement #2 (Arabic), March 21, 2008.

224 Mueller ended the meeting: Michael Isikoff, "A Tense Impasse in Yemen," *Newsweek*, April 26, 2008.

224 "loud firecrackers": This phrase was used by a Western scholar of Yemen at a not-for-attribution conference held in London by the Foreign and Commonwealth Office in July 2008.

225 Ahmad al-Mashjari: Abu Umar al-Hadrami, "The Doctor Marytr" (Arabic), *Sada al-Malahim* 8 (March 2009), 42–43.

225 "The blood of Muslims is not free": Soldiers' Brigades of Yemen, statement 11 (Arabic), July 26, 2008.

226 destruction and violence: This is based on my own observations and discussions in Yemen as well as those of several Yemenis.

226 watching the house for months: Muhammad al-Ahmadi, "Al-Ghad

reveals new details about the operation that killed the commander of the military wing of al-Qaeda in Yemen" (Arabic), *al-Ghad*, October 26, 2008.

227 "The women aren't here": Ibid.

227 When the police patrol arrived: This account of the fighting has been compiled from three different reports: Ahmadi, "Al-Ghad reveals new details"; "Marib Press exclusive on the Operation in Tarim" (Arabic), *Marib Press*, August 11, 2008; and an account published on the jihadi Internet forum al-Ikhlas: Shadad3, "Details of the storming operation of the Yemeni security forces on a house of mujahidin in Tarim, Hadramawt" (Arabic), *al-Ikhlas*, August 14, 2008.

228 Of the seven-man cell: Muhammad al-Ahmadi, "Yemen and al-Qaeda" (Arabic), *al-Ghad*, August 18, 2008.

228 relax travel warnings: Gregory D. Johnsen, "Assessing the Strength of al-Qa'ida in Yemen," *CTC Sentinel* 1, no. 10 (September 2008), 10–13.

228 "The proof": Soldiers' Brigades of Yemen, statement 13 (Arabic), August 19, 2008.

229 *jambiya*: Wright, *The Looming Tower*, 318.

230 seven attackers in two modified Suzuki jeeps: See Thomas Hegghammer's excellent article in Bruce Hoffman and Fernando Reinares, eds., *Leader-led Jihad* (forthcoming, 2012).

231 Three of the embassy attackers: Author e-mail communication with a Yemeni political analyst, Sanaa, November 2008. Name withheld by request. Also see "The Furqan Raid: the attack on the embassy nest" (Arabic), al-Malahim, 2009.

231 "We must do more": Robert Worth, "10 are killed in bombings at embassy in Yemen," *New York Times*, September 18, 2008.

232 the men knew Shihri from Guantánamo: Suhayl, "The repentant al-Fayfi relates the story of the banquet" (Arabic), *al-Sharq al-Awsat*, January 5, 2011.

232 Fayfi didn't say much: Ibid.

233 "selling out your religion": "The Just Punishment" (Arabic), al-Malahim video, released in 2009.

233 parcel bomb: The bomb is shown in "The Just Punishment"; also see "Assassination of chief of security in Marib by a letter bomb" (Arabic), *Mareb Press*, October 20, 2008.

234 "Anyone whose hands are stained": Al-Qaeda in the South of the Arabian Peninsula, "The Just Punishment" (Arabic), *Sada al-Malahim* 6 (November 2008).

Chapter 17: The Merger

235 Shaya interview: Abdalilah Haydar Shaya, "An Interview with Nasir al-Wihayshi" (Arabic), January 2010, www.abdulela.maktoobblog.com.

238 Fayfi watched the weeks of war: Suhayl, "The repentant al-Fayfi."

239 "restore the standards": "Obama signs order to close Guantánamo Bay facility," *CNN News*, January 22, 2009.

239 "Either we will come": Al-Qaeda in the Arabian Peninsula, "From Here We Begin and at al-Aqsa We Meet," al-Malahim, January 2009. Translation by Global Islamic Media Front.

240 tiny Yemeni village: Suhayl, "The repentant al-Fayfi."

240 "This is chaos": Ibid.

240 Wihayshi told his men: Ibid.

241 "This is nothing": Ibid.

242 four-inch-deep metal box: "I swear by the Lord of the Ka'bah, I won," Part 1 (Arabic), al-Malahim, 2009.

242 "This is my suicide vest": Ibid.

243 "expel the infidels": Abu Amr al-Faruq, "Statement of Explanation Regarding the Ruling on the Targeting of Tourists" (Arabic), al-Malahim, 2009.

244 suicide attack in Saudi Arabia: Turki al-Sahayl, "New Details From the Attempted Assassination of Muhammad bin Nayif" (Arabic), *al-Sharq al-Awsat*, January 12, 2011.

244 Yemen was not a friend: "General Petraeus' Visit to Yemen," US diplomatic cable, December 6, 2008. Released via Wikileaks.

244 "Without restrictions or conditions": "Saleh Tells Petraeus: 'No Restrictions' on CT," US diplomatic cable, August 9, 2009. Released via Wikileaks.

244 "a dangerous poison": Ibid.

245 asked them to publicly repent: Al-Qaeda in the Arabian Peninsula, "The Battle of Marib" (Arabic), video and text released via al-Malahim.

246 "He was a 9/11 loose end": Hannah Allam, "Is imam a terror recruiter or just an incendiary preacher?" *McClatchy Newspapers*, November 20, 2009.

246 lack of evidence: "Yemeni–American Awlaqi Released from ROYG Custody," US diplomatic cable, December 18, 2007. Released via Wikileaks.

246 message to Awlaki: Michelle Shephard, "The powerful online voice of jihad," *Toronto Star*, October 18, 2009.

247 for the Nigerian to join the jihad: This section relies on Doc. #130 in *United States v. Umar Farouk Abdumutallab*, Case No. 2:10-cr-20005, Supplemental Factual Index. Available at: https://www.documentcloud.org/documents/291667-abdulmutallab-sentencing-memorandum.html.

247 "Pray for the one who will wear this": Suhayl, "The repentant al-Fayfi."

248 volunteering for laundry duty: Najdi, "Biography of Abu al-Khayr," 55–56.

248 Ibrahim whispered in his brother's ear: Al-Qaeda in the Arabian Peninsula, "The Descendants of Muhammad al-Muslamah" (Arabic), al-Malahim, 2009.

248 "Peace and blessings": Turki al-Sahayl and Yusif al-Hamadi, "Jeddah suicide bomber took advantage of the issue of Shihri's wife and her son (Arabic), *al-Sharq al-Awsat*, September 2, 2009.

249 broke their Ramadan fast: "Countdown to Asiri's death," *Saudi Gazette*, September 2, 2009.

249 "Speak up": "The Descendants of Muhammand bin Maslamah" (Arabic), al-Malahim, 2009.

250 "It was a mistake": Margaret Coker, "Assassination attempt targets Saudi prince," *Wall Street Journal*, August 29, 2009.

Chapter 18: Targets

251 a terrorist organization: Josh Gerstein, "Clinton named al-Qaeda Yemen as terror group a month ago," *Politico*, January 18, 2010.

251 Two days later: Daniel Klaidman, *Kill or Capture: The War on Terror and the Soul of the Obama Presidency* (Boston and New York: Houghton Mifflin Harcourt, 2012), 200–201

251 The military wanted to kill three men: Klaidman, *Kill or Capture*, 199–202.

251 Akron, the main target: Ibid., 199.

251 Listening to the military's clipped presentation: Ibid., 209–10.

252 In Washington: Ibid., 209–11.

252 "You see goats and sheep": Quoted in Richard Rowley and Jeremy Scahill, *America's Dangerous Game in Yemen*, film broadcast by al-Jazeera English, February 2012.

253 "If I were Catholic": quoted in Klaidman, *Kill or Capture*, 210.

253 "to stop a massive freight train": quoted in ibid., 202.

253 to invite such wrath: Rowley and Scahill, *America's Dangerous Game in Yemen*.

253 no sign of Raymi: Muhammad al-Ahmadi, "Yemen's war on al-Qaeda" (Arabic), *al-Ghad*, December 28, 2009.

254 "Ask them to come up": This account relies on Jeremy Scahill's interview with Salih bin Farid, January 2012. Used with permission.

255 "Al-Qaeda's war in Yemen . . . God's community": "al-Awlaqi appears in public, threatening revenge for those killed" (Arabic), *News Yemen*, December 22, 2009.

255 scanning the crowd for threats: "Qaeda makes rare public appearance at Yemen rally," Reuters, December 21, 2009.

256 "Either they will kill me": Jeremy Scahill interview with Salih bin Farid.

256 small stone house: "News Report" (Arabic), *Sada al-Malahim* 12 (January 2010), 33.

256 "religious sciences": Arafat Madabish, "Areas of unrest in southern Yemen, Part 1" (Arabic), *al-Sharq al-Awsat*, December 19, 2010.

257 to survey the damage: Robert Worth, "Is Yemen the Next Afghanistan?" *New York Times Magazine*, July 11, 2010.

257 series of brief text messages: Karen DeYoung and Michael Leahy, "Uninvestigated terrorism warning about Detroit suspect called not unusual," *Washington Post*, December 28, 2009; Jeremy Scahill, "Washington's War in Yemen Backfires," *The Nation*, February 14, 2012.

257 "Forgive me": Andrew Gregory, "Syringe bomber Umar Abdulmutallab chilling text messages to dad," *The Mirror*, January 1, 2010.

257 met with US officials at the embassy: DeYoung and Leahy, "Uninvestigated terrorism warning."

257 revoke the US visa: Ibid.

257 failed miserably: Deborah Charles, "System to keep air travel safe failed: Napolitano," Reuters, December 28, 2009.

258 possible plots against the US: Eric Lipton, Eric Schmitt, and Mark Mazzetti, "Review of jet bomb plot shows more missed clues," *New York Times*, January 17, 2010.

258 second meeting devoted to Yemen: Ibid.

259 partially melted syringe: Kenneth Chang, "PETN, explosive found on flight 253, is among most powerful," *New York Times*, December 27, 2009.

259 "a bit of an issue": John Brennan, "US Policy Toward Yemen," remarks delivered at the Carnegie Endowment for International Peace, December 17, 2010.

259 "but we didn't know": White House briefing, January 7, 2010, available at: http://www.whitehouse.gov/the-press-office/briefing-homeland-security-secretary-napolitano-assistant-president-counterterrorism.

259 "an extension of al-Qaeda core": White House briefing, January 7, 2010, available at: http://www.whitehouse.gov/the-press-office/briefing-homeland-security-secretary-napolitano-assistant-president-counter terrorism.

260 "We dodged a bullet": Jeff Zeleny and Helene Cooper, "Obama says 260 could have been disrupted," *New York Times*, January 5, 2010.

260 "He could have gotten it right": Quoted in Jo Becker and Scott Shane, "Secret 'Kill List' Proves a Test of Obama's Principles and Will," *New York Times*, May 29, 2012

260 "You cannot enter . . . lied": "General Petraeus' Visit with Saleh on Security," US diplomatic cable, January 4, 2010. Released via Wikileaks.

260 Unless there was explicit intelligence: Becker and Shane, "Secret 'Kill List' Proves a Test of Obama's Principles and Will."

261 without a scratch: "Doubts regarding the claims of 6 al-Qaeda members killed" (Arabic), *News Yemen*, January 17, 2010.

261 "I didn't put": Abdalilah Shaya, "Interview with Anwar al-Awlaki" (Arabic), al-Jazeera, December 23, 2009.

261 "I had communications": Robert Worth, "Cleric in Yemen admits meeting airliner plot suspect, journalist says," *New York Times*, January 30, 2010.

262 "I did not tell him": Ibid.

262 Office of Legal Counsel: Charlie Savage, "Secret U.S. memo made legal case to kill a citizen," *New York Times*, October 8, 2011.

263 "The Constitution guarantees": Eric Holder, speech at Northwestern Law School, March 5, 2012. Available at: http://www.justice.gov/iso/opa/ag/speeches/2012/ag-speech-1203051.html.

263 After the Christmas Day attempt: Becker and Shane, "Secret 'Kill List' Proves a Test of Obama's Principles and Will."

263 "We are not going to war with Yemen": Ibid.

263 "scalpel": Scott Shane, Mark Mazzetti, and Robert Worth, "Secret assault on terrorism widens on two continents," *New York Times*, August 14, 2010.

264 300 members of AQAP: Stefano Ambrogi, "Yemen says may harbour up to 300 Qaeda Suspects," Reuters, December 29, 2009.

264 "The US sees al-Qaeda": Jeremy Scahill, "Washington's War in Yemen Backfires," *The Nation*, February 14, 2012.

264 "How could this have happened": Quoted in Klaidman, *Kill or Capture*, 255.

265 "We think we got played": Adam Entous, Julian E. Barnes, and Margaret Coker, "US doubts intelligence that led to Yemen strike," *Wall Street Journal*, December 29, 2011.

265 "wasn't as up to speed": Ibid.

265 "armed men": Jeremy Scahill, "Why Is President Obama Keeping a Journalist in Prison in Yemen?," *The Nation*, March 13, 2012.

266 acquiring ricin: Eric Schmitt and Thom Shanker, "Qaeda tries to harness toxin for bombs, US officials fear," *New York Times*, August 12, 2011.

267 French intelligence: "France Warned of al-Qaeda Threat," al-Jazeera English, October 18, 2010.

267 a pair of bombs on cargo planes: Mark Mazzetti and Robert Worth, "U.S. sees complexity of bombs as link to al-Qaeda," *New York Times*, October 30, 2010.

267 "smiling and shaking his head": This observation by Iona Craig was quoted in Scahill, "Why Is President Obama Keeping a Journalist in Prison in Yemen?"

267 "media man": Scahill, "Why Is President Obama Keeping a Journalist in Prison in Yemen?"

268 "When they hid . . . suspicion": Ibid.

Chapter 19: Out of the Shadows

269 "Yemen is not Tunisia": Mohammed Jamjoom, "No Egypt-style protests in Yemen, says Prime Minister," *CNN News*, February 7, 2011.

269 "show restraint": "Readout of President's Call with President Saleh of Yemen," The White House, February 2, 2011, available at: http://www.whitehouse.gov/the-press-office/2011/02/03/readout-presidents-call-president-saleh-yemen.

269 "expressed concern": Ibid.

271 looking for ammunition: Sudarasan Raghavan, "Yemen crisis intensifies with factory explosion," *Washington Post*, March 29, 2011.

271 killing more than 120 looters: Tom Finn, "Yemen munitions factory explosion leaves over 120 dead," *Guardian*, March 29, 2011.

271 "the right time," "enough steel": Greg Miller, "Bin Laden document trove reveals strain on al-Qaeda," *Washington Post*, July 1, 2011.

271 "Today we control Jaar . . . arrange these affairs": Adil al-Abab, "Online Question and Answer Session," translated by the International Centre for the Study of Radicalisation and Political Violence, April 18, 2011.

272 mission to Pakistan: Nicholas Schmidle, "Getting Bin Laden," *New Yorker*, August 8, 2011.

273 sleep on the decision: This description relies on Schmidle, "Getting Bin Laden."

273 "hope and pray": "Clinton describes Sit-room mood," *Politico,* May 6, 2011.

274 massive bear hug: Schmidle, "Getting Bin Laden."

274 "God decided to take you": Nasir al-Wihayshi, "Eulogy for the Shaykh of the Mujahidin Osama bin Laden—may God have mercy upon him," statement #33 *al-Qaeda in the Arabian Peninsula* (Arabic) May 11, 2011.

274 Anwar al-Awlaki had been spotted: Martha Raddatz, "US missiles missed Awlaki by inches in Yemen," *ABC News*, July 19, 2011.

274 After bin Laden: Klaidman, *Kill or Capture*, 261.

274 "I want Awlaki": quoted in ibid., 261.

274 "Bring it to me": quoted in ibid., 263–64.

275 southern Shabwa: "Two brothers from al-Qaeda killed in Shabwa" (Arabic), *News Yemen*, May 5, 2011.

275 missile lock: Raddatz, "US missiles missed Awlaki."

275 "Speed up": Harith al-Nadar, "My Story with al-Awlaki," *Inspire* 9 (Winter 2012).

275 accelerating out of the explosion: Ibid.

275 two local al-Qaeda operatives: "Two killed in US airstrike" (Arabic), *Mareb Press*, May 5, 2011.

276 "increased my certainty": Nadar, "My Story with al-Awlaki."

276 fifty stragglers: Abd al-Raziq al-Jamal, "Interview with Fahd al-Qusa" (Arabic), al-Malahim, September 13, 2011.

277 Sumali later told journalists: Scahill, "Washington's War in Yemen Backfires."

277 stomped on it with his sandals: Ansar al-Shariah video, released August 2011.

277 Sumali was told: The outline of this conversation has been confirmed by two different Yemeni government sources familiar with the discussion. Names withheld by request.

278 green canvas pouch: Abd al-Raziq al-Jamal, "Mujahidin of Abyan speak to the media for the first time" (Arabic), *al-Wasat*, September 18, 2011.

279 A judge had ordered: Scahill: "Washington's War in Yemen Backfires."

279 "I'm not a thief": Amjad Khashaqa, "From Azzan to Zanjubar," *al-Wasat*, no date.

279 "to start a new life": Ibid.

279 "It is like a dream": "Eye on the Event #10," *al-Madad* (Arabic), released April 2012.

279 On June 10: Klaidman, *Kill or Capture*, 253–56.

280 Across the room, John Brennan listened: Klaidman, *Kill or Capture*, 254–55.

280 The deputies pared back the target list: Ibid., 255–56.

280 "We're not in Yemen to get involved": quoted in ibid., 256.

280 massive prison break: "Al-Qaeda fighters escape from Yemen jail," al-Jazeera English, June 22, 2011.

281 cracks down the glass: Scahill, "Washington's War in Yemen Backfires."

281 "Our soldiers' morale": Muhammad Jamih, "Interview with Muhammad al-Sumali" (Arabic), *al-Sharq al-Awsat*, July 26, 2011.

282 Throughout August: Khashaqa, "From Azzan to Zanjubar"; Jamih, "Interview with Muhammad al-Sumali."

282 melted away: Khashaqa, "From Azzan to Zanjubar."

282 "We are not happy at all": Anna Fifield, Roula Khalaf, and Abigail Fielding-Smith, "Yemeni president accused of tricking Saudis," *Financial Times*, September 27, 2011.

283 "I am sorry": Quoted in Michelle Shephard, "Drone death in Yemen of American teenager," *Toronto Star*, April 13, 2012.

283 The prisoner had provided the US: Klaidman, *Kill or Capture*, 262–64.

283 Buzzing overhead: Ibid.

283 "The death of Awlaki": "Obama: Awlaki death 'major blow to terrorism,'" *CBS News*, September 30, 2011.

284 The first missile plowed into the fire: the scene of this strike and the two missile is discussed by Ghaith Abdul-Ahad in the *PBS Frontline* film, al-Qaeda in Yemen, aired on May 29, 2012.

284 group of teenagers: Michelle Shephard, "Drone death in Yemen."

284 "coup against the constitution": "President Salih signs GCC deal ending 33 years in power," *al-Arabiya*, November 23, 2011.

285 Months earlier, MI5: Duncan Gardham, "British secret agent was al-Qaeda mole who cracked new 'underpants' bomb plot," *Daily Telegraph*, May 10, 2012.

285 chemicals from military laboratories: Yahya Ibrahim, "Winning on the Ground," *Inspire* 9 (Winter 2012), 57.

285 His cover story: Nic Robertson, Paul Cruikshank, and Brian Todd, "Saudi agent in bomb plot held UK passport, source says," *CNN News*, May 11, 2012.

286 The death sentence al-Qaeda posted: "Eyes on the Event #4," al-Madad (Arabic), released February 2012.

287 The video al-Qaeda made: "Eyes on the Event #5," al-Madad (Arabic), released March 2012.

287 "That's the traitor": "Martyrs of the Arabian Peninsula #10: Mawhid al-Maribi" (Arabic), al-Malahim, March 2012.

287 two triggering mechanisms: Robertson, et al., "Saudi agent in bomb plot."

288 terrorist-attack-disruption strikes: Jo Becker and Scott Shane, "Secret 'Kill List' Proves a Test of Obama's Principles and Will," *New York Times*, May 29, 2012.

288 "And to America": "Statement of Condolence on the Martyrdom of Shaykh Fahd al-Qusa al-Awlaki," Al-Qaeda in the Arabian Peninsula statement #49 (Arabic), May 9, 2012.

INDEX

Abab, Adil al-, 271–72, 276
abayas (black cloaks), 84, 267
Abbottabad, 272–74
Abdullah (secretary for British company), 45–46
Abdullah, King of Saudi Arabia, 250, 282
Abidah, 216
Abqaiq oil refinery, 201, 204
Abu Ghraib prison, 174
Abuja, 257, 258
Abyan Province, 22–24, 30, 32–33, 35–36, 40, 49, 55, 57, 61, 63, 208, 247, 265, 268, 271, 276–79, 281, 284, 287, 290
Accra, 258
Aden, 17, 19, 20, 21, 29–36, 40, 41–47, 60–61, 71, 73, 77, 108, 116, 130–31, 180, 181–82, 192, 217, 223, 272, 277–78, 281, 291
  bombing strikes in, 30–36 52
  sack of, 44–47, 63, 78
Aden-Abyan Islamic Army, 59
Aden Free Zone, 181–82
Aden Hotel, 44
Aden International Airport, 41–42
Afghanistan, xiv, 3–18, 22, 23–24, 27–29, 33–36, 48–50, 52, 53, 54–59, 64, 65, 66, 67–68, 79, 82, 87, 97–108, 113–14, 128, 135, 162, 167, 168, 191, 195, 200, 210, 211, 216, 217, 233, 241, 280, 290–91, 292, 293
Afghanistan War, xiv, 97–104, 107, 113, 150, 163, 196, 238, 280, 290–91, 293
Afghan-Soviet War, 3–18, 24, 31, 98, 107
Ahdal, Muhammad Hamdi al- (Abu Assam), 91–94, 105–6, 108, 129, 131–32, 135, 144, 184, 289, 293
Ahmar, Ali Muhsin al-, 22, 44–45, 78, 148–49, 178, 289
Ahmar, Shaykh Abdullah al-, 7–8, 40–41, 78, 149, 178, 289
Air Force Two, 111
airliner attacks, 257–62, 263, 291
AK-47 rifle, 120–21

Akbari, Ali al-, 228, 280–81
Akron code name, 251–53
Ali, Hazarat, 100, 102
Ali, Umm, 66
Ali, Zayd bin, 145
Alimi, Rashad al-, 131, 260–61
al-Qaeda:
  Afghanistan network of, 5, 12, 14, 28–29, 52, 55, 56, 57, 65, 66, 79, 82, 97–104, 113–14, 128, 167, 168, 191, 195, 200, 233
  airliners attacked by, 257–62, 263, 291
  as al-Qaeda in the Arabian Peninsula (AQAP), xiv–xv, 57–58, 235–38, 239, 240–43, 244, 247, 251, 262, 265, 266, 267–68, 271–72, 278–82, 284, 285, 286–88, 290, 291, 292, 293
  arms supplies of, 112, 154, 157, 258–67
  arrests of, 61, 62, 77–78, 130–32, 135–36, 144, 161, 164, 165, 184, 186, 206–8, 215–16, 246, 253, 265–68
  assassinations by, 14, 98, 233, 247–50, 266–67, 281, 284, 285, 291
  audio statements issued by, 204, 212–13
  bin Laden as leader of, 28–29, 36–38, 52, 55, 56, 57, 64, 65, 66, 69, 71, 79, 82, 97–104, 128, 143, 161, 164, 195, 204, 208–10, 228–29, 233, 235, 237, 271–74, 291
  bombings by, 30–36, 52, 65, 71–73, 109–10, 111, 112–13, 117–18, 150, 152, 186, 196–99, 205, 209, 213–15, 225–26, 230–31, 236–37, 241–43, 244, 247–50, 251, 257–60, 266–67, 276, 285–86, 289–90
  bounties offered for members of, 210, 223
  casualties of, 206–8, 216–17, 226–28
  CIA investigations of, 12, 13, 20–21, 70–71, 79, 90–94, 97, 100–103, 111, 114–15, 121, 122, 166–67, 184, 195, 203, 257, 258, 263, 267, 272, 284–85
  decentralized organization of, 66, 69, 71, 208–10
  defector and informants in, 123–29, 210–12, 240–41, 243, 266–67, 286–87
  explosives used by, 241–43, 244, 258, 266–67, 276, 285
  factionalism in, 210–12
  FBI investigations of, 74–78, 81–88, 90, 111–12, 123–30, 131, 169–74, 195, 217, 218, 223–24, 257, 258, 288, 289, 291, 292
  financial support for, 18, 22, 24, 123–29, 170
  flag used by, 199, 239, 277
  Huthi rebellion compared with, 149, 159
  imprisonment of, 103–4, 113–15, 130–31, 159–75, 191–205, 206, 209, 210, 211, 213, 223, 226, 251, 266, 280–81, 290, 292, 293
  intelligence information on, 12, 13, 21, 53–56, 70–71, 79, 93–95, 114–15, 121–23, 131–32, 136, 152, 195, 228–29, 235, 236, 239, 251–52, 257, 260, 262, 264–67, 283, 284–88
  Islamic fundamentalism of, 121–22, 137–47, 156, 160–65, 167–69, 198–200, 237–38, 278–79, 282
  Jews as targets of, 52–53, 56–57, 58, 65, 128, 145, 147, 148, 162, 164, 201

"jihadis" in, 32–37, 39–40, 42, 44–47, 49, 51–57, 59, 60–64, 67, 71, 80, 81, 94, 127, 143, 146, 151, 160–65, 168–69, 182, 196, 200, 204, 207, 208–9, 210, 211, 212, 216, 217, 221, 232–33, 266, 290, 293
leadership of, 107–8, 129–30, 142, 144, 174–75, 220–21, 235–38, 239, 263–64, 266, 280–81, 286–88
media coverage of, 171–72, 220–21, 224, 235–38, 239, 245–46, 256, 261–62, 265–72, 281, 292
membership strength of, 264
military operations against, 78, 94, 97, 148–59, 206–8, 215–17, 226–28, 244–45, 255–56, 276–82, 289
Muslim victims of, 197–98, 225–26, 231, 243
oath of allegiance (*bay'a*) to, 30, 68–69, 140–41, 193, 208–9, 240, 241, 257–58
Pakistan as refuge for, 14, 97, 98, 103–4, 271–74
popular support for, 107, 109, 197–98, 225–26, 231, 243, 271–72, 279
prison escapes of, 130–31, 175, 191–205, 206, 209, 210, 211, 213, 223, 226, 251, 266, 280–81, 290, 292, 293
propaganda of, 204, 212–13, 220–21, 224, 228–29, 234, 235–38, 239, 245–46
recruitment by, 3–18, 66–69, 161–65, 208–11, 212, 214, 217, 240–41, 261–62, 264, 271–72
in rehabilitation program, 135–44, 151, 186–87, 191, 231, 232, 239
resurgence of, 174–75, 186–87, 194, 200–201, 203, 206–19
safe houses used by, xiii, 49–50, 55–56, 113, 116, 117, 130, 198, 201, 202, 206–7, 211–12, 216–17, 226–28, 235–38, 247
Salih's suppression of, 22, 32–33, 38, 39, 44, 49, 51–52, 58–59, 63, 78, 84, 88, 89–94, 95, 110, 111, 116, 129–32, 135–37, 140–41, 142, 146, 156, 164, 180, 184, 185, 186, 195, 206–7, 212–19, 223–24, 237–38, 244, 245, 246, 260–61, 265, 267, 269–70, 293
in Saudi Arabia, 196–202, 239
simultaneous attacks by, 30–34, 65, 196–97, 230–31
suicide missions by, 71–73, 117–18, 186, 196–99, 205, 209, 213–15, 225–26, 230–31, 236–37, 241–43, 244, 247–50, 251, 257–60, 285–86, 289–90; *see also specific missions*
as terrorist organization, 36–38, 64, 65, 82, 108–9, 144, 161–65, 217–19, 223–25, 235–38, 251, 264
tourists attacked by, 213–15, 221–22, 241–43, 251
training camps of, 49–50, 57–58, 62–63, 65, 78, 82, 88, 110, 129, 165, 191, 217, 221, 252–53, 254, 258, 264
US citizens as members of, 262–63
US embassy attacked by, 229–31, 233, 251
US interests attacked by, 25, 29–34, 52–53, 56–57, 58, 65, 68, 70, 107, 128, 143, 145, 147, 148, 162, 164, 165–75, 198, 201, 209, 230–31, 239, 245, 246, 251, 255–60, 266–67

al-Qaeda (*continued*)
US targeted strikes against, 251–68, 280–81, 282, 283–84, 286, 288, 290, 291, 292
videos released by, 214–15, 225, 228–29, 239, 245, 258, 279, 286, 287
Yemeni cells of, xiv–xv, 17, 24, 29, 30–40, 46, 50, 52–58, 80, 160–65, 208–10, 213–17, 226–28, 233–38, 239, 240–43, 244, 247, 251, 252, 262, 265, 266, 267–68, 271–72, 278–82, 284, 285, 286–88, 290, 291, 292, 293
al-Qaeda in the Arabian Peninsula (AQAP), xiv–xv, 57–58, 235–38, 239, 240–43, 244, 247, 251, 262, 265, 266, 267–68, 271–72, 278–82, 284, 285, 286–88, 290, 291, 292, 293
ambushes, 213–15, 221–22
amirs (commanders), 208–9
amnesties, 240–41, 243–44
Amnesty International, 253*n*
amputation, 279
Amran, 147, 149
Amri, Yahya al-, 149
Anbari, Jamil al-, 263–64
Ansar al-Shariah (Supporters of Islamic Law), 272, 278
Ansi, Muhammad al-, 123–29, 169–74, 289
anti-Semitism, 52–53, 56–57, 58, 65, 126, 127, 128, 137–38, 145, 147, 148, 162, 164, 201
Arab, Husayn, 54
Arab Contractors Co., 114
Arabian peninsula, xix, 4, 28, 29–30, 59, 78, 81, 95, 213, 237
Arabic language, 127–28, 168, 176, 183, 247, 285–86
Arab-Israeli War (1967), 10
Arab League, 25
Arab Mind, The, 166–67
Arafat, Yasir, 128
Arhab, 268
Ariqi, Ramzi al-, 286–87
Armitage, Richard, 88
Ashcroft, John, 129
Ashtal, Abdullah al-, 26–27
Asiri, Abdullah, 198–202, 209, 235, 244, 247–50, 289–90
Asiri, Hasan, 198
Asiri, Ibrahim, 198–202, 235, 244, 247–48, 258, 285, 287–88, 290
Asir Province, 201–2
assassinations, 48, 49–51, 209–12, 272–76, 281, 284, 285, 291
by al-Qaeda, 14, 98, 223, 247–50, 266–67
attempted, on bin Laden, 28–29, 36–38, 40, 66
in bin Laden's death, 272–74
in Yemen, 20, 27–28, 119–23, 218, 233–34
Associated Press (AP), 123, 186–87
Atanasov, Atanas, 118
Atta, Muhammad, 69
Awfi, Muhammad al-, xv, 239, 240–41, 244, 266, 285
Awlaki, Abd al-Rahman al-, 283, 284, 285
Awlaki, Anwar al-, 245–47, 257, 261–63, 274–76, 283–84, 290
Awaliq, al-, tribe 73, 254–57
Axelrod, David, 263
ayatollahs, 156
Azerbaijan, 52, 115
Azzam, Abdullah, 10, 11–12, 13, 14–16, 17, 37, 98
Azzam, Muhammad, 15
Azzan, 286–87

Badawi, Hasan al-, 117
Badawi, Jamal al-, 73, 77, 130–31, 192–93, 195, 217–18, 219, 222–23, 224, 290
Badi, Mustafa (Abu Ibrahim), 8–10
Badr, battle of, 229–30
Baghdad, 165, 180
Bahrain, 72, 74, 199
Bahri, Nasir al- (Abu Jandal), 66–69, 71, 86–88, 142, 290
Bajammal, Abd al-Qadir, 178
Baker, James, 26–27
Bakil tribe, 7
Baku, 115
Banna, Ibrahim al-, 49, 284
Banna, Jabir al-, 195, 222–23, 224, 231, 290
Banna, Susan al-, 231, 237
Batis, Abdullah, 227
Bawaydhan, Muhammad, 228, 280–81
bay'a (oath of allegiance), 30, 68–69, 140–41, 193, 208–9, 240, 241, 257–58
Bayhani, Mansur al-, 213
Baz, Abd al-Aziz bin, 156
BBC, 123
bedouins, 222, 252–53, 254, 255
Berntsen, Gary, 100
Bible, 10, 214
Bid, Ali Salim al-, 19, 32–33, 38–39, 42–43, 44, 47
Biden, Joe, 273
Bill of Rights, 263
bin Laden, Abdullah, 37–38
bin Laden, Muhammad, 16–17
bin Laden, Osama:
- Abbottabad attack on, 272–74
- Aden attacks ordered by, 30–34
- in Afghanistan, 5, 12, 14, 24, 28–29, 52, 55, 56, 57, 65, 66, 79, 82, 97–104, 128, 233
- as al-Qaeda leader, 28–29, 36–38, 52, 55, 56, 57, 64, 65, 66, 69, 71, 79, 82, 97–104, 128, 143, 161, 164, 195, 204, 208–10, 228–29, 233, 235, 237, 271–74, 291
- assassination attempts against, 28–29, 36–38, 40, 66
- audio messages sent by, 204
- bodyguards of, 37–38, 57, 66–69, 86, 290
- code name for, 56
- couriers used by, 66, 271
- death of, 272–74
- fatwa issued by, 52–53, 56–57, 65
- funding provided by, 18, 22, 24
- as Islamic fundamentalist, 121–22, 139–40, 142, 143, 156
- Jews as targets of, 52–53, 56–57, 58, 65
- last will and testament of, 103
- marriages of, 66, 69, 103, 274
- oath of allegiance to (*bay'a*), 68–69, 140–41, 193, 208–9
- offices used by, 36–38
- in Pakistan, 14, 271–74
- passport of, 40
- as Saudi Arabian, 16–18, 24–25, 28–29, 36, 37, 40, 66, 163, 196, 198
- September 11 attacks planned by, 197
- in Sudan, 29–30, 35–38, 40, 50–51, 52, 65, 291
- as terrorist, 36–38, 64, 65, 82
- US interests attacked by, 25, 29–34, 52–53, 56–57, 58, 65, 68, 70, 107, 143, 198, 239
- videos released by, 228–29
- Yemeni background of, 16–17, 226

bin Laden, Osama (*continued*)
Yemeni operations directed by, 17–18, 19, 22, 23–24, 27, 29, 30–34, 35, 38, 46, 55, 56, 64, 107–9, 110, 191, 271–72, 279, 292
Black, Gideon, 173
Black Panthers, 125, 126, 127
"black sites," 169
Blair, Tony, 63
Bloomfield, Lincoln, Jr., 153–55
Bodine, Barbara, 59–60, 74–75, 77, 81–82, 85, 88, 89, 109
bodyguards, 37–38, 57, 66–69, 86, 290
bomb-making operations, 241–43, 244, 258, 266–67, 276, 285
Bosnia, 67
bounties, 210, 223
Bremer, Paul, 180
Brennan, John, 258, 259, 262, 263, 267, 274, 280, 288
breweries, 46–47
British Empire, 17, 19, 35
Bureau of Intelligence and Research, US, 182
Bush, George H. W., 25–27, 29, 82, 90
Bush, George W., 82, 88–92, 123, 132, 162, 168, 172, 197, 203, 217, 219, 223
Salih's relationship with, 89–92, 93, 142, 179–80, 184

C-4 explosive, 273–74
C-5 Galaxy aircraft, 30–31
C-17 aircraft, 111
C-130 cargo planes, 154–55
Cairo, 114–15, 136
capitalism, 25
car bombs, 196–99, 201, 205, 213–15, 225–26, 230–31
cell phones, 121–23
Central Command, US (CENTCOM), 60, 122, 244, 260, 279–80
Central Intelligence Agency (CIA), 12, 13, 21, 70–71, 79, 90–94, 97, 100–103, 111, 114–15, 121, 122, 166–67, 184, 195, 203, 257, 258, 263, 267, 272, 284–85
Central Security Forces, 105, 116, 179–80, 183, 231, 276, 277
Chafee, USS, 213
Chechnya, 64, 91, 200
Cheney, Dick, 111, 142
Christian Science Monitor, 123
civilian casualties:
in al-Qaeda attacks, 197–98, 213–15, 221–22, 225–26, 231, 241–43, 251
in U.S strikes, 251–54, 260–61, 264, 265, 268, 280
Cleveland code name, 251
Clinton, Bill, 82, 88, 90
Clinton, Hillary, 251, 273
cluster bombs, 252
CNN, 88, 123, 203
Coast Guard, Yemeni, 180
Cohen, William, 82
Cold War, 6, 11–12, 19, 25, 180
Cole, USS, attack on (2000), 71–77, 81–84, 85, 86, 90, 108, 109, 111, 112, 130–31, 157, 192, 195, 215, 217, 229, 256, 288, 290, 291–92
"collective presidency," 21
Communism, 7, 9, 13, 17, 18
Confidential Informant One (CI1), 126
Congress, US, 88, 91, 129, 203
Constitution, US, 263
counterterrorism, 89, 111, 123–29, 179–80, 215–19, 226–28, 244, 251–53, 257, 258, 272, 284–85

crucifixions, 286, 287
cruise missiles, 213, 252–53, 256–57, 260–61, 263, 268
"crystal ball memo," 118

Daisy Cutter bomb, 101–2
Darwish, Kamal, 122–23
Daylami, Abd al-Wahhab al-, 3–6, 8, 39, 63–64, 135–36
Daylami, Hisham al-, 3–6, 8, 10
Daylami, Muhammad al-, 120–21, 206–7
death penalty, 169, 175, 192–93, 286–87
defectors, 123–29, 210–12, 240–41, 243, 266–67, 286–87
Defense Department, US, 34, 101, 166–67, 251–52
Delta Force, 102
democracy, 27, 176–77, 183–85, 195
Democratic Party, 203, 231
"detainees," 166–67, 186, 195
Dhahabi, Muhammad al-, 136
Dhayani, Khalid al-, 242–43
diesel fuel, 182–83
Djibouti, 44, 119, 121, 283
Doha, Ali, 209–10, 213–17
Donilon, Tom, 263
drones, xii, 119, 121–23, 132, 185, 209, 211, 263, 264, 275–76, 283–84, 286, 288, 290, 291, 292
Dubai, 119, 267
Dubai Ports International, 181–82
due process, 263
Duwaydar, Ahmad, 215–16

Egypt, 10–11, 38, 48, 49–51, 52, 114–15, 136, 182, 216, 270
Empty Quarter, 95
"enemy combatants," 167
"enhanced interrogations," 168
Ethiopia, 50
explosives, 241–43, 244, 258, 266–67, 276, 285

F-5 fighters, 155
Fadhli, Nasir al-, 16–17
Fadhli, Tariq al-, 16, 17, 19, 21–24, 27–28, 30, 32–33, 39–40, 42, 45, 49, 52, 55, 58–59, 78, 290
Fadl, Dr. (Sayyid Imam al-Sharif), 49
Fahd, King of Saudi Arabia, 27
Farid, Salih bin, 254–57
Faruq, Abu Amr al-, 243
Faruq, al-, training camp, 65
fatwas, 11, 39, 52–53, 56–57, 65, 293
Fayfi, Jabir al-, 99, 101, 104, 166, 167–69, 232–33, 238, 239–40, 241, 266–67, 290–91
Federal Bureau of Investigation (FBI), 74–78, 81–88, 90, 111–12, 123–30, 131, 169–74, 195, 217, 218, 223–24, 257, 258, 288, 289, 291, 292
Federal Express (FedEx), 267
Fifth Amendment, 263
Finsbury Park Mosque, 59
First Armored Division, Yemeni, 40, 78, 149, 270–71, 289
"fiver" Shi'ism, 144*n*, 145, 156
food prices, 147, 177
Fort Hood shootings (2009), 261, 290
France, 93, 267
Franks, Tommy, 142
Freedom House, 185
Friendship Bridge, 12
fuel subsidies, 177–78, 182–83
Fuller, Robert, 124, 171
Fury, Dalton (pseud.), 100–103
futa (cloth skirt), 255, 278

Gaza, 238, 239
Germany, 127–29, 169–70, 224, 231, 291
Ghamsharik, Haji Zaman, 100, 102
Ghana, 258
Ghashmi, Ahmad al-, 20
"ghost employees," 105
Giuliani, Rudolph, 219, 223
God, 121–22, 139–40, 146, 162, 165, 199–200, 201, 232, 245
Gold Mohur hotel, 32
Gore, Al, 38–39, 82
Great Britain, 45–46, 59, 60, 63, 224–25, 228, 246, 254, 284–85, 288
Great Mosque (Sanaa), 147, 148
Green Zone, 180
Griffin missiles, 275
Gromov, Boris, 12
Guantánamo Bay detention center, xiii, xiv–xv, 104, 113, 165–75, 186, 195, 207, 218, 232, 235, 237, 238–39, 240, 253, 262, 291, 292
guerrilla warfare, 13, 18, 98, 152–53
guided missiles, 213, 252–53, 256–57, 260–61, 263, 268
Gulf Cooperation Council, 278, 284
Gulf of Aden, 29, 44, 57, 95, 108, 130, 213, 221
Gulf of Oman, 81
Gulf War, 24–27, 28, 42, 43, 59, 74, 80, 88

Hada, Samir al-, 113
Hadi, Abd Rabu Mansur, 43, 284, 286, 288
hadiths (commentaries), 24
Hadramawt, 30, 204–5, 221–22, 225, 226–28, 241–43
hajj, 5
Hajjah, 147
Hamas, 126, 127, 128, 172–74, 238
Hamdan, Salim, 66, 87
Hammadi, Khaled al-, 186–87
Harad, Abdullah al-, 275, 276
Harad, Musad al-, 275, 276
Harhara, Malik, 61
Harithi, Abu Ali al-, 33–36, 42, 46, 64, 91–92, 94, 95–97, 107–8, 109, 110, 112, 117, 119, 121–23, 129, 132, 184, 185, 211, 275, 291
Harrier jets, 275–76
Hasan, Nidal, 261, 290
Hashid tribe, 7–8, 149*n,* 289
Hatshepsut, Queen, 52
Hayat, al-, 210
health care, 108–9, 119, 161, 233
Hellfire missiles, 122, 123
hijrah (migration), 28–29
Hijri, Abd al-Wahhab al-, 88–89
Hilah, Abd al-Salam al-, 54–55, 69–71, 76, 109, 114–15, 169, 195, 291
Hilah, Abd al-Wahhab, 115
Hindu Kush, 14
Hitar, Hamud al-, 137–44, 151, 152, 186–87, 191, 231, 232
Holder, Eric, 263
Homeland Security Department, US, 257, 258
hospitals, 108–9, 119, 233
House of Representatives, US, 91
Hudaydah, 41, 108, 116, 231
hudud (punishment categories), 279
Hull, Edmund, 89, 90, 94, 108–9, 116, 119–21, 123, 125, 129–31, 142, 180–81, 233, 291
Hunt Oil, 121, 129, 154, 174
Husn, al-, 95–97

Hussein, Saddam, 24–27, 28, 42, 80, 92
Huthi, Abd al-Malik al-, 158–59
Huthi, Badr al-Din al-, 155–57, 158
Huthi, Husayn al-, 145, 146, 148–53, 155
Huthi, Yahya al-, 150, 155
Huthi rebellions, 145–59, 164, 177, 184, 195–96, 202–3, 218, 241, 270, 278, 289

Ibb, 66
Ikhlas, al-, forum, 228-29
imams, 83, 138, 145, 246
India, 38, 40
infidels, 7, 24, 25, 36–37, 146, 201, 213
informants, 123–29, 210–12, 240–41, 243, 266–67, 287–88
Intercontinental Semiramis, 115
Interior Ministry, Yemeni, 186–87, 210
International Monetary Fund (IMF), 177
Internet, xiv, 221, 225, 228–29, 245–46, 247, 271, 286
interrogations, 85–88, 105–6, 111, 165–75, 262
Iran, xiii, 103, 144, 156, 163, 196, 293
Iraq, 24–27, 28, 144
Iraq War, xiv, 142, 164–65, 174, 180, 186–87, 198, 203, 208, 210, 211, 220, 225, 264, 280
Iryani, Abd al-Karim al-, 89–90
Islah, 38, 41, 289
Islam:
  alcohol prohibited by, 46–47, 199
  beards as traditional in, 200
  calendar of, 228, 229
  caliphate of, 16, 140
  clerics of, 5, 8, 39, 59, 83, 125–29, 135–47, 156, 197, 224, 225–26, 243, 245–47, 261–62, 271–72
  fatwas in, 11, 39, 52–53, 56–57, 65, 293
  founding of, xi–xii
  fundamentalist, 10–11, 121–22, 137–47, 156, 160–65, 167–69, 198–200, 237–38, 278–79, 282
  hajj performed in, 5
  infidels opposed by, 7, 24, 25, 36–37, 146, 201, 213
  jihad ideology of, xiii, xiv, 5–6, 7, 8–10, 11, 12, 15–18, 19, 22, 23, 24–25, 27, 39, 52–53, 79–80, 87, 99, 121–22, 125–29, 132, 135–47, 160–65, 200, 228–29, 238, 247, 257
  marriage in, 66, 69, 126–27, 204, 274
  martyrdom in, 212, 221, 241–43, 257–60
  mosques of, 5, 8, 9–10, 15, 19, 37, 70, 83, 125–26, 147, 148, 174, 191, 193–94, 197, 198–200, 225–26, 246, 270, 278, 285
  political systems based on, 7, 19, 135–47, 198–200
  prayers in, 166, 191–92, 194, 199, 247
  radical interpretations of, 10–11, 144–47, 156, 159
  religious institutes for, 56–57, 146, 165
  Shariah law of, 51, 63, 66, 79–80, 87, 135–47, 168, 199–200, 212–13, 272, 278–79, 282, 286
  Shi‘a, 144–47, 156
  Sunni, 144, 145, 146, 159
  takfir (excommunication) in, 49, 168, 169

Islam (*continued*)
Wahhabi, 146
women's role in, 28, 79, 80, 84, 152–53, 155, 156, 226–27, 267
in Yemeni culture, xi–xii, 38, 41, 46–47, 51, 56–57, 64, 137–47, 165, 212–13, 271
Islamabad, 51
Islamic University, 9
Israel, 10, 42, 126, 127, 128, 172–74, 238
Italy, 69–71, 114

Jaar, 271–72, 279, 280, 282, 286
Jacob, 4
Jacobs, Howard, 173
jah (reputation), 41
Jalal, Al, family, 95
Jalal, Hamad bin Ali, 95–96
Jalalabad, 12–14, 16, 68, 98, 99, 272, 290
jambiya (curved dagger), 138, 229
Jarallah, Umar, 205
Jawf, al-, 95, 147, 208, 283–84
Jazeera, al-, 84, 88, 238, 256, 265, 270
Jeddah, 17–18, 24, 28, 249
Jensen, Bruce, 167
Jews, 52–53, 56–57, 58, 65, 126, 127, 128, 137–38, 145, 147, 148, 162, 164, 201
Jifri, Abd al-Rahman al-, 43
Jihad, al-, 48, 50, 51, 52–57
"Jihad Against the Jews and Crusaders," 52–53
jihad ideology, xiii, xiv, 5–6, 7, 8–10, 11, 12, 15–18, 19, 22, 23, 24–25, 27, 39, 52–53, 79–80, 87, 99, 121–22, 125–29, 132, 135–47, 160–65, 200, 228–29, 238, 247, 257
Johnson, Jeh, 251–53
Joint Special Operations Command, 265, 273
Jordan, 164
judicial process, 263
Justice Department, US, 169–74

Kaabah, 5
Kabul, 7, 12, 98
Kandahar, 56, 65
Karachi, 9, 113–14
Kazami, Muhammad al-, 251–53, 260
Kenya and Tanzania embassy attacks (1998), 65, 82, 112, 231
Khamiri, Hassan al-, 72
Khan, Samir, 283
Khanabashi, Salih al-, 31–32, 33, 35, 36, 40, 46, 291
Khartoum, 29–30, 35, 36, 37–38, 50
Khost, 57
Khoury, Nabeel, 182
Khulayfi, Muhammad al-, 36–38
Khyber Pass, 11, 13
kidnappings, 62–64, 114–15, 169, 265–66, 292
Kill TV, 252–53
Kilwi, Muhammad al-, 255–56, 257, 258
Kindi, Nasir al-, 117
King Abd al-Aziz International Airport, 249
Krajeski, Thomas, 180–84
Kuwait, 24–27, 43, 49, 74, 88

Lackawanna Six, 195, 223, 290
last wills and testaments, 103, 205, 242, 258
"learned helplessness," 167
Leiter, Michael, 272
Lenin, V. I., 23

Lippold, Kirk, 72
Los Angeles International Airport, 65
Luxor massacre (1997), 52

Maasada, 5
Madhbah neighborhood, 130
mail bombs, 233–34, 266–67
Majalla, al-, 252–53, 254, 260–61, 264, 265, 292
Manaa, Faris al-, 218
"Manhattan of the desert," 241
man-portable air-defense systems (MANPADS), 153–54
Mansurah, al-, prison, 35
Maraqishah, al-, Mountains, 22–23
Marib, battle of, 244–45, 246
Marib oil refinery, 205
Marib Province, 22, 34, 92–95, 105, 108–9, 110, 119–23, 124, 129, 205, 208–10, 213–17, 228, 231, 233, 244–45, 246, 251
Marib Travel, 124
Marines, US, 30–34, 74
marriage, 66, 69, 126–27, 204, 274
martyrdom, 212, 221, 241–43, 257–60
Marxism, 19, 23
Mashjari, Ahmad al-, 225–26
Masri, Abu Hamza al-, 59, 60, 62, 63
Massoud, Ahmad Shah, 14, 98, 233
mass weddings, 126–27
Mattis, James, 279–80
Mawn, Barry, 77
Mazar-i-Sharif, 97–98
McRaven, William, 273
Mecca, xi, 5, 28–29, 199, 229
Medina, 141, 199, 229
Medina, Treaty of (622), 141
mercenaries, 100–107
MH-60 Black Hawk helicopters, 273
MI5, 285
MI6, 285
migrant workers, 27, 80
Mihdhar, Zayn al-Abidin al-, 58, 60, 61, 62–64, 73
Millennium Challenge Corp. (MCC), 181, 182, 184, 219
Mir, Hamid, 98
missiles, 213, 252–53, 256–57, 260–61, 263, 268
Mitchell, James, 167
mosques, 5, 8, 9–10, 15, 19, 37, 70, 83, 125–26, 147, 148, 174, 191, 193–94, 197, 198–200, 225–26, 246, 270, 278, 285
Movenpick Hotel, 32, 52, 60
MSNBC, 88
Muayyad, Muhammad al-, 125–29, 169–74, 224, 231, 289, 291
Mubarak, Hosni, 49–51, 53, 270
Mueller, Robert, 131, 223–24
Muhammad, xi–xii, xiii, 7, 24, 28–29, 48, 58, 68, 137, 138, 141, 146, 162, 213, 229–30
Muhammad, Ali Nasr, 21
Muhaya, al-, housing compound, 197–98
Muhsin, Ali, 40, 42, 147–48, 271, 277, 282
mujahidin, 10, 11–14, 28–29, 234
Mujali, Arif, 117, 120–21, 129, 204
Mujali, Hizam, 109, 116, 117, 120–21, 130, 174, 204
Mujali, Yahya, 116, 117, 119, 204
Mukalla, al-, 22, 43, 44, 108, 116–18, 280–81
Mukayras region, 57
murder, 137–38, 175, 197–98, 207
Murphy, Caryle, 171

Musayk neighborhood, 213
Mutallab, Umar Farouk Abdu, 247, 257–62, 263, 285, 290, 291
mutatawwa (morality police), 79–80
Mutawakkil, Yahya al-, 123
MV Limburg oil tanker attack (2002), 111–12, 116–18, 119, 157, 184, 215, 292

Nabi Shuayb, 4
Nahdi, Jamal al- (Abu Jandal), 30–34, 35, 38, 46, 52, 60, 86–87
Najjar, Ahmad al-, 49, 51
Najran, 249
Napolitano, Janet, 257, 258
Nashiri, Abd al-Rahim al-, 65–66, 71, 76, 108, 109, 111, 112, 116, 117, 119
Nasrallah, Ahmad, 53–56, 58
Nasser, Gamal Abd al-, 11
Nassib, Rauf, 122
National Counterterrorism Center, 257, 258, 272
National Security Agency (NSA), 121–23
National Security Bureau, 182–83
Navy, US, 30–31, 59, 71, 179, 213, 252, 272–74
Nayif, Muhammad bin, 197, 201, 202, 239, 243–44, 247–50, 258, 266, 267, 284–85, 289–90, 291
Nayif, Prince, 197
"negative leaders," 169, 232
new world order, 25
New York Times, 172
Nigeria, 247, 257, 258
9/11 attacks, *see* September 11, 2001, terrorist attacks
9/11 Commission, 246
Northern Alliance, 97–104, 233
Northwest Airlines flight 253 bombing attempt (2009), 258–60
Numan, Ahmad, 179

Obama, Barack, xv, 269–74
  Abbottabad raid authorized by, 272–74
  on Awlaki, 274, 283–84
  on failed 2009 Christmas bombing, 259–60
  Guantánamo closing plans of, xiii, xiv, 238–39
  Salih's relationship with, 269 292
  "signature strikes" as viewed by, 262–65, 280
  on 2008 Yemen US embassy bombing, 231
  Yemeni al-Qaeda's challenge to, xiii, xiv, 239, 280–84
Office of Legal Counsel, 262–63
oil industry, 20, 24, 108, 116–18, 201, 204–5
Old Testament, 10
Oman, 44
119th Mechanized Brigade, Yemeni, 277–78
O'Neill, John, 74–77, 81, 84–85, 217, 291
Operation Copper Dune, 251–52
Operation Restore Hope, 29
Organization of African Unity (OAU), 50

package bombs, 233–34, 266–67
Pakistan, 6, 9–10, 12, 14–15, 17, 24, 38, 49, 59, 88, 103–4, 113–14, 167, 196, 290
Pakistani Army, 103–4
Palestinians, 10, 126, 238, 239
Panetta, Leon, 272

Parlier, James, 72–73
passports, 36, 40, 53, 70, 71, 285
Penal Primary Court, Yemeni, 137–44
People's Democratic Republic of Yemen, 19–22
Persian Gulf, 204
Peshawar, 6, 9–10, 14–15, 17, 24, 49, 59
PETN explosive, 258, 267
Petraeus, David, 244, 260–61, 279
police forces, 201–2, 226–28, 279
Political Security Organization (PSO), 53–56, 75–78, 79, 80, 85–88, 90–91, 105–6, 109–10, 114–15, 130–31, 132, 160–65, 174–75, 182–83, 192, 194, 203, 218, 225, 265–66, 291
Powell, Colin, 89
Predator drones, xii, 119, 121–23, 132, 185, 209, 211, 263, 264, 275–76, 283–84, 286, 288, 290, 291, 292
propaganda, 204, 212–13, 220–21, 224, 228–29, 234, 235–38, 239, 245–46

Qahtani, Nayif al-, 220–21, 263
Qamish, Ghalib al-, 75–77, 85–86, 90–91, 93, 105, 175, 225, 291
Qasaylah, Ali Mahmud, 209–10, 213
Qasimi, Muhammad Ali al-, 151–52, 154–55
qat, 20, 214
Qatn, al-, 227
Qirbi, Abu Bakr al-, 150, 264
Quayti, Hamza al-, 161–62, 221–22, 225, 226–28, 281
Quds al-Arabi, al-, 186–87
Quran, 4, 11, 57, 78, 94, 138–40, 143, 162, 165, 191–92, 198–200, 229–30, 245, 248, 256
Qusa, Fahd al-, 73–74, 77–78, 85–87, 130–31, 256–57, 288, 291–92
Qutb, Muhammad, 10–11
Qutb, Sayyid, 4, 10–11, 48

Rabi'i, Abu Bakr al-, 109, 110, 112–13, 120–21, 207
Rabi'i, Fawaz al-, 79–80, 81, 107–8, 109, 110, 112–13, 116, 119–21, 129, 130, 154, 161–65, 169, 175, 184, 191, 203, 204–8, 292
Rabi'i, Hasan al-, 207
Rabi'i, Salman al-, 80, 99–100, 207
Rabi'i, Yahya al-, 207–8
Raes, Peter, 118
Rafdh, 256–57
Ramadan, 100, 103–4, 131, 141, 186, 228, 230, 249
Rass, al-, 198
Raymi, Faris al-, 211–12
Raymi, Qasim al-, xv, 161–62, 169, 175, 193–94, 203, 208, 211–12, 213, 216–17, 235–36, 239, 243–44, 245, 247, 251, 253, 261, 264, 266, 282, 292
Red Crescent, 49
refugees, 152, 202
rehabilitation programs, 135–44, 151, 186–87, 191, 231, 232, 239
"rendition," 111
Republican Guards, Yemeni, 78, 179, 277
Republican Party, 123, 219
retribalization policy, 22
Rice, Condoleezza, 184–85
ricin, 266
Riyadh, 196–202, 226, 233, 238, 267, 284

rocket-propelled grenades (RPGs), 264
Rubaysh, Muhammad, 233–34
Rubaysh, Shaykh, 108–9, 119, 233
Ruhayqah, Abdu Muhammad al-, 213–15
Ruzami, Abdullah al-, 152
Rwanda, 44

Sabr, Nasir, 179
Sada al-Malahim ("The Echo of Battles"), 221, 224, 234, 263
Sadah, Amal al-, 66
Sadah Province, 144–47, 150, 157, 184, 196, 240, 278
safe houses, xiii, 49–50, 55–56, 113, 116, 117, 130, 198, 201, 202, 206–7, 211–12, 216–17, 226–28, 235–38, 247
sales tax, 178
Salih, Ahmad, 78, 179, 267
Salih, Ali Abdullah:
- al-Qaeda suppressed by, 22, 32–33, 38, 39, 44, 49, 51–52, 58–59, 63, 78, 84, 88, 89–94, 95, 110, 111, 116, 129–32, 135–37, 140–41, 142, 146, 156, 164, 180, 184, 185, 186, 195, 206–7, 212–19, 223–24, 237–38, 244, 245, 246, 260–61, 265, 267, 269–70, 293
- arms requests of, 153–55
- background of, 7, 19–21
- Bush's relationship with, 89–92, 93, 142, 179–80, 184
- in civil war, 32–33, 38–47, 49, 58, 78
- corruption in, 105, 147, 179, 181–86
- economic policies of, 20, 25–27, 80, 88, 108–9, 125–26, 147, 149, 153, 176–87, 219, 222
- elections of, 38, 39, 176–77, 195, 203, 205, 206, 237–38, 269
- Gulf War policy of, 25–26, 29, 43, 80, 90
- Huthi rebellions suppressed by, 145–59, 164, 195–96
- immunity agreement for, 284
- as Islamic leader, 7, 140–42, 143
- media coverage of, 84, 88
- medical treatment for, 278, 282
- military support for, 38–47, 63, 78, 93–94, 151–55, 220, 270–71, 276–78, 289
- as North Yemen president, 7, 19–22
- Obama and, 269, 292
- political rivals of, 178–79, 265
- as president, 21–22, 25–26, 29, 38–39, 51–52, 58–60, 78, 80, 84, 88, 164, 176–87, 195, 203, 205, 206, 212, 233, 237–38, 269–71, 276–78, 284, 286, 289, 290, 292
- proposed resignation of, 176–79
- public opposition to, 177–78, 270–71, 282
- rehabilitation program supported by, 135–37, 140–41, 142
- terrorism opposed by, 78, 84, 88, 89–94, 95, 110, 111, 116, 129–32, 135–37, 140–41, 142, 146, 156, 160–62, 164
- tribal relations of, 21, 22, 93–94, 95, 110, 129, 156, 176, 204, 216
- in unification period, 19–22, 25
- US relations with, 21, 29, 35–36, 43, 59–60, 78, 88, 89–92, 93, 111, 116, 131, 135–36, 142, 153–55, 157, 161, 162, 176–87, 195, 203, 217–18, 223–24, 260–61, 265, 269–70, 278, 282

Salih, Ali Muhammad, 111
Salih, Yahya, 105, 179–80, 183
Salim (son of al-Qaeda operative), 287
Sallal, Abdullah al-, 145
Sanaa, xii, 4, 6, 7–8, 19, 20, 21, 25, 34, 38, 39, 40, 41–42, 43, 48, 49, 53, 54, 55–56, 60, 64, 78, 82–86, 88, 89, 93, 95, 105, 108, 109–10, 111, 112, 115, 116–26, 129–32, 135–38, 145, 147, 149, 155–58, 160, 163, 170, 176, 180, 186, 203, 204, 206–7, 209, 210, 211–12, 213, 215–16, 217, 223, 224, 230, 235–36, 244, 245, 247, 257, 267, 270, 271, 278, 282, 283, 288, 292
Sanaa University, 270
Sanabani, Faris, 183–84
Sanhan tribe, 151
sanitation, 192
Saudi Arabia, xiii, 5, 10, 12, 16–18, 22, 24–29, 34, 36, 37, 40, 43, 59, 66, 79–80, 107, 146, 163, 168, 196–202, 208, 209, 221, 226, 232, 233, 235, 239–41, 243–44, 247–50, 262, 266–67, 278, 281–86, 288, 291
Sawani, Ali al-, 175
Sayyid, Abd al-Qadir al- (Abu Salih), 69–71, 78
sayyids (descendants of Muhammad), 145–46
"scalpel" approach, 263
Schuringa, Jasper, 259
Scud missiles, 42
SEALs, 179, 272–74
Seche, Stephen, 218–19
Secret Service, US, 172
Semtex, 112
Senate Judiciary Committee, 129
September 11, 2001, terrorist attacks, 71, 80, 84–92, 98, 107, 108, 111, 114, 123–24, 128, 163, 165, 167, 191, 197, 199, 200, 211, 217, 228, 229, 233, 246, 257, 258, 276, 290, 291, 292
Services Bureau, 9–10, 11, 14, 24
Shabwani, Aidh al-, 245, 264
Shabwani, Jabir al-, 264–65
Shabwa Province, 32, 33, 34, 42, 92, 95, 96, 208, 247, 256, 257, 261, 268, 271, 274–75, 278–79, 283–84, 286
shahada (Islamic profession of faith), 199
Shalan, Hani, 253
Sharaf, Kamal, 265
Shariah law, 51, 63, 66, 79–80, 87, 135–47, 168, 199–200, 212–13, 272, 278–79, 282, 286
Sharif, Sayyid Imam al- (Dr. Fadl), 49
Sharon, Ariel, 225
Sharq al Awsat, al-, 281
Shaya, Abdalilah, 235–38, 239, 261–62, 265–70, 292
shaykhs, 5, 8, 9–10, 20, 33, 40–41, 63, 69, 93–94, 96, 108, 125–29, 135, 165, 176, 196, 216, 217, 237, 244–45, 254–57, 269, 270, 274
Sheba, Queen of, 214
Shephard, Michelle, 246–47
Sheraton Hotel (Sanaa), 83
Shi'a Islam, 144–47, 156
Shibam, 241–43
Shibh, Ramzi bin al-, 113–14
Shibh, Walid al-, 113
Shihhi, Marwan al-, 87
Shihri, Said al-, xiv–xv, 104, 169, 232–33, 235, 237, 239, 243–44, 248, 292

Sidqi, Atif, 48
"signature strikes," 263, 280–81, 288
simultaneous attacks, 30–34, 65, 196–97, 230–31
Siyam, Muhammad, 127
snipers, 157–58, 216, 270, 281
Socialists, 18, 19–22, 23, 24, 25, 27–28, 30, 31, 32, 35, 36, 38–39, 40, 41, 42, 43, 44, 49, 51, 55, 58–59, 148, 175, 270, 279, 289, 290, 293
solitary confinement, 160–61, 175, 191
Solomon, King, 214
Somalia, 29, 67, 213
Soufan, Ali, 74, 77, 78, 81, 82–88, 111–12, 116, 118, 125, 291, 292
Southern Command, Yemeni, 281
South Korea, 241–43
Soviet Union, 3, 6, 7, 11–12, 19–20, 21, 25, 43, 107, 180
Special Forces, US, 92, 97–104, 179, 260, 265
Special Forces, Yemeni, 78, 179
"specially designated global terrorist," 293
Square of Change, 270
State Department, US, 77, 89, 178, 182, 184–85, 186, 223, 259
Stinger missiles, 13
Sudan, 29–30, 35–38, 40, 50–51, 52, 65, 147, 291
suicide belts, 247–50
suicide missions, 71–73, 117–18, 186, 196–99, 205, 209, 213–15, 225–26, 230–31, 236–37, 241–43, 244, 247–50, 251, 257–60, 285–86, 289–90
see also specific missions
suicide vests, 236–37, 241, 242
Sulawi, Uthman al-, 165
Sumali, Muhammad al-, 277–82
Sunnah, 138
Sunni Islam, 144, 145, 146, 159
Supermax prisons, 174
Suq al-Talh, 112, 157
surface-to-air missiles, 154
"surgical strikes," 288
Surmi, Muhammad al-, 54, 109
Syria, 164

Taif, 232–33, 235, 238
Taizz, 53, 55
Tajikistan, 14, 67, 68
Tajik tribesmen, 98
takfir (excommunication), 49, 168, 169
Takfir wa Hijra, 54
Taliban, 16, 98, 107, 279
Tanzania and Kenya embassy attacks (1998), 65, 82, 112, 231
Tarim, 226–28, 281
Tel Aviv, 127
Tenet, George, 90–91
terrorism, xiii–xv, 36–38, 64, 65, 82, 89, 91–92, 111, 123–29, 165–75, 179–80, 215–19, 226–28, 244, 251–53, 257, 258, 263, 272, 280, 284–85, 288
see also suicide missions; *specific terrorist organizations*
terrorist-attack-disruption strikes (TADS), 288
"Terror Tuesday," 263, 280
tha'r (revenge killing), 161
Thawrah, al-, hospital, 49
Thawar, Ibrahim al-, 72
theft, 279
Third Armored Division, Yemeni, 32
Toledo code name, 251
tombs, 146

Tora Bora, 97–104, 107, 113, 150, 163, 196, 238, 290–91, 293
Toronto Star, 246
torture, xiii, 35, 159, 160, 161, 167, 225
tourism, 61–62, 124, 213–15, 221–23, 228, 233, 241–43, 251
Townsend, Frances, 217–18, 223
tracking chips, 286
travel warnings, 222–23, 228
tribal law, 96–97, 105, 117
tribal oaths, 255
tribes, Yemeni, 7–8, 22, 23, 33, 40–41, 48–49, 51, 55, 63, 73, 83, 92, 93–97, 98, 105–6, 108–9, 110, 111, 117, 129, 135–36, 141, 144–47, 149*n,* 157, 160, 161, 176, 180, 186, 208, 216, 222, 233, 241, 247, 252–57, 261, 264, 278, 289
Tunisia, 269
Turab, Abu, 9–10
Turabi, Hasan al-, 29, 40, 52
"twelver" Shi'ism, 144–45, 156
Twenty-Fifth Mechanized Brigade, Yemeni, 276–82

"underwear bombs," 285, 290
unemployment rate, 148
UNESCO World Heritage Site, 241
United Arab Emirates (UAE), 33, 288
United Nations, 25–27, 29, 43–44, 59, 141, 278
United Parcel Service (UPS), 267
United States:
  economic aid from, 27, 88, 108–9, 119, 176–87, 195, 218–19, 222–23
  elections in, 123, 180, 203, 219, 231
  foreign interests of, 25, 29–34, 52–53, 56–57, 58, 65, 68, 70, 107, 128, 143, 145, 147, 148, 162, 164, 165–75, 198, 201, 209, 230–31, 239, 245, 246, 251, 255–60, 266–67
  judicial system of, 262–63
  military aid from, 116, 153–55, 179–87
  as superpower, 6, 11–12, 19, 25, 180
  targeted strikes by, 251–68, 280–81, 282, 283–84, 286, 288, 290, 291, 292
  in war on terror, 91–92, 123, 165–75
  Yemeni relations of, xii–xv, 21, 24–27, 29, 35–39, 43, 59–60, 74–75, 78, 82–83, 88–92, 93, 108–9, 111, 115, 116, 119, 121, 123, 131, 135–36, 142, 143, 153–55, 157, 161, 162, 176–87, 194, 195, 203, 211, 212–13, 217–19, 222–24, 225, 228, 229–31, 233, 237, 251, 260–61, 265, 269–70, 278, 282
UN Security Council, 25–27, 29, 43–44, 59
'urf (tribal code), 96–97
Uyayri, Yusuf al-, 197
Uzbekistan, 12, 98

veils, 80, 226
Vietnam War, 11–12, 101

Wadi'i, Muqbil al-, 146, 156
Wahhabism, 146
wali al-amr (religious term of responsibility), 140
Wall Street Journal, 114
Waqar, 279
war on terror, 91–92, 123, 165–75
Washington Post, 21, 171–72, 246

water supplies, 279
Wihayshi, Nasir al-, xv, 57–58, 100, 163, 164, 174, 191–92, 193, 203–4, 208–11, 213, 217, 220–21, 224–25, 233, 235, 237–38, 240–41, 242, 251, 266, 271, 274, 278–79, 281, 293
Wolfowitz, Paul, 123, 185
women, 28, 79, 80, 84, 152–53, 155, 156, 226–27, 267
World Bank, 177, 185
World Trade Center (WTC), 81, 84–85

Yafai, Zakariya al-, 211
Yemen:
- Afghanistan recruits from, 3–18, 22, 23–24, 27–28, 34–36, 48–50, 53, 54–59, 64, 67–68, 87, 107–8, 135, 162, 191, 195, 210, 211, 216, 217, 241, 290–91, 292, 293
- agriculture in, 147, 150
- air force of, 41–42, 150, 152, 154–55
- airspace of, 260–61
- al-Qaeda cells in, xiv–xv, 39–40, 46, 52–58, 80, 160–65, 208–10, 213–17, 226–28, 233–38, 239, 240–43, 244, 247, 251, 252, 262, 265, 266, 267–68, 271–72, 278–82, 284, 285, 286–88, 290, 291, 292, 293
- Arab fighters in, xii–xiii
- arms sales to, 43, 70, 112, 153–55, 157, 218
- arrests in, 61, 62, 77–78, 130–32, 135–36, 144, 161, 164, 165, 184, 186, 206–8, 215–16, 246, 253, 265–68
- assassinations in, 20, 27–28, 119–23, 218, 233–34
- black market in, 182–83
- bombings in, 30–36, 52, 65, 71–73, 109–10, 111, 112–13, 117–18, 150, 152, 186, 196–99, 205, 209, 213–15, 225–26, 230–31, 236–37, 241–43, 244, 247–50, 251, 257–60, 266–67, 276, 285–86, 289–90
- borders of, 95, 111, 112, 164, 180, 201–2, 221, 239–40, 243–44, 247–48, 261, 266, 278, 283
- British relations with, 45–46, 224–25, 228, 254
- ceasefires in, 43–44, 150, 155–57
- cemeteries in, 46
- civil war in, 17–18, 32–33, 38–47, 49, 55, 58, 60, 78, 83, 145, 146, 148, 176, 270, 293
- constitution of, 138–39, 284
- corruption in, 105, 147, 179, 181–86
- currency of, 27
- diplomatic initiatives of, 39, 42, 88–92, 181–82, 284, 286
- economy of, 20, 25–27, 80, 88, 108–9, 125–26, 147, 149, 153, 176–87, 219, 222
- elections in, 38–39, 176–77, 184–85, 195, 203, 205, 206, 237–38, 269
- electrical grid of, 81
- expatriates from, 124, 170, 179, 195
- food prices in, 147, 177
- foreign aid to, 19–20, 25, 27, 39, 42, 43–44, 62, 88–92, 108–9, 119, 176–87, 195, 216, 218–19, 222–23, 284, 286
- fuel subsidies in, 177–78, 182–83
- geography of, 95, 150, 279

government of, 38–39, 41, 78, 105, 135–37, 146–47, 148, 149, 150, 155–56, 158, 179, 181–87, 212, 219, 221, 225, 254, 256, 260–61, 269, 270, 288
health care in, 108–9, 119, 161, 233
history of, xi–xii, 144–47
Huthi rebellions in, 145–59, 164, 177, 184, 195–96, 202–3, 218, 241, 270, 278, 289
intelligence information on, 12, 13, 21, 53–56, 70–71, 75–78, 79, 80, 85–88, 90–95, 105–6, 109–10, 114–15, 121–23, 130–32, 136, 152, 160–65, 174–75, 182–83, 192, 194, 195, 203, 218, 225, 228–29, 235, 236, 239, 251–52, 257, 260, 262, 264–67, 283, 284–88, 291
international support for, xii–xiii, 19–20, 25, 39, 42, 43–44, 62, 88–92, 177, 181–82, 185, 216, 284, 286
Iraq recruits from, 164–65, 186–87, 208, 210, 211, 225, 264
Islamic traditions of, xi–xii, 38, 41, 46–47, 51, 56–57, 64, 137–47, 165, 212–13, 271
Jewish population of, 137–38
judicial system of, 135–44
kidnappings in, 62–64, 114–15, 169, 265–66, 292
looting in, 44–47
map of, ix
mass weddings in, 126–27
media coverage of, 21, 84, 88, 111, 123, 142, 159, 178, 179, 183–84, 186–87, 191, 203, 210, 215, 216
migrant workers from, 27, 80
military forces of, 78, 94–97, 148–59, 206–8, 215–17, 255–56, 289
militias in, 152
mosques of, 5, 8, 9–10, 15, 19, 37, 70, 83, 125–26, 147, 148, 174, 191, 193–94, 197, 198–200, 225–26, 246, 270, 278, 285
North, 7, 19–22, 27–28, 39–47
northern area of, 147, 148–59, 195, 202–3, 292
oil industry of, 20, 108, 116–18, 204–5
parliament of, 38–39, 41, 78, 146–47, 149, 150, 155, 260–61
police forces of, 201–2, 226–28, 279
political reforms in, 181–87, 219, 269, 270
poverty in, 108–9, 125–26
prisons in, 105–6, 109–10, 111, 130–31, 135–44, 155, 159, 160–65, 168, 174–75, 191–96, 203, 204, 208, 209, 212, 213, 221, 223, 225, 242–43, 251, 265–68, 269
refugees in, 152, 202
rehabilitation program in, 135–44, 151, 186–87, 191, 231, 232
religious institutes in, 56–57, 146, 165
riots in, 177–78
safe houses in, xiii, 49–50, 55–56, 113, 116, 117, 130, 198, 201, 202, 206–7, 211–12, 216–17, 226–28, 235–38, 247
Saudi relations with, 25, 34, 43, 80, 196–202, 239
security situation in, 110–11, 123
Socialist rule in, 18, 19–22, 23, 24, 25, 27–28, 30, 31, 32, 35, 36, 38–39, 40, 41, 42, 43, 44, 49, 51, 55, 58–59, 148, 175, 270, 279, 289, 290, 293

South, 19–22, 27–28, 39–47
southern area of, 29–34, 44–47, 60–61, 271
Soviet influence in, 19–20, 21
terrorist groups in, 19–20, 56–57, 119, 179–80, 184, 233; *see also* al-Qaeda
tourism in, 61–62, 124, 213–15, 221–23, 228, 233, 241–43, 251
training camps in, 49–50, 57–58, 62–63, 65, 78, 82, 88, 110, 129, 165, 191, 217, 221, 252–53, 254, 258, 264
travel warnings for, 222–23, 228
tribes of, 7–8, 22, 23, 33, 40–41, 48–49, 51, 55, 63, 73, 83, 92, 93–97, 98, 105–6, 108–9, 110, 111, 117, 129, 135–36, 141, 144–47, 149*n,* 157, 160, 161, 176, 180, 186, 208, 216, 222, 233, 241, 247, 252–57, 261, 264, 278, 289
unemployment in, 147
unification of, 19–22, 25, 38–39, 45–47, 55, 90
as UN member, 25–27, 29, 43–44, 59, 141, 278
US economic aid to, 27, 88, 108–9, 119, 176–87, 195, 218–19, 222–23
US embassy in, 82–83, 108–9, 111, 115, 121, 157, 178, 179, 180–84, 186, 213, 217–19, 223, 225, 228, 229–31, 233, 237, 251
US military aid to, 116, 153–55, 179–87
US relations with, xii–xv, 21, 24–27, 29, 35–39, 43, 59–60, 74–75, 78, 82–83, 88–92, 93, 108–9, 111, 115 116, 119, 121, 123, 131, 135–36, 142, 143, 153–55, 157, 161, 162, 176–87, 194, 195, 203, 211, 212–13, 217–19, 222–24, 225, 228, 229–31, 233, 237, 251, 260–61, 265, 269–70, 278, 282
water supplies in, 279
women in, 28, 79, 80, 84, 152–53, 155, 156, 226–27, 267
Zaydi rebellion in, 144–57
Yemen Observer, 183–84

Zanjubar, 272, 276–82, 283, 285
Zarqawi, Abu Musab al-, 80, 203
Zawahiri, Ayman al-, 48–56, 103, 114, 139, 141, 195, 235, 274, 291
Zawahiri, Muhammad, 49, 53
Zayadi, Ghalib al-, 93–94, 105–6, 160–61, 163, 293
Zaydi rebellion, 144–57
Zindani, Abd al-Majid al-, 8, 14–15, 39, 63–64, 78, 135–36, 293
Zinni, Anthony, 60